The INDUSTRIAL RAILWAYS of the WIGAN COALFIELD

Part I

West and South of Wigan

by

C.H.A. Townley
F.D. Smith
J.A. Peden

Runpast Publishing
Cheltenham

To all those whose recollections about the railways in South Lancashire inspired us to further research. Especially to Vince Burns, Joe Brown and Ebenezer Rudd, whose knowledge of the Wigan Coal and Iron Company's locomotives has contributed so much to the present work.

© **C.H.A. Townley**
F.D. Smith
J.A. Peden
March 1991

Townley etc
 The Industrial Railways of the Wigan Coalfield
 History, operation and railways
 Pt. 1 West and South of Wigan
 1.
 I. Title

ISBN 1-870754-18-2

All rights reserved. Except for normal review purposes no part of this book may be reproduced or utilised in any form or by any means, electrical or mechanical including photocopying, recording or by an information storage and retrieval system, without the prior consent in writing of Runpast Publishing

Typeset by Ryburn Typesetting Ltd
and printed by
Ryburn Book Production, Halifax, West Yorkshire

Runpast Publishing
10 Kingscote Grove
Cheltenham
GL51 6JX

CONTENTS

CHAPTER 1	INTRODUCTION	5
CHAPTER 2	THE DEVELOPMENT OF THE CANAL AND RAILWAY SYSTEM	15
CHAPTER 3	ORRELL AND NORLEY HALL	54
CHAPTER 4	PEMBERTON	71
CHAPTER 5	WINSTANLEY AND WORSLEY MESNES	85
CHAPTER 6	THE EARLY INCE COLLIERIES	98
CHAPTER 7	DEVELOPMENTS AT INCE – 1845 TO 1900	109
CHAPTER 8	INCE IN THE TWENTIETH CENTURY	128
CHAPTER 9	PEARSON AND KNOWLES INCE COLLIERIES	147
CHAPTER 10	AMBERSWOOD AND STRANGEWAYS HALL	163
CHAPTER 11	PLATT BRIDGE, BAMFURLONG AND MAINS	176
CHAPTER 12	LOW HALL, MAYPOLE AND WIGAN JUNCTION	186
CHAPTER 13	EDGE GREEN, BRYNN AND GARSWOOD	198
CHAPTER 14	SKELMERSDALE AND BICKERSTAFFE	229
CHAPTER 15	RAINFORD, UPHOLLAND AND ORRELL	252

This view at John Pit, Standish, captures the atmosphere of the colliery railways as they used to be. Although the photograph was taken in 1955, the scene has changed little from the early years of the century. Two locomotives stand outside the engine shed, their work finished for the week. Beyond, a single track leads to the west coast main line at Rylands Sidings. To the left, a rake of wooden wagons has been unloaded in the pit-prop yard. Beyond, there are more empty wagons, waiting to be loaded with coal. The original Standish Washery lies in the middle distance, while the chimney and spoil heaps of Giants Hall Colliery are just visible on the horizon. The late B. Roberts

CHAPTER 1

INTRODUCTION

The authors have had a lifelong interest in the colliery railways of South Lancashire and particularly those in and around Wigan. This interest started during visits made on foot and by bicycle in the late 1940s and early 1950s. There was plenty to be seen in those days – old locomotives, old wagons, old tracks and old employees who were only too glad to talk about their jobs and how it had been in the past. With our enthusiasm aroused, we set out to learn all we could about the railway systems and the collieries which they served.

Although the coalfield had been in decline for several decades, there were, in 1948, still around twenty-five collieries in existence in the area covered by this book. The network of main line railways, which had been built up in Victorian times, was largely intact and many of the larger collieries still had their own private railway systems.

Now only one major colliery remains, together with a few small licensed mines. Very little is left on the ground to remind us of the enterprises which once dominated the landscape. Coal mines and factories have been demolished. The railways which served them have been dismantled. Opencast coal mining and redevelopment have made it impossible in most instances even to identify the sites. It is none too soon for us to record what we have been able to piece together about the history of industrial transport in and around Wigan during the past two hundred years. Our story concludes in the middle of 1990, when the text of our book was completed.

Mining, albeit on a very limited scale, goes back to medieval times and as early as the fifteenth century Wigan had become well known for its cannel as well its coal. The cannel was a hard, compact form of coal. It had a high calorific value and a low ash content. It was much sought after for gas making from the 1820s onwards and it commanded a premium price. By the end of the nineteenth century it was all but worked out.

Up to the middle of the eighteenth century, mining was restricted to shallow workings at those places where the seams outcropped to the surface. Lack of proper means of transport meant that sales were, for the most part, restricted to a few customers within easy reach of the pit-head. Major changes started to take place as soon as the River Douglas had been made navigable from Wigan to the Ribble Estuary in the period 1737 to 1742. Coal could now reach markets in Liverpool and Preston and this provided the stimulus to open up the new mines, particularly around Orrell. Further expansion of the industry to the west of Wigan followed the opening of a direct canal to Liverpool in the late 1770s.

The first railways in Lancashire date from this period. They were all narrow gauge. They were built to carry coal from the pits to the river and to the canal, and replaced the packhorses and horse drawn carts which had previously been the only means of transport. The earliest lines were constructed with wooden rails, but these were later replaced by cast or wrought iron rails, laid on stone sleeper blocks. Although one of these railways employed steam locomotives early in the nineteenth century, this was the exception. Horses were normally used to pull trains of a few small wagons, each carrying two to three tons of coal.

Introduction

At this time coal mining was still almost a cottage industry. The pits themselves were quite shallow, no more than 50 or 60 yards deep, with up to ten men and women being employed. After three or four years the coal would be exhausted, and a new pit would be sunk nearby, the railway being moved to serve it.

To the north east of Wigan, the opening of the canal from Bark Hill, near Whelley, to Chorley and Preston at the turn of the century led to a similar expansion of coal mining activities in Haigh, Aspull and Blackrod. However, by 1820 when the last canal links had been completed, from Wigan to Bark Hill through Ince and from Wigan to Leigh through Platt Bridge, a much more intensive phase of colliery activity was just beginning. Hit and miss exploration was being replaced by more scientific methods based on an understanding of geology. With improved steam engines for winding as well as for pumping it was now possible to exploit the deeper seams and the collieries themselves became larger and more capital intensive.

For a few years, the canal, and the tramroad which linked it to the pit-head, remained the main means of transport. Then in the 1830s, as the pace of the industrial revolution accelerated, the first public railways appeared on the scene. The new manufacturing industries were powered by the steam engine. The steam engines needed coal and the mining industry expanded to meet the demand.

A connection with the public railway system became essential if a colliery were to take advantage of the wider markets which were now available. A network of new private railways developed to link the mines with the nearest main line. Water borne transport, however, still remained important and a branch to a pier head on the canal was included wherever possible. Many of the older horse worked lines giving access to the canal were converted to the standard 4' 8½" gauge.

The more prosperous colliery firms adopted steam locomotives from the outset, to perform the shunting around the pit-head and to work traffic to the main line sidings. Horses still provided the motive power at many of the smaller establishments, a practice which continued, in some instances, until the end of the nineteenth century and beyond.

Certain coal owners were permitted to run their own trains over the main line railways, using their own locomotives. We have been able to trace at least eight colliery concerns which took advantage of this facility in the late 1840s and 1850s. The principal destinations were Liverpool and Preston, although some trains ran as far afield as Bolton, Rochdale and Winsford. The majority of these workings seem to have ceased in the 1860s, although those to Liverpool seem to have continued until about 1870.

The coal industry continued to expand during the second half of the nineteenth century. Many of the collieries were now employing over 1500 men. The largest, such as Pemberton and Bickershaw, had over two thousand on their payroll. Increased output of coal required better transport facilities. New railways were built and and existing ones were improved. Higher capacity wagons and more powerful locomotives were introduced.

This growth in coal mining was accompanied by a growth in those industries which were allied to it. Kirkless Iron Works was founded in the 1850s and at one time ten blast furnaces were in production. Puddling furnaces and rolling mills were erected to process the pig iron. Foundries and engineering works, specialising in equipment for the collieries, were set up. Some, such as the Haigh Foundry, Ince Forge and Walker Brothers were for a time engaged in locomotive construction, albeit on a small scale. There were also firms dealing in second hand machinery of all types, often including railway equipment.

Introduction

Up to the second world war, much of the coal traffic was carried in privately owned wagons belonging to colliery companies. Many of the larger concerns had their own repair shops where both internal user wagons and wagons for main line service were overhauled. The smaller companies, as well as the larger ones when their own facilities were overstretched, relied on specialist firms. As well as undertaking repairs these firms were often engaged in the manufacture of new wagons, for which there was a continuing steady demand well into the 1920s and 1930s.

Ince became one of the main centres in Lancashire for wagon building and wagon repairing, being well situated at the centre of the coalfield. Most of these works were located on the Springs Branch where, after the closure of the older collieries, ample land was available with existing rail connections.

By the beginning of the twentieth century the coal industry in the Wigan area had reached its peak. Very few new collieries opened up during the period up to the first world war and there were no significant additions to the railway systems, either private or public. The post war period, with its trade depressions, led to the start of the decline. A number of old established colliery companies went out of business in the 1920s and 1930s. Others took advantage of legislation [1,2] which encouraged amalgamation and rationalisation. Output was regulated and Lancashire Associated Collieries Ltd was formed, in July 1935, to market all the coal produced in Lancashire and Cheshire. This firm took over all landsale yards and acted as sales agents for bulk supply to industrial customers.

Mineral rights were taken over by the Government from the landowners in 1939 [3] and the coal mines themselves were nationalised as from 1st January 1947 [4]. Those that we are dealing with here all became part of the North Western Division of the National Coal Board.

Production was maintained during the second world war and opencast mining was started to recover coal left behind in the shallower seams by the earlier methods of extraction. However, the post war period saw a falling demand nationally and a falling export trade. Most of the better coal had been worked out and what was left could not compete in price with that from other coal fields. The result was that there was an accelerated programme of colliery closures.

Bickershaw Colliery was the only one to be redeveloped with up to date equipment and modern mining methods. With its associated man riding shaft at Parsonage, it still survives at the time of writing, although with a very much reduced railway system. The coal, all of which is destined for power stations, is loaded directly into 36-ton merry-go-round wagons.

Opencast mining continues, although on a somewhat diminished scale. Formerly it had been the practice to take the coal to specially constructed screening plants at Pemberton and Abram, where it was loaded into railway wagons. Although the screening plant at Abram still remains, it is no longer served by rail. Coal now goes direct to the customer by road vehicle.

It is against this background of the rise and decline of the coal industry around Wigan that our book has been written. Although the main purpose is to trace the history and development of the various colliery railway systems and the locomotives which worked on them, these cannot be studied in isolation. To understand the subject properly we need to know how the collieries themselves developed. It is however outside the scope of the book, and indeed outside the competence of the authors, to deal with the methods of working the coal and the geology of the coal seams. For those who wish to learn more about these topics, we would refer them to the books published in recent years by Mr Donald Anderson [5,6,7].

Our task has not been an easy one, despite the restrictions on scope. Very few of the colliery company records have survived. Even where fragmentary material is available, there is little mention of transport in general and railways in particular.

Introduction

Among our most important sources of information about the early history are the leases granted by the coal owners to the colliery proprietors. As only a relatively small proportion of the coal was held freehold by the colliery companies, these leases provide at least partial evidence for the dates of opening of the various collieries and their transfer to new ownership. In case of bankruptcy of the colliery proprietor, or surrender of the lease for other reasons, the fixed plant at the colliery and the railways associated with it usually reverted to the lessor, and this is sometimes recorded.

Before the days of the Limited Liability Company, the *London Gazette* provides information about the partnerships which worked the collieries and the changes which took place. Subsequently, records are available from the Registrar of Public Companies. From the mid 1850s until 1881, details of mine ownership were recorded in the *Mineral Statistics* published by the Geological Survey[8]. These also provide information on blast furnaces and wrought iron manufacture. From 1882 onwards, lists of coal mines were provided in the the *Reports of the Inspectors of Mines,* published annually by the Stationary Office. From the 1890s onwards we have also made use of the various trade publications which are available, such as *Potts Mining Register*[9], the *Colliery Year Book*[10] and the *Guide to the Coalfields*[11]. Another important source has been the books by Anderson, referred to earlier.

Local papers have proved an invaluable source for information about all aspects of colliery activities – new mines, bankruptcies, sales of plant, new owners and final closure. Often there are references to the colliery railways, sometimes the opening of a new line, more usually to an accident on an existing one.

Maps of Lancashire are particularly sparse for the Victorian period when the greatest expansion of the coal industry took place. Of the pre-Ordnance Survey maps, only that produced by Stanley in 1833[12] has proved to be of use. The first series 1" Ordnance survey map is, because of its many revisions, difficult to interpret and, for most areas, is at too small a scale for our purpose. The first edition of the 6" Ordnance Survey Map was published shortly before 1850, so that the earliest lines which had disappeared by then have largely gone unrecorded. There was a partial revision of sheets 93 and 94 around 1850 and another in the mid 1860s[13,14,15]. However, these do not provide any new information except, in some instances, near to new main line railways.

The next complete revision of the 6" Ordnance Survey map did not appear until the end of the 1880s, a gap of 40 years during which time complete colliery railway systems had been built and had been abandoned without trace. For this period we have had to make do with the the few estate plans which are available and one large scale plan of 1876, which only covers the Borough of Wigan[16]. Some of the deficiencies have been made good by consulting the Deposited Plans and associated Books of Reference relating to railways in South Lancashire. These, however, only cover a limited amount of ground on each side of the proposed line.

We have been fortunate in being able to refer to a considerable amount of material originating with the railway companies, which provide useful information about the colliery systems at least as far as their junctions with the main lines are concerned. All the railway companies produced Line Plans showing the layout of their tracks and the sidings which connected into them. Often there are annotations referring to agreements with the colliery companies and the landowners. Changes in track layout subsequent to publication have been inserted by hand. Usually such plans were produced at a scale of 2 chains to 1 inch, although the most recent are at a scale of 1/1250. Through the courtesy of the Estates Surveyor, British Rail Property Board, North Western Region, we have been able to inspect the complete set of

Introduction

plans for the area which we cover in this book. We have also referred to some older issues of the Line Plans which are available in the Greater Manchester Records Office.

The railway companies also produced a series of diagrams, one for each of the private sidings which connected with their system. Like the Line Plans, these give invaluable information about connections with colliery railway systems. We have been able to examine those for the Lancashire and Yorkshire Railway, dating from the 1900 to 1914 period, again through the courtesy of the Estates Surveyor. Those for the London and North Western Railway have been lent to us by the Librarian of the Manchester Locomotive Society. We have been unable to trace any sidings diagrams relating to the Great Central Railway and the London and North Eastern Railway.

We have also had access to xerox copies, in private hands, of a number of handwritten and typescript sheets which summarise information about private sidings in the Wigan area. Those for the London and North Western Railway are the most comprehensive and some of the sheets appear to date back perhaps as far as the 1880s. There are also some sheets produced more recently by the LNWR and by the London Midland and Scottish Railway. For the Lancashire and Yorkshire lines, the sheets were compiled in LMS times and lack much of the earlier information. Those for the former Great Central lines were prepared after British Railways took over, and are obviously based on incomplete information supplied from another office.

The opening and closing dates for the various sections of main line railway have been obtained from standard works of reference. The publications of the Branch Line Society have proved to be of great help in establishing the dates of closure. We were, however surprised to find, when we finally analysed the information we had, that, despite the plethora of railway books which have been published, some opening and closing dates had gone unrecorded.

For our locomotive information we have relied heavily on data contained in the various locomotive manufacturers' records which have survived. We have also referred to lists compiled by organisations such as the Industrial Locomotive Society and the Industrial Railway Society, but we have chosen to omit information which could not be verified independently. Finally we have made considerable use of the notes which we made, mostly in the 1945 to 1955 period, during our conversations with the older generations of employees at the collieries. Their memories went back to railways and the locomotives as they were in late Victorian times.

Our book deals with Wigan and its immediate surroundings and any definition of the boundaries must be to a large extent arbitrary. We have gone as far north as the edge of the coal mining area at Charnock Richard and Chorley, and have then followed the Bolton and Preston railway line as far as Lostock Junction. For our eastern boundary we have taken the Bolton and Leigh Railway, on the grounds that, beyond it, the history of the collieries and the railways have been the subject of recent publications [17,18]. From Leigh we have drawn an imaginary line across country to Edge Green and another from there to Rainford. In doing so, we have left out the area around St Helens and Widnes; this needs a book of its own to describe what is an extremely complex story of industry and transport. Finally, we have included the collieries in the neighbourhood of Skelmersdale, Rainford and Upholland.

Within the boundaries which we adopted we had considerable debate about the best way to present all the information which we had gathered together. In the end, we decided to divide the book on a geographical basis. Part 1 deals with an area generally to the south and west of Wigan, while Part 2 deals with an area generally to the north and east.

Introduction

In conclusion we wish to express our gratitude to all our friends and colleagues who have assisted in preparation of our book. Our special thanks go to Ken Plant for making information freely available from his extensive locomotive builders archives, to John Ryan for information about the private sidings agreements, to Tony Walker for filling in the gaps in our knowledge of the wagon works, to Richard Maund for answering our many queries about recent railway history, to Ted Cheetham for enabling us to bring our story up to date, and to Alex Appleton for his constructive criticism and comment on our original manuscript.

We wish to acknowledge all the help which we have freely received from members of staff at the Public Libraries at Bolton, Leigh, Preston and Wigan, at the Mining Museum at Buile Hill, Salford and at the Greater Manchester, Preston and Wigan Record Offices. We also wish to express our appreciation for being able to examine the Line Plans and Sidings Diagrams held by the British Railways Property Board at their Manchester Office. We are particularly grateful to David Lawrence for arranging this for us and to Alan Cherry, the Estates Surveyor, and to Mike Arnold, the Chief Draughtsman, for their help in answering our questions.

We are particularly indebted to Geoff Monks for producing an excellent set of maps from some very rough drafts. In the majority of cases we have been able to provide a set of maps to accompany each chapter. In a few instances geography and the overlapping nature of the different railway systems have conspired against us. We apologise in advance if any of our readers find difficulty with the compromises which we have had to adopt.

Finally, we must thank all our friends who have so generously made available photographs from their collections to provide the illustrations to the book. Individual acknowledgements are given in the captions.

Locomotive Summaries

A summary is provided at the end of most of the chapters which gives, in tabular form, details of the locomotives referred to in the text.

The tables are set out in order of name or number; type of locomotive (wheel arrangement, position of tanks, position of cylinders); maker; makers number (where known); cylinder dimensions (bore and stroke); diameter of driving wheels.

The Whyte system of classification has been used to describe the wheel arrangements of the engines, with the addition of 4w and 6w to indicate four or six wheels with gear or chain drive.

The position of the water tanks is denoted by ST for saddle tank, T for side tank and WT for well tank. Tk indicates that we lack information, other than knowing that the locomotive in question was a tank rather than a tender engine.

Cylinder position is denoted by IC for inside the frames and by OC for outside the frames. VC indicates vertical cylinders.

A vertical boiler is denoted by V and a geared drive, on a steam engine, by G.

Diesel locomotives are identified by a D after the wheel arrangement, with M added for mechanical drive, H for hydraulic drive and E for electric drive.

In the case of electric locomotives, OHW denotes current collection from an overhead wire system.

We have used the conventional abbreviations for the locomotive builders, with a few extra ones which are relevant to the Wigan area. A full list of the abbreviations is given below.

Introduction

AB	Andrew Barclay, Sons & Co Ltd, Caledonia Works, Kilmarnock
AE	Avonside Engine Co Ltd, Bristol
AP	Aveling and Porter Ltd, Invicta Works, Canterbury
AtW	Atkinson Walker Wagons Ltd, Frenchwood Works, Preston
BH	Black, Hawthorn & Co Ltd, Gateshead
BP	Beyer, Peacock & Co Ltd, Gorton, Manchester
CC	Clarke, Chapman & Co Ltd, Gateshead
DK	Dick, Kerr & Co Ltd, Britannia Works, Kilmarnock
EB	Edward Borrows & Sons, St Helens
EE	English Electric Co Ltd
Fbn	William Fairbairn and Sons, Canal Street Works, Manchester
FJ	Fletcher, Jennings & Co, Lowca Works, near Whitehaven
FH	F C Hibberd & Co Ltd, Park Royal, London
FMJ	Fenton, Murray and Jackson, Water Lane, Leeds
FW	Fox, Walker & Co, Atlas Works, Bristol
GE	George England & Co, Hatcham Ironworks, New Cross, London
GECT	GEC Traction Ltd, Vulcan Works, Newton le Willows
HC	Hudswell, Clarke & Co Ltd, Railway Foundry, Leeds
HCR	Hudswell, Clarke & Rodgers, Railway Foundry, Leeds
HE	Hunslet Engine Co Ltd, Leeds
HF	Haigh Foundry Company, Wigan
HH	Henry Hughes & Co, Falcon Works, Loughborough
HL	R & W Hawthorn, Leslie & Co Ltd, Newcastle on Tyne
Hor	Lancashire & Yorkshire Railway Co, Horwich Works
HU	Robert Hudson Ltd, Leeds
HW	Head, Wrightson & Co, Stockton on Tees
IWB	Isaac Watt Boulton, Ashton under Lyne
JF	John Fowler & Co Ltd, Leeds
J&P	Jones and Potts, Viaduct Foundry, Newton-le-Willows
JSW	James Scarisbrick Walker and Brother, Wigan
K	Kitson & Co, Airedale Foundry, Leeds
KS	Kerr, Stuart & Co Ltd, California Works, Stoke on Trent
L	R A Lister & Co Ltd, Dursley, Gloucestershire
MW	Manning, Wardle & Co Ltd, Boyne Engine Works, Leeds
N	Neilson & Co, Glasgow
NBL	North British Locomotive Co Ltd, Glasgow
NG	Nasmyth, Gaskell & Co, Bridgewater Foundry, Patricroft
NW	Nasmyth, Wilson & Co Ltd, Bridgewater Foundry, Patricroft
P	Peckett & Sons Ltd, Atlas Works, Bristol
P&J	Parfitt and Jenkins, Cardiff
PK	Pearson & Knowles Coal & Iron Co Ltd, Warrington
RH	Ruston and Hornsby Ltd, Lincoln
RS	Robert Stephenson & Co Ltd, Newcastle, later Darlington
RSH	Robert Stephenson and Hawthorns Ltd, Newcastle and Darlington
RWH	R & W Hawthorn & Co, Newcastle on Tyne

Introduction

S	Sentinel Waggon Works Ltd, Shrewsbury (and also at Chester for a time). Later Sentinel (Shrewsbury) Ltd
SR	Sharp, Roberts & Co, Atlas Works, Manchester
SS	Sharp, Stewart & Co, Atlas Works, Manchester. Later Atlas Works, Glasgow
TH	Thomas Hill (Rotherham) Ltd, Vanguard Works, Kilnhurst
VF	Vulcan Foundry Ltd, Newton le Willows
WB	W G Bagnall Ltd, Castle Engine Works, Stafford
WCI	Wigan Coal & Iron Co Ltd, Kirkless Workshops, Wigan
WkB	Walker Brothers & Co, Pagefield Works, Wigan
YE	Yorkshire Engine Co Ltd, Meadow Hall Works, Sheffield

Also mentioned are :

Chaplin	Alexander Chaplin & Co, Cranstonhill, Glasgow
Clarke Chapman	Clarke, Chapman & Co Ltd, Gateshead on Tyne
Crewe	Crewe Locomotive Works, Grand Junction Railway. After 1846, London and North Western Railway
H'worth	Timothy Hackworth, Shildon, Durham
H'dock	Haydock Workshops of Richard Evans & Co
Hick	Benjamin Hick, Soho Ironworks, Bolton
L'hall	Lilleshall Iron Co, Wellington, Salop
Pemberton	Workshops of the Pemberton Colliery Co Ltd
Rylands	Wigan Workshops of Rylands & Sons Ltd
St H Rly	Sutton Locomotive Works of St Helens and Runcorn Gap Railway Co, later St Helens Railway and Canal Co
St Rollox	St Rollox, Glasgow, locomotive works of the Caledonian Railway Co
Tayleur	Charles Tayleur & Co, Vulcan Foundry, Newton le Willows; subsequently the Vulcan Foundry Co (qv)

References

References to the background literature are given at the end of each chapter. The following abbreviations have been used:–

GMRO	Greater Manchester Records Office
LRO	Lancashire Records Office, Preston
PRO	Public Records Office, Kew
WRO	Wigan Metropolitan Borough Records Office, Leigh
BC	Bolton Chronicle
BEN	Bolton Evening News
BJ	Bolton Journal
CG	Colliery Guardian
LC	Leigh Chronicle
LEN	Lancashire Evening News
LG	London Gazette

Introduction

OA	Ormskirk Advertiser
PC	Preston Chronicle
PG	Preston Guardian
PP	Preston Pilot
MG	Manchester Guardian
MJ	Mining Journal
MM	Machinery Mart
WEx	Wigan Examiner
WO	Wigan Observer
WT	Wigan Times

Maps

The following symbols are used throughout on the maps, with the exception of those in Chapter 2.

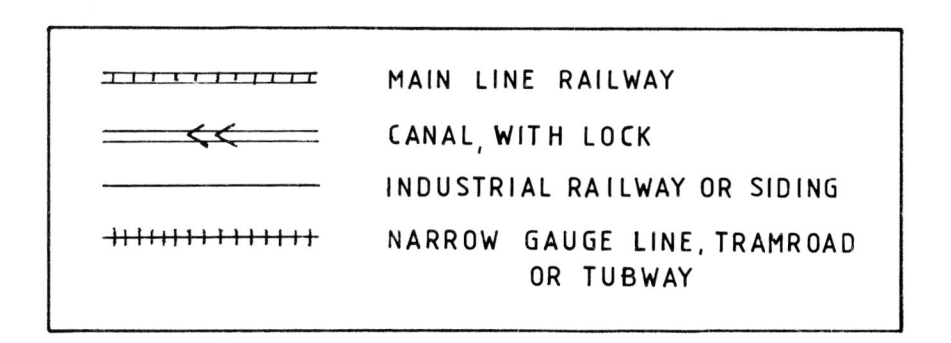

⊥⊥⊥⊥⊥⊥⊥	MAIN LINE RAILWAY
══«══	CANAL, WITH LOCK
───	INDUSTRIAL RAILWAY OR SIDING
┼┼┼┼┼┼┼┼	NARROW GAUGE LINE, TRAMROAD OR TUBWAY

In the text we have used "tramroad" to describe a narrow gauge horse worked line, except in the chapter dealing with Orrell. Here we have followed the example of previous historians and we have referred to these earliest lines as "railways". We have used the term "tubway" to denote a narrow gauge railway on which the tubs from the pit were used to convey coal overground, often over considerable distances and usually employing endless rope haulage.

References to Chapter 1

1 Mining Industries Act – 16 & 17 Geo 5 cap 28; 4th August 1926
2 Coal Mines Act – 20 & 21 Geo 5 cap 34; 1st August 1930
3 Coal Act – 1 & 2 Geo 6 cap 52 ; 29th July 1938
4 Coal Industry Nationalisation Act – 9 & 10 Geo 6 cap 59; 12th July 1946
5 *The Orrell Coalfield, Lancashire, 1740–1850*, D. Anderson, Moorland Publishing Co, Buxton, 1975

Introduction

6. *"Blundell's Collieries 1776–1966"*, D. Anderson, Reprinted for the author, 1986, from the *Transactions of the Historic Society of Lancashire & Cheshire*, Vol 116:1964:Vol 117:1965; Vol 119:1967
7. *The Standish Collieries, Wigan, Lancashire, 1653–1963*, D. Anderson, J. Lane and A. A. France, published D. Anderson, Quaker House Colliery, Ashton in Makerfield, 1984
8. *"Mineral Statistics of the United Kingdom of Great Britain and Ireland"*, Robert Hunt, Keeper of Mining Records, *Memoirs of the Geological Survey of Great Britain and of the Museum of Practical Geology*, annually from 1853/4 to 1881
9. *Potts Mining Register and Directory for the Coal and Ironstone Trades of Great Britain and Ireland* – W J Potts, North Shields
10. *The Colliery Year Book* and *Coal Trades Directory*, The Lewis Cassier Co Ltd, London, published annually from 1923 to about 1948
11. *Guide to the Coalfields*, The Colliery Guardian Co Ltd, London, published annually from 1948 to date
12. *"A Plan Showing the Situation of the Collieries Communicating with the Canals and Railways in Lancashire"*, W.Stanley, 1833. Approx 1 inch to 1 mile. Liverpool Library, Binn's Collection, Vol 23, Item 68
13. The original first edition sheets for Lancashire are in Lancashire Records Office
14. The circa 1850 revisions of the first edition 6" map of Lancashire, including sheets 93 and 94, are in the British Library Map Room
15. The mid 1860 revision of sheet 93 is at Cambridge University Library. That of sheet 94 is in the authors' possession.
16. *"Map of the Borough of Wigan, surveyed and corrected up to 1st January 1876, and further corrected up to December 1876"*, J Hunter, Borough Engineer, 220ft to 1 inch.
17. *The Coal Pits of Chowbent*, Kenneth Wood, published by K. Wood, Bolton, 1984
18. *Collieries in the Manchester Coalfields*, Geoffrey Hayes, De Archaeologische Pers, Eindhoven, n.d., circa 1986

CHAPTER 2

THE DEVELOPMENT OF THE CANAL AND RAILWAY SYSTEM

The Canals

In the early years of the eighteenth century thoughts began to turn towards establishing river navigations as an alternative to the inadequate roads which then existed. Supported by Liverpool interests, schemes were prepared for the Mersey and the Irwell, for the Sankey Brook and for the Douglas. The first true canal projects appeared in the 1740s and 1750s.

For readers who wish to study the history of the inland waterways of South Lancashire in depth, we refer them to Hadfield and Biddle's *Canals of North West England* [1], which we have used as a source document for much of what follows. In the present work we must confine ourselves to a brief resume of the principal events, as background to the development of the collieries and the transport systems which served them. Before the advent of locomotive railways in the nineteenth century, the collieries were almost entirely dependent on water transport in order to distribute their products to other than very local markets. Conversely, the canals relied to a very large extent on the coal trade for their traffic and their profits.

An Act of Parliament to make the River Douglas navigable from Wigan to the Ribble Estuary was passed in 1720 [2]. Locks were provided and the channel deepened where necessary. The works were completed between Gathurst and the Ribble in 1736 or 1737 and throughout, to wharves near Miry Lane at Wigan, in 1742. Despite the small size of the boats then in use, the opening of the navigation led to considerable expansion of coal mining activities to the west of Wigan during the second half of the eighteenth century.

Proposals for a canal from Manchester to Wigan, passing through Worsley and Leigh, were put forward in the 1750s. The canal would have led to the opening up of the coalfield around Platt Bridge and Westleigh, but the project did not proceed. Schemes for a canal from Liverpool to Wigan prepared in the 1770s included branches to Ince and Pemberton which would have served collieries there. Although a Bill was presented to Parliament in 1772, this was subsequently withdrawn and the project allowed to lapse.

In the 1760s the first proposals began to take shape for a canal across the Pennines, from Liverpool to Leeds. An Act was obtained in 1770 [3] which authorised a line from the north side of Liverpool to Newburgh, where the River Douglas was intersected. Beyond Newburgh, the canal would have gone through Eccleston and Leyland, avoiding Wigan and passing to the south of Preston.

Construction work was confined to the sections between Liverpool and Newburgh, in Lancashire, and between Leeds and Gargrave, in Yorkshire. To obtain access to Wigan, the Leeds and Liverpool Canal Company purchased the Douglas Navigation. The Navigation Company appears to have started construction of an artificial cut parallel to the river some years earlier and this was completed by the Leeds and Liverpool company.

Development of the Canal and Railway System

The waterway was opened from Liverpool as far as Dean Locks, near Gathurst, in October 1774. East of Dean Locks, the original river navigation was used until the canal was finally completed to Wigan Basin in 1780. The lower portion of the Douglas Navigation was replaced by a canal from Burscough to Sollom, opened in October 1781.

The Yorkshire section of the canal was opened throughout from Leeds to Gargrave on 4th June 1777. Shortage of funds prevented further construction for the time being, and this provided the opportunity for reconsideration of the route to be taken by the intervening section of the canal. It was eventually decided to adopt a line which would pass to the east of Chorley, to the north of Blackrod and then through Red Moss and Kirkless to join the completed Lancashire section of the canal at Wigan. This would have the advantage of tapping collieries around Chorley, Blackrod and Aspull. There would also be a connection with Manchester, as the Manchester, Bolton and Bury Canal was proposing an extension of its system to join the Leeds and Liverpool at Red Moss. An Act of Parliament was obtained for the revised line in 1794[4], but there were further changes of plan because of the recently authorised Lancaster Canal.

The Lancaster Canal was intended to run from Kendal to Westhoughton and had obtained its Act of Parliament in 1792[5]. South of Preston, the line passed through Chorley, Adlington and the north eastern outskirts of Wigan. A short branch to Duxbury was also authorised and an extension from Westhoughton to join the Duke of Bridgewater's Canal at Worsley was under consideration.

The north end of the Lancaster Canal was opened from Tewitfield, near Kendal, to Preston on 22nd November 1797 and part of the south end, from Bark Hill, near Whelley, to Chorley, in February 1798. The proposed aqueduct over the Ribble at Preston proved too expensive and a tramway was built instead, from Walton Summit to the basin at Preston. The tramway and the connecting portions of canal were opened in 1803. Coal from Chorley, Blackrod and in the area north east of Wigan was now able to reach markets in the Fylde and north Lancashire as well as Preston itself.

The Leeds and Liverpool, aware that two competing lines of canal in the district south of Chorley would not be viable, came to an arrangement with the Lancaster to use that canal between Whittle le Woods and Wigan. A short branch was built by the Lancaster company at Johnson's Hillock, north of Chorley, to meet the Leeds and Liverpool's line, then under construction from Blackburn.

At the southern end, the Leeds and Liverpool built the long flight of locks from the basin in Wigan as far as Kirkless, where there was a junction with a short extension from Bark Hill provided by the Lancaster company. The Leeds and Liverpool Canal, together with the connecting link provided by the southern section of the Lancaster Canal, was ceremonially opened from end to end on 23rd October 1816.

The Leeds and Liverpool abandoned its proposed route through Red Moss and Blackrod beyond the top lock at Kirkless. The Lancaster undertook no work between Kirkless and Westhoughton, except for a short length near the top lock, built in 1836 in an unsuccessful attempt to block the North Union Railway's Springs Branch. The proposed extension of the Manchester, Bolton and Bury to Red Moss was dropped, as was the scheme for a canal from Worsley to Westhoughton.

The link with Manchester and the main English canal network was provided by the Leigh branch of the Leeds and Liverpool, authorised in 1819[6]. This canal was opened in December 1820 and provided the stimulus for colliery developments south and south east of Wigan.

Development of the Canal and Railway System

The Leeds and Liverpool Canal at Wigan. The nineteenth century warehouses on the left are now occupied by the Wigan Pier museum. The original terminal basin lies beyond. The raised portion of the towpath on the right marks the site of the Winstanley Colliery coal tip.
J.A. Peden

Less than a decade later the first main line railways appeared in South Lancashire, and, as we shall describe later, were soon to challenge the supremacy of the canals as carriers of coal. In many parts of the country, the canals were bought out by the railways and were no longer permitted to compete for traffic. That did not happen around Wigan. Apart from the period from 1850 to 1874, when it was leased to a group of railway companies, the Leeds and Liverpool Canal remained independent until nationalised under the Transport Act of 1947.

The Lancaster Canal had a more complicated history. The Preston and Walton Summit tramroad was leased to the Bolton and Preston Railway in January 1837, part of the deal being that the railway company would provide sidings to serve the canal basin in Preston. These sidings, and the coal yards which were developed around them, became a focal point for railway traffic from the Wigan collieries. Some of the coal was transhipped for onward conveyance by the canal, while a large part was distributed by road to industrial and domestic consumers in Preston. Traffic on the Canal Company's tramroad soon declined. The portion north of Bamber Bridge was formally abandoned in 1864 and the remainder in 1879 [1].

The Lancaster Canal itself was leased in 1864, the northern part to the London and North Western Railway and the southern part to the Leeds and Liverpool Canal. The Lancaster Canal company sold out completely to the London and North Western Railway in July 1885. This, however, did not affect the lease of the southern section and the Leeds and Liverpool Canal was able to continue its operations without railway interference.

17

Development of the Canal and Railway System

The canals which served Wigan were thus able to offer an alternative method of coal transport, albeit at considerably reduced profit. No doubt the colliery owners made good use of this competition to negotiate favourable rates from the railway companies.

To keep down costs, horse haulage of the canal barges began to be replaced as early as the 1850s. In May 1853, successful trials were carried out of a twin screw tug, CONQUEROR, which operated on the 31 mile level section between Appley Bridge Locks and Liverpool. Converted from a passenger boat and powered by a 6 HP steam engine, it was capable of towing four loaded barges, each weighing 40 tons, at 2½ mph [7]. By the 1890s the Leeds and Liverpool Canal Company was ordering large numbers of self propelled steam barges [8,9]. In the 1920s and 1930s, diesel engines began to take over, although several steam barges survived until the 1950s.

Both the Lancaster Canal and the Leeds and Liverpool Canal passed to the Docks and Inland Waterways Executive of the British Transport Commission on 1st January 1948, and were transferred to the British Waterways Board in 1955. Commercial traffic continued until well after the second world war and finally ceased in the Wigan area on 11th August 1972, when the last load of coal was delivered from Bickershaw Colliery to Westwood Power Station [10]. The Leeds and Liverpool Canal and the South End of the Lancaster Canal, with the exception of the branch from Johnson's Hillock to Walton Summit, remain open as cruising waterways.

A scene on the Leeds and Liverpool Canal in the 1950s, before commercial traffic ceased. A barge, loaded with coal for Blackburn, leaves Lock No 4 at Kirkless. The National Coal Board workshops and steel stockyard can be seen on the right. These were all that survived of the once prosperous Kirkless Iron Works. Collection J.A. Peden

Development of the Canal and Railway System

The Early Public Railways

The first major railway development in Lancashire was the Liverpool and Manchester line, which was opened on 15th September 1830[11]. This did not directly serve the Wigan coalfield, but soon afterwards a short connecting line was built by the independent Wigan Branch Railway Company. The Company's Act[12] authorised a railway from the Liverpool and Manchester at Parkside to the centre of Wigan, together with a branch to New Springs, intended to serve the collieries in Ince and to the north east of Wigan. The line from Parkside to Wigan opened on 3rd September 1832[11], but construction of the Springs Branch was delayed.

Meanwhile plans were being made to extend northwards. The Preston and Wigan Railway received its Act in 1831[13] and, in addition to the main line, branches were authorised to the Leeds and Liverpool Canal in Wigan, to the Preston and Walton Summit Tramway, to Welch Whittle and to mines near Adlington. In 1834, before construction was completed, the Preston and Wigan amalgamated with the Wigan Branch Railway, the combined enterprise becoming the North Union Railway.

No work had been done on the Springs Branch and the coal owners were becoming impatient. The Act of 1834 creating the North Union[14] required that it should be completed and open for traffic before the main line from Wigan to Preston. In the event, both the main line and the Springs Branch came into use on 31st October 1834[11]. Originally the Springs Branch was single track and the work needed to double it between the main line and Manchester Road was ordered on 16th January 1845[15]. The other branches from the North Union main line, authorised under the 1831 Act, were not built.

The North Union Act of 1834 also contained a number of measures, introduced in the interest of the colliery proprietors and the landowners. In addition to being given protection against interference with existing private tramroads and railways, they were granted very wide powers to make new sidings and connections.

They made especially good use of the powers which permitted them to run their own locomotives and trains over the North Union system. We have been able to trace seven colliery concerns which exercised these rights in respect of coal traffic to Preston over the period from the 1840s to the 1870s. Although the majority of these workings seem to have ceased in the late 1860s, the powers were not formally revoked until 20 years later, by Section 75 of the London and North Western Act of 1888[16], which however did not apply to the Springs Branch. Section 76 preserved the rights of the Wigan Coal and Iron Co Ltd to run over the West Coast main line between Rylands Sidings and Broomfield Colliery.

The north eastern part of the area with which we are dealing was served by the Bolton and Preston Railway. This started from an end on junction with the Manchester and Bolton Railway and was authorised in 1837[17]. The original intention was to use the track bed of the Preston and Walton Summit tramroad to gain access to Preston, and, as recorded earlier, the tramroad was leased from the Lancaster Canal Company in January 1837. That idea was abandoned and a further Act in 1838[18] provided for a new route from Chorley to Euxton, from where the company was able to run over North Union tracks to Preston.

The line was opened from Bolton to Rawlinson Bridge on 4th February 1841 and thence to Chorley on 22nd December of the same year[11]. After delays due to difficult earthworks, it was finally opened throughout to Euxton Junction on 22nd June 1843[11]. A short branch line, the Waterhouse Branch, was constructed to join the Earl of Crawford and Balcarres' private railway from his collieries at Haigh and Aspull. In 1844[19] the Bolton and Preston sold out to

Development of the Canal and Railway System

the North Union Railway, and we shall be following its subsequent history a little later.

To complete our brief study of the earliest public railways in and around Wigan we must turn our attention to the Bolton and Leigh Railway. This was originally planned to connect the collieries around Leigh and Atherton with Bolton and with the Bridgewater Canal. It was authorised in 1825 [20] and was opened for goods traffic on 1st August 1828 [11]. Passenger traffic started on 11th June 1831 [11]. Modelled on the early railways in County Durham, the Bolton and Leigh consisted of a series of rope worked inclines connected by short level sections. The inclines were worked by stationary engines, and it was not until 2nd February 1885 [11] that a series of deviations had been completed which permitted the line to be adhesion worked throughout.

The Bolton and Leigh line was continued to join the Liverpool and Manchester Railway at Kenyon Junction by the nominally independent Kenyon and Leigh Junction Railway. Authorised in 1829 [21], this extension was opened for goods traffic in January 1831 and for passengers on 11th June 1831 [11].

There was also a proposal in 1835 for a line from Leigh to Hindley, which was not proceeded with. The Deposited Plans [22] show that it would have terminated near the Bird in Hand Public House. One branch would have served the collieries at Hindley Green owned by Mr Worsley, Mr Gough, Mr Edwards and Mr Scowcroft. A second would have connected with Abraham Ackers' pits at Bickershaw, while a third would have served John Hargeaves' estate near Hindley.

Competing Schemes in the 1840s

The Railway Mania of the 1840s saw the promotion of a number of schemes to link Liverpool with Preston and Wigan, Southport with Wigan, and Wigan with Bolton and Manchester.

Between Liverpool and Preston, there were at least three competing companies which reached the stage of submitting Parliamentary Plans. Each intended to follow the direct route through Ormskirk. The rather obviously named Liverpool, Ormskirk and Preston Railway prepared proposals in 1844 and 1845 [23,24]. Rival schemes put up by the Manchester, Wigan and Southport and by the West Lancashire appeared in 1845 [25,26].

The decision went in favour of the Liverpool, Ormskirk and Preston, which received its Act of Parliament in 1846 [27]. As well as the main line from Liverpool to Preston, the Act authorised a branch from Ormskirk to Skelmersdale, which was intended to serve the collieries there. The main line was opened on 2nd April 1849 [11], and the branch probably at the same time. Although the official date has not been recorded, the Skelmersdale line was certainly in existence as far as Blaguegate when a revision of the 1st edition of the 6" map was published about 1850.

The Bolton, Wigan and Liverpool Railway prepared plans [28] in 1844 for a line from Liverpool to join the Bolton and Preston Railway near Lostock. From Pemberton to Ince the line was to keep to the south side of the Leeds and Liverpool Canal, passing near to Pottery Lane. There were also to be branches from the west end of the tunnel at Upholland to a junction with the Liverpool, Ormskirk and Preston's line at Skelmersdale and from Hindley to Haigh. The latter was to terminate at the Wigan to Blackrod road near the Blucher Inn.

The proposals were merged with those for a line from Bolton to Bury, under the title of the Liverpool and Bury Railway, and were authorised by Parliament in 1845 [29]. The Haigh Branch seems to have been dropped, but powers were granted for a connection with North Union main line. A second Act [30], in 1846, authorised a junction with the Springs Branch and a line from

Development of the Canal and Railway System

the Springs Branch to Whelley. It also authorised a branch from Lostock to a point near the White Horse Public House at Westhoughton.

In 1845 there were proposals by the Blackburn, Chorley and Liverpool Railway for a line from Errwood Bridge, on the Blackburn and Bolton Railway, to a junction with the Liverpool and Bury at the east end of Upholland Tunnel[31]. This would have passed through Chorley and then through Coppull and Shevington, crossing the River Douglas near Dean Locks. There would have been connections with the Bolton and Preston Railway near Chorley and with the North Union Railway near Coppull, and the line would have served the colliery area north and west of Wigan. The scheme does not seem to have obtained Parliamentary sanction and nothing further is heard of it.

Several rival projects were promoted for railways serving Southport. The Manchester, Wigan and Southport Railway proposals of 1845[32] were for a line from Pendleton on the Manchester and Bolton Railway, through Atherton, Hindley and Ince to a junction with the North Union near the bridge over the Leeds and Liverpool Canal at Ince. Through Wigan it was intended to run over the North Union Railway, using that company's station. Immediately north of the station, the Manchester Wigan and Southport's line would have left the North Union and, keeping to the north bank of the canal throughout, would have passed through Appley Bridge and Burscough to reach its terminus. At Burscough, junctions were to be built to connect with the Company's projected line from Liverpool to Preston. Numerous branches were proposed, including one to Southport Pier. In the Wigan area there was to be connection at Ince with the Liverpool and Bury Railway and a branch from Hindley across Amberswood Common to join the North Union at the canal bridge at Bamfurlong.

The West Lancashire Railway put forward an alternative proposal, also in 1845[33], for a line from Southport to Wigan. This would have started at a junction with the Liverpool and Bury Railway at Ince and would have followed the same course through Wigan as that later adopted by the Lancashire and Yorkshire Railway. Beyond Douglas Bank, its route was almost identical to that of the rival Manchester Wigan and Southport Railway, again keeping to the north side of the canal. There would have been connecting lines to the North Union north and south of that company's Wigan station and to the Manchester, Wigan and Southport Railway's proposed Manchester line at Ince.

Neither of the 1845 schemes came to fruition, and a further proposal[34] was prepared in 1846 by a new company, the Manchester and Southport Railway. East of Ince and west of Gathurst the route was essentially the same as that put forward by the Manchester, Wigan and Southport in 1845. From Ince, where there was a spur to the Liverpool and Bury Railway, the line followed the West Lancashire's projected route as far as Douglas Bank. From here to Gathurst, the line now took to the south side of the canal, on the course later followed by the Lancashire and Yorkshire Railway.

The Manchester and Southport Railway, in its amended form of 1846, was authorised in 1847[35]. As well as the main line from Southport to Pendleton, the Act also sanctioned a number of branches. These included connecting lines to the Liverpool, Ormskirk and Preston Railway near Burscough, to the Bolton and Leigh Railway at Atherton and to the Liverpool and Manchester Railway at Barton Moss. There were also three short lines serving collieries at Little Hulton and Tyldesley and a branch to Pungle Lane in Westhoughton. In the neighbourhood of Wigan, two lines were to connect with the Liverpool and Bury Railway's authorised route, which passed to the south of the town. One left the Southport line to the west of the site of Wigan station and joined the Liverpool and Bury near Pemberton. The other was a short spur at a point where the two lines crossed near Ince. Two connections with the North Union were also authorised. One was at the south end of the North Union station, where the two lines were adjacent. The second was a branch from the Manchester and Southport near Hindley to the North Union at Bamfurlong. In the event, much of the main line and the majority of the branches were never constructed.

A further line which would have passed through the southern and eastern parts of the Wigan coalfield was the Liverpool and Bolton Direct Railway. This company prepared plans[36] in 1845 for a line from Garston to Bolton, connecting with the Liverpool and Manchester at Huyton. Its route would have taken it through Prescot, St Helens, Ashton, Hindley and Westhoughton. Its primary purpose seems to have been for the transport of passengers and merchandise, with little emphasis on coal traffic, as it by-passed the collieries which were then in operation.

The Amalgamations of 1845 and 1846

Amalgamation of many of the smaller railways operating in South Lancashire took place in the second half of the 1840s, leading to the creation of the two large companies which were to dominate the scene for the next seventy five years. The Grand Junction Railway, which extended from Newton le Willows to Birmingham, took over the Liverpool and Manchester, the Bolton and Leigh and Leigh and Kenyon railways on 1st July 1845[37]. The next year, on 16th July 1846, the Grand Junction amalgamated with the Manchester and Birmingham and London and Birmingham Railways to form the London and North Western Railway[38].

The Liverpool and Bury Railway was taken over by the Manchester and Leeds Railway in 1846[39], as part of a policy of expansion. On 23rd July 1847[40], the Manchester and Leeds changed its name to the Lancashire and Yorkshire Railway. The Manchester and Southport was leased to the Lancashire and Yorkshire from May 1848, but was not taken over until April 1855[41].

The Liverpool, Ormskirk and Preston became part of the East Lancashire Railway in October 1846. The latter remained independent of the Lancashire and Yorkshire until 13th July 1859, when the two companies amalgamated[42].

The North Union was in effect split between the London and North Western and the Lancashire and Yorkshire. It had been leased jointly by the Grand Junction and Manchester and Leeds as from 1st January 1846 and the property was vested jointly in them from July 1846[43]. The section from Parkside to Euxton Junction was operated and maintained by the LNWR and became part of the West Coast main line from London to Scotland. The Lancashire and Yorkshire operated and maintained the section from the Bolton to Euxton Junction, while that from Euxton Junction to Preston was operated and maintained jointly by the two companies.

The North Union Company was dissolved as from 1st July 1888 and absorbed by the two lessees[44]. The physical assets were split between them in July 1889[45]. Parkside to Euxton Junction became the sole property of the London and North Western, Bolton to Euxton Junction became the sole property of the Lancashire and Yorkshire, and Euxton Junction to Preston became jointly owned.

In the late 1840s the newly formed Lancashire and Yorkshire Railway had need to economise and this led to considerable changes in the plans for the Liverpool and Bury and the Manchester and Southport Railways. Construction of the former continued, with the exception of the portion to the south of Wigan, from Pemberton to Ince. Between these points the route of the Manchester and Southport was adopted instead, passing through what was later to become Wallgate station. The line was opened throughout on 20th November 1848[11].

Work on the other parts of the Manchester and Southport, between Pendleton and Ince and between Wigan and Southport, did not proceed. No construction was carried out on the Liverpool and Bury Railway's branches to Skelmersdale, Haigh, Whelley and Westhoughton. Of the many authorised branches of the Manchester and Southport Railway, only those from Wigan to Pemberton and the very short connecting line to the North Union at Wigan were completed.

Developments in the 1850s and 1860s

There was an enforced revival of the Wigan to Southport line in August 1852, when Southport interests obtained a writ of mandamus requiring the Lancashire and Yorkshire to complete the railway. Construction commenced and the line was opened throughout on 9th April 1855, the section from Burscough Bridge into Southport being jointly owned with the East Lancashire Railway. The section from Burscough Bridge to Wigan was constructed as single line. It was subsequently doubled, the second track being opened on 1st November 1861[41].

Proposals were also drawn up in 1852, in the name of the Manchester and Southport Railway, to proceed with a direct line from Wigan to Manchester. The Deposited Plans, submitted to Parliament in November 1852[46], show that it was intended to follow the route of the Manchester and Southport Railway, as authorised in 1847, as far as Howe Bridge. Between here and Manchester the new line was intended to to take a more northerly course, passing near Little Hulton and Walkden, to join the Manchester and Bolton line near Clifton.

The 1852 scheme did not proceed, but, in 1860, the Lancashire and Yorkshire Railway Company again turned its attention to a direct line to Manchester[47]. This was to run from Hindley to Clifton Junction with various branches, including one from Hindley towards Moss Hall Colliery. The proposals, which were submitted to Parliament in 1861, were in competition with the London and North Western's projected Eccles, Tyldesley and Wigan line, and served much the same district[48].

The outcome was that the Lancashire and Yorkshire proposals were defeated and the London and North Western scheme obtained its Act[49]. The LNWR line was duly opened from a junction with the former Liverpool and Manchester line at Eccles to the North Union Railway at Springs Branch Junction on 1st September 1864. A connecting line from Tyldesley via Leigh to join the Bolton to Kenyon line and a short spur from Chowbent East Junction to Atherton Junction were opened at the same time. A second spur, from Chowbent West Junction to Atherton Junction was opened in 1883[11].

The Lancashire and Yorkshire also turned its attention again to a loop line to the south of Wigan. Proposals[50] were submitted to Parliament in 1862, following the route authorised by the Liverpool and Bury Act of 1845, for which the powers had presumably expired. Later Line Plans show that the land needed for the new line was purchased by the railway company. The 1st edition of the 25" map, published in 1893, shows that a start had been made with the earthworks. The line was, however, never completed on its proposed course.

There were also developments at Skelmersdale during this period. Although the branch from Ormskirk to Blaguegate, authorised by the Liverpool, Ormskirk and Preston Act of 1846, had been opened around 1849, there still was no rail connection to the south. The powers, granted to the Liverpool and Bury Railway in 1845 for a branch from Upholland, had not been exercised and subsequent proposals had come to nothing.

Development of the Canal and Railway System

The St Helens and Southport Railway had been promoted in 1851 and had intended to build two lines [51]. The first would have run from a junction with the St Helens Railway to the LO&P's Blaguegate Branch, with two spurs to the Liverpool and Bury line at Rainford. The second line would have left the LO&P's main line south of Ormskirk and run via Halsall to Southport.

There had been earlier schemes for a line from St Helens as far as Rainford. The Liverpool and Manchester Railway had obtained an Act in 1845 [52] for a railway between these two places and, in 1847, the St Helens Canal and Railway Company had made arrangements to lease the line [53]. The powers appear to have lapsed and the scheme was revived by the St Helens Company in its Act of 1853 [54]. The line, which provided an alternative route from the collieries at Wigan to Garston and Liverpool, was opened for coal traffic on 5th December 1857 [55]. Passenger trains started on 1st February 1858 [11].

It was left to the East Lancashire Railway to complete the link between Skelmersdale and Rainford. An Act [56] was obtained in 1853 for a railway from the terminus of the Blaguegate Branch to an end on junction with the St Helens line. The railway was opened for traffic on 1st March 1858 [11]. The connecting link to the Lancashire and Yorkshire at Rainford Junction, apparently built without express Parliamentary authority, was opened at the same time [41]. As noted earlier, the East Lancashire Railway amalgamated with the Lancashire and Yorkshire on 13th August 1859. The St Helens Canal and Railway Company became part of the LNWR system on 29th July 1864 [57].

The Lancashire Union Railways

The early 1860s saw moves by the principal coal owners to provide an independent rail outlet from the Wigan area. In the one direction they wanted a shorter route to Liverpool by way of St Helens. In the other, they wanted a direct route to markets in Blackburn and north-east Lancashire. This resulted in the formation of the Lancashire Union Railways Company, to which many of the Wigan colliery proprietors subscribed. The list was headed by the Earl of Crawford and Balcarres, Lord Lindsay, John Lancaster and Alfred Hewlett, whom we shall meet later in connection with the Wigan Coal and Iron Company and other major colliery undertakings.

There had been an earlier proposal, in 1862, for an independent Blackburn, Chorley and Wigan Railway [58], which seems to have been dropped in favour of the Lancashire Union scheme. The 1862 line was intended to leave the North Union Railway south of Coppull and to run through Duxbury and Chorley to its own terminal station in Blackburn.

In 1863, the Parliamentary Plans [59] for the Lancashire Union Railway were drawn up. These showed a main line starting at a junction with the North Union Railway at Boars Head and running to an independent terminus in Blackburn. Between Adlington and Chorley the Lancashire Union was to be separate from the existing Bolton and Preston line and to the east of it.

A second main line was to run from the St Helens Railway near Parr to a junction with the first line at Haigh. Between St Helens and Hindley the course was to the south of that eventually adopted, passing through Haydock and Ashton and crossing over the North Union Railway at Bamfurlong. There were to be connections with the North Union at Bamfurlong, with the LNWR Eccles, Tyldesley and Wigan line at Platt Bridge, with the Springs branch of the North Union, and with the L&Y at Hindley, Adlington, Chorley and Blackburn. A branch was proposed near Adlington to serve the Ellerbeck collieries.

Development of the Canal and Railway System

Although the Lancashire Union was nominally independent, it had the backing of the London and North Western Railway. This aroused the opposition of the Lancashire and Yorkshire, which promoted its own scheme for railways linking Blackburn, Chorley and Wigan [60]. Two new lines were proposed, from the Bolton and Preston line at Chorley to the Preston and Blackburn line near Cherry Tree and from the Bolton and Preston line at Red Moss to the Wigan and Bolton line at Hindley. There was also to be a branch from Blackrod to Horwich.

In the 1864 Parliamentary Session the merits of both schemes were considered. The Lancashire and Yorkshire proposals were accepted in their entirety and authorisation [61] was given for the Chorley to Blackburn and Red Moss to Hindley lines, together with the Horwich Branch. The Lancashire Union received authorisation [62] for its line from St Helens to Haigh but only that portion of its Blackburn line from Boars Head as far as the Bolton and Preston line at Adlington. The connection with the North Union main line at Bamfurlong was thrown out, as was a short spur at St Helens. The Ellerbeck Branch was retained, as were the spurs to the Eccles, Tyldesley and Wigan line, to the Lancashire and Yorkshire at Hindley and to the Springs Branch.

Further negotiations between the Lancashire Union and Lancashire and Yorkshire companies resulted in an agreement to transfer the lines between Boars Head and Adlington and between Chorley and Blackburn to joint ownership. This was confirmed by the Lancashire and Yorkshire and Lancashire Union Act of 1865 [63].

At this time, the Lancashire Union was reconsidering its line west of Wigan. A competing scheme, put forward by the South Lancashire Railway and Dock Company, had appeared in 1864 [64] which would parallel the already authorised route. This company proposed to build a new dock south of Liverpool, at Dingle, and a railway from there to the southern outskirts of Wigan, passing through Childwall, Prescot and St Helens. There were to be connections with the North Union main line near Ince Moss, with the Springs Branch in the vicinity of Ince Forge, with the Eccles, Tyldesley and Wigan line at Platt Bridge and with the Lancashire and Yorkshire Railway near Hindley.

The outcome was that the Lancashire Union abandoned its earlier route and applied to Parliament for a revised line from St Helens to Hindley, which closely followed that proposed by the South Lancashire Railway and Dock Company. The new Lancashire Union line was authorised by Parliament in 1865 [65]. The Act also authorised a branch from Brynn to the Norley Hall Colliery Company's railway together with a spur to the Lancashire and Yorkshire at Pemberton, a spur to the North Union line at Ince Moss, a revised connection with the Eccles, Tyldesley and Wigan line and a branch from Roundhouse to Kirkless Hall Ironworks. The proposed branch to Rose Bridge Colliery, shown on the Deposited Plans [66], was not authorised.

The 1865 Act confirmed the arrangements whereby the London and North Western was to work the line. The Lancashire and Yorkshire Railway was given access to St Helens. There was also a provision, which does not seem to have been implemented, that the Earl of Crawford and Balcarres and the Kirkless Hall Coal and Iron Company would have to work their own trains to Widnes, Runcorn and Garston if required to do so by the LNWR.

Further Acts in 1866 [67], 1868 [68] and 1871 [69] concerned short branches in the neighbourhood of St Helens, which are outside the scope of the present study. It is however of interest to note that the 1866 Act permitted Richard Evans and Company, the Haydock colliery proprietors, to work to Widnes, Runcorn and Garston with their own locomotives, an option which does not seem to have been taken up.

25

Development of the Canal and Railway System

The Lancashire and Yorkshire's line from Red Moss to Hindley opened on 15th July 1868 for goods traffic and for passengers on 14th September 1868 [41]. The Horwich branch was opened for goods traffic on 15th July 1868 and for passengers on 14th February 1870 [41]. The Lancashire and Yorkshire and Lancashire Union Joint lines between Boars Head and Adlington and between Chorley and Blackburn were opened, according to Greville [11] for goods traffic on 1st November 1869. The opening to passenger traffic should have taken place on 15th November, but was deferred to 1st December, in order to comply with certain requirements imposed by the government inspector [70].

The Lancashire Union line from Ince Moss to the St Helens Railway at Gerards Bridge was also opened for goods traffic on 1st November 1869 [11] and for passengers on 1st December [70]. The Pemberton Branch and its spur to the L&Y, neither of which carried regular passenger trains, are believed to have opened at the same time as the St Helens line, although no official record appears to have survived.

The Whelley line of the Lancashire Union, from Ince Moss Junction to Haigh Junction was opened on 1st November 1869 for goods traffic only [11]. The connection with the Eccles, Tyldesley and Wigan line, the Roundhouse Branch and the connection to the Springs Branch are all believed to have opened on the same date, although again no official record appears to have survived. Passenger stations were subsequently built at Whelley and Hindley and, for a short period from 1st January 1872, a service was provided from Whelley to Liverpool. Lack of patronage caused the trains to be withdrawn as from 1st March 1872 [70].

On the former Lancashire Union line between Amberswood East Jct and De Trafford Jct in 1961, an ex-LNWR 0-8-0 goods engine hauls a coal train from Bamfurlong Sorting Sidings to Kearsley Power Station. An ex-LMSR "Jubilee" Class 4-6-0, No 45600, is at the rear. The train will reverse at De Trafford Jct and will then travel over the spur to Hindley and the former Lancashire and Yorkshire line to Bolton.　　　　　　　　　　　　　　　　　　A.C. Gilbert

Development of the Canal and Railway System

There was delay in completing the Ellerbeck Branch, and an extension of time was granted by the Lancashire and Yorkshire and Lancashire Union Act of 1868 [71]. Completion was to be by 25th January 1870 under penalty of legal action by Edward Cardwell, the owner of the mineral rights. The line was reported to be ready for traffic on 19th June 1871. It was presumably opened shortly afterwards, despite the date being given in the official Lancashire and Yorkshire records as 6th January 1877 [70]. The line only carried goods and mineral traffic and was never used by regular passenger trains.

The final section to be constructed under auspices of the Lancashire Union Railways was a single line connection from Whelley Junction to the North Union at Standish. This was authorised under an Act of 1877 [72,73]. A second line, forming a burrowing junction with the North Union, was authorised by the LNWR (New Railways) Act of 1881 [74,75]. The usually quoted opening date for the connection from Whelley to Standish is 5th June 1882, [11] but we do not know whether this refers to the first or the second of the two lines.

The independent existence of the Lancashire Union Railways Company came to an end on 1st July 1883, when it was absorbed by the London and North Western [76]. The LNWR later adapted the Lancashire Union route through Whelley as an avoiding line for Wigan. Although mainly intended for freight traffic, it began to be used by certain passenger trains, following the opening of the Hindley Junction and Platt Bridge Junction lines. The first recorded services were through trains from Manchester to Blackpool and elsewhere, which started to run from the summer of 1887 over the section from Amberswood East Junction to Standish Junction [70]. Much later, from July 1924, some of these services were diverted over the spur from Hindley No 2 Cabin, joining the Whelley Loop at De Trafford Junction.

The Wigan Junction Railway

In the 1870s another railway appeared on the scene, which was to provide competition, albeit on a limited scale, to the monopoly held by the London and North Western and the Lancashire and Yorkshire companies. The Wigan Junction Railway was promoted to provide an independent outlet from the Wigan coalfield to the Cheshire Lines Railway, which was in the joint ownership of the Manchester, Sheffield and Lincolnshire, the Midland and the Great Northern Railways.

The proposal of 1873 [77] was for a line commencing at a junction with the Cheshire Lines at Glazebrook and running almost due north to Wigan. The line was to cross the North Union south of the canal bridge at Ince and terminate at the foot of Queen Street. There was to be a branch to Ackers Whitley's Bickershaw Railway, two spurs to the Lancashire Union at Strangeways, a spur to the Springs Branch and a short branch from near the Wigan terminus to Pottery Lane.

The scheme received Parliamentary authorisation in 1874 [78], with the exception of the sections of line west of the North Union. The branch to the Bickershaw Railway was to be extended to James Diggle's colliery. A further Act in 1875 [79] authorised an extension to a new Wigan station in Standishgate and a new branch from Ince under the North Union to Parsons Meadow Bridge. Also authorised was a deviation of the 1874 line between the junction with the Bickershaw Branch and Strangeways, an extension of the Bickershaw Branch to the Wigan Coal and Iron Company's railway at Westleigh and a branch from Wigshaw Lane to join the Cheshire Lines Railway near Padgate. A proposed extension [80] from Standishgate past the

Development of the Canal and Railway System

Gidlow and Swinley Collieries and Holme House Colliery to link up with the Wigan Coal and Iron Company's Standish railway system near Rylands Sidings was thrown out.

The Wigan Junction Company experienced considerable difficulty in raising sufficient money for the construction of its railway, and turned to the Manchester, Sheffield and Lincolnshire for help. This company was authorised to subscribe funds by the Wigan Junction Act of 1878 [81]. The Act also authorised minor deviations in the branch to the Bickershaw Railway and the Wigan Coal and Iron Company's Westleigh system.

The line as far as Strangeways Colliery was formally opened on 16th October 1879, when an engine and three first class carriages, conveying directors and officials, left Stoney Lane Bridge at Hindley for Glazebrook [82]. Regular passenger trains did not start running until five years later, only coal and general goods traffic being conveyed initially [83]. The branch to Ackers Whitley's Bickershaw Railway also appears to have been opened at the same time, although official confirmation is lacking. It is shown as completed on the Plans [84] prepared in November 1879 for the MS&L Bill of 1880.

There was delay in constructing the spurs to the Lancashire Union and to the Springs Branch. Although Dow [83] quotes an opening date of July 1880 for both connections to the Lancashire Union, we believe this to be incorrect. An extension of time up to 16th July 1881 was granted under Section 36 of the MS&L Act of 1879 [85] for the completion of the connection to Amberswood West Junction. Under Section 37 of the Act, the LNWR was granted running powers from Amberswood West to Strangeways Colliery. As we shall describe more fully in Chapter 10, the owners of Strangeways Hall Colliery assisted in the construction works. The line was eventually opened before the end of 1882, being shown on the Deposited Plans [86] for the Hindley Junctions line of the LNWR, prepared in November of that year.

The scheme for a passenger station in Standishgate was dropped in favour of a site on the south side of Darlington Street. Abandonment of the proposed route north of this point and also of the branch from Wigshaw Lane to Padgate was confirmed by the MS&L (New Works) Act of 1881 [87]. Further alterations to the Westleigh branch were authorised. Working arrangements with the Manchester, Sheffield and Lincolnshire, in force since the opening of the line, were confirmed. Three proposals which are shown on the Deposited Plans [88] were thrown out. One was a branch which started near the end of the authorised but incomplete connection to the Lancashire Union at Amberswood East and ran through Hindley to join the Wigan Coal and Iron Company's railway from Kirkless to Hindley. The others were two short spurs at Lower Ince to the Lancashire and Yorkshire's Wigan to Bolton line.

Further extensions of time were granted by the MS&L and Cheshire Lines Act of 1882 [89]. A completion date of 16th August 1885 was set for the main line to Darlington Street, for the branch from Ince to Parsons Meadow Bridge and for the connections to the Springs Branch and to the Lancashire Union at Amberswood East. The Act actually refers to the connection to Amberswood West, but we believe this was due to an error in drafting the Bill.

The main line was eventually opened to Darlington Street on 1st April 1884, when passenger trains first started to use the line from Glazebrook [83]. Some construction took place on the spur to the Springs Branch, as can be seen from the 1st edition of the 25" map; the rails never seem to have been laid. Land was purchased for the Parsons Meadow branch [90], but there is no evidence that any work was undertaken. The branch to Westleigh was also dropped.

The Amberswood East connection with the Lancashire Union Railway had not been completed by November 1882, when the Deposited Plans [91] were submitted by the London and North Western for their Hindley Junctions Railway. The plans show that rails had been laid by

Development of the Canal and Railway System

the Wigan Junction Company on the curve to Amberswood East but had not been joined to the Lancashire Union tracks.

The LNWR proposal was for a connection from the Eccles, Tyldesley and Wigan line to the Lancashire Union at Amberswood East, on a course parallel to, but independent of, the Wigan Junction Company's spur. This was modified by Parliament and the LNWR (New Railways) Act of 1883 [92] only authorised a connection from the Eccles, Tyldesley and Wigan line to the Wigan Junction Railway south of that company's Hindley and Platt Bridge Station. At the same time, the Act granted running powers to the LNWR through the station and over the yet to be completed Wigan Junction spur to Amberswood East. The Hindley Junctions line was opened for traffic on 25th October 1886 [70], which means that the Wigan Junction Company's spur to Amberswood East must have been completed on or before that date.

A major extension of the Wigan Junction Railway was planned by the Manchester, Sheffield and Lincolnshire in 1883, when application was made to Parliament [93] for a line from the Darlington Street station at Wigan to join the West Lancashire Railway at New Longton, thus gaining access to Preston and beyond. The line would have followed the Douglas valley past the town centre and then struck off past Holme House, crossing the North Union line a little to the north of Rylands Sidings, where there would have been a short spur to the Wigan Coal and Iron Company's Standish railway system. From here, the new line would have passed close to the collieries at Broomfield, Langtree, Welch Whittle and Pemberton House.

The line was authorised by the MS&L (Additional Powers) Act of 1883 [94]. The only portion to be built was the short extension from Darlington Street to the new Wigan Central Station,

46448 at the head of a Wigan Central to Manchester Central passenger train, entering Bickershaw Station on the former Wigan Junction Railway. Photographed in May 1956, after British Railways had taken over.   C.H.A. Townley

Development of the Canal and Railway System

which was opened on 1st August 1892 [11]. Discussions about the viability of the remainder dragged on until 1896, when the scheme was finally dropped [83].

The independent life of the Wigan Junction Railway came to end on 1st June 1906 [95], when it was taken over by the Great Central Railway, the name adopted by the Manchester, Sheffield and Lincolnshire Company on 1st August 1897.

The London and North Western Railway in the 1880s and 1890s

No doubt spurred on by the threat of competition from the Wigan Junction Railway, the London and North Western took steps to provide an improved southern outlet for collieries in the neighbourhood of Bickershaw and West Leigh. Powers for the West Leigh Branch Railways were obtained in 1880 [96], which authorised a line from Pennington on the Bolton to Kenyon railway to join Ackers, Whitley's private Bickershaw Railway to the north of the Leeds and Liverpool Canal at Plank Lane. Also authorised was a branch from the Pennington to Plank Lane line to join Diggle's private railway from Westleigh Colliery to the canal.

As we shall describe in a later chapter, the Bickershaw Railway was used by a number of colliery concerns in addition to its owners, Ackers, Whitley & Co Ltd. The Abram Coal Company, John Scowcroft & Co Ltd and the Hindley Field Coal Company all shipped coal on the canal at Plank Lane. In the opposite direction the railway was used to convey coal from these collieries to the LNWR Eccles, Tyldesley and Wigan line.

An ex-LNWR 0-8-0 engine at the head of a coal train, coming off the Bickershaw Branch on to the Eccles, Tyldesley and Wigan line. The photograph was taken in 1960 and the remains of John Scowcroft and Company's Hindley Green Colliery, closed some 30 years earlier, can be seen in the left background.   W.S. Garth

Development of the Canal and Railway System

To make this territory more secure the LNWR promoted a further application to Parliament to purchase the Bickershaw Railway and the associated coal tip on the canal at Plank Lane. This was authorised by the LNWR (New Railways) Act of 1881 [97] which also provided for a new south to west connection with the Eccles, Tyldesley and Wigan line. There were naturally many clauses protecting the interests of the former users of the line, including concessionary rates for coal taken to the canal and to Messrs Stocks' glass works at Plank Lane. Coal had to be conveyed free of charge to the Eccles, Tyldesley and Wigan line during the construction period.

The line was opened throughout from Pennington to the Eccles, Tyldesley and Wigan on 9th March 1885 for goods and coal traffic only [11] (The second edition of reference 11 gives the opening date as 2nd February 1885). It is assumed that the short branch to join Diggle's railway opened at the same time. Further developments took place later, when the line was brought up to passenger standards. A direct flyover was provided from the Tyldesley to Pennington line at Pennington East Junction to join the original line at Pennington West Junction. The connection with the branch to Diggle's railway was moved to Pennington South Junction. The new arrangements were brought into use for goods traffic on 2nd June 1903 [11]. Passenger trains started to run through from Pennington East Junction to Bickershaw Junction on 1st October 1903 [11].

Meanwhile, increasing traffic locally in South Lancashire and on the West Coast main line had required additional facilities. The London and North Western Railway as early as 1874 had prepared plans [98] for an extra pair of tracks between Bamfurlong and Standish. South of Wigan these would have taken an independent course to the east of the North Union line, but north of the station they would have been adjacent to the existing formation. This scheme was not pursued and instead it was decided to use the Lancashire Union line through Whelley as a by pass to Wigan. Although there were further abortive proposals for widening between Wigan and Standish in 1891 [99], this section has always remained double track.

We have already described how, at the northern end of what was to become the Whelley Loop, connecting lines had been provided between Whelley Junction and Standish Junction. At the southern end, the Hindley Junctions Railway, which we have also mentioned previously, gave access from the Manchester direction. To provide through running for trains to and from the main line from Warrington and the south, the Platt Bridge Junction Railway [86] was built from Bamfurlong to Amberswood West. This was authorised by the LNWR (New Railways) Act of 1883 [92] and, like the Hindley Junctions line, was opened on 25th October 1886 [70].

An additional pair of tracks was provided on the main lines south of Wigan and north of Standish. The widening between Golborne and Springs Branch Junction was authorised in 1883 [86,92] and brought into use on 29th October 1888 [70]. That between Springs Branch Junction and Wigan was authorised in 1894 [100] and brought into use in the autumn of 1894 [70] and that between Standish and Euxton Junction was authorised in 1888 [101,102] and brought into use in the autumn of 1895 [103].

An enlarged passenger station at Wigan was opened in the autumn of 1894 [103]. On the former Lancashire Union line, widening between Carr Mill and Ince Moss was authorised in 1887 [104,105] and the third and fourth lines were opened on 16th October 1892 [70]. Additional tracks between Ince Moss and Springs Branch Junction were authorised in 1890 [106] and opened in the autumn of 1894 [70].

Further improvements were brought about by the construction of the Bamfurlong Junction Railways, authorised in 1887 [104,105]. Part of the work was completed on 10th February 1889 and the remainder on 1st October 1889 [70]. The junction from the main passenger lines was altered,

Development of the Canal and Railway System

the down Whelley line being carried under the Wigan lines. Two additional connections were provided which passed under the Wigan lines from the goods lines on the down side. One gave access to the sidings on the up side at Springs Branch Junction. The other pair of tracks joined the Whelley Loop at Fir Tree House Junction.

Finally, the sidings layout at Bamfurlong was enlarged and modernised, so that all marshalling of goods trains in the Wigan area could be concentrated there. The land which was needed was acquired under the 1890 Act [106] and the new Bamfurlong Sorting Sidings were brought into use in the summer of 1895 [70]. At the same time a through siding connection was opened giving access, at Ince Moss Junction, to the former Lancashire Union line to St Helens.

The Lancashire and Yorkshire Railway in the 1880s and 1890s

There were improvements, too, on the Lancashire and Yorkshire Railway during this period. Following further tentative proposals for a direct line from Wigan to Manchester in the 1870s [41], a comprehensive plan was drawn up in the early 1880s for new lines in South Lancashire, with the object of providing improved routes between Manchester and Preston and Manchester and Liverpool. An Act of 1883 [107] authorised a railway from Pendleton, on the Manchester and Bolton line, to Crow Nest Junction on the Hindley to Blackrod line. Then in 1884 an Act [108] was obtained for a connection from this line at Dobbs Brow to the Hindley and Blackrod branch. Finally, in 1885, there was an Act [109] for the Wigan Loop, from Pemberton to Hindley, and for the Horwich Fork, giving direct access to the Horwich Branch from the Bolton direction. Between Pemberton and Ince, the former took a route to the south of that proposed in 1845 and 1862. Between Ince and Hindley it followed the earlier course.

The Pendleton to Hindley line was constructed with four tracks. One pair of tracks was opened for goods traffic as far as Atherton on 2nd July 1888 and from there to Crow Nest Junction on 1st October of the same year. The second pair of tracks was opened on 1st June 1889, on which date passenger traffic commenced [41].

The Pemberton Loop was opened for goods traffic on 1st May 1889 and for passengers on 1st June [41]. The connection from the Atherton line at Dobbs Brow Junction to the Hindley and Blackrod Branch was opened for both goods and passenger trains on 1st June 1889 [41]. The Horwich Fork had been opened the previous year, for goods on 20th June 1887 and passengers on 1st July 1887 [41]. The connection between the Hindley and Blackrod Branch and the Bolton and Preston line was moved from Red Moss to Horwich Fork Junction at this time. This did not involve a new route north of Hilton House, as has been suggested by a recent series of historical maps [110]. What was done was to provide an additional pair of tracks between the site of the original junction and the new junction at Horwich Fork.

The line between Crow Nest Junction and Hindley No 3 Cabin, where the Pemberton Loop diverged, was widened with an extra pair of tracks, which were ready for traffic on 26th July 1887 [41]. Powers were then obtained to widen the whole of the main line between Pemberton and Walton Junction on the outskirts of Liverpool. An Act of 1891 [111] authorised the portion from Rainford Junction to Walton Junction and an Act of 1899 [112] covered that from Pemberton to Rainford Junction, including the construction of a second tunnel at Upholland. Very little work was actually carried out, except for the provision of up and down goods loops between Winstanley Sidings and Orrell East, between Ditton Brook Sidings and Holland Moss and between Rainford Colliery and Simonswood.

Development of the Canal and Railway System

A freight train bound for Liverpool passes Winstanley Colliery Sidings Signal Box, hauled by an ex-LMSR Class 8F, No 48515. The photograph was taken in November 1961. The exchange sidings with the Winstanley Colliery railway system occupied the level ground at the right of the picture
A.C. Gilbert

The Liverpool, St Helens and South Lancashire Railway

In the southern part of our territory, plans [113] were drawn up by the St Helens and Wigan Junction Railway for a line from St Helens to Lowton St Mary's . This was promoted, mainly by St Helens interests, as an independent company, and was authorised in 1885 [114]. In 1886 proposals were submitted to Parliament for a westward extension to a junction with the Cheshire Lines Railway at Fazakerley, from where access to Liverpool could be obtained [115]. Also proposed were a west to north curve at Lowton and a short branch to what later became the passenger station in St Helens. These were authorised by the St Helens and Wigan Junction Act of 1886 [116]. In 1889, the more pretentious name of the Liverpool, St Helens and South Lancashire Railway was adopted, but the Act [117] which permitted this change also rather ominously granted extension of time for previously authorised lines.

Financial difficulties were only overcome with the assistance of the Manchester, Sheffield and Lincolnshire Railway, which was authorised to subscribe funds [117]. The extension to Liverpool was formally abandoned by the Liverpool, St Helens and South Lancashire Act of 1897 [118]. The line from St Helens to Lowton was eventually opened for goods and coal traffic on 1st July 1895. MS&L engines worked the trains between Lowton and Golborne. Beyond Golborne, locomotives owned by the contractor, S W Pilling, took over [83,119]. The MS&L became responsible for operation of the whole line on 21st October 1895 [83].

Development of the Canal and Railway System

The Lowton to Ashton section was inspected by the Board of Trade in January 1899 and excursion trains were run to Haydock Park on 3rd and 4th February[120]. The formal opening of the whole line for passenger traffic took place on 2nd January 1900. Regular public services started the next day[83,121].

Like the Wigan Junction Railway, the Liverpool, St Helens and South Lancashire was absorbed by the Great Central Railway, as successors to the MS&L, on 1st January 1906[95].

More Proposed Lines

Towards the end of the century a number of schemes were put forward, in most instances independently of the existing railway companies. They came at a time when industry in South Lancashire was no longer expanding rapidly and were too late to stand any real chance of success. Nevertheless, those which would have passed through the Wigan area merit a brief mention.

The most ambitious, and the least likely to succeed, was the Lancashire Plateway. This was promoted by Liverpool business interests in an attempt to offer an alternative to the Manchester Ship Canal. The Ship Canal was intended to break the monopoly of raw cotton imports held by Liverpool and the railway companies which served it. The Plateway would would maintain the status of Liverpool and the enable imports through the port to be distributed throughout the whole of Lancashire. No doubt coal was one of the commodities which would have been carried in the opposite direction.

It was intended to revert to the style of railway adopted a hundred years previously for short feeder lines to the canals. The Plateway was to make use of a form of Barlow rail, to which was riveted an upstand which provided the guidance system[122]. The wagons were to have flangeless wheels so that they could be hauled by horses on ordinary roads within the port of Liverpool and could similarly be taken on ordinary roads from the Plateway termini to the mills. It was intended to use steam locomotives on the plateway proper.

The Plateway was planned to serve all the principal cotton manufacturing towns and would have been some 85 miles in total length[123]. Only parts of the scheme fall within the scope of the present book. One line would have passed through Ashton in Makerfield and then on to Bolton by way of Leigh and Atherton, eventually terminating in Rochdale. At Ashton in Makerfield a branch diverged which would have passed to the west of Wigan and then through Boars Head to Chorley, Preston, Accrington and Burnley. A further short branch from the Chorley line at Goose Green was intended to give access to a terminus in the southern outskirts of Wigan. A Bill for the Plateway was presented to Parliament in 1882, but withdrawn. The scheme was resubmitted in 1883, but again failed to gain Parliamentary sanction[122].

The Leigh and South Central Lancashire proposals of the late 1890s were for a network of conventional railways intended to provide access to the newly opened Manchester Ship Canal, on which coal shipping facilities had been established. The Deposited Plans[124], drawn up in 1894, show a main line running from the Lancashire and Yorkshire at Ince to the Lancashire and Yorkshire at Walkden, passing Low Hall Colliery and Wigan Junction Colliery and then striking across country to Leigh. A second main line, intersecting the first between Leigh and Astley, was to run from collieries south of Tyldesley to a junction with the Cheshire Lines Railway at Cadishead.

Development of the Canal and Railway System

There were to be as many as ten branches to serve individual collieries, numerous connections with existing railways, and a branch to the Partington North Coaling Basin on the Ship Canal, near Irlam. In the Wigan area there would have been spurs to the Wigan Junction Railway south of Bickershaw and Abram Station, to the London and North Western Railway's Bickershaw Branch north of Plank Lane, to Abram Colliery, to the Westleigh Colliery Company's railway and to the Wigan Coal and Iron Company's Westleigh railway system. Opposition of the established railway companies was considerable. When the Leigh and South Central Lancashire Bill was considered in Parliament in May 1895, the Preamble was not proved and nothing more is heard of the scheme.

Proposals in the early years of the present century sought to provide a northern outlet for Wigan coal, through the Midland Railway's recently opened port at Heysham. The Deposited Plans prepared for the 1907 session of Parliament[125] by the Wigan and Heysham Railway show a line which was intended to start from an end on junction with the Wigan Junction line at Wigan Central Station, to pass through Preston and to join the Midland's line from Leeds to Morecambe and Heysham at Lancaster. Blackpool was to be served by a branch from Freckleton. Through Wigan it was proposed to follow the valley of the River Douglas for the first one and a half miles. Then, after crossing the North Union north of Boars Head, the line was to pass near to the collieries at Broomfield, Chisnall Hall and Welch Whittle. There was to be a branch from the Douglas valley, south of Brock Mill, which was to cross the North Union near Elms Colliery and connect with the Wigan Coal and Iron Company's Standish railway system. The project did not receive support and was subsequently dropped.

Railways in the Twentieth Century

By the turn of the century the railway system in South Lancashire had reached its maximum extent. In the period up to the first world war coal production had reached its peak, and no new traffic was on offer. Developments in the coalfield were confined to the extension and modernisation of the existing pits rather than opening up new collieries on fresh sites, so no new branch lines were required. With two minor exceptions, the railway network remained unchanged until closures commenced in the 1930s.

In 1903, the alterations to the Bickershaw Branch and the new junctions at Pennington, referred to earlier, were completed. Then, in 1913, the Lancashire and Yorkshire obtained authorisation[126] for a short west to north spur between the Wigan and Bolton and the Bolton and Preston lines at Lostock Junction. Although the spur and an associated fan of sidings were subsequently built, it seem unlikely that they were ever connected to the Bolton and Preston line[41].

In the immediate post war period, the railway companies were brought together in four main groups, as from 1st January 1923, under the provisions of the Railways Act of 1921[127]. The Lancashire and Yorkshire Railway and the London and North Western Railway, which had previously amalgamated on 1st January 1922, became part of the London Midland and Scottish Railway. The former Great Central lines in the Wigan area passed to the London and North Eastern Railway, while the Cheshire Lines became the joint property of the two companies.

During the 1920s and 1930s the traffic carried by the railways dropped significantly. As the older and less economic collieries were closed there was a corresponding fall in the amount of coal to be transported. Passenger journeys also declined, due to competition from the rapidly expanding bus services. While the loss of revenue affected the profitability of the railway companies and led to

35

Development of the Canal and Railway System

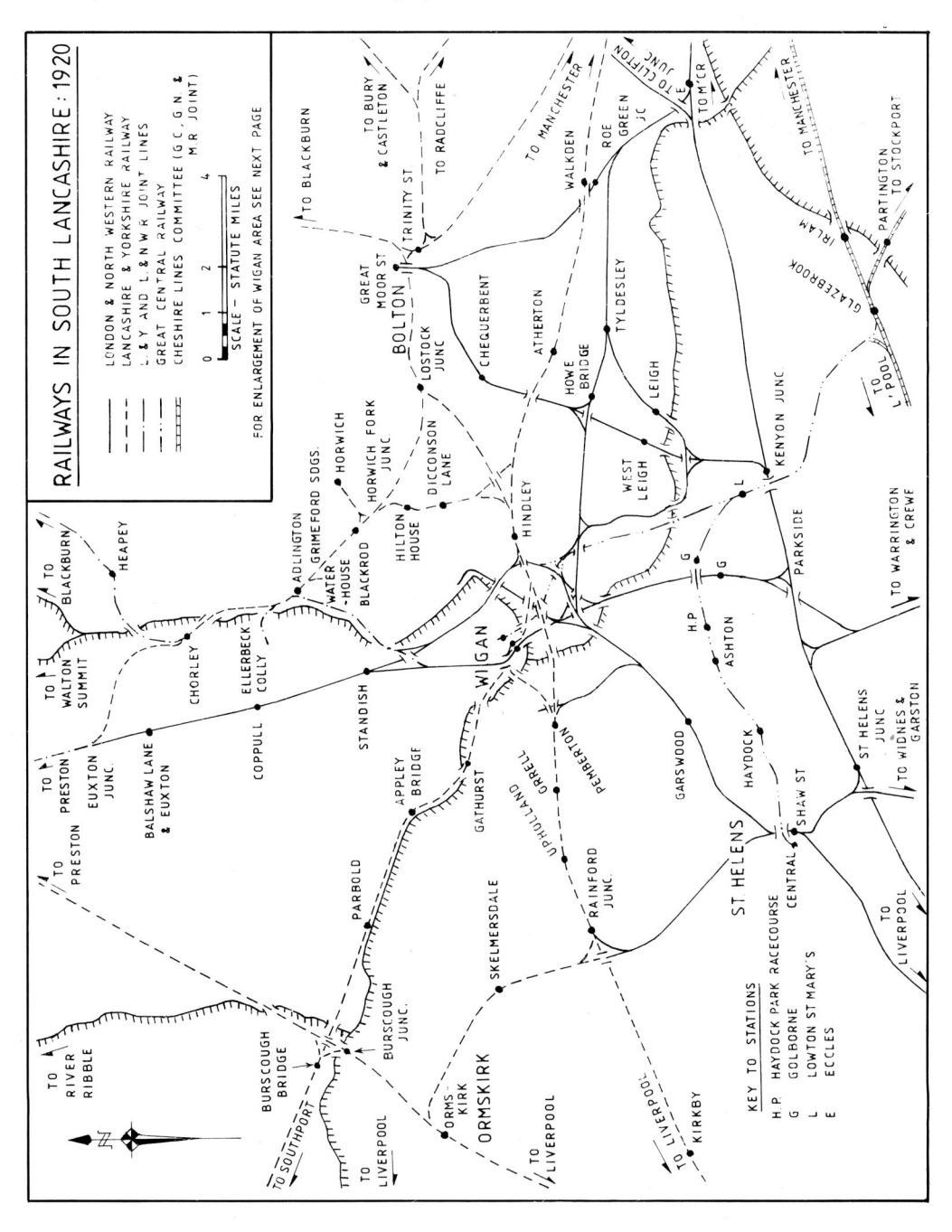

Development of the Canal and Railway System

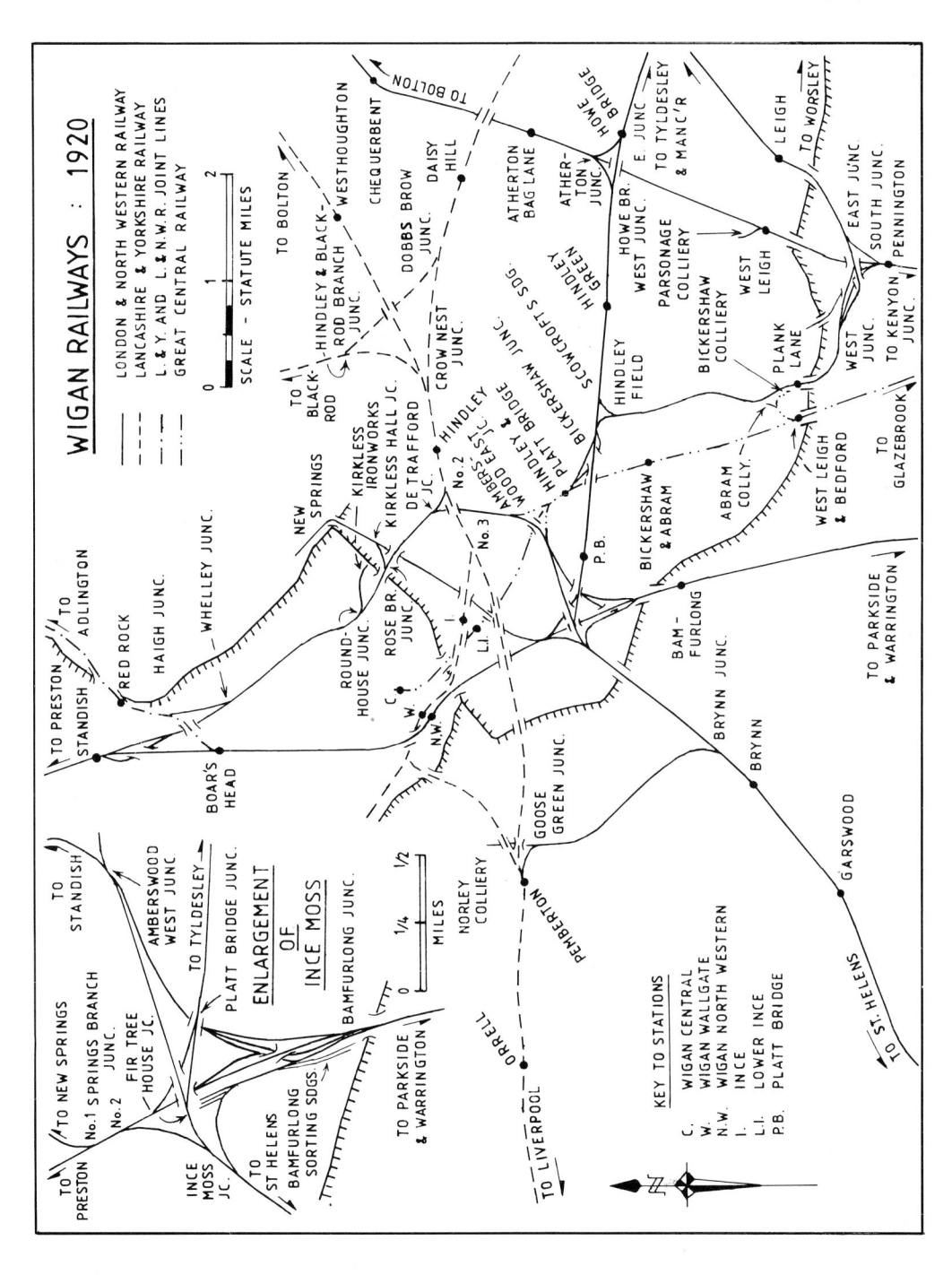

Development of the Canal and Railway System

economies in operating methods, very few lines were actually closed during this period. Those that were were all short freight-only branches – Pennington South Junction to the Westleigh Colliery railway, Goose Green Junction to the Norley Colliery railway, the Ellerbeck Branch and three branches serving the Wigan Coal and Iron Company's Kirkless Ironworks and Haigh collieries.

On 1st January 1948, further rationalisation took place when the railways passed into public ownership as a result of the Transport Act of 1947 [128]. The London Midland and Scottish lines in the Wigan area, together with those of the London and North Eastern, became part of the London Midland Region of British Railways.

The period after the second world war brought another very heavy downturn in the railway traffic. Many of the remaining collieries were closed down, either worked out or uncompetitive with more productive pits elsewhere. It was no longer economic to transport general merchandise by rail, apart from a few types of specialised traffic. For local passenger transport, the growth of private car ownership completed the process which had started with the street tramways at the turn of the century and had been continued with the spread of bus services in the 1920s and 1930s. The railways were no longer able to compete and wholesale withdrawal of passenger and freight facilities took place in the 1960s and 1970s. Most of the goods stations were closed and complete sections of railway were abandoned. Information about closure dates for the various sections of line will be found in the summary at the end of the chapter.

British Railways began to look to its long distance traffic as the most profitable source of revenue, and proceeded to modernise its west coast main line through Wigan. The first regular electric trains on this section ran on 23rd July 1973. On other routes, diesel locomotives and diesel multiple unit trains replaced steam engines.

A train of coal for the washery at Bickershaw Colliery passes the site of Hindley Field Colliery. The photograph was taken in August 1972, after diesel had taken over from steam. I.A. Sommerfield

Development of the Canal and Railway System

At the time of writing the west coast main line continues to carry a heavy traffic, both passenger and long distance freight, and the original Liverpool and Manchester and Bolton and Preston lines still see considerable use. Local passenger trains, operated by diesel multiple units and subsidised by the local authorities still operate on a few other lines – Wigan to Manchester, via Westhoughton and via Atherton, Wigan to Southport, the L&Y route from Wigan to Liverpool (cut back to Kirkby since May 1977) and the LNWR/LUR route from Wigan to Liverpool via St Helens.

Apart from these, the whole of the network of lines around Wigan has disappeared with two exceptions. Portions of the Eccles, Tyldesley and Wigan line and the Bickershaw Branch have been retained to provide a connection to Bickershaw Colliery. Traffic is confined to trains conveying coal in 36 ton merry-go-round wagons, for the most part destined for Fiddlers Ferry Power Station, near Widnes. There is also a short spur which was constructed in British Railways times to provide a link from the west coast main line to the former LNER branch to St Helens. This is still used by bitumen trains serving the Kelbit plant at Edge Green.

References to Chapter 2

1. *The Canals of North West England* Charles Hadfield and Gordon Biddle – David and Charles, Newton Abbot 1970
2. 6 GeoI cap xxviii; 7-4-1720
3. 10 Geo III cap cxiv; 19-5-1770
4. 34 Geo III cap xciv; 9-5-1794
5. 32 Geo III cap ci; 11-6-1772
6. 59 Geo III cap cv; 21-6-1819
7. *Railway and Commercial Gazette* 28-5-1853
8. WO 1-8-1894
9. WO 29-2-1896
10. WO 12-8-1972
11. "Chronological List of the Railways of Lancashire, 1828–1939" M D Greville – *Transactions of the Historic Society of Lancashire and Cheshire*, Vol 105, 1953
    Also, Revised Edition (combined with Cheshire) – Railway and Canal Historical Society – 1981
12. 11 Geo IV cap lvi; 29-5-1830
13. 1 Wm 4 cap lvi; 22-4-1831
14. 4 Wm 4 cap xxv; 22-5-1834
15. North Union Railway Minutes 1/7
16. 51 & 52 Vic cap clxxvi; 7-8-1888
17. 1 Vic cap cxxi; 15-7-1837
18. 1 & 2 Vic cap cvi; 4-7-1838
19. 7 & 8 Vic cap ii; 10-5-1844
20. 6 Geo IV cap xviii; 31-3-1825
21. 10 Geo IV cap xxxvi; 14-5-1829
22. LRO PDR 244
23. LRO PDR 408
24. LRO PDR 447
25. LRO PDR 488
26. LRO PDR 499
27. & 10 Vic cap ccclxxxi; 18-8-1846
28. LRO PDR 411
29. 8 & 9 Vic cap clxvi;31-7-1845
30. 9 & 10 Vic cap cccxii; 3-8-1846
31. LRO PDR 504
32. LRO PDR 503
33. LRO PDR 499
34. LRO PDR 539
35. 10 & 11 Vic cap ccxxi; 22-7-1847
36. LRO PDR 481
37. 8 & 9 Vic cap cxcviii; 8-8-1845
38. 9 & 10 Vic cap cciv; 16-7-1846
39. 9 & 10 Vic cap cclxxxii; 22-7-1846
40. 10 & 11Vic cap clxiii; 9-7-1847
41. *The Lancashire and Yorkshire Railway* John Marshall – David and Charles, Newton Abbot, 1969
42. 22 & 23 Vic cap cx; 13-6-1859
43. 9 & 10 Vic cap ccxxxi; 27-7-1846
44. 51 & 52 Vic cap clxxvi; 7-8-1888 – Sec 60
45. 52 & 53 Vic cap xcviii; 26-7-1899
46. LRO PDR 592
47. LRO PDR 707
48. LRO PDR 717
49. 24 & 25 Vic cap cxxx; 11-8-1861
50. LRO PDR 728
51. LRO PDR 572
52. 8 & 9 Vic cap cxxiii; 21-7-1845
53. 10 & 11 Vic cap cclxxii; 22-7-1847
54. 16 & 17 Vic cap cxxxiv; 4-8-1853
55. WO 11-12-1857
56. 16 & 17 Vic cap clxiii, 4-8-1853
57. 27 & 28 Vic cap ccxcvi; 29-7-1864
58. LRO PDR 741
59. LRO PDR 768

Development of the Canal and Railway System

60	LRO PDR 764	61	27 & 28 Vic cap cclxx; 25-7-1864
62	27 & 28 Vic cap cclxxiii; 25-7-1864	63	28 & 29 Vic cap xxi; 26-5-1865
64	LRO PDR 800	65	28 & 29 Vic cap cxciii; 29-6-1865
66	LRO PDR 797	67	29 & 30 Vic cap ccxxxiii; 16-7-1866
68	31 & 32 Vic cap cxv; 13-7-1868	69	34 & 35 Vic cap x; 25-7-1871
70	*"The Lancashire Union Railways"* John Marshall – *Railway Magazine* April, May and June 1970		
71	31 & 32 Vic cap cxiv; 13-7-1868	72	LRO PDR 1037
73	40 & 41 Vic cap lvii; 28-6-1877	74	LRO PDR 1142
75	45 & 46 Vic cap cxli; 18-7-1881 Section 41	76	46 & 47 Vic cap cx; 16-7-1883
77	LRO PDR 970	78	37 & 38 Vic cap cxvii; 16-7-1874
79	38 & 39 Vic cap clxxxix; 2-8-1875	80	LRO PDR 990
81	41 Vic cap xcvii; 17-6-1878	82	WO 17-10-1879
83	*Great Central* – Vols II and III – George Dow – Locomotive Publishing Company, London – 1962 and 1965		
84	LRO PDR 1145	85	42& 43 Vic cap cli; 21-7-1879
86	LRO PDR 1220	87	44 & 45 Vic cap cxxxvi; 18-7-1881
88	LRO PDR 1145	89	45 & 46 Vic cap cxvi; 12-7-1882
90	Line Plan of Wigan Junction Railway – Henry Fowler – 1883 – 2 chains to 1 inch – at BRPB, Manchester Office		
91	LRO PDR 1220	92	46 & 47 Vic cap cx; 16-7-1883
93	LRO PDR 1222	94	45 & 46 Vic cap clvii; 2-8-1883
95	5 Ed 7 cap clxxviii; 4-8-1905	96	43 & 44 Vic cap cxlv; 6-8-1880
97	44 & 45 Vic cap cxli; 18-7-1881	98	LRO PDR 994
99	LRO PDR 1435	100	53 & 54 Vic cap cliv; 4-8-1890
101	LRO PDR 1316	102	51 & 52 Vic cap clxxvi; 7-8-1888
103	*Railway Reminiscences* – G P Neele – McCorquodale, London, 1904		
104	LRO PDR 1309	105	50 & 51 Vic cap cxxxi; 19-7-1887
106	53 & 54 Vic cap cliv;4-8-1890	107	46 & 47 Vic cap clxix; 2-8-1883
108	47 & 48 Vic cap cxlv; 14-7-1884	109	48 & 49 Vic cap xcix; 16-7-1885
110	*Lancashire and Yorkshire Railway Historical Maps* – R A Cook – Railway and Canal Historical Society – 1974		
111	54 & 55 Vic cap xcix; 3-7-1891	112	62 & 63 Vic cap lxxxv; 13-7-1899
113	LRO PDR 1274	114	48 & 49 Vic cap cxxi; 22-7-1885
115	LRO PDR 1295	116	50 Vic cap xxxiii; 25-9-1886
117	52 & 53 Vic cap xci; 26 7-1889	118	60 & 61 Vic cap cxi; 15-7-1897
119	WO 25-5-1895	120	WO 28-1-1899
121	WO 6-1-1900		
122	*An Account of the Proposed Lancashire Plateway Company* – Alfred Holt, Liverpool, 1883, with Appendix dated 1899		
123	LRO PDR 1215	124	LRO PDR 1491
125	LRO PDR 1907	126	3 & 4 Geo 5 cap lxvi;15-8-1913
127	11 & 12 Geo5 cap 55; 19-7-1921	128	10 & 11 Geo 6 cap 49; 6-8-1947

RAILWAY CHRONOLOGY

LONDON AND NORTH WESTERN RAILWAY

Bolton to Kenyon Junction

Originally Bolton and Leigh Railway from Bolton to Leigh;
  Kenyon and Leigh Junction Railway from Leigh to Kenyon Junction

Bolton and Leigh Railway absorbed by Grand Junction Railway	1. 7. 1845	(1)
Kenyon and Leigh Junction Railway absorbed by Grand Junction Railway	1846	(1)
Became LNWR	16. 7. 1846	(1)
Became LMSR	1. 1. 1923	
Became British Railways	1. 1. 1948	

Opened:
Bolton to Leigh for goods	1. 8. 1828	(1)
Bolton to Leigh for passengers	11. 6. 1831	(1)
Leigh to Kenyon Jct for goods	1. 1831	(1)
Leigh to Kenyon Jct for passengers	11. 6. 1831	(1)

Closed:
Bolton to Pennington South Jct for passengers	29. 3. 1954	(9)
Atherton Jct to Pennington South Jct for goods	17. 6. 1963	(2)
Bolton to Hultons Sidings for goods	16.10. 1967	(3)
Hultons Sidings to Atherton Jct for goods	6. 1. 1969	(4)
Pennington South Jct to Kenyon Jct	5. 5. 1969	(4)

Parkside to Wigan

Originally Wigan Branch Railway

Became North Union Railway	22. 5. 1834	(1)
Leased to Grand Junction and Manchester & Leeds Rlys	1. 1. 1846	(1)
Became LNWR and L&YR joint property	7. 8. 1888	(1)
Became sole property of LNWR	26. 7. 1889	(5)
Became LMSR	1. 1. 1923	
Became British Railways	1. 1. 1948	

Opened:
Throughout for passengers and goods	3. 9. 1832	(1)

Widening:
Golborne Jct to Springs Branch Jct	29.10. 1888	(5)
Springs Branch Jct to Wigan	Autumn 1894	(5)

Electrified:
  Golborne Jct to Bamfurlong
First goods trains	19. 3. 1973	(11)
First passenger trains	23. 7. 1973	(11)

  Bamfurlong to Wigan
First goods trains	11. 6.1973	(11)
First passenger trains	23. 7. 1973	(11)

Still open:
  Throughout, including third and fourth lines from Golborne Jct to Wigan

41

Railway Chronology

Wigan to Preston

Originally Preston and Wigan Railway		
Became North Union Railway	22. 5. 1834	(1)
Leased to Grand Junction and Manchester & Leeds Rlys	1. 1. 1846	(1)
Became LNWR and L&YR joint property	7. 8. 1888	(1)
Wigan to Euxton Jct became sole property of LNWR	26. 7. 1889	(1)
Became LMSR	1. 1. 1923	
Became British Railways	1. 1. 1948	

Opened:
Throughout for passengers and goods	31.10. 1838	(1)

Widening:
Standish Jct to Euxton Jct	Autumn 1895	(7)

Third and fourth lines removed:
Standish Jct to Balshaw Lane	5.11. 1972	(8)

Electrified:
Overhead lines energised	28. 5. 1973	(6)
First goods trains	11. 6. 1973	(11)
First passenger trains	23. 7. 1973	(11)

Still open:
    Throughout, including third and fourth lines from Balshaw Lane to Preston.

Springs Branch Junction to New Springs (Springs Branch)

Originally authorised by Wigan Branch Railway		
Powers transferred to North Union Railway	22. 5. 1834	(1)
Leased to Grand Junction and Manchester & Leeds Rlys	1. 1. 1846	(1)
Became LNWR and L&YR joint property	7. 8. 1888	(1)
Became sole property of LNWR	26. 7. 1889	(1)
Became LMSR	1. 1. 1923	
Became British Railways	1. 1. 1948	

Opened:
Throughout for goods	31.10. 1838	(1)

Closed:
Kirkless Workshops to New Springs	See Note 1	
Belle Green Lane to Kirkless Hall Jct		
(and Rose Bridge Jct to Kirkless Hall Jct reopened)	13. 4. 1958	(9)
Kirkless Hall Jct to Kirkless Workshops	15. 5. 1965	(10)
Central Wagon Works to Belle Green Lane	See Note 2	
Springs Branch Jct to Central Wagon Works and Ince Forge	See Note 3	

Notes:

1   Probably about 1932
2   Probably 13. 4. 1958
3   Late 1970s or early 1980s. Portion from Springs Branch Jct to bridge over former Wigan Junction line retained for wagon storage.

Railway Chronology

Eccles to Springs Branch Junction and Branches (Eccles, Tyldesley and Wigan line)

Originally London and North Western Railway
Became LMSR	1. 1. 1923	
Became British Railways	1. 1. 1948	

Opened:
Eccles to Springs Branch Jct	1. 9. 1864	(1)
Chowbent East Jct to Atherton Jct for passengers	1864	(3)
Chowbent East Jct to Atherton Jct for goods	See Note 1	
Bickershaw Jct to Moss Hall sidings [Note 2]		
Chowbent West Jct to Atherton Jct for passengers	1883	(3)
Chowbent West Jct to Atherton Jct for goods [Note 4}	See Note 3	

Closed:
Howe Bridge East Jct to Atherton Jct for passengers	4. 5. 1942	(9)
Tyldesley to Springs Branch Jct for passengers	2.11. 1964	(12)
Howe Bridge West Jct to Atherton Jct for goods	18. 1. 1965	(4)
Bickershaw Jct to Moss Hall [Note 5]	31.10. 1966	(4)
Tyldesley to Howe Bridge West for goods [Note 6]	7.10. 1968	(4)
Tyldesley to Springs Branch Jct for parcels	6. 1. 1969	(4)
Howe Bridge East Jct to Atherton Jct for goods	6. 1.1969	(13)
Eccles to Tyldesley for passengers (all)	5. 5. 1969	(4)
Howe Bridge West Jct to Bickershaw Jct for goods [Note7]	11. 2. 1975	(4)

Notes:
1 Probably 1864
2 Built by LNWR, but regarded as colliery company's property; worked by railway company's locomotives. Opened late 1880s
3 Probably 1883
4 Chowbent East Jct renamed Howe Bridge East Jct; Chowbent West Jct renamed Howe Bridge West Jct.
5 Official date. Out of use a number of years previously
6 Dates should probably be 6.1.1969 for goods traffic Tyldesley to Howe Bridge East and 7.10.1968 for goods traffic Howe Bridge East to Howe Bridge West
7 Official date for line taken out of use. Last traffic 8.1974 at same date as N.C.B line from Howe Bridge West to Parsonage Colliery

Gerards Bridge Junction to Springs Branch Junction

Originally Lancashire Union Railways
Absorbed by LNWR	1.10. 1883	(5)
Became LMSR	1. 1. 1923	
Became British Railways	1. 1. 1948	
Opened:		
Throughout for goods	1.11. 1869	(1)
Throughout for passengers	1.12. 1869	(14)
Widening:		
Carr Mill Jct to Ince Moss Jct	16.10. 1892	(5)
Ince Moss Jct to Springs Branch Jct	Autumn 1894	(5)
Third and fourth lines removed:		
Carr Mill Jct to Garswood Hall	4. 5. 1958	(5)
Garswood Hall to Springs Branch Jct	25. 8. 1958	(5)
Still open:		
Throughout for goods and passenger traffic		

Railway Chronology

Brynn Junction to Pemberton Jct and Norley Hall

Originally Lancashire Union Railways
Absorbed by LNWR   1.10. 1883   (5)
Became LMSR   1. 1. 1923
Became British Railways   1. 1. 1948

Opened:
   Throughout for goods (no passenger traffic)   See Note 1

Closed:
   Goose Green Jct to Norley Hall Sidings [Note 2]   5. 1926   (16)
   Brynn Jct to Pemberton Jct [Note 3]   22. 3. 1947   (9)

Notes:

1 Probably November 1869
2 No traffic after this date; lifting of track completed by 24th November 1932
3 Alternative versions are 26.10.1948 (8) and 1946 (15)

Ince Moss Jct to Haigh Jct and Branches

Originally Lancashire Union Railways
Absorbed by LNWR   1.10. 1883   (5)
Became LMSR   1. 1. 1923
Became British Railways   1. 1. 1948

Opened:
   Ince Moss Jct to Haigh Jct for goods   1.11. 1869   (1)
   Ince Moss Jct to Whelley for passengers [Note 1] 1. 1. 1872   (5)
   Fir Tree House Jct to Platt Bridge Jct for goods See Note 2
   De Trafford Jct to Hindley for goods   See Note 2
   Rose Bridge Jct to Kirkless Hall Jct for goods   See Note 2
   Round House Jct to Kirkless Ironworks for goods   See Note 2
   Whelley Jct to Standish Jct (single line) for goods   5. 6. 1882   (5)
   Whelley Jct to Standish Jct (second line) for goods   NK
   Amberswood East Jct to Standish Jct for passengers   Summer 1887   (5)
   De Trafford Jct to Hindley for passengers   7. 1924   (5)

Closed:
   Round House Jct to Kirkless Ironworks   About 1930
   Rose Bridge Jct to Kirkless Hall Jct [Note 3]   7. 1938   (9)
   Haigh Jct to Whelley Jct [Note 4]   23. 1. 1967   (5)
   Ince Moss Jct to Ambersood West Jct for goods   19. 5. 1969   (4)
   Fir Tree House Jct to Platt Bridge Jct for goods 19. 5. 1969   (15)
   Ambserswood East Jct to De Trafford Jct to Standish Jct for seasonal passengers   5. 9. 1964   (4)
   Hindley to De Trafford Jct to Standish Jct
      Regular passengers   15. 6. 1969   (4)
      Seasonal passengers   2. 9. 1972   (4)
   Hindley to De Trafford Jct for goods   2.10. 1972
   Ambserswood West Jct to Standish Jct for goods [Note 5]   2.10. 1972 (4)

Notes:

1. Whelley to Liverpool passenger service withdrawn 1.3.1872
2. Probably November 1869
3. Reopened 13.5. 1958 (9); finally closed 15.5.1965 (10)
4. Officially taken out of use on this date; no booked traffic since 25.4.1965. Line had been singled on 16.11.1952 (5)
5. Officially closed on this date. Used for diversions from 12.1.1973 to 15.1.1973 and by engineers trains until 1976

Connecting Lines at Bamfurlong and Hindley

Originally London and North Western Railway
Became LMSR   1. 1. 1923
Became British Railways   1. 1. 1948

Opened:
Bamfurlong Jct to Amberswood West Jct (Platt Bridge Junction Railway)   25.10. 1886   (5)
Bamfurlong to Platt Bridge Jct – burrowing junction to main line and
  new low level goods lines (Bamfurlong Jct Railways)   See note 1
Bamfurlong Sorting Sidings Jct to Springs Branch Junction low level lines   See note 1
Bickershaw Jct to Hindley and Platt Bridge (Hindley Junctions Railway)
  For goods [Note 2]   25.10. 1886   (5)
  For passengers   Summer 1887   (5)
Bamfurlong Sorting Sidings Jct to Ince Moss Jct [Note 3]   Summer 1895   (5)

Closed:
Bickershaw Jct to Hindley South
  For seasonal passengers   5. 9. 1964   (4)
  For goods [Note 4]   6.11. 1967   (3)
Bamfurlong Jct to Platt Bridge Jct – Down Whelley Main Line   22. 9. 1968   (8)
Platt Bridge Jct to Bamfurlong Jct – Up Whelley Main Line [Notes 5 and 8]   2.10. 1972   (8)
Bamfurlong Sorting Sidings Jct to Amberswood West Jct [Notes 6, 7 and 8]   2.10. 1972   (8)

Still Open:
Bamfurlong Jct to Springs Branch Junction (Low level lines)
Bamfurlong Sidings Jct to Ince Moss Jct

Notes:

1. Part opened 10.2.1889, part 1.10.1889 (5)
2. Strangeways East Jct renamed Hindley and Platt Bridge Jct, and later Hindley South Jct
3. Originally through siding connection. Converted to through line during demolition of marshalling yard about 1972. Bamfurlong Sorting Sidings Jct renamed Bamfurlong Sidings Jct
4. Retained until this date for goods trains to Wigan GCR
5. Portion of line from Platt Bridge Jct to point short of Bamfurlong Jct retained as siding to serve CWS Glass Factory (8)
6. Officially closed on this date but used for diversions between 12.1.1973 and 15.1.1973 and by engineers trains until 1976 (8)
7. After 1976, portion of up line from Platt Bridge Jct to Bamfurlong Sidings Jct retained as siding to connect with stub end of Up Whelley Main Line, serving CWS Glass Works (8)
8. Siding from Bamfurlong Sidings Jct to site of Platt Bridge Jct to CWS Glass Works taken out of use July 1986 and lifted at end of 1989 (8)

45

Railway Chronology

Bickershaw Lines

Originally London and North Western Railway
(Plank Lane to Scowcrofts Sidings purchased from Ackers, Whitley & Co Ltd)
Became LMSR   1. 1. 1923
Became British Railways   1. 1. 1948

Opened:
    Pennington South to Bickershaw Jct for goods only [Note 1]   9. 3 .1885   (1)
    Diggles Colliery S.B. to Diggles Siding for goods only [Note 2]   See Note 3
    Hindley Field to Scowcrofts Sidings for goods only   See Note 3
    Pennington East Jct to West Jct for goods   2. 6. 1903   (1)
    Pennington East Jct to West Jct for passengers   1.10. 1903   (1)
    Pennington West Jct to Bickershaw Jct for passengers [Note 4]   1.10. 1903   (1)

Closed:
    Pennington East Jct to Bickershaw Jct for passengers [Note 5]   4. 5. 1942   (9)
    Pennington South Jct to Diggles Siding for goods   19. 3. 1944   (9)
    Hindley Field to Scowcrofts Sidings for goods   27.12. 1944   (9)
    Pennington East Jct to Pennington West Jct for goods [Note 6]   26. 8. 1951   (8)
    Pennington South Jct to Plank Lane for goods   13. 9. 1965   (4)

Still open:
    Plank Lane to Bickershaw West Jct for goods

Notes:

1   Second edition of reference 1 gives 9.2.1885
2   Point of junction changed to Pennington South on opening connecting line from Pennington East to Pennington West in 1903
3   Probably same date as Pennington South to Plank Lane to Bickershaw Jct
4   Line brought up to passenger standards
5   Temporarily closed for passengers 20.12.1915 to 3.6.1922 (1),(9)
6   Date when officially taken out of use; no traffic from about 1943 (8)

Connecting Line at Golborne

Provided by British Railways

Opened:
    Golborne LNW to Edge Green GC for goods [Note 1]   22. 4 .1968   (4)
Still in use:
    Throughout

Note:
1   Used for special passenger trains to Ashton in Makerfield, in connection with Haydock Park Races, during 1975 (21)

LANCASHIRE AND YORKSHIRE RAILWAY

Bolton to Euxton Junction and Branches

Originally Bolton and Preston Railway		
Absorbed by North Union Railway	1. 1. 1844	(1)
Leased to Grand Jct and Manchester & Leeds Rlys	1. 1. 1846	(1)
Became LNWR and L&YR joint property	7. 8. 1888	(1)
Bolton to Euxton Jct became sole property of L&YR	26. 7. 1889	(5)
Absorbed by LNWR	1. 1. 1922	
Became LMSR	1. 1. 1923	
Became British Railways	1. 1. 1948	

Opened:
Bolton to Rawlinson Bridge for passengers and goods	4. 2. 1841	(1)
Rawlinson Bridge to Chorley for passengers and goods	22.12. 1841	(1)
Chorley to Euxton Junction for passengers and goods	22. 6. 1843	(1)
Waterhouses Branch for goods only	Mid 1843	(17)

Closed:
Waterhouses Branch for goods　　　　　　　　　　　See note 1

Still open:
Bolton to Euxton Junction for goods and passenger traffic

Note:
1　Last traffic sometime between 1928 and 1930

Lostock Jct to Walton Jct

Originally Liverpool, Bolton and Bury Railway (Portion between Hindley and Pemberton was Manchester and Southport Railway)

Absorbed by Manchester and Leeds Railway	1.10. 1846	(1)
Became L&YR prior to opening	23. 7. 1847	(18)
Absorbed by LNWR	1. 1. 1922	
Became LMSR	1. 1. 1923	
Became British Railways	1. 1. 1948	

Opened:
Lostock Jct to Walton Jct for passengers and goods	20.11. 1848	(1)
Connecting line to LNWR at Wigan	See Note 1	
New connnection to LNWR at Wigan	1. 9. 1880	(18)

Widening:
Crow Nest Jct to Hindley No 3 Cabin [Note 2]	Mid 1889	(18)

Third and fourth lines removed:
Crow Nest Jct to Hindley No 3 Cabin	NK	

Still open:
Throughout (between Wigan and Walton Jct, passenger service only [Note 3])

Notes:
1　Probably November 1848
2　Ready for traffic on this date
3　With change of trains at Kirkby as from 2.5.1977

Railway Chronology

Wigan to Southport

Originally Manchester and Southport Railway
Leased to L&YR prior to opening	5. 1848	(18)
Absorbed by L&YR	4. 1855	(18)
Absorbed by LNWR	1. 1. 1922	
Became LMSR	1. 1. 1923	
Became British Railways	1. 1. 1948	

Opened:
Throughout for passengers and goods [Note 1]	9. 4. 1855	(1)

Still open:
  Throughout

Note:
1   Originally single track Burscough to Wigan. Double track brought into operation 1.11. 1861 (18)

Ormskirk to Rainford

Ormskirk to Skelmersdale
  Originally Liverpool, Ormskirk and Preston Railway
Became East Lancashire Railway	10. 1846	(18)
Amalgamated with L&YR	13. 8. 1859	(18)

Skelmersdale to Rainford
  Originally East Lancashire Railway
Amalgamated with L&YR	13. 8. 1859	(18)

Both sections
Absorbed by LNWR	1. 1. 1922
Became LMSR	1. 1. 1923
Became British Railways	1. 1. 1948

Opened:
  Ormskirk to Skelmersdale (Blaguegate Sdg)
For goods	See Note 1	
For passengers	1. 3. 1858	(18)
Skelmersdale to Rainford Jct		
For passengers and goods	1. 3. 1858	(18)
Bushey Lane Jct to jct with LNWR for goods	1. 3. 1858	(18)
Branch to Bickerstaffe Colliery Moss Pits	Prob 1860	

Closed:
Branch to Bickerstaffe Colliery Moss Pits	About 1936	
Ormskirk to Rainford Jct for passengers	5.11. 1956	(18)
White Moss Crossing to Bushey Lane Jct for goods	16. 9. 1961	(8)
Skelmersdale to White Moss Crossing for goods	4.11. 1963	(8)
Ormskirk to Skelmersdale for goods	18.11. 1963	(8)
Bushey Lane Jct to Rainford Jct for goods	See Note 2	

Notes:
1   Believed to be in 1849 or 1850
2   Probably 16.9.1961

Hindley to Red Moss Junction (Hindley and Blackrod Branch)

Originally Lancashire and Yorkshire Railway
Absorbed by LNWR   1. 1. 1922
Became LMSR   1. 1. 1923
Became British Railways   1. 1. 1948

Opened:
  Throughout for goods   15. 7. 1868   (18)
  Throughout for passengers   14. 9 .1868   (18)
  Junction moved from Red Moss to Horwich Fork on opening of
    Dobbs Brow Jct to H and B Branch Jct line   1. 6. 1889

Closed:
  Hindley to Horwich and Blackrod Branch Jct for passengers   4. 1. 1960   (12)
  Hindley and Blackrod Branch Jct to Horwich Fork Jct for passengers   6. 9 .1965   (12)
  Throughout for goods   9. 9. 1968   (4)

Pendleton to Crow Nest Jct (Hindley)

Originally Lancashire and Yorkshire Railway
Became LMSR   1. 1. 1923
Became British Railways   1. 1. 1948

Opened:
  Pendleton to Swinton for goods   13. 6.1887   (18)
  Swinton to Atherton for goods   2. 7.1888   (18)
  Atherton to Crow Nest Jct for goods   1.10. 1888   (18)
  Pendleton to Crow Nest Jct for passengers   1. 6. 1889   (18)
Third and fourth tracks removed:
  Pendleton to Crow Nest Jct [Note 1]   NK
Still open:
  Throughout

Note:
1   These were the Fast Lines, which did not serve intermediate stations

Railway Chronology

Dobbs Brow Jct to Hindley and Blackrod Branch Jct

Originally Lancashire and Yorkshire Railway
Absorbed by LNWR   1. 1. 1922
Became LMSR   1. 1. 1923
Became British Railways   1. 1. 1948

Opened:
    Throughout for goods and passengers   1. 6. 1889   (1)

Closed:
    Throughout for passengers [Note 1]   6. 9. 1965   (12)
    Throughout for goods   9. 9. 1968   (4)

Note:
1   Local passenger services withdrawn 1.2.1954

Hindley to Pemberton (Pemberton Loop Line)

Originally Lancashire and Yorkshire Railway
Absorbed by LNWR   1. 1. 1922
Became LMSR   1. 1. 1923
Became British Railways   1. 1. 1948

Opened:
    Throughout for goods   1. 5. 1889   (18)
    Throughout for passengers   1. 6. 1889   (18)

Closed:
    Throughout (latterly only passenger traffic)   14. 7. 1969   (4)

LONDON AND NORTH WESTERN AND LANCASHIRE AND YORKSHIRE JOINT LINES

Boars Head Junction to Adlington Junction

Originally Lancashire and Yorkshire and Lancashire Union Rlys
Became Lancashire and Yorkshire and London and North Western joint property   1.10. 1883   (5)
Became sole property of LNWR   1. 1. 1922
Became LMSR   1. 1. 1923
Became British Railways   1. 1. 1948

Opened:
  Throughout for goods   1.11. 1869   (1)
  Throughout for passengers   1.12. 1869   (14)

Closed:
  Throughout for passengers   4. 1. 1960   (9)
  Throughout for goods   5.10. 1971   (15)

Ellerbeck Junction to Ellerbeck Colliery

Originally Lancashire and Yorkshire and Lancashire Union Rlys
Became Lancashire and Yorkshire and London and North Western joint property   1.10. 1883   (5)
Became sole property of LNWR   1. 1. 1922
Became LMSR   1. 1. 1923

Opened:
  Throughout for goods [Notes 1 and 2]   6. 1. 1877   (18)

Closed:
  Throughout   See Note 3

Notes:
1. This is official date; note in (18) says line complete and ready for traffic 19th June 1871. Appears to have been in use well before 1877
2. Traffic worked by colliery locomotives
3. Probably about 1932

Railway Chronology

GREAT CENTRAL RAILWAY

Glazebrook to Wigan and Branches

Originally Wigan Junction Railway		
Worked by MS&LR and later by GCR		
Absorbed by GCR	1. 1. 1906	(1)
Became LNER	1. 1. 1923	
Became British Railways	1. 1. 1948	

Opened:
Glazebrook to Strangeways Colliery for coal	16.10. 1879	(19)
Glazebrook to Strangeways Colliery for goods	17.10. 1879	(19)
West Leigh and Bedford to Plank Lane for goods	See Note 1	
Strangeways Colliery to Amberswood West Jct for goods	See Note 2	
Strangeways West Jct to Amberswood East Jct for goods [Notes 3 and 4]	25.10. 1886	
Strangeways West Jct to Wigan (Darlington St) for goods	1. 4. 1884	(1)
Glazebrook to Wigan (Darlington St) for passengers	1. 4. 1884	(1)
Wigan (Darlington St) to Wigan (Central) for passengers	3.10. 1892	(1)

Closed:
Glazebrook to Wigan (Central) for passengers	2.11. 1964	(12)
Hindley South to Amberswood East Jct		
For seasonal passengers	5. 9 .1964	(4)
For goods	22. 2. 1965	(2)
Hindley South to Amberswood West for goods	15. 3. 1965	(4)
Lowton St Marys to Hindley South for goods	4. 1. 1965	(2)
Hindley South to Wigan (Goods) for goods [Note 5]	6.11. 1967	(2)
West Leigh and Bedford to Plank Lane	NK	

Notes:
1. Probably 1879
2. Reference 19 gives July 1880, but the junction with the Lancashire Union line at Amberswood West does not seem to have been completed until 1881 or 1882 (See Chapter 2)
3. Strangeways West Jct renamed Hindley and Platt Bridge Jct and later Hindley South Jct
4. Reference 19 gives July 1880, but this is incorrect. The junction with the Lancashire Union line at Amberswood East had not been completed in November 1882. The date quoted here is when LNWR goods trains from Bickershaw Junction first started to use the line. It may have been opened earlier. LNWR passenger trains started to use it in July 1887 (5)
5. Served from Bickershaw Jct

Lowton St Marys to St Helens

Originally St Helens and Wigan Junction Railway		
Became Liverpool, St Helens and South Lancashire Railway	26. 7. 1889	(1)
Worked by MS&LR and later GCR		
Absorbed by GCR	1. 1. 1906	(19)
Became LNER	1. 1. 1923	
Became British Railways	1. 1. 1948	

Opened:
Throughout for goods [Note 1]	1. 7. 1895	(19)
Throughout for passengers [Note 2]	3. 1. 1900	(19)

Railway Chronology

Closed:
    Throughout for passengers [Note 3]   3.3.1952   (12)
    Ashton in Makerfield to St Helens Central for goods [Note 4]   4.1.1965   (2)
    Lowton St Marys to Edge Green for goods [Note 5]   22.4.1968   (4)
    Edge Green to Ashton in Makerfield for goods   3.1987   (8)

Still open:
    Edge Green, junction with chord line from Golborne to connection with Kelbit Ltd's sidings and headshunt.

Notes:
1. Worked by contractor's locos between Golborne and St Helens until 21.10.1895 (19)
2. Special trains from Lowton to Haydock Park Race Course from early 1899 (19) (20)
3. Special trains to Haydock Park Race Course Station ran via Lowton St Marys up to and including 1963. Special trains for the Races also ran, for one year only, in 1975, to Ashton in Makerfield via the new chord line. Dates of operation were 22-5-1975, 7-6-1975, -7-1975, 9-8-1975 and 4-10-1975 (21)
4. Ashton in Makerfield to Haydock Oil Depot reopened July 1968. Closed again between Ashton in Makerfield and Haydock in February 1983. (8)
5. New chord line opened from Golborne to Edge Green on this date (8)

References

1. *"Chronological List of the Railways of Lancashire 1828 –1939"*, – M D Greville – *Transactions of the Historic Society of Lancashire and Cheshire*, Vol 105, 1953.
   Also Revised Edition (including Cheshire) published by Railway and Canal Historical Society, 1981
2. Circulars of the GLO Organisation, various dates
3. Information supplied by Mr Cobb
4. *Branch Line News*, various dates
5. *"The Lancashire Union Railways"* – John Marshall – *Railway Magazine*, April, May and June 1970
6. *Electric from Euston to Glasgow* – O S Nock – Ian Allan, London, 1974
7. *Railway Reminiscences* – G P Neele – McCorquodale, London, 1904
8. Information supplied by Mr Richard Maund
9. *LNWR Chronology 1900–1960* – C R Clinker – David and Charles, Newton Abbot, 1961
10. Information supplied by Mr Addison
11. *A Chronology of the Electric Railways of Great Britain and Ireland* – Electric Railway Society, 1981
12. *Passengers No More* – Daniels and Dench – 3rd Edition – Ian Allan, London, 1980
13. Note on Line Plan of Eccles, Tyldesley and Wigan Railway – LNWR, 1892 – At BRPB Manchester Office
14. Lancashire Union Railway Minutes
15. Note on Line Plan of Lancashire Union Railway – BR, 1952 – At BRPB Manchester Office
16. Sidings Schedules
17. Bolton and Preston Railway Half Yearly Report – July 1843
18. *The Lancashire and Yorkshire Railway* – John Marshall – David and Charles, Newton Abbot, 1969
19. *The Great Central Railway, Vol 2* – George Dow – Ian Allan, London, 1962
20. *Wigan Observer* 28-1-1899
21. Information supplied by Mr Bob Miller

CHAPTER 3

ORRELL AND NORLEY HALL

Our story starts to the west of Wigan, in and around Orrell. The collieries here were the first to be opened out to serve anything other than very local needs. The River Douglas had been made navigable from Wigan to the Ribble Estuary in 1742 and by 1774 a canal had been opened to Liverpool. The colliery owners were quick to expand their production to satisfy the demands of the new customers who could readily be served by the improved transport facilities.

The need to provide efficient means of transport from the pits to the River Douglas, and later the Leeds and Liverpool Canal, was solved by the construction of wooden railways. In this the colliery proprietors followed a practice which had already been well tried elsewhere and which had been developed to a high degree of sophistication on Tyneside. From the end of the 18th century cast iron rails were substituted for the wooden ones, and the new lines built after this time adopted iron rails from the beginning.

The history of these lines, the earliest in Lancashire, is difficult to trace in the absence of comprehensive records and of detailed plans and maps for the period. Ownership of the railways changed quite frequently as new colliery proprietors took over the mining leases. The lines were extended to serve new workings, and branches to old ones were taken up. The average life of a coal pit in Orrell at this period was four or five years, so the railway layout was never static. Finally, to complicate the historian's task still further, several colliery owners often made use of the same railway to transport their coal to the canal. We are fortunate in having available Anderson's account[1] of the Orrell collieries at this period, which provides us with much of the historical background.

By 1845, these early collieries had all been worked out. Some small scale mining activity continued at Orrell during the remainder of the nineteenth century. Around Upholland and Dalton, it went on well into the twentieth century. Operations were mostly on too small a scale to need rail transport. Those few that had rail connections are described in chapter 15.

Major new colliery development in the latter half of the nineteenth century was confined to an area to the east of Orrell, on the Norley Hall and Walthew House Estates. This was encouraged by the construction of the Lancashire and Yorkshire Company's line from Wigan to Southport, opened in 1855. The collieries here were also served by the Pemberton Branch of the Lancashire Union Railway, opened in 1869.

Jackson's Collieries

The first railway to be constructed seems to have been from John Jackson's Orrell House Colliery to the River Douglas near Gathurst. A partnership of Liverpool merchants, Warren and Company, had contracted to take over the whole output of Jackson's colliery and the railway was an essential link in the transport chain. A contemporary advertisement[2], quoted

Orrell and Norley Hall

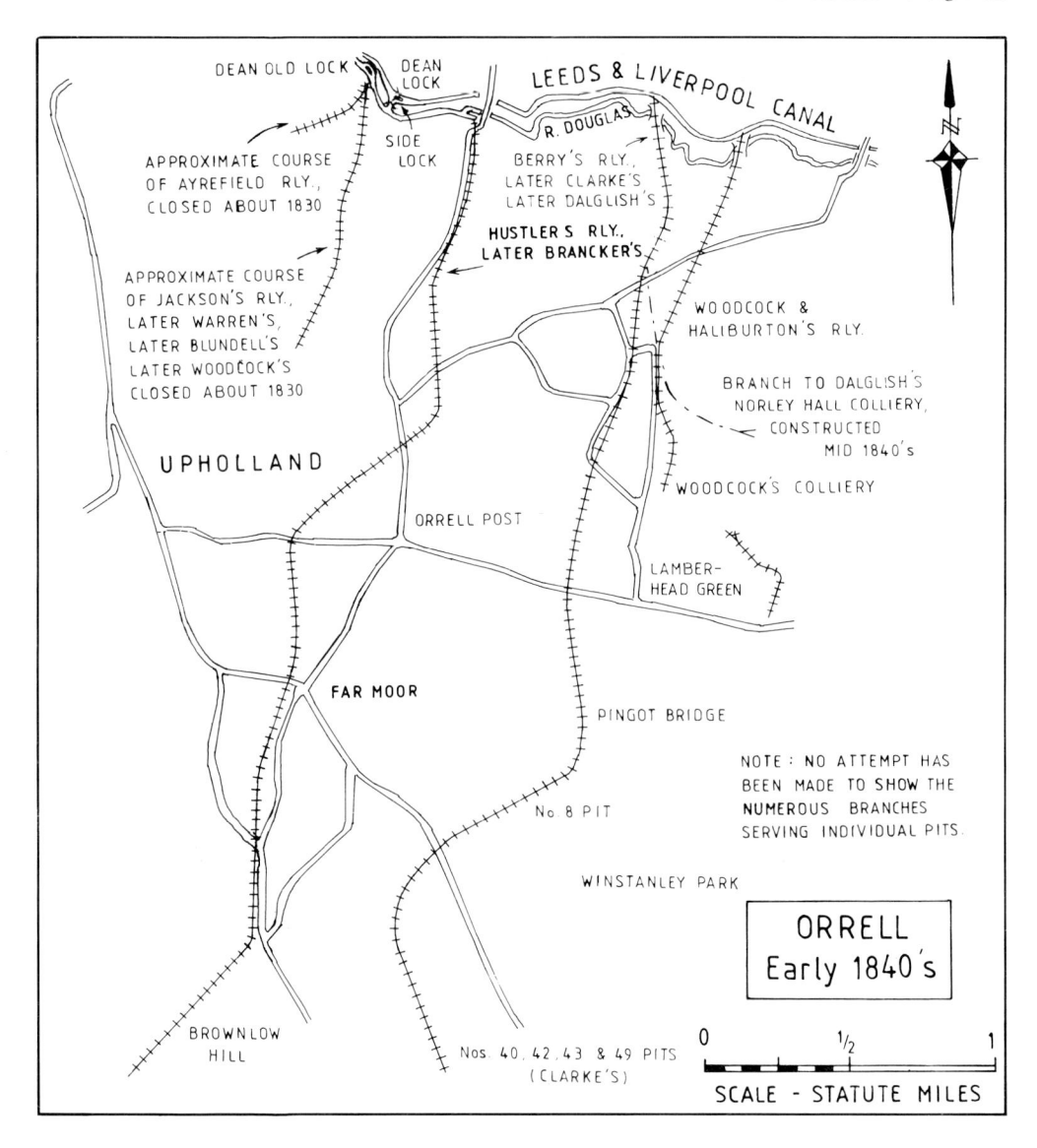

Orrell and Norley Hall

by Anderson, shows that it had been opened by November 1776, and implies that it had been constructed by Warren and Company rather than by John Jackson. Michael Jackson, John's son, took over shortly afterwards, but was declared bankrupt in 1780.

The colliery and its plant, including 13 railway waggons, were advertised for sale on 15th May of that year[3]. Subsequently Warren and Company took over the working of the colliery and, by 1873, Jonathan Blundell, who had been a prominent member of the partnership, had became sole proprietor. By the end of the century the colliery had been worked out, but the railway, or at least part of it, seems to have been retained for further use.

In 1813 Woodcock and Haliburton took a lease of coal near Upholland, and it is believed that they extended the line to their new collieries. The reconstruction of the line with cast iron rails, as shown in Anderson's book, may have been carried out then. If not, it must have been earlier, during the Blundell period. Stanley's map of 1833[4] shows this railway, with the note that it was then owned by Woodcock. Woodcock and Haliburton's colliery seems to have closed in the late 1830s or early 1840s, and this would seem to mark the demise of the railway.

Ayrefield Colliery

The railway from the Ayrefield Colliery, at that time worked by John Longbotham, seems also to date from the mid 1770s. A lease of 1775 authorised a line from Ayrefield colliery to join into Jackson's railway, but the two seem to have remained separate, terminating at adjacent wharves on the River Douglas. It is probable that these occupied the site where, according to Anderson, Alexander Leigh, had, in 1748, formed an arm of the river at the lower end of the Dean Brook, to load coal brought from his collieries by horse drawn carts.

When the Leeds and Liverpool Canal was extended from Dean Locks to Wigan, it was suggested that the Canal company should pay for both Jackson's railway and the Ayrefield Colliery railway to be extended over the river to new loading basins on the canal. There is no evidence that this work was carried out. It seems, from what can be deduced from the 1st edition of the 6" map, that the old wharves were retained and that boats gained access to them through a side lock from the canal to the river at Dean.

In 1776 or 1777, Longbotham's pits were taken over by a partnership of John Hustler, Thomas Hardcastle and John Chadwick. By 1790 the collieries were in the sole ownership of William Hustler, John's son. They are thought to have been worked out by the end of the century and the railway was presumably closed then. It is not shown on Stanley's map of 1833 nor on the 2" drawings prepared around 1840 for the 1st edition of the 1" map.

Hustler's Collieries

We must now turn our attention to a railway which, if a little later than the pioneering efforts of Warren and Company, eventually developed into one of the most extensive in the Orrell district. John Hustler, chairman of the Leeds and Liverpool Canal Company, with his partners Thomas Hardcastle and John Chadwick, took over the working of the Orrell Hall Colliery in 1776 or 1777. As with the Ayrefield Colliery, William Hustler had become sole proprietor by 1790. A railway was constructed from Orrell Hall Colliery to Gathurst. The pier head here was located on the River Douglas and again reached through the side lock at Dean.

Orrell and Norley Hall

Although no date has been discovered, it is believed that the line opened in the 1780s or early 1790s. It is not known whether wooden rails were originally used. It certainly had cast iron rails of the fish belly type later, as an example is illustrated in Anderson's book.

By 1790 the railway had been extended southwards to serve collieries which were being developed by Jonathan Blundell and his son. Stanley's map of 1833 shows the line terminating to the south of the Wigan to Upholland turnpike road. The owner is given as Hustler. The railway was again extended in the early 1840s to Hustler's new colliery at Brownlow Hill.

Anderson gives the total length of the line from here to Gathurst as four miles, with a fall of 470 feet. From the Brownlow Hill pits, the line ran in a north easterly direction until it reached the road from Orrell Post to Billinge. Here it turned north, for the first quarter mile or so at the side of the road. Striking off across the fields from Far Moor, it crossed the Wigan to Upholland turnpike on the level between Orrell Post and Abbey Lakes. From the turnpike it turned north east again, crossing the Orrell Post to Gathurst road, again on the level. Once in the fields to the east of the road, it took a northerly course, skirting Orrell Hall Farm and rejoining the road near Harvey House.

The last half mile to Gathurst was on a steep gradient through a small ravine on the east side of the road. It is here that one of the few tangible remains of the early Orrell railways can still be found – the small arch at the side of the main road bridge, constructed in the 1850s to take the Wigan to Southport line of the Lancashire and Yorkshire over the colliery railway.

Blundell's collieries at Orrell had all closed by the 1830s, and Hustler's Orrell House Colliery was advertised for sale on 23rd December 1844[5]. The plant on offer included a 45 HP pumping engine with a 45" cylinder, a 6 HP engine with a 10" cylinder and a 7 HP atmospheric engine. In the early 1840s, William Hill Brancker, who we shall meet again later in this chapter, took over Hustler's collieries in the Brownlow Hill area.

Brancker retained the railway to Gathurst to provide an outlet for his coal to the canal. Soon after the opening of the Wigan to Liverpool railway in 1848, a spur was constructed from the colliery line to Upholland station, which at that time was located at the east end of the tunnel. Here a loading dock was provided, where coal could be transhipped to standard gauge wagons. Although we do not have a precise date for this development, it must have taken place before 1850 as the spur appears on a revision of the 1st edition of the 6" map published at about that date.

As far as we are aware, Brancker's railway was never modernised and remained narrow gauge, using horse traction. It seems finally to have closed in 1861, as in August that year it was recorded that Brancker's Bispham and Shaley Brow Collieries were worked out[6].

The Bispham Colliery was a later name for the Brownlow Hill pits, while Shaley Brow Colliery was further to the south. Shaley Brow was not connected with Brancker's main railway system. However the 1st edition of the 6" map, surveyed in 1844 and 1847, shows that it had a short tramroad, partly on an inclined plane, leading to a coal yard alongside the lane to Billinge Hall.

Towards the end of the century there was a renewal of mining activity on the northern slopes of Brownlow Hill. We shall be following these developments in Chapter 15.

Clarke's Collieries

The origins of our next early railway, usually known as Clarke's, go back to 1780. In that year William Berry, who was opening out a colliery on the Post House Estate, applied for

Orrell and Norley Hall

permission to build a railway to the Leeds and Liverpool Canal opposite Crooke. An advertisement of April 1781, quoted by Anderson, stated that a "good and commodious railed or plank road" connected the colliery to the canal, "the road made of new oak timber". William Clarke appears on the scene at this time, with others, as trustees of the estate of William Berry and Company. In 1789 John Clarke, in partnership with William Roscoe, William German and Charles Porter, took a lease of coal near Gathurst. In 1790 John Clarke, his brother William and William German took another lease at Lamberhead Green. The railway was extended to serve the new collieries. Around 1792 it was again extended to new sinkings by Clarke and his partners near the Pingot.

The final extension came some time around 1812, when Clarke and German opened out new pits on the west side of Winstanley Park. From here to the canal the railway was just under 4 miles in length. A map reproduced in Anderson's book shows a double track line from No 8 Pit at Winstanley through to the canal, with single track on the branches. An estate plan of 1812[7] shows the southern extremity of the railway, serving Nos 40, 42 and 43 Pits, together with a new branch serving No 49 Pit.

The main line of the railway crossed the valley of the Smithy Brook at a point near the Pingot by means of an eleven arched viaduct. This is illustrated in Anderson's book, together with a photograph of the cast iron bridge which replaced two arches of the viaduct to accommodate the Liverpool and Bury line of the Lancashire and Yorkshire Railway. From the Pingot the line took a northerly course to three pier heads[8] on the canal almost opposite to Crooke village. There were level crossings over the Wigan to Upholland turnpike near Oldham's Fold and over Prescot Lane and Walthew House Lane.

Robert Daglish was appointed manager of Clarke's collieries in 1810 or 1811. Daglish had previously been manager of the Haigh Foundry, and had been responsible for a wide range of improvements to colliery equipment. It was his arrival at Orrell which led to the introduction of the first steam locomotives to be used in Lancashire. One was built in 1812, at the Haigh Foundry, and put into operation in 1813. Two others were in service before the end of 1816. To overcome difficulties due to lack of adhesion, the locomotives were fitted with cog wheels which engaged with a rack on the outer edge of the running rails. The railway had meanwhile been relaid with cast iron fish belly rails with rack attached. A drawing of one such rail is given in Anderson's book.

Some interesting technical details about the locomotives and their work has survived and is reproduced in Appendix 1. A letter, written by Benjamin Hick, quoted by Dendy Marshall[9], appeared in the *The Kaleidoscope or Literary and Scientific Mirror* for 8th October 1822. This stated that there were three locomotives, two being in use and with the third as a spare. One worked from the pits to the summit of the line, which would have been near the level crossing of the Wigan to Upholland turnpike. The other worked between the summit and the canal. They drew twelve wagons, weighing 3 tons each, at a speed of three miles an hour. Each engine performed the work that formerly required fourteen horses.

The inference of the 1822 correspondence is that all three were rack engines. However, Robert Daglish, writing in 1856, when he was in his eighties, recorded that "I worked two of my locomotive engines on a cog railway ... and one of them by adhesion ...". Perhaps, some time after 1822, the rack was only used on the steep gradient down to the canal. According to Daglish the locomotives were in use upwards of 36 years, until the colliery finished.

The Orrell engines were based on a design prepared by John Blenkinsop of Leeds a year or two earlier for the Middleton Colliery railway and patented by him in 1811. In a letter to the

Orrell and Norley Hall

Repertory of Arts, Manufactures and Agriculture for 1818, quoted by Dendy Marshall, Blenkinsop stated that his design of locomotive was in use at four collieries, including Orrell. It is not certain how far the Daglish locomotives followed the Blenkinsop design in detail, as no contemporary drawings have survived for the Orrell engines.

The term "Yorkshire Horse" seems to have been in general use in Orrell and vicinity to describe the locomotives. A ⅛th inch to 1 foot model of one of the engines, constructed by Mr Eli Banks of Pemberton, is preserved in the Lancashire and Cheshire Miners Convalescent Home at Blackpool. However, it is not clear how far this truly represents the Daglish design. It was constructed from drawings supplied by the Science Museum, and these are likely to have been for a Blenkinsop engine.

To conclude the story of Clarke's Railway, Clarke himself went bankrupt in 1816. Robert Daglish continued to manage the collieries on behalf of the creditors. The Orrell pits had been worked out by the 1830s. According to Anderson those to the west of Winstanley Park continued until 1852, but the greater part of the railway seems to have closed in the mid 1840s. The 2" drawings, surveyed in 1840 to 1842 and used in the preparation of the 1st edition of the 1" map, show it terminating to the west of Winstanley Park. By the time the surveys were carried out for the 6" map, in 1845 and 1846, it had been cut short to Kitt Green, and now served the Norley Colliery which we shall deal with later in this chapter.

Woodcock and Halliburton's Walthew House Colliery

The Woodcock and Haliburton partnership took out leases at Lamberhead Green in 1815 and under the Walthew House Estate in 1822. The collieries seem to have had a short life, and, according to Anderson, closed down about 1840.

A tramroad was constructed from the pits to the Leeds and Liverpool Canal opposite Crooke. This was in existence before 1833, as it is shown on Stanley's Map, under the ownership of Woodcock. It also appears on the 1st edition of the 1" map, surveyed in 1840 to 1842.

The 1st edition of the 6" map also marks a short tramroad from pits near Norley House to a coal yard adjacent to the Wigan to Upholland turnpike. We have not been able to identify the owners of these pits, but we think that they may have been part of Woodcock and Haliburton's colliery at Lamberhead Green.

Roby Mill

We now move west to record a tramroad which ran to the Leeds and Liverpool canal west of Gathurst and which served underground quarries and collieries in the vicinity of Roby Mill. The line seems to have been built early in 1845, under a lease from the Revd Charles Kenrick Preston to John Laithwaite, which was to run for 21 years from 2nd February of that year [10]. This is consistent with the fact it does not appear on the 1st edition of the 1" map, surveyed in 1840 to 1842, but is shown on the 1st edition of the 6" map, surveyed in 1845 to 1846.

The features of the tramroad are described in an article by Bill Newby [11]. Towards the river, the line followed the course of the earlier Ayrefield Colliery tramroad, but at a higher level. According to the lease it passed on the north or north-westerly side of the old dock and terminated at the River Douglas.

Orrell and Norley Hall

The tramroad, together with the coalpits and quarries, seems to have passed into the occupation of a Mr R Townsend. The plant at his Belle Vue Colliery and Stone Quarry, which included a beam engine, was auctioned on 10th June 1867[12]. We think the tramroad may have closed at this time. It had certainly gone by 1892, when the survey was made for the 2nd edition of the 6" map.

Cassicar Colliery

We complete our survey of the early railways in the neighbourhood of Orrell with two short lines for which we only have scant information.

The 1st edition of the 1" map shows a tramroad, about half a mile in length, which served the Cassicar Colliery near Holland Lees. It ran in a northerly direction, across the River Douglas, to a wharf on the Leeds and Liverpool Canal at Appley Locks.

The line had disappeared when the 1st edition of the 6" map was surveyed in 1845 and 1846. The 6" map, however, shows a short tramroad from another colliery, further south near Welshman's Delf, which ran as far as a coal yard on the side of Lees Lane.

Norley Hall Colliery

The Norley Hall Colliery was opened up by Robert Daglish and his brother John about 1845. It is evident from the 1st edition of the 6" map, surveyed in 1845 and 1846, that Daglish took over the northern portion of Clarke's railway. According to Anderson, the connection from this line to the new colliery was the subject of an agreement in 1845 between the Daglishs and Richard Eccles, the landowner. It crossed the formation of Woodcock and Halliburton's railway, which we described earlier, on the level, just north of Orrell City.

The Norley Colliery railway was presumably 4'0" gauge, like Clarke's line. That it was worked by horses is confirmed by the recollections of Joseph Hilton, an Orrell octogenarian writing in 1930[13], although we cannot rule out the possibility that the rack locomotives were used here for a few years. The same writer also stated that parts of one of these engines were fitted up in the stables at Norley Colliery for cutting hay and mixing provender and were only disposed of when the colliery closed in the 1920s.

In 1852 John Daglish's executors sold out to a partnership headed by Thomas Whaley[14,15] which traded as the Norley Hall Coal Company until 1875. After that date the Mines Lists refer to the firm as the Norley Coal and Cannel Company.

Conversion of the railway to standard gauge took place about 1860. From a point just north of Kitt Green, then known as Orrell City the old tramroad alignment was abandoned. The new railway ran on a course a little to the east and passed under the Lancashire and Yorkshire's Wigan to Southport line by what had originally been an occupation bridge.

The land which was required for the deviation was leased by Richard Eccles to the Norley Coal Company under an agreement dated 15th July 1859[16]. The lease was for a term of 31 years from 2nd February 1859, the colliery company paying £200 per annum for the wayleave and £2 per Cheshire Acre for the land they occupied. Only traffic from the Norley Colliery could be carried. On the expiry of the lease, use of the railway was extended on an annual tenancy by an indenture of 31st March 1891, which also reduced the certain rent to £50 per annum.

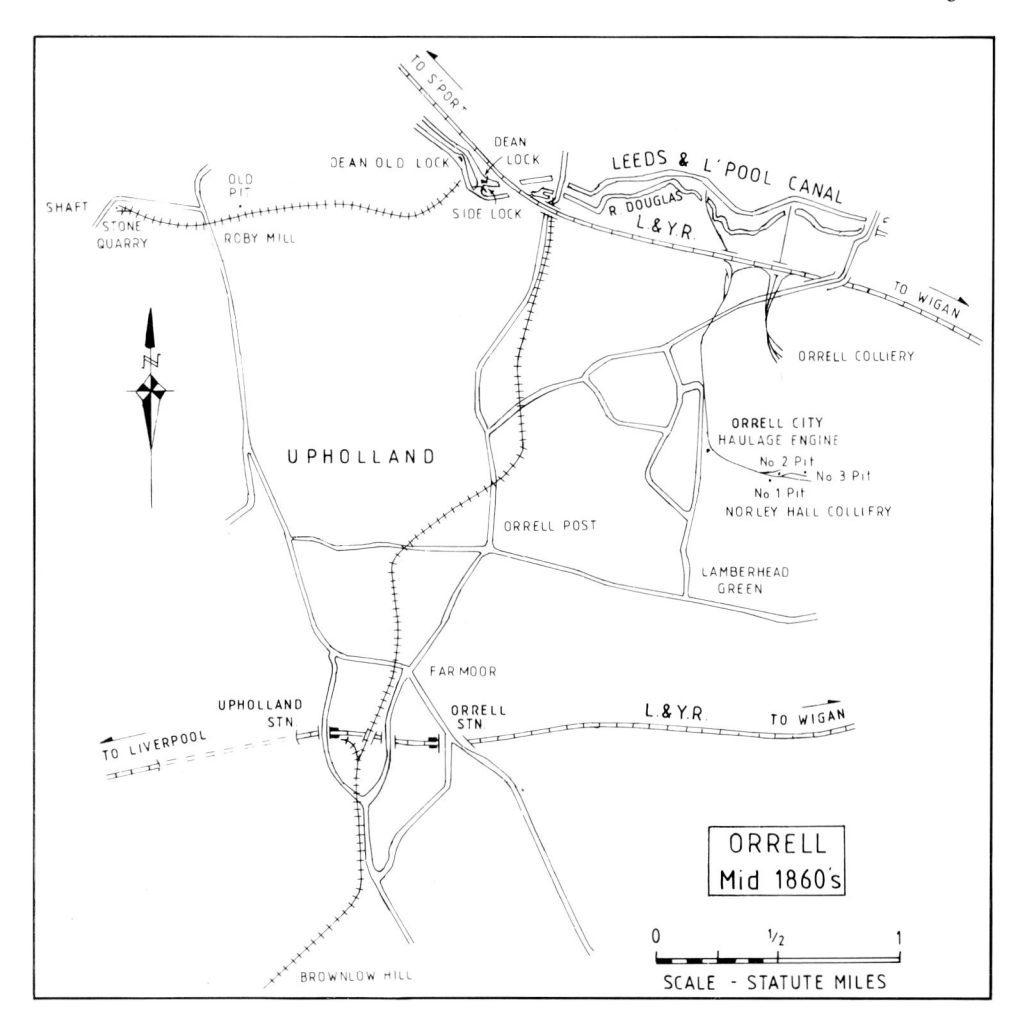

A spur was constructed to join the Lancashire and Yorkshire Railway. The siding connections were provided under an agreement dated 11th April 1860[17]. A second spur, facing towards Southport, was put in later.

A stationary steam engine was built at Kitt Green for working the incline down to the main line and to the canal. A clause in the lease required the rope on the incline to pass below the level of the roadway at all level crossings "as is done on the railways at the colliery of Mr Charles Scarisbrick" or as otherwise agreed.

Presumably horses were employed initially, to haul the standard gauge wagons between the pits and the Orrell City engine. Two locomotives were obtained from Fletcher, Jennings and Company of Whitehaven in 1864 and 1865, known as NORLEY No 1 and NORLEY No 2 respectively. The Fletcher, Jennings records note that both were cut down to enable them to pass through low bridges, No 2 having a collapsible chimney. Both were stated to work on an incline, so presumably the rope haulage down to the canal was dispensed with after they arrived.

Orrell and Norley Hall

NORLEY No 2 was returned to the builders in 1872, in part exchange for a new locomotive of the same type, NORLEY No 3. We think that No 2 may have been damaged in an explosion of a stationary boiler at the No 2 Pit, when debris fell on the locomotive shed [18].

Meanwhile there had been plans to extend the railway system. The Norley Coal Company had negotiated with the Bridgewater Trustees to mine coal under land to the east of the Norley Estate. The lease [16], which ran for fifty years from 1st June 1863, permitted construction of railways on the land covered by the lease and also on adjacent land owned by the Bridgewater Trustees. The firm was also authorised to erect a coke works on a site adjacent to that where No 4 Pit was later sunk. The coke works was apparently later leased to the Ditton Brook Coal and Iron Company. Following the bankruptcy of this firm, plant at the coke works, including 20 8-ton wagons, was advertised for sale in September 1882 [19].

A plan attached to the Bridgewater Estates lease shows that a railway was contemplated from the existing Nos 1, 2 and 3 Pits to the Leeds and Liverpool Canal at Harrison's Meadow, about a quarter of a mile north of Seven Stars Bridge. Here the cutting of a "basin or waterbay" to hold four boats was authorised. There was also to be another line which started from a junction near the future No 4 Pit and ran to the Lancashire and Yorkshire railway at Pemberton. The terms of the lease provided that the Norley Coal Company's works should not interfere with the canal basins and railways which Hollinshead Blundell and Jonathan Lamb were intending to build.

Except for the tramroad which Lamb constructed from his Newtown Colliery, these schemes came to nothing. Blundell, as we shall describe later, found an alternative access to the canal. The Norley Coal Company extended their railway system from Nos 1, 2 and 3 Pits to form an end on junction with Lancashire Union Pemberton Branch, instead of the Lancashire and Yorkshire Railway. The Sidings Schedules show that the connection was provided under a Private Sidings Agreement between Thomas Whaley and the London and North Western Railway Company dated 1st January 1871.

The new line built by the colliery company provided access to No 4 Pit, sunk in 1874, No 5 Pit sunk in 1881 [14] and to a landsale yard near Ormskirk Road. The agreement provided for the London and North Western Railway to work traffic over the colliery line as far as a point near No 4 Pit, provided Mr Whaley kept his track in good repair. For this the railway company charged $¼d$ per ton.

Thomas Whaley died on 15th July 1879 [20] and Charles Herbert Whaley was admitted to the partnership on 10th July 1880. C H Whaley died on 1st March 1885 [21] and the partnership was dissolved on 11th March 1887 [22], prior to the formation of the Norley Coal and Cannel Co Ltd. An inventory made in June 1885 refers to one saddle tank engine No 1 and one saddle tank engine No 2. Perhaps NORLEY No 3 had been renumbered.

The Norley Coal and Cannel Company ran into financial difficulty towards the end of the century. No 4 pit closed in the middle of 1896 [23] and the remaining pits on 15th February 1897 [24]. Nos 4 and 5 Pits were purchased by Sharrock and Gaskell [25] and worked in conjunction with their Orrell Colliery, which we shall describe later. The surplus plant of the Norley Coal and Cannel Company was auctioned on 2nd December 1897 [26].

Norley No 2 Pit was reopened by Mr S W Higginbotham on 2nd July 1897 [27]. The Mines Lists show he also took over the nearby No 3 Pit and that both passed to Mr H S Higginbotham in 1906. The firm of H S Higginbotham Ltd was formed in 1908 [28]. No 2 Pit finally ceased work in 1914 [29] and, presumably, No 3 Pit closed at the same time.

Orrell and Norley Hall

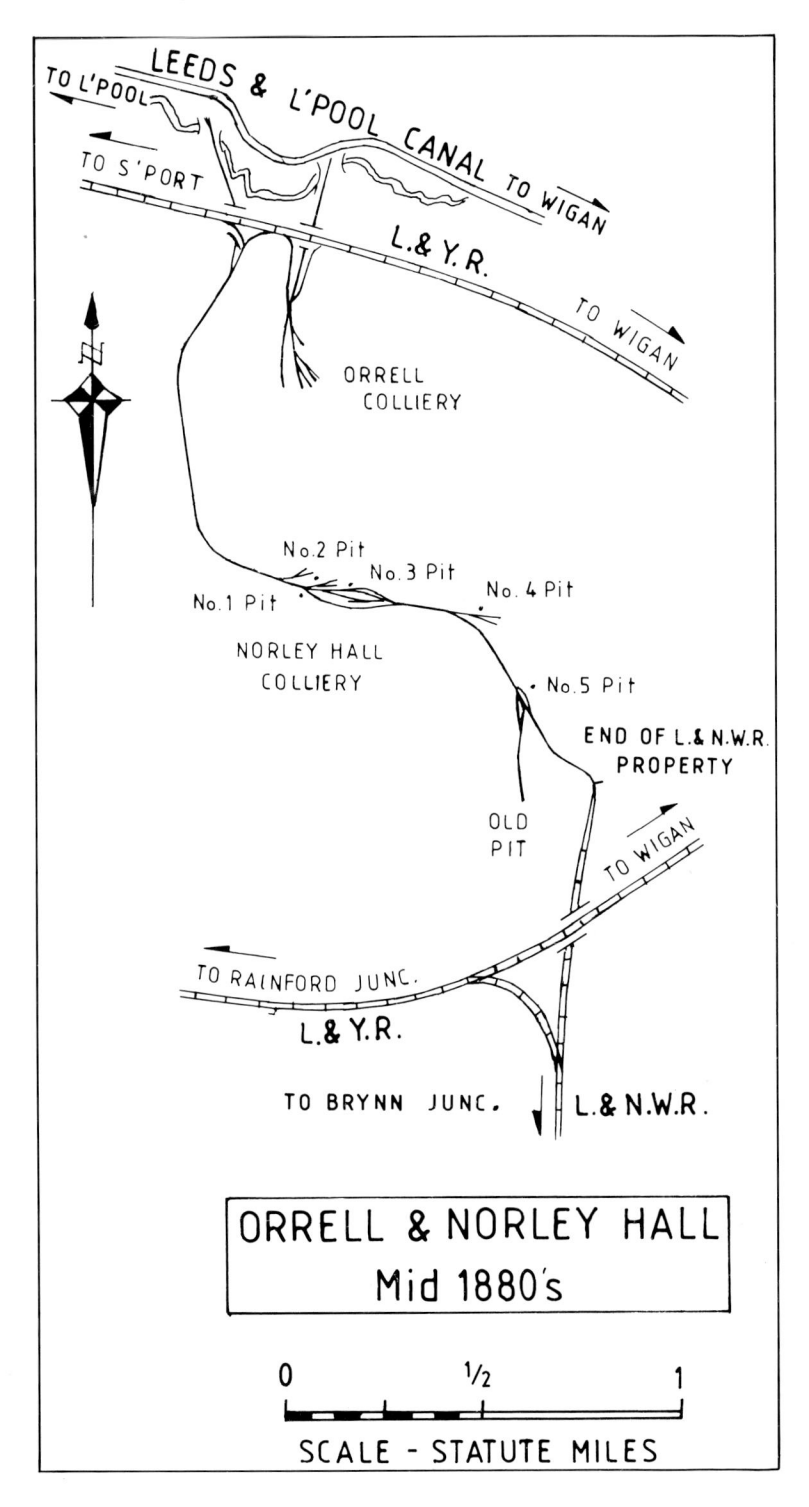

Orrell and Norley Hall

Orrell Colliery

Mildred Hustler, son of William Hustler whom we have met in connection with the early railway to Gathurst, went into partnership with William Hill Brancker, of Liverpool, in 1845 or 1846. They opened out their Orrell Colliery on the Walthew House Estate, where the mines had previously been leased to Woodcock and Haliburton. An article in the Colliery Guardian [30] suggests that No 1 Pit dated from 1834, and, if this is correct, the pit must have been sunk during the short period when Woodcock and Haliburton were in occupation. Nos 2 and 3 Pits were sunk in 1849.

To provide access to the Leeds and Liverpool Canal, Hustler and Brancker made use of the northern end of the railway originally constructed by Woodcock and Haliburton around 1820 and abandoned by them when their Lamberhead Green and Walthew House Collieries closed down. We presume these new arrangements date from around 1850, as the revised railway layout is not shown on the 1st edition of the 6" map, surveyed in 1845 and 1846.

If the railway from the Hustler and Brancker's Orrell Colliery to the canal was originally narrow gauge, it must have been converted to standard gauge shortly after the opening of the Lancashire and Yorkshire Railway's Wigan to Southport line in 1855.

A connection with the new line was put in at a point which later became known as Branckers Sidings. Although neither the Sidings Schedules nor the Sidings Diagrams [31] provide a precise date for this work, the main line connection is shown on the second revision of the 1st edition of the 6" map, published in the late 1850s.

ORRELL in the early years of the century. This locomotive is believed to have been built at the Haigh Foundry.
J.A. Peden Collection

Orrell and Norley Hall

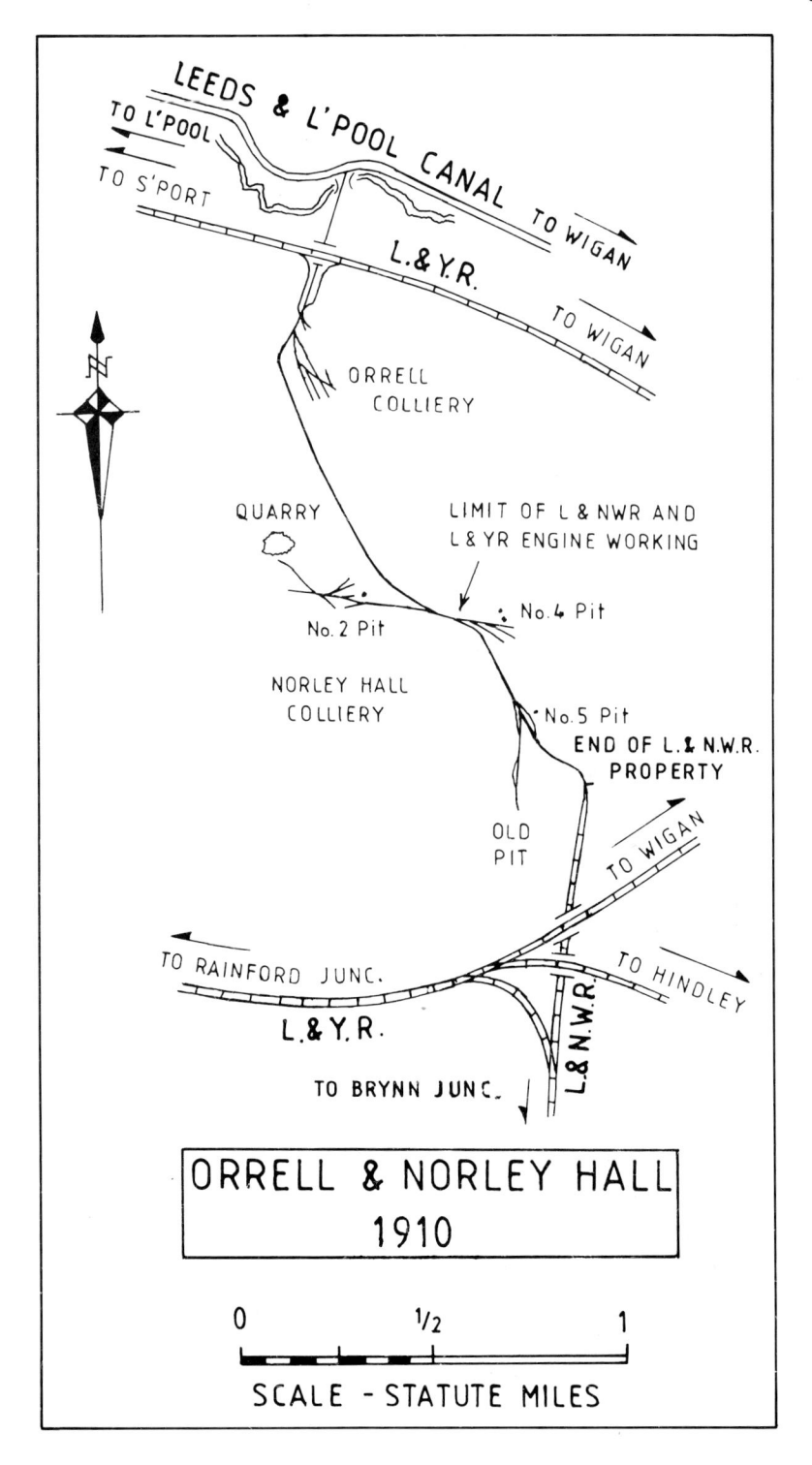

ORRELL & NORLEY HALL
1910

Orrell and Norley Hall

The Orrell Coal and Cannel Co Ltd was formed on 8th July 1875[32], with the Brancker family as principal shareholders. However, the colliery never seems to have been a financial success. It closed early in 1895 and the company was in liquidation in June of the same year[33].

The plant was put up for sale on 23rd to 25th April 1895[34,35]. Included in the auction were two four coupled saddle tank locomotives ARTHUR and ORRELL. The sales catalogue at Wigan Public Library states that ARTHUR had 11" x 14" inside cylinders and had been built by the Haigh Foundry. From the description in the catalogue, ORRELL seems to have been almost identical, except that it had 10" x 14" cylinders. These are the only two locomotives at Brancker's Orrell Colliery for which we have records, and we presume that they went back to the earliest days of the standard gauge railway system there.

The colliery and much of its equipment, including the two locomotives, were purchased by Sharrock and Gaskell, who also had interests in the Newtown and Meadows Collieries. Nos 2 and 3 Pits at Orrell Colliery were reopened by them later in 1895[36]. As we have described earlier, this same firm also took over Nos 4 and 5 pits of the Norley Hall Colliery in 1897. In July 1900, the partners formed the Orrell Colliery Co Ltd[37].

The amalgamation of the Norley and Orrell collieries led to a reorganisation of the railway system, which the Colliery Guardian article[30] suggests had been completed by 1899. The Norley Hall Company's line from No 2 Pit through Kitt Green to the canal was abandoned. The connection between this line and the Lancashire and Yorkshire Railway was taken up in October 1897[38] and the agreement for the Orrell Company's connection at Brancker's Sidings renegotiated on 5th May of the same year[31]. A new line was built by the colliery company running directly from Orrell Colliery to Norley Nos 4 and 5 pits and the Lancashire Union sidings. A short section of the original line from No 4 Pit remained to serve No 2 Pit, now under the ownership of S W Higginbotham.

Sharrock and Gaskell, at least for the first few years of their occupation, seem to have had to make do for their motive power with the two old Haigh Foundry locomotives purchased from the previous owners of the colliery.

To supplement these veterans, a second hand engine was purchased. This was KATHLEEN, a four coupled saddle tank, originally built by the Hunslet Engine Company of Leeds in 1882 for T A Walker on his Manchester Ship Canal contract, where it was named GREENFIELD. The manufacturer's records last report it at Orrell in 1917 and by September 1918 it had been sold to the Admiralty for use at Portbury Dock.

KATHLEEN was replaced by a further second hand locomotive, a six coupled saddle tank which carried the name BUTTERLEY. This had been built by the Hunslet Engine Company in 1894 and went new to Huddersfield Corporation to be used on the construction of their Butterley reservoir. It was later used by John Scott, a public works contractor, and came to Orrell Colliery some time before 1917, after the completion of the new docks at Birkenhead[39].

In addition, Higginbotham's had their own locomotive at their No 2 Pit. We have been unable to discover much about it. It is reputed to have been a six coupled saddle tank, bearing the name SAMSON. We presume that it worked the traffic between No 2 Pit and the Norley Company's line at No 4 Pit. It may also have worked through to the LNWR sidings. When Higginbotham's Pit closed in 1914, the line between No 2 Pit and No 4 pit seems to have been retained to serve the Norley Quarry. The locomotive, according to old employees, became the property of the Orrell Colliery Company.

The arrangements for main line engines to work as far as No 4 Pit were reconfirmed by an agreement dated 29th November 1918, referred to in the Sidings Schedules. Since the

Lancashire and Yorkshire Railway was permitted to run over the Pemberton Branch to work coal traffic to certain destinations, the agreement covered both LNW and L&Y locomotives[40].

Charges were increased to ½d per ton for coal and slack as from 1st August 1918. From 1st January 1919, The Orrell Colliery Company had to pay 2d per ton on all traffic other than coal and slack, while Norley Quarries Ltd, situated near No 2 Pit, paid 2d per ton on their stone traffic. From 15th January 1920 there were further increases to 1d per ton on coal and slack and 3d per ton on stone.

According to the Mines Lists, the former Norley No 5 Pit closed in 1921 and No 4 Pit in 1922. No 3 Pit of the original Orrell Colliery was abandoned on 30th October 1924. No 2 Pit there had closed around the turn of the century. Subsequently a brick works was built on the Orrell Colliery site and opened in 1925[41].

The whole of the railway system was taken out of use, with the exception of the sidings to the former Lancashire and Yorkshire line, which were retained to serve the brickworks. A note in the Sidings Schedules records that there was no traffic over the connection with the former Lancashire Union branch after May 1926 and that the private siding agreement was cancelled in February 1932.

According to the Sidings Schedules, the London Midland and Scottish Railway originally planned to take up the track between the boundary with the colliery company's property and Victoria Street Crossing, where the branch crossed the road from Wigan to Billinge. It was intended to leave the portion between Blundells Siding and Victoria Street for storage of empty wagons. However the whole of the branch was removed, apart from 30 wagon lengths at Goose Green, because of concern about pilferage. The work was completed by 24th November 1932.

An early photograph of BUTTERLEY on the construction of the reservoir for Huddersfield Corporation.
M. Swift Collection

Orrell and Norley Hall

According to old employees, ORRELL and ARTHUR, the two locomotives taken over from the Brancker concern, survived until the collieries closed in 1924. They were then cut up, along with the six coupled saddle tank, latterly apparently unnamed, which had been acquired from Higginbotham. BUTTERLEY was retained for use in the brick works.

The Sidings Schedules record that the brick works was taken over by the Wigan Brick Co Ltd from 1st June 1933. The new company continued to use the short branch to what was now the London Midland and Scottish line at Branckers Sidings. BUTTERLEY went to the new owners.

Rail traffic ceased in or before 1940, and the the Sidings Schedules state that the Private Sidings Agreement was terminated on 30th June 1940. Work to remove the siding connection was ordered on 28th July 1941. According to the Wigan Brick Company, BUTTERLEY, the only locomotive to have been used here, was sold for scrap in May 1943 [41].

The brick works closed in July 1965, still under the ownership of the Wigan Brick Co Ltd. The Sharrock family, who had worked the Orrell Colliery, were joint owners with Joseph Simpkins [42].

LOCOMOTIVE SUMMARY

Clarke's Orrell Colliery

1789–1816	John Clarke and partners
1816–c1845	Creditors of John Clarke (Robert Daglish, manager)

Gauge 4'0"

	0-4-0G	VC	HF	1812	8"

New
Scrapped, possibly about 1850

	0-4-0G	VC	HF	before 1816	8"

New
Scrapped, possibly about 1850

	0-4-0G	VC	HF	before 1816	8"

New
Scrapped, possibly about 1850

One of the above to Norley Hall Colliery. Taken out of service and used in stables

Norley Hall Colliery

c1845–1887	Various Whaley partnerships
1887–1897	Norley Hall Coal and Cannel Co Ltd
1897	No 2 Pit taken over by S W Higginbotham
1897	Nos 3 and 4 Pits taken over by Sharrock and Gaskell

Orrell and Norley Hall

Gauge 4'0" c1845 to c1860
Standard gauge c1860 to 1897

NORLEY NO 1	0-4-0ST	OC	FJ	43	1864	12"x20"	3'6"

   New
   Scrapped or sold

NORLEY NO 2	0-4-0WT	OC	FJ	50	1865	12"x20"

   New
   Retd to Fletcher Jennings in 1872 in part payment for NORLEY No 3

NORLEY NO 3	0-4-0ST	OC	FJ	102	1872	12"x20"

   New
   Scrapped or sold

Orrell Colliery

c1845–1875	Hustler and Brancker
1875–1895	Orrell Coal and Cannel Co Ltd
1895–1900	Sharrock and Gaskell
1897	Norley Hall Nos 3 & 4 Pits purchased from Norley Hall Coal and Cannel Co Ltd and railway system combined
1900–1933	Orrell Colliery Co Ltd
1924	All collieries closed, but brickworks retained
1933	Brickworks taken over by Wigan Brick Co Ltd
c1940	Rail traffic at brickworks ceased

ORRELL	0-4-0ST	IC	HF?			10"x14"	

   For sale 23 to 25-4-1895
   Taken over by Sharrock and Gaskell
   Scrapped about 1924

ARTHUR	0-4-0ST	IC	HF			11"x14"	

   For sale 23 to 25-4-1895
   Taken over by Sharrock and Gaskell
   Scrapped about 1924

KATHLEEN	0-4-0ST	OC	HE	282	1882	12"x18"	3'0"

   Ex T A Walker
   To Admiralty, Portbury in 1917 or 1918

SAMSON	0-6-0ST

   Reputed to have been taken over from H S Higginbotham Ltd in 1914

BUTTERLEY	0-6-0ST	OC	HE	617	1894	12½"x18"	2'9"

   Ex J Scott, Birkenhead Dock, 1917
   To Wigan Brick Co Ltd 1933
   Sold for scrap May 1943

Orrell and Norley Hall

Norley No 2 Pit

1897	Purchased by S W Higginbotham
1906–1908	H S Higginbotham
1908–1914	H S Higginbotham Ltd
1914	Colliery closed

SAMSON　　　　　　　　0-6-0ST
Reputed to have been taken over by Orrell Colliery Co Ltd in 1914

References to Chapter 3

1. *The Orrell Coalfield, Lancashire 1740 to 1850* – D. Anderson Moorland Publishing Co Ltd, Hartington – 1975
2. *Liverpool Advertiser* 1-11-1776
3. *Liverpool Advertiser* 27-4-1780
4. "*Plan Showing the Situation of the Collieries Communicating with the Canals and Railways in Lancashire*" – W. Stanley – 1833 – Liverpool Library – Binns Collection Vol 28, item 68
5. BC 21-12-1844
6. WO 26-7-1861
7. In the possession of Mr Donald Anderson
8. "*List of All Coal Staithes and Other Landing Places on the Line of the Leeds and Liverpool Canal*" – undated in Specification Book at Skipton Museum
9. *History of Railway Locomotives Down to the End of the Year 1831* – C F Dendy Marshall – Locomotive Publishing Company, London – 1953
10. WRO DDX Ta 30/1
11. "*Tramways of the Douglas Valley*" – Bill Newby – *Journal of North Western Society for Industrial Archaeology and History* – No 2, 1974
12. WO 7-6-1867
13. WO 20-12-1930
14. Article on Norley Collieries CG 18-11-1892, p918
15. WRO DDX El 122/3
16. In possession of Mr John Ryan
17. L&YR Sdgs Diag No 90, dated 24-10-1896
18. WO 10-5-1872
19. WO 2-9-1882
20. WO 16-7-1879
21. Probate Records
22. WO 2-4-1887
23. WO 23-5-1896
24. BJ 6-2-1897
25. WO 17-7-1897
26. WEx 13-11-1897
27. WO 3-7-1897
28. WRO DDX El 257/2
29. WO 8-12-1917
30. Article on Orrell Collieries CG 3-3-1899, p381
31. L&YR Sdgs Diag No 16A, dated 27-7-1897
32. WO 23-7-1875
33. WO 4-5-1895
34. CG 11-4-1895
35. WEx 6-4-95
36. WO 4-5-1895
37. WO 28-7-1900
38. Note on L&YR Sdgs Diag No 90, dated 24-10-1896
39. *Reservoir Railways of the Yorkshire Pennines* – H D Bowtell – The Oakwood Press – 1979
40. LNWR Sdgs Diag No 116, dated June 1920
41. Letter from Wigan Brick Co Ltd to Mr Frank Smith, dated 21-6-1954
42. Information supplied by Mr Ted Cheetham

CHAPTER 4

PEMBERTON

As the collieries in Orrell were being run down, Henry Blundell started to sink new pits further east. His Pemberton Colliery remained in the Blundell family for over a hundred years and, in late Victorian times, became one of the most productive in the Wigan coalfield.

The Lancashire and Yorkshire Company's Wigan to Liverpool line passed through Pemberton and the colliery had the advantage of a main line railway connection from as early as 1848. A second main line outlet was provided by a branch of the Lancashire Union Railway, opened in 1869.

Before this, Pemberton Colliery had been linked to the Leeds and Liverpool Canal near Seven Stars Bridge by a horse worked, narrow gauge tramroad. For most the distance the line ran parallel to an earlier tramroad which had been constructed to serve pits worked by the German family. We start with a brief study of Germans' activities before devoting the remainder of the chapter to Blundell's Pemberton Colliery.

German's Collieries

The earliest railway in the district was built by the German family, which owned a group of coal pits situated between Pemberton and Goose Green, to the south of the main road from Wigan to Upholland. The first workings here date from the early years of the nineteenth century, and are shown in the occupation of J F German in 1815[1]. By 1824[2] they had passed to his trustees and subsequently came into the possession of William German. They were later taken over by Martha Ann German, who we believe was William German's widow.

We presume that she must have remarried, as the colliery was later shown under the ownership of Martha Ann Williams. In 1848[3] it was being worked by her trustees. By 1851[4] the pits had been taken over by John Stephen, who had been agent to Martha Williams' trustees. The colliery continued to be operated by him until the mid 1860s, last appearing in the Mines Lists in 1864.

The railway, which was rather less than a mile and a half in length, terminated at the Leeds and Liverpool Canal near Seven Stars Bridge. According to the 1st edition of the 6" map, much of it consisted of an inclined plane, leading down to the wooden bridge where it crossed the River Douglas. It was, we believe, narrow gauge, probably 4'0", and laid with iron edge rails on stone sleepers. We have no doubt that it was worked by animal power throughout its existence.

We have been unable to trace when the line was constructed. We think that it was probably around 1825 or 1826. There is a record of repairs in 1826[5] to a canal boat, the "Hero", owned by William German, so we presume that the pier head was in existence by that date. The railway was certainly in operation by 1833, as it is shown on Stanley's map[6] of that date.

Pemberton

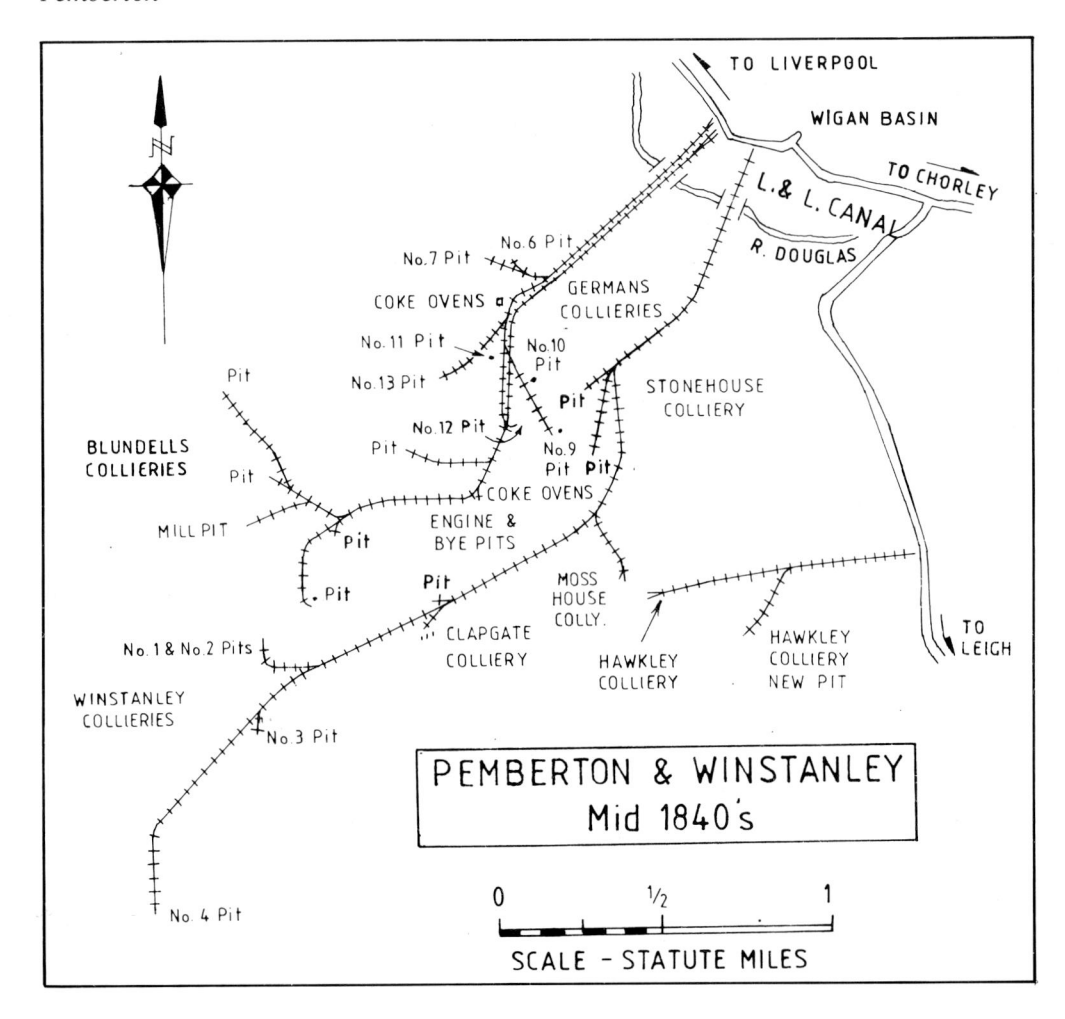

[Map: PEMBERTON & WINSTANLEY Mid 1840's]

We know that, in September 1827, Mr Daglish, the landowner, applied to the canal company, on behalf of Thomas German, to construct a side basin for loading coal[7]. We believe that this application, which was not approved, related to an extension of the installations at Seven Stars Bridge. There is also record of a lease of land from Robert Claughton to Martha Ann German on 4th August 1837, for the construction a railway[8]. However it is clear that this must refer to a branch which was being built to serve a new pit.

The railway seems to have been abandoned around 1865, following the closure of the colliery.

Blundell's Pemberton Colliery before 1850

To the west of German's collieries, Henry Blundell Hollinshead sank a series of pits at Pemberton between 1815 and 1827. Henry was the son of Jonathan Blundell, whom we have already met in connection with coal mining at Orrell in the closing years of the eighteenth century. He had adopted the surname of Hollinshead in 1802 as a condition for inheriting estates at Blackrod. He died in 1832, and his colliery properties at Orrell, Pemberton and Blackrod passed to his son, Richard Hollinshead Blundell. As well as initiating further developments at Pemberton, Richard Blundell expanded his coal mining activities by opening new collieries at the Mesnes and Amberswood and by purchasing others at Chorley from John Whittle and Partners.

A railway had already been built from Pemberton to the Leeds and Liverpool Canal at Seven Stars Bridge during Henry Blundell Hollinshead's period of ownership and this is described in considerable detail in Anderson's book [9] on Blundell's collieries. Leases for the land needed for its construction were taken in December 1827 and the line seems to have been opened sometime in 1828 or 1829. It is certainly shown on Stanley's map of 1833.

Starting at Ferrymans Pit, almost two miles from the canal, the railway ran past the Engine and Bye pits. A branch served the Venture Pit. For the last mile to the canal, Blundell's and German's railways followed the same course. It is apparent from the Pemberton Tithe Map of 1848 [10] and from the 1st edition of the 6" map that there was a double line of tracks for most of this distance. Each seems to have been operated independently, German using the northernmost track and Blundell the southernmost one. The Ordnance Survey 1/1056 Town Plan of Wigan, surveyed in 1847, shows that at the canal there were two separate pier heads. Germans line crossed to the north of the main road before Seven Stars Bridge. Blundell's line remained to the south of the road. The same features are shown on the Land Plan for the Liverpool, Bolton and Bury Railway, undated, but about 1846 [11].

In August 1838, Blundell was granted permission for a side basin on the canal [12], presumably to extend his coal loading facilities. It is also recorded that, in April 1841, Blundell was about to construct a boat yard near Seven Stars Bridge [13].

Like many of the early lines, in the district Blundell's railway was built to a gauge of 4'0" and laid with iron edge rails on stone sleeper blocks. The gradient was 1 in 80 down to the canal in favour of the loaded wagons.

Pemberton Colliery 1850 to 1870

Shortly after the opening of the Wigan and Liverpool line of the Lancashire and Yorkshire Railway, in 1848, standard gauge sidings were laid in to serve Pemberton Colliery. A revision of the 1st edition of the 6" map, published about 1850, shows a network of sidings opening out from the Lancashire and Yorkshire near Pemberton Station. These served the Lady Lane Pit, the Engine and Bye Pits, the Mill Pit and the Venture Pit. The narrow gauge lines intersected the standard gauge at a number of points, and constituted what at that time was a virtually independent system. Anderson states that, by 1852, three locomotives had been purchased to replace horses for shunting at Pemberton and that 389 wagons of 3½ and 5 ton capacity were then in use. It is interesting to note that an engine shed is shown on the 6" map alongside the Pemberton Foundry. We have almost no information about these early locomotives. We presume that they were all standard gauge, since, according to tradition, the narrow gauge line to the canal was always worked by horses.

As we shall see in Chapter 10, the Blundells had been locomotive owners since the early 1840s, and were hauling their own coal trains from their Mesnes and Amberswood Collieries over the North Union line to Preston and to Liverpool, via Parkside and the Liverpool and Manchester Railway. We assume, without any concrete evidence, that, at least up to 1848, these engines were based at Amberswood Colliery.

Pemberton

PEMBERTON & WINSTANLEY Mid 1860's

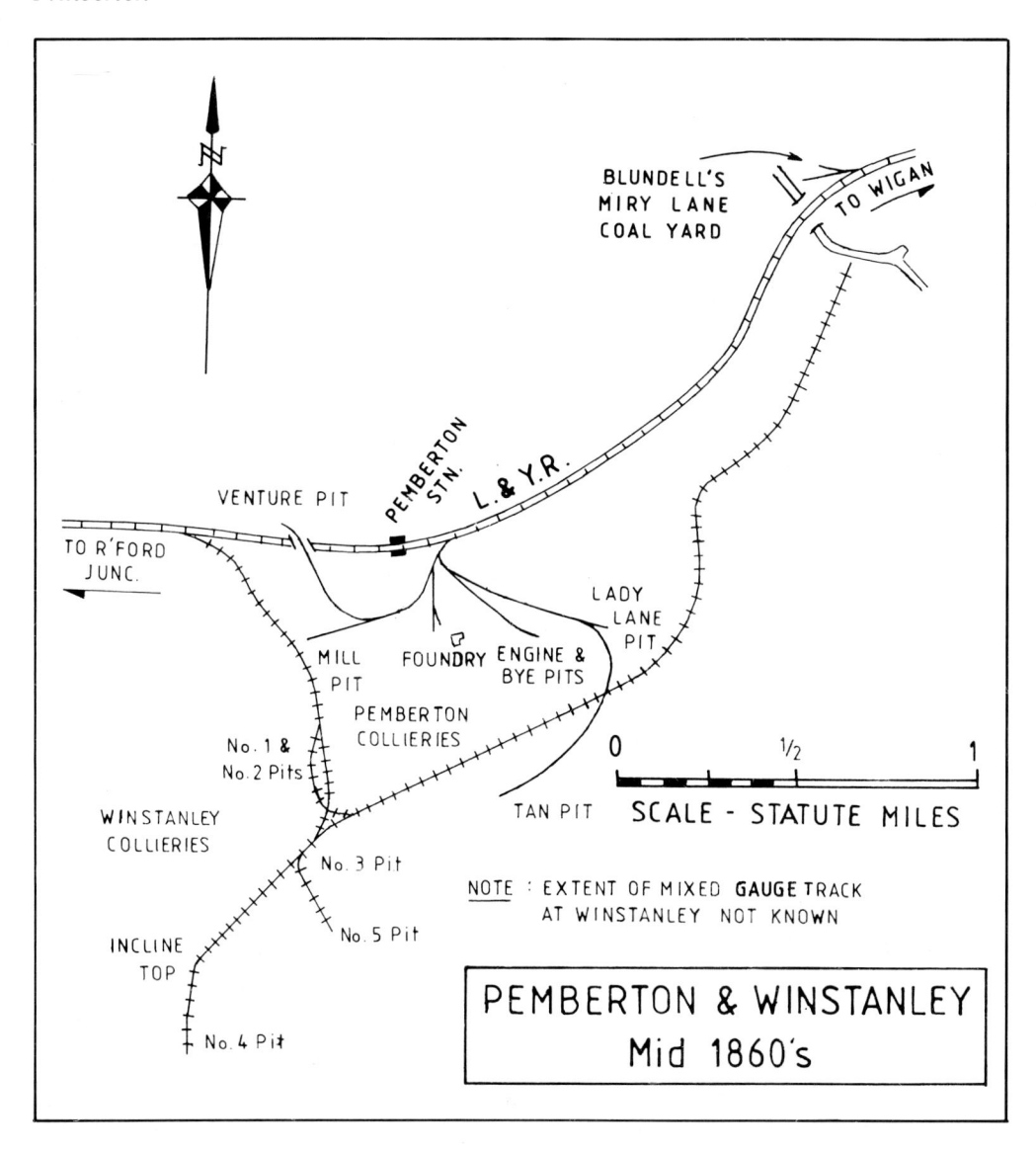

What happened after 1848 has gone unrecorded. It seems likely that Blundells extended their operations to include trains from Pemberton to Preston, using the L&Y tracks as far as Wigan. It also seems likely that they worked their own coal traffic to Liverpool via the Lancashire and Yorkshire route, in the same way as the Earl of Crawford and Balcarres. We think that these main line workings, which we treat more extensively in Chapter 10, ceased some time before 1860.

Richard Blundell was succeeded as head of the firm by his son Henry in 1853. During Henry's term of office, which lasted until 1906, the company concentrated on further expansion at Pemberton. Blackrod colliery inherited by his grandfather in 1802 had already been closed in 1849. Of the other collieries acquired by his father around 1840, that at Chorley was sold to James Darlington, who had mining interests nearby at Coppull. Mesnes was given up by 1854 and Amberswood by 1873.

Pemberton Colliery 1870 to 1900

The first major development during this period was the opening of two modern shafts to replace the original pits and to exploit the deeper seams. Sinking of the King and Queen Pits started in December 1867, and the latter reached coal on 2nd September 1870. Of the earlier shafts, the Bye Pit and Pumping Pit were retained, together with the Venture Pit, which lasted until 1884. The Tanhouse Pit had previously been transferred to the Winstanley colliery concern, as a result of an exchange of mining leases between Henry Blundell and Meyrick Bankes.

In 1869 the Pemberton Branch of the Lancashire Union Railway was opened. This provided a rail outlet independent of the Lancashire and Yorkshire Railway and the Sidings Schedules show that a connection was put in under an agreement dated 14th December 1869. The construction of the Lancashire Union line resulted in alterations to the colliery company's line to Tan Pit. An independent track was provided on LUR land, at the expense of the railway company, on the west side of the its line. Lady Lane Pit closed at this time, and the colliery line which served it was taken up.

A makers photograph of the first PEMBERTON of 1872.   V.J. Bradley Collection

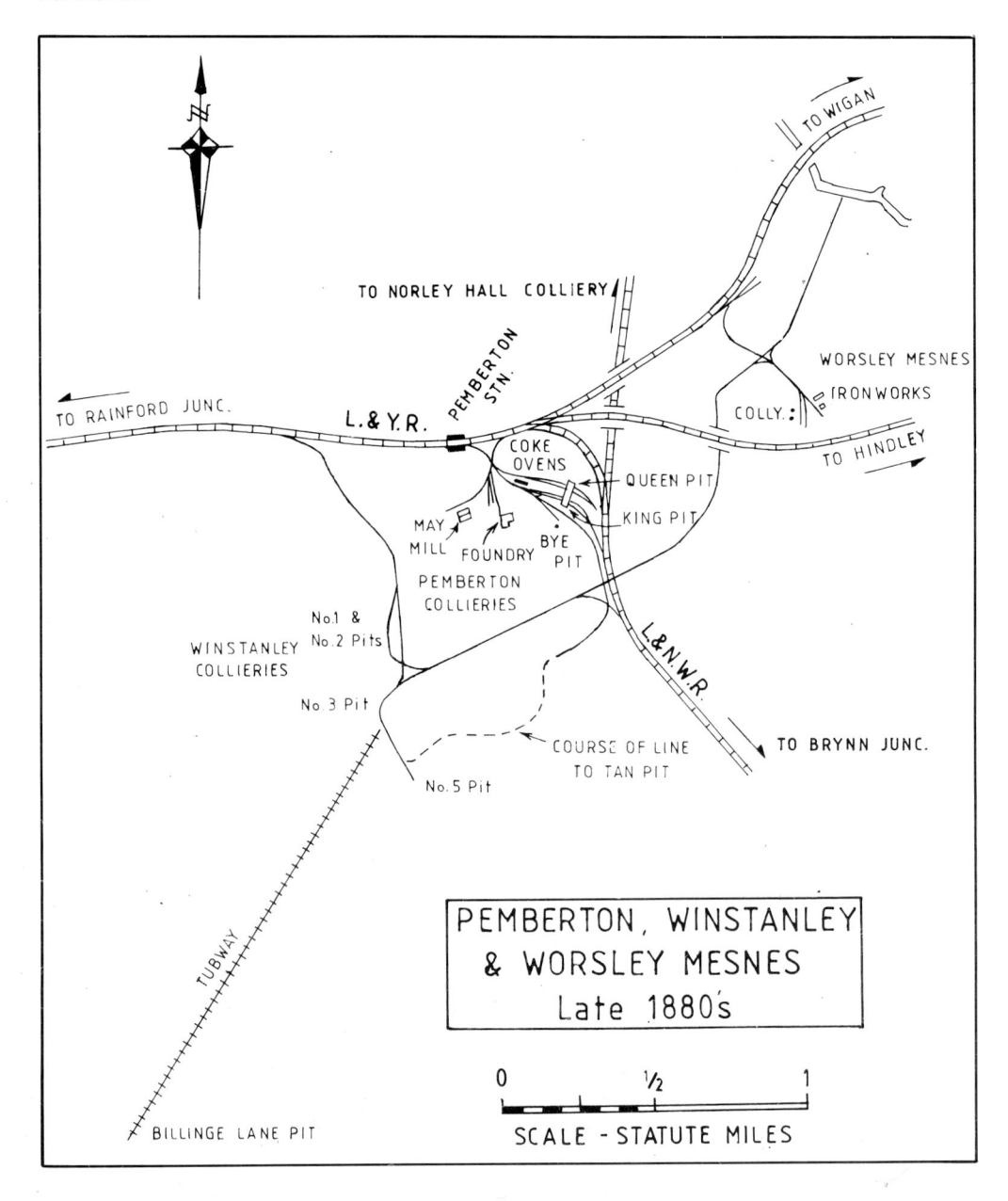

By this time Blundell's narrow gauge line to the canal had been abandoned. The leases of the land which it occupied were given up on 1st April 1868. The course of the line, including most of the two track section shared by German and Blundell, was later used to provide a direct road from Pemberton to Wigan – the present Victoria Street.

We know, from information contained in a lease[14] from the Bridgewater Trustees to the Norley Coal Company, that in the mid 1860s Blundell was considering the construction of a standard gauge line from Pemberton to the Leeds and Liverpool Canal at Harrison's Meadow. However, he did not proceed with this project. Instead, around 1865, a new coal yard was established at Miry Lane, on the north bank of the canal almost opposite the wharves where the narrow gauge railway had terminated. Coal, brought here by the Lancashire and Yorkshire Railway from Pemberton Colliery, could be loaded into horse drawn carts for local delivery. Alternatively, it could be transhipped to barges, thus maintaining deliveries to customers served by the canal.

We have rather more information about the locomotives used at Pemberton Colliery at this period. Unlike some of their predecessors, they were employed solely in shunting duties around the colliery yard. The first locomotive that we have on record was a four coupled saddle tank which came from the Vulcan Foundry at Newton-le-Willows in 1863.

The next locomotive that we have been able to trace came in 1866. This was a small four coupled saddle tank built by Manning, Wardle of Leeds, which carried the name HENRY. Two further four coupled saddle tanks, named PEMBERTON and QUEEN, were purchased from the Hunslet Engine Company of Leeds in 1872 and 1875 respectively.

Pemberton Colliery 1900 to 1929

The Pemberton Colliery Co Ltd was registered on 7th December 1900 to take over the colliery, with control still in the hands of the Blundell family[15]. A third new shaft, the Prince Pit, had been started in 1898, and first wound coal in January 1901. A new Venture Pit was sunk during 1910 to 1912, but lasted only until 1916.

Pemberton Colliery about the turn of the century. View from Lancashire and Yorkshire Railway exchange sidings.
John Ryan Collection

Pemberton

Coke had been made at Pemberton since the earliest days and by 1904 118 beehive ovens were in operation. In that year, according to Anderson, a battery of 23 Semet-Solvay by-product recovery ovens were installed. The number of the new ovens was increased to 30 in 1914, and 40 in 1924. Slack was evidently purchased from neighbouring collieries for the coke ovens, because there is correspondence between Meyrick Bankes and the Lancashire and Yorkshire Railway Company concerning rates for carriage from Winstanley to Pemberton[16].

These developments were accompanied by alterations and improvements to the network of private railways serving the three pits and the coking plant. The colliery company also worked traffic to and from the main line sidings on behalf of several other establishments which were connected to their railway system. The Sidings Schedules record that Messrs R S Clare and Company, Tar Distillers, Oil Grease and Varnish makers, had a branch works here which had been built about 1905. The May Mill Company, which had been established here in the nineteenth century, received traffic exclusively from the Lancashire and Yorkshire Railway. There was also a small amount of traffic for farmers which came from the Lancashire and Yorkshire Railway and was worked by Pemberton Colliery engines to the Tan Pit sidings.

From 1900 onwards, the earlier locomotives began to be supplemented by larger and more powerful designs. In that year a six coupled saddle tank, PRINCE, came from Peckett and Sons of Bristol. KING, a four coupled saddle tank, built in the colliery workshops, was completed about 1905. Two six coupled saddle tanks were purchased from the Avonside Engine Company of Bristol in 1913 and 1918. These were named PHYLLIS and BLUNDELL, the former subsequently having its name changed to DOUGLAS.

Anderson states that, in the period 1900 to 1925, Pemberton Colliery possessed nearly 2000 wagons, 6 locomotives and over 15 miles of track in the sidings. This is consistent with the information which we have gathered together about the locomotives. The Vulcan Foundry engine of 1863 seems to have disappeared at an early date. PEMBERTON and QUEEN appear to have been withdrawn from service in the early years of the century, the manufacturer's records showing that spare parts were last supplied in February 1906 and October 1904 respectively. According to old employees, HENRY, or Little Harry as it seems to have been known, was scrapped just before the first world war.

Pemberton Colliery 1929 to 1945

In 1929, the Blundell family relinquished its interests in the colliery and control passed to the Pemberton Colliery (1929) Ltd. By this time coal reserves were beginning to be worked out. Production was down to 300,000 tons per year compared with over double that figure during the peak years before the first world war.

At least on the railway side, the new owners seem to have carried out a certain amount of modernisation. Two new four coupled saddle tanks were purchased from Hawthorn, Leslie and Co Ltd of Newcastle in 1936 and 1937, named PEMBERTON and BESS respectively. Of the locomotives taken over from the previous company, BLUNDELL and DOUGLAS were retained. KING, the locomotive built in the colliery workshops, is believed to have lasted until about 1938.

Under the new company output continued to decline. The brickworks, built in 1910, was sold to the West Lancashire Brick Co Ltd in July 1936. A financial reorganisation resulted in a change in name to Pemberton Colliery Ltd in August 1938. The coke ovens were shut down soon after the outbreak of war in 1939. The colliery closed on 3rd November 1946, when the last tub of coal was wound. Since 1943, when the Lancashire Union Pemberton Branch was closed, all traffic had been handled over the former Lancashire and Yorkshire Railway connections.

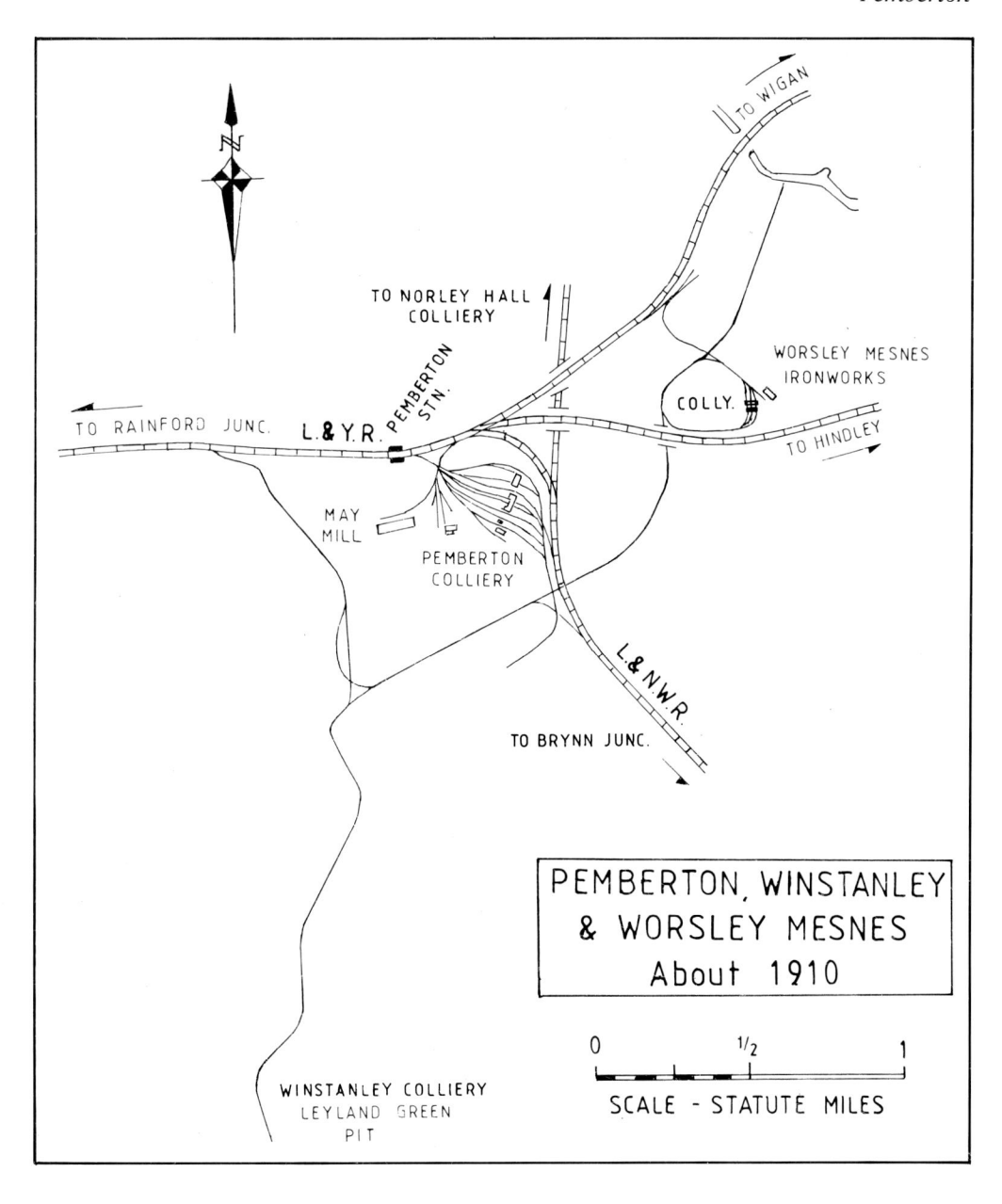

Production continued in a small way at the Summersales Drift, which was opened out towards the end of the second world war. The coal was taken by road to Pemberton station, where it was loaded into railway wagons, the Sidings Schedules stating that this traffic commenced on 3rd September 1945.

Pemberton

The second PEMBERTON, photographed in National Coal Board days, working at John Pit, Standish.
Industrial Railway Society, Ken Cooper Collection

Summersales Drift was taken over by the National Coal Board on 1st January 1947 and finally closed on 18th March 1966[9]. The National Coal Board also acquired the Pemberton Colliery site and much of the equipment. According to *Guide to the Coal Fields*[17], pumping continued here until 1959.

The locomotives PEMBERTON and DOUGLAS became the property of the Coal Board. The former was still at the Pemberton site in July 1947 and was sent to Ince Moss Colliery before the end of the year. Its subsequent movement are dealt with in other chapters. DOUGLAS was moved to Kirkless Workshops on 31st December 1947 and was scrapped there in 1948.

BLUNDELL seems to have been broken up at about the time that the colliery closed. BESS was sold to Hough and Sons Ltd, the Wigan machinery merchants, and later went to Pilkington Brothers Ltd, of St Helens.

Pemberton after 1945

Part of the railway sidings at Pemberton Colliery remained in use to serve a screening plant for opencast coal which was being mined south west of Wigan. The coal was brought by road from the various sites to Pemberton for despatch by rail. The Sidings Schedules record that the first wagons had been sent away on 16th July 1943.

The opencast disposal point was initially under the control of the Ministry of Fuel and Power's Directorate of Opencast Coal Production. Responsibility passed to the Opencast

Executive of the National Coal Board on 1st April 1952. Operations at the screening plant were carried out under contract by William Todd and Co (Pemberton) Ltd, at least in later years.

The disposal point was closed about 1964, but was maintained in working order for several years afterwards. The private sidings agreement was terminated on 31st August 1967[18].

At the start the opencast plant seems to have been served by the locomotives owned by the Pemberton Colliery Company. Following the closure of the colliery, six coupled saddle tanks of the Austerity type were employed and a new wooden locomotive shed was constructed to house them. These engines had been built during the second world war for military use and were based on a design which originated with the Hunslet Engine Company of Leeds. After the war many were sold for industrial use and new engines of the same design were purchased by the National Coal Board and other companies.

The engines at Pemberton were drawn from a pool maintained by the Ministry of Fuel and Power, and subsequently by the Opencast Executive, for use at disposal points around the country. Usually only one locomotive was here at a time, being moved elsewhere as circumstances dictated. The last to be used at Pemberton, WD 71507, was repainted with the name William Todd and Co (Pemberton) Ltd on the tanks. It does not, however, seem to have been purchased by them, as it was transferred to another opencast disposal point at Glyn Neath when the Pemberton site was cleared.

For a short period in 1962, a small four coupled saddle tank, named WESTWOOD, was also based at Pemberton, presumably while the regular engine was undergoing repair. WESTWOOD had been built by Hudswell, Clarke and Company of Leeds in 1913 for Platt Brothers and Co Ltd, for use at their Moston Colliery near Manchester. It had subsequently been taken over by the North Western Division of the National Coal Board.

After the opencast disposal point was closed, part of the site was retained by William Todd. For some years the Industrial Steam Preservation Group stored one of its locomotives here. This was a four coupled saddle tank, built in 1908, which came to Pemberton from the Millom Hematite Ore and Iron Co Ltd, in Cumbria, in 1968. It was moved away in 1974 and since 1982 it has been at the Mining Museum at Astley Green.

Another part of the colliery site was occupied by S Littler Ltd, scrap merchants and machinery dealers. A diesel locomotive, built by John Fowler and Company of Leeds, which they had purchased from Blackpool Corporation Highways Department, arrived here about 1962. It was used from time to time during the period from 1969 to 1974 by the Industrial Steam Preservation Group. It was still in the yard in February 1984 but has subsequently disappeared.

At the time of writing, the group of buildings at the end of Foundry Lane, which at one time formed the colliery workshops and offices, are still in existence and are occupied by a variety of small firms. The locomotive shed remains more or less intact and is used by a road haulage company. The site of the colliery itself has been landscaped.

Pemberton

LOCOMOTIVE SUMMARY

Pemberton Colliery

1815 to 1900	Various Blundell family partnerships
1900 to 1929	Pemberton Colliery Co Ltd
1929 to 1938	Pemberton Colliery Co (1929) Ltd
1938 to 1946	Pemberton Colliery Co Ltd
1947 to 1966	National Coal Board (Summersales Drift only, no rail connection)

For early tender engines see Chapter 10

		0-4-0ST	OC	VF	505	1863	14"x20"	4'0"

New
Scrapped or sold

HENRY		0-4-0ST	OC	MW	214	1866	9½"x14"	

New
Scrapped or sold

PEMBERTON		0-4-0ST	OC	HE	90	1872	14"x20"	3'6"

New
Scrapped or sold after 1906

QUEEN		0-4-0ST	OC	HE	140	1875	14"x20"	3'6"

New
Scrapped or sold after 1904

KING		0-4-0ST	OC	Pemberton		1905?	14"x20"	

New
Scrapped about 1938

PRINCE		0-6-0ST	IC	P	876	1900	16"x22"	

New
To Hough and Sons Ltd, Wigan, 1929

PHYLLIS		0-6-0ST	OC	AE	1654	1913	14"x20"	3'3"

New
Renamed DOUGLAS
To National Coal Board 1-1-1947
Scrapped at Kirkless Workshops 1948

BLUNDELL		0-6-0ST	OC	AE	1812	1918	14"x20"	3'3"

New
Scrapped or sold about 1946

PEMBERTON		0-4-0ST	OC	HL	3878	1936	14"x22"	3'6"

New
To National Coal Board 1-1-1947
Transferred to Ince Moss 1947

BESS		0-4-0ST	OC	HL	3933	1937	14"x22"	3'6"

New
To Pilkington Bros, St Helens, via Hough and Sons Ltd, Wigan

Pemberton

Pemberton Opencast Disposal Point

1943 to 1952   Ministry of Fuel and Power, Directorateof Opencast Coal Production
1952 to c1964   National Coal Board, Opencast Executive
                          Operated under contract by William Todd and Co (Pemberton) Ltd

75060   0-6-0ST   IC   RSH   7096   1943   18"x26"   4'3"
   From Coton Park in February 1947
   To Hafod in September 1948
   Returned to Pemberton from Wentworth about January 1951
   To Hafod July 1951

75137   0-6-0ST   IC   HE   3188   1944   18"x26"   4'3"
   Arrived here before January 1948
   To Watnall after August 1953

71508   0-6-0ST   IC   RSH   7162   1944   18"x26"   4'3"
   From Skiers Spring August 1953
   To Walkden Yard under own steam 22-3-1956, returned April 1957
   To Gatewen by November 1958

71507   0-6-0ST   IC   RSH   7161   1944   18"x26"   4'3"
   From Watnall to Walkden Yard 21-12-1956 and thence to Pemberton
   under own steam 16-3-1956
   Sent away for repairs and returned by road in late 1962
   To Glyn Neath about January 1967

WESTWOOD   0-4-0ST   OC   HC   1036   1913   16"x24"   3'8"
   Temporarily here from Walkden Yard January to July 1962

Industrial Steam Preservation Group, Pemberton Colliery Site

                              0-4-0ST   OC   AE   1563   1908   12"x18"
   Ex Millom Hematite Ore and Iron Co Ltd, Hodbarrow, September 1968
   Stored here until 1974 and occasionally steamed.
   Now at Astley Green Mining Museum

S Littler Ltd, Pemberton

                              0-4-0D   JF   22598   1938   40 HP
   Ex Blackpool Corporation Highways Dept, about 1962
   Scrapped or sold after February 1984

Pemberton

References to Chapter 4

1. *The Commercial Directory for 1814–15* – Wardle and Bentham, Manchester.
2. *History, Directory and Gazeteer of the County Palatine of Lancashire* – Edward Baines – Liverpool 1824–5
3. *Royal National Commercial Directory and Topography of the County of Lancaster* – Isaac Slater – Manchester, 1848
4. *Royal National Commercial Directory and Topography of the County of Lancaster* – Isaac Slater – Manchester, 1851
5. WRO DDX Ta 37/8
6. "*Plan Showing the Situation of Collieries Communicating with the Canals and Railways in Lancashire*" – W. Stanley – 1833 – Liverpool Library – Binn's Collection Vol 28, item 68
7. Leeds and Liverpool Canal Company's Minutes, 22-9-1827
8. WRO DDX El 28/67
9. "*Blundell's Collieries 1776 to 1966*" – Donald Anderson – *Transactions of the Historic Society of Lancashire and Cheshire* – Vol 116, 1964, Vol 117, 1965 and Vol 119, 1967
10. LRO DRL 1/62
11. Land Plan of Liverpool and Bury Railway at GMRO
12. Leeds and Liverpool Canal Company's Minutes, 24-8-1838
13. Leeds and Liverpool Canal Company's Minutes, 17-4-1841
14. In possession of Mr John Ryan
15. WO 22-12-1900
16. "*A Nineteenth Century Colliery Railway*" – Joyce H M Bankes – *Transactions of the Historic Society of Lancashire and Cheshire* – Vol 114, 1962
17. *Guide to the Coal Fields* – Colliery Guardian Co Ltd, London, published annually
18. Schedule attached to Line Plan of Liverpool Bolton and Bury Railway – LMSR Euston 1938 to 1940 – At BRPB, Manchester

CHAPTER 5

WINSTANLEY AND WORSLEY MESNES

We now turn to an adjacent district, lying to the south of the collieries which we described in the preceding chapter. A large part of the land was owned by the Bankes family of Winstanley Hall. Two articles [1,2] written by Mrs Joyce Bankes, drawing on family records, provide a wealth of information about the history of mining and transport in the area up to the 1880s. The articles have been used as source material for much of what follows.

The maps relating to the tramroad and railway systems will be found in Chapter 4.

Stonehouse, Moss House and Clapgate Collieries

Thomas Claughton purchased the Stonehouse Estate in 1819, and, in 1822, obtained leases to mine in the adjoining properties owned by Meyrick Bankes. In 1822 or 1823 he built a railway from the pits he was sinking to the Leeds and Liverpool Canal at Parsons Meadow. In the early years of the present century, the coal tip here became known as Wigan Pier, a cognomen which has persisted ever since. As we shall see in Part 2, Chapter 21, there had been a previous Wigan Pier.

As a result of the bankruptcy of Claughton, who had no doubt overstretched himself financially in the venture, a new partnership of John Daglish and Peter Bromilow took over the colliery and the railway in 1830.

The railway is shown under their ownership on Stanley's map of 1833 [3]. An undated Estate Plan in the authors' possession, thought to have been drawn in 1830, indicates that there were branches from four separate pits, all located to the west of the main Wigan to Ashton road between Stonehouse and Smithy Brook. The branches converge near Hindley Hall to form the "main line" to the canal.

In 1840 John Daglish became the sole proprietor [4], and in 1850 the collieries at Stonehouse and Hindley Hall (near Newtown, not to be confused with the estate of the same name at Hindley) had passed to Dr George Daglish. The Mines Lists for 1853/4 show that they had been taken over Thomas Fisher, the Fisher family remaining in occupation until the mines closed in 1864. After 1868 the remaining coal at Hindley Hall was worked by Henry Blundell and was conveyed underground for winding at Pemberton.

Moss House Colliery was situated to the north of Hawkley Bridge, between Poolstock Lane and the Wigan to Ashton Turnpike. Coal under the Moss House Estate had been leased by Messrs Bradshaw and their mortgagees to James Whaley in 1837 [5], but the pits do not seem to have been sunk until the early 1840s. The colliery is not shown on the 2" drawings, prepared between 1840 and 1842 for the 1st edition of the 1" map. By the time that the 1st edition of the 6" map was surveyed in 1845 and 1846, the colliery was in operation and connected to the Stonehouse railway system.

Winstanley and Worsley Mesnes

James Whaley appears as the proprietor of Stonehouse Colliery in directories for 1848[6] and 1851[7], and the Mines Lists show that it was worked by his executors between 1853 and 1857. It seems to have closed in 1858 or 1859 and the plant was up for sale on 7th November 1859[8,9]. The Moss House Estate was purchased in 1863 from Thomas Whaley by Henry Blundell, who worked the coal from Pemberton Colliery.

Further west there was Clapgate Colliery. This had been opened around 1800 by Stopford and Briden, who had obtained a lease from Meyrick Bankes the elder. Still worked by this partnership in 1824[10], it had been taken over by Henry Harrison before 1848[6]. The Mines Lists show that Henry Harrison continued to work the colliery until 1865, when it closed.

We know, from the 1st edition of the 6" map, that Clapgate Colliery was served by a branch of the narrow gauge railway running from Winstanley Colliery to the canal. As we shall see later, the Winstanley line, east of Goose Green, made use of the railway constructed by Thomas Claughton. We have not been able to discover whether Clapgate Colliery had to wait for a rail connection until the Winstanley line was built or whether Claughton's line had been extended to Clapgate at an earlier date.

Hawkley Colliery

We now move east again to Hawkley Colliery. Thomas Jenkinson and James Richard Grimshaw leased mineral rights here from Brian William Molyneux and his mortgagees for a forty year period on 10th April 1837[11]. Anderson[12] records that the lease was renewed when Meyrick Bankes purchased the Hawkley Estate in 1840.

The colliery may have originally been served by a branch from Daglish's railway at Smithy Brook, as the 2" drawings show what could be an abandoned tramroad from here to a point near Hawkley Hall. The 2" drawings also make it quite clear that, by the time the survey was carried out in 1840 to 1842, the Hawkley pits had an independent line to the Leigh Branch of the Leeds and Liverpool Canal.

The railway is not shown on Stanley's map of 1833, but must have been opened before 1838. The Ince Rate Book for April of that year[13] shows that Jenkinson and Grimshaw were the occupiers of a tramroad and pier head at Bryn Moss, on land owned by John Walmesley.

James Richard Grimshaw is shown as the proprietor in 1848[6] and again 1851[7], but the colliery closed during 1853. The plant was auctioned on 10th January of that year, when there were stated to be four shafts in use. Amongst the items to be sold were 3000 yards of tram rails and sleepers, together with a unspecified number of coal wagons[14]. There was a further sale on 2nd May 1853, as a result of the bankruptcy of the firm[15].

Hawkley Colliery does not seem to have reopened and the railway to the canal must have been abandoned at this time. The remaining coal was later worked from Pemberton Colliery.

Winstanley Colliery – the Early History

In the 1830s Meyrick Bankes Junior started to exploit coal under his own estate at Winstanley. Four pits were sunk, and Bankes sought to provide an outlet to the canal. Approaches to Blundell Hollinshead for use of the Pemberton Colliery railway were rejected. Attention was then turned to forming a junction with the line operated by Daglish and Bromilow, for which provision had been made in the lease of 1822 from Meyrick Bankes.

The line from the Winstanley Nos 1, 2 and 3 pits to the junction with Daglish and Bromilow's railway seems to have been opened in the mid 1840s. The section from here to the canal was purchased by Bankes in the same year. It appears that the lower end of the line continued to be used by the other colliery concerns which we have described above.

The Winstanley railway, and the events leading up to its construction, are fully described in *A Nineteenth Century Colliery Railway* by Joyce H M Bankes [2]. The complete line from Winstanley No 4 Pit, at Windy Arbour, to the canal, a distance of about 3½ miles was opened in 1845. It was laid with T section wrought iron rails, 15 feet long, supported on stone sleeper blocks. The gauge was 4'0", presumably to conform with that of Claughton's earlier railway.

There were two inclined planes on the main line to the canal, where trains of six to eight wagons were let down under the control of two brakesmen. The horses, which were needed to haul the empty wagons on their return journey to the pits, apparently travelled down the inclines in special wagons known as dandy carts.

The line between No 4 Pit and No 3 Pit was worked by rope. The loaded trucks from No 4 Pit were drawn up to the summit of the line near Smith's Farm by a haulage rope, which according to local tradition was attached to a drum on the No 4 Pit winding engine. From Smith's Farm the waggons were then let down a self-acting incline to No 3, or Baxter Pit.

A branch was constructed in 1848 or 1849 to sidings adjacent to the Lancashire and Yorkshire Railway's Wigan to Liverpool line, so that coal could be transferred directly from narrow gauge to standard gauge wagons. There is a suggestion that this branch was also operated by a stationary engine. A further branch was laid in to No 5 Pit, which appears to have been sunk about 1860.

The four foot gauge locomotive LOUISA working at Brixworth in Northamptonshire, in later ownership.
The late G. Alliez

Winstanley and Worsley Mesnes

By 1867 a third rail had been laid on the greater part of the railway system at the collieries and a standard gauge connection provided with the Lancashire and Yorkshire Railway. Coal could now be loaded at the pits either into standard gauge wagons for despatch by main line railway or into narrow gauge wagons if it was destined for the canal.

At this period there was an exchange of leases between Meyrick Bankes and Henry Blundell. As a result, the Tan Pit was transferred to Meyrick Bankes, and was used for raising water until abandoned in 1897. A standard gauge line was laid in from Winstanley No 5 Pit to the Tan Pit, which was already linked to the Pemberton Colliery railway system. In this way, the Winstanley collieries were provided with an alternative main line outlet when the Lancashire Union Pemberton Branch was opened in 1869.

Horses continued to haul both standard and narrow gauge wagons on the Winstanley Railway until a little before 1880. A four coupled saddle tank, bearing the name ELEANOR, was ordered from the Wigan firm of Walker Brothers. It seems to have been delivered on 23rd June 1879, according to a diary of a former employee, whose son, George Melling, made it available to us. The colliery ledgers show that Walker Brothers' bill for £1000 was paid on 18th December that year [16]. With only one locomotive, arrangements had to be made to provide a substitute when ELEANOR needed repairs. On at least one occasion HARRY was hired from Walker Brothers at a cost of £30 [16].

At this time consideration was being given to modernisation of the line to the canal which was still narrow gauge and using horses for motive power. A proposal to erect a stationary engine and employ rope haulage was turned down. It was decided to relay the line so that it could be worked by a locomotive, but still retaining the narrow gauge. A 4'0" gauge engine was obtained from the Hunslet Engine Company, of Leeds, in 1882, which was named LOUISA.

Winstanley Collieries from 1885 to 1928

On 9th July 1885 [16] the Winstanley Colliery, together with its railway system, was leased to Tomlinson, Rogers and Simpson. Winstanley Collieries Co Ltd was formed on 27th October 1885, with these three individuals having a controlling interest [17,18]. The same partnership had already taken over the adjacent Worsley Mesnes Colliery and had control of the Ellerbeck Colliery, which we deal with later, and a colliery at Cross Hands in South Wales.

The new company proceeded with the conversion of the remaining narrow gauge lines. The railway to the canal seems to have been changed to standard gauge in 1886 or 1887. The old route to the Lancashire Union, via Tan Pit, was abandoned, except for a short length at its eastern end which continued to be worked from Pemberton Colliery, presumably for the conveyance of wagons of coal and general merchandise to farmers in the neighbourhood of Harvey House. A new connection to the Lancashire Union line was provided from the Winstanley Company's now standard gauge line to the canal, the Sidings Schedules stating that the work was carried out under the authority of LNWR Board Minute 6376 of July 1886.

The spur from the Winstanley line to the Lancashire Union crossed the Pemberton Colliery Company's line to Harvey House on the level and at least one accident took place here. The Sidings Schedules record that in early part of 1913 a collision occurred between a set of loaded wagons being lowered by gravity along the Winstanley line to the main line sidings and some

The level crossing keeper's cabin at Goose Green where the Winstanley railway to the canal crossed the Ashton road. After conversion to standard gauge.
J.A. Peden Collection

empty wagons belonging to Pemberton Colliery which were being propelled by a Pemberton Company's engine over the Tan Pit sidings. A signal was therefore erected on the Tan Pit Siding in December 1914 to prevent future collisions. The signal was normally "all right" and was put to danger when traffic was passing along the Winstanley line.

Towards the end of the century the earlier Winstanley pits were becoming worked out. The Mines List show that by 1894 only Nos 3 and 5 Pits remained in production and these seem to have closed around 1900. Meanwhile, a new shaft had been sunk further south at Billinge Lane. Work started here in 1888[19] and the colliery came into production a few years later. It was linked by a tubway to a tippler near No 3 Pit, where standard gauge railway wagons were loaded.

Billinge Lane colliery does not seem to have been successful. It was closed for coal production about 1900 but retained for ventilation purposes. It was replaced by Leyland Green Colliery which first appears in the Mines Lists for 1899. The tubway from Billinge Lane was dismantled and the standard gauge railway extended from No 5 Pit to Leyland Green.

Winstanley Collieries Ltd acquired the two locomotives ELEANOR and LOUISA when they took over in 1885. In the lease of that year, they were valued at £1200. LOUISA became redundant following the conversion of the line to the canal to standard gauge. According to old employees of the company, it was mounted on blocks at No 3 Baxter Pit. Coupled to rods which extended down the shaft, it worked an underground pump.

We were told that when it was no longer needed for this purpose it was sold to Henry Flint of Ince, machinery merchant. It later turned up as a working locomotive at the ironstone quarries of Attenborough and Timms, at Spratton in Northamptonshire, where it arrived in

Winstanley and Worsley Mesnes

May 1900. It was later transferred to the firm's nearby Brixworth quarries, where it remained until 1947. It was broken up at the Clay Cross Works, near Chesterfield, about 1953 [20].

On the standard gauge, ELEANOR was joined by several other locomotives which were obtained in the period up to 1900. Records are incomplete and are complicated by the fact that engines were transferred between the different collieries in which the Tomlinsons had a financial interest.

We have a photograph of a small four coupled saddle tank named LEYLAND which was provided by a former employee at Winstanley Colliery. From its general appearance and from the ogee shape of the tank, we conclude that it had built by one of the Scottish locomotive manufacturers, probably at Kilmarnock.

LEYLAND at Winstanley. An early product of the Scottish locomotive builders. J.A. Peden Collection

We also know that there was a four coupled saddle tank, built by Walker Brothers, which carried the name WALTER. This engine had been ordered about 1873 by Mr Edward Johnson for use at his Swan Lane Colliery at Hindley Green. Former employees recall that it was at Winstanley in the 1890s. Walker Brothers records show that it was still at Winstanley in 1904, when spare parts were supplied. Our old employees also remembered a six coupled saddle tank named LION which also apparently came to Winstanley second hand. So far we have been unable to trace any other information about it.

To cater for the extra traffic and the extended length of railway following the opening of the Leyland Green Pit, an additional locomotive was purchased in 1905, This came from the firm of Andrew Barclay Sons and Company of Kilmarnock, and was a four coupled saddle tank named WINSTANLEY. A second similar locomotive came from Andrew Barclays in 1916 and was named BILLINGE.

Winstanley and Worsley Mesnes

WALTER at Winstanley. Originally built by Walker Brothers for the collieries at Swan Lane.   J.A. Peden Collection

WINSTANLEY, the Barclay of 1905, photographed at the level crossing by the weigh cabin near No 3 Pit.
J.A. Peden Collection

Winstanley and Worsley Mesnes

The earlier locomotives seem to have been taken out of service at this period, leaving the two new engines to work the traffic between Leyland Green Colliery and the exchange sidings with the Lancashire and Yorkshire Railway and with the London and North Western Railway. They do not seem to have worked through to the canal tip as, according to old employees that we interviewed, wagons for this destination were handed over to a Worsley Mesnes locomotive at the LNWR sidings. There were exceptions to this rule. Sometimes the Winstanley drivers would take their engine as far the Farriman's Arms at Goose Green for refreshment. They would have to leave in a hurry if the Worsley Mesnes locomotive appeared, heading for the LNWR !

In spite of this, the engines must have been quite busy, as we were told by George Melling that, at this time, Leyland Green Colliery was producing 1000 tons of coal per day, needing 100 10-ton wagons. These were worked in rakes of between twelve and sixteen each trip. Two engines were required to take the empty wagons to the colliery, one at the front of the train and one at the rear. The leading engine was detached at the loop near the level crossing over the Winstanley to Ashton road and, from here, the banking engine propelled the wagons in to the pit yard. There were three trips in the morning and three in the afternoon.

Leyland Green Colliery was, according to the Mines Lists, abandoned on 8th July 1927, and the railway system was taken out of use. The Sidings Schedules state that the company went into liquidation on 29th July of the same year. Bankes Sidings on the former Lancashire and Yorkshire Railway were taken up in January 1928. The Lancashire Union connection survived for another year or so, serving the Worsley Mesnes Colliery. Work of removal was reported complete on 15th December 1933.

The Collieries at Winstanley after 1928

Winstanley No 3 Pit, also known as Baxter Pit, had been reopened by the Worsley Mesnes Colliery Co Ltd in 1924. By 1929, it had been transferred to a firm known as Baxter Pit Ltd, which continued to work here until April 1950, when Lee and King took over [21]. Baxter Pit seems to have finally closed in 1960 as it is not shown in *Guide to the Coal Fields* [22] after that date. Since 1927 all coal had been sent away by road transport.

Some small scale mining operations took place in the vicinity of the old Winstanley Nos 1 and 2 Pits in the period after the second world war. The *Guide to the Coal Fields* records that the Pony Dick Colliery was established here in 1952 by a Mr Harold Brimson. In the 1960s the firm was known as Pony Dick Colliery Company. Mining seems to have finished around 1970. A planning application in December 1971 by the Windy Arbour Colliery Co Ltd for further development here was not granted [23].

The Windy Arbour Colliery Co Ltd had been formed in the early 1920s to mine coal in the area previously worked from Winstanley No 4 Pit. Windy Arbour Colliery was sufficiently large to be nationalised on 1st January 1947, but later reverted to its original owners. Operations ceased around 1980, the last year that the colliery is shown in *Guide to the Coal Field*. Again the coal was sent away by road transport.

In the vicinity of Billinge Lane, mining was restarted by the New Billinge Lane Colliery Company around 1920. By 1930 the owners had become the Billinge Lane Colliery Co Ltd and from 1936 the workings had been taken over by the Billinge and Winstanley Colliery Co Ltd. The colliery finally closed about 1952.

Quaker House Colliery was opened in the late 1940s, near the site of Leyland Green Colliery. It was originally worked by the Dalton Coal and Fireclay Co Ltd and later by the Quaker House Colliery Co Ltd. Mr Donald Anderson, mining engineer and surveyor and author of historical works on the Orrell, Pemberton and Standish collieries, was the principal partner in both firms.

The Quaker House Colliery Co Ltd opened up a new drift mine on the opposite side of Winstanley Road in 1979. This has now closed but the original colliery remains in operation at the time of writing.

In December 1976, Mr Anderson and colleagues purchased the former Wigan Coal and Iron Company's locomotive LINDSAY from Maudland Metals Ltd at Preston, who had bought it from the National Coal Board for scrap. The engine was restored to working order at Quaker House by the colliery company. It was repainted in the livery adopted by the Wigan Coal and Iron Company in Victorian times. It was sent, on loan, to Steamtown Railway Museum at Carnforth on 10th March 1981, where it can be seen today.

Worsley Mesnes Colliery and Iron Works

The Mines Lists for 1856 and 1857 show that Barton and Gilroy had a colliery at Worsley Mesnes. We believe that these operations were on a very small scale. There seems to have been no major development until Nathaniel Eckersley sank two pits here which first appear in the Mines Lists in 1873. Eckersley also took over the running of the Worsley Mesnes Ironworks at about this time. The works had been owned by the firm of R, J and E Coupe in the 1860s. Contemporary advertisements [24] show that stationary steam engines were one of their main products, a line of business which was continued by later owners.

In 1883, the pits were being worked by the Worsley Mesnes Colliery Company, a firm in which Eckersley was the principal partner. In July 1886, following his death, the Ironworks was up for sale as a going concern [25]. It was subsequently purchased by the Melling family and run in conjunction with their Ince Forge [26,27]. The colliery was acquired by Tomlinson, Rogers and Simpson who formed the Worsley Mesnes Colliery Co Ltd. The partners, as we have seen earlier in this chapter, took over the Winstanley collieries at about this time. They were also proprietors of the Ellerbeck Colliery Company and owned a colliery at Cross Hands in South Wales.

Worsley Mesnes Colliery was linked by its own private railway to the Lancashire and Yorkshire line at a point immediately to the south of the bridge over the main road from Wigan to Upholland. We think that it was constructed in the early 1880s, as the first agreement which we have been able to trace relating to the main line connection is dated 13th February 1884 [28]. The private railway also served the ironworks.

We have already mentioned that the Winstanley railway to the canal was converted to standard gauge soon after the take-over by the Tomlinson partnership. With both Winstanley and Worsley Mesnes under the same ownership, steps were taken to join up the two railway systems. Previously the standard gauge Worsley Mesnes line had crossed the narrow gauge Winstanley line on the level. Now two spurs were put in so that coal from Worsley Mesnes could reach the canal tip and also the Lancashire Union Pemberton Branch.

With trains of two nominally separate companies using the same single line track collisions were likely to happen. One fatal accident occurred on 20th January 1912 at night, when a train of wagons being propelled by a Winstanley locomotive ran into a train of Worsley Mesnes wagons [29]. It was perhaps after this that Winstanley engines ceased to work beyond Goose Green.

Winstanley and Worsley Mesnes

In the early years of the twentieth century the railway layout at Worsley Mesnes was remodelled. A new connection was made with the Winstanley line at the point where it passed under the Lancashire and Yorkshire Pemberton Loop. From here a lead to the colliery yard enabled empty wagons to be delivered to a siding above the screens. They could then run by gravity through the screens to the loaded wagon sidings at the north end of the yard. At the same time the south to east spur at crossing between the Winstanley and Worsley Mesnes lines was removed . The work was completed by 1907, when the survey was carried out for the 2nd edition of the 25" map.

According to old employees interviewed in 1953, the first locomotive to be used at Worsley Mesnes, and the last to remain in use, was a four coupled saddle tank, built by Manning, Wardle and Company of Leeds, and carrying the name JANE. The makers records show that this engine had originally been delivered to the Lincolnshire Iron Smelting Company at Frodingham in 1878 and was subsequently resold to Worsley Mesnes Colliery. Our informants also recalled a small four coupled inside cylinder saddle tank, named DRAGON. We have been unable to uncover further particulars about it.

The next locomotive for which we have information was TOMLINSON, a four coupled saddle tank built by Andrew Barclay, Sons and Company of Kilmarnock and delivered in 1893. The manufacturer's records show that it had been transferred to Tomlinson's colliery at Cross Hands, worked by S R Anthracite Collieries Ltd. Here it was renamed ADAMANT. The engine arrived some time before May 1918 and does not seem to have returned to Lancashire.

Around the turn of the century, it was the practice to arrange with the Worsley Mesnes Iron Works to carry out repairs and make spare parts for the colliery locomotives. Fragmentary records from the period 1896 to 1898 refer to all three engines – JANE, DRAGON and TOMLINSON.

A second four coupled saddle tank, similar to TOMLINSON, was delivered from Andrew Barclay, Sons and Company in 1909 and carried the name WORSLEY. It was followed by MESNES, a four coupled saddle tank, which came new from Manning, Wardle and Company in 1915.

We were told by old employees that the locomotives worked chimney first up the incline to the Lancashire and Yorkshire exchange sidings and in the direction of Winstanley. Wagons for the canal at Wigan Pier were propelled to a point about half a mile short of the tip. From here they were hauled by horses.

Worsley Mesnes Colliery was abandoned, according to the Mines Lists, on 21st September 1929. Following a Chancery Court judgement, the plant was advertised for sale by auction on 21st to 24th January 1930 [30]. The sale was actually postponed until 28th to 31st January and included one saddle tank locomotive [31].

According to our informants only JANE remained here until the end, the other engines having been disposed of before the colliery closed. We know that MESNES was transferred to S R Anthracite Collieries Ltd, the manufacturer's records showing that spare parts were delivered to the new owners from March 1930 onwards.

The railway giving access to the former Lancashire and Yorkshire line fell into disuse with the closure of the colliery. The remaining section of the Winstanley railway was also abandoned, the Sidings Schedules noting that instructions were given to remove the Lancashire Union connection 20th December 1933. The railway from Leyland Green through to the canal was dismantled by E Calderbank and Sons Ltd [32]. The coal tip at Wigan Pier was broken up for scrap by the same firm, only to be rebuilt fifty years later as a tourist attraction.

Worsley Mesnes Ironworks Ltd continued in business as general engineers. Although the works was no longer served by rail at least one railway engine was repaired after the second

Winstanley and Worsley Mesnes

world war. HARTSHEAD, a fireless locomotive belonging to the Central Electricity Generating Board's power station of the same name, was here in 1963 and was photographed leaving the works on a low loader on 17th October[33].

In 1966, Worsley Mesnes Engineering Ltd was formed as a subsidiary of Readson Ltd of Manchester, to take over from Worsley Mesnes Ironworks Ltd[34]. The works was closed towards the end of the 1970s and was later demolished to make room for a new housing development.

LOCOMOTIVE SUMMARY

Winstanley Collieries

c1830 to 1885	Meyrick Bankes
1885 to 1927	Winstanley Collieries Ltd
1927	Colliery closed and rail traffic ceased

Standard Gauge

ELEANOR　　　　　　　　　0-4-0ST　　OC　　Wkb　　1938　　1878　　12"x20"
　New
　Scrapped by 1914

HARRY　　　　　　　　　　0-4-0ST　　IC　　Wkb　　1018　　c.1876　　10"x16"　　2'9"
　On hire from Walker Bros 1879

WALTER　　　　　　　　　0-4-0ST　　OC　　Wkb　　444　　c.1873　　14"
　Ex Swan Lane Brick and Coal Company
　Scrapped by 1914

LEYLAND　　　　　　　　0-4-0ST　　OC
　Reputed to be from Ellerbeck Colliery, where it was named ELLERBECK
　Scrapped or sold before colliery closed

LION　　　　　　　　　　　0-6-0ST
　Second hand
　Scrapped or sold before colliery closed

WINSTANLEY　　　　　　0-4-0ST　　OC　　AB　　1067　　1905　　14"x22"
　New
　Scrapped or sold after 1927

BILLINGE　　　　　　　　0-4-0ST　　OC　　AB　　1465　　1916　　14"x22"　　3'5"
　New
　To Hough and Sons Ltd, Wigan, after 1927

4'0" Gauge

LOUISA　　　　　　　　　0-4-0ST　　OC　　HE　　298　　1882　　9"x14"　　2'8½"
　New
　Taken out of service about 1887 and used as stationary engine
　To Attenborough and Timms, Spratton Ironstone Pits, May 1900 reputedly via Henry Flint, Ince.

Winstanley and Worsley Mesnes

Quaker House Colliery

c1950 to date   Quaker House Colliery Co Ltd

LINDSAY	0-6-0ST	IC	WCI	1887	16"x20"	4'3"

Ex Maudland Metals Ltd, Preston, December 1976
To Steamtown, Carnforth, 10th March 1981.
Property of Mr Donald Anderson and others. Loco here for restoration only.

Worsley Mesnes Colliery

1883 to 1886(?)   Worsley Mesnes Colliery Company
1886(?) to 1929   Worsley Mesnes Colliery Co Ltd
1929   Colliery closed and rail traffic ceased

JANE	0-4-0ST	OC	MW	702	1878	14"x18"	3'0"

Ex Lincolnshire Iron Smelting Company, Frodingham
To Thompson and Company, Ince 1930

DRAGON	0-4-0ST	IC	

TOMLINSON	0-4-0ST	OC	AB	728	1893	15"x22"	3'5"

New
To S R Anthracite Colls Ltd, by May 1918, and renamed ADAMANT

WORSLEY	0-4-0ST	OC	AB	1169	1909	15"x22"	3'5"

New
Disposal before colliery closed

MESNES	0-4-0ST	OC	MW	1889	1915	15"x22"	3'10"

New
To S R Anthracite Colls Ltd, by March 1930

References to Chapter 5

1. *"Records of Coal Mining in Winstanley and Orrell, near Wigan"* – Joyce H.M.Bankes – *Transactions of the Lancashire and Cheshire Antiquarian Society*, Vol LIV
2. *"A Nineteenth Century Colliery Railway"* – Joyce H.M.Bankes – *Transactions of the Historic Society of Lancashire and Cheshire*, Vol 114
3. *"Plan Showing the Situation of the Collieries Communicating with the Canals and Railways in Lancashire"* – W. Stanley – 1833 – Liverpool Library – Binns Collection – Vol 28, item 68
4. LG 20-3-1840
5. WRO DDX El 96/1
6. *Royal National Commercial Directory and Topography of the County of Lancaster* – Isaac Slater – Manchester, 1848
7. *Royal National Commercial Directory and Topography of the County of Lancaster* – Isaac Slater – Manchester, 1851
8. WO 4-11-1859
9. MG 5-11-1859
10. *History, Directory and Gazeteer of the County Palatine of Lancaster* – Edward Baines – Liverpool, 1824–5
11. WRO DDX Ta 28/7
12. *"Blundell's Collieries 1776–1966"* – Donald Anderson – *Transactions of Historic Society of Lancashire and Cheshire* – Vol 116, 1964, Vol 117, 1965 and Vol 119, 1967
13. Formerly in Ince UDC Offices
14. BC 8-1-1853
15. BC 30-4-1853

16	Letter Mrs J H M Bankes to Mr J A Peden, dated 9-1-1970		
17	CG 6-11-1885	18	*Iron* 6-11-1885
19	WO 24-4-1892		
20	*The Ironstone Quarries of the Midlands – Part III The Northampton Area* – Eric Tonks, Runpast Publishing, Cheltenham, 1989		
21	WO 8-4-1950		
22	*Guide to the Coal Fields* Colliery Guardian Co Ltd, London – published annually		
23	WO 24-12-1971	24	CG 22-10-1864
25	CG 16-7-1886	26	WEx 28-1-1949
27	WEx 4-2-1949	28	L&YR Sdgs Diag No 304, dated 26-6-1903
29	WO 3-2-1912	30	CG 10-1-1930
31	CG 17-1-1930	32	Information supplied by E Calderbank and Sons Ltd
33	*Post and Chronicle* 18-10-1963		
34	*Industry In South Lancashire* – South Lancashire Development Corporation – Publ Ed Burrow & Co Ltd, Cheltenham and London, n.d., about 1970		

CHAPTER 6

THE EARLY INCE COLLIERIES

Although there are records of mining at Ince from 1748 onwards [1,2,3,4], it was the opening of the Leeds and Liverpool Canal from Wigan Basin to the Top Lock in 1816 which provided the stimulus for the first phase of a major development. Further expansion of the industry followed the construction of the North Union Railway's Springs Branch in 1838. By the middle of the nineteenth century there were probably more coal pits to the square mile than in any other comparable part of Great Britain.

The history of the collieries is far from simple. The pits themselves changed hands at frequent intervals, particularly in early Victorian times and, as a consequence, the railways which served them altered their course just as frequently. To compound the difficulties of the historian, most of the firms operating in the district used the words Ince Hall in their title.

We shall first consider the collieries which date from the first quarter of the nineteenth century, leaving subsequent developments to later chapters. We shall work our way up the west side of the canal from Britannia Bridge as far as the 8th Lock and then return down the east side.

Birkett Bank Colliery

Birkett Bank Colliery was situated on the west side of the canal, below Lock 17. It was worked by Ralph Thicknesse from the early 1820s [5] until about 1847, when there was a lease to the Ince Hall Colliery Company, not, we suspect, associated with other earlier and later firms with similar names [6]. By 1854 the Mines Lists show that it had become the property of John Part. In 1855 it was taken over by John Lancaster, who worked it until 1857. It is shown as suspended in 1858.

The Mines Lists for 1859 show that it had reopened and was being worked by the Ince Hall Coal Company, a firm not to be confused with the contemporary Ince Hall Coal and Cannel Company. William Crompton and George Nuttall Shawcross seem to have been involved in Birkett Bank Colliery in the early 1860s. The Birkett Bank Colliery Company, in which they were partners, was dissolved on 16th April 1862 [7], the firm carrying on as Crompton and Shawcross. They appear in the Mines List at Birkett Bank for the first time in 1864.

By 1873 the colliery had been taken over by the Ince Hall Coal and Cannel Company. It appears to have closed down following the bankruptcy of that firm in 1884. It was included in a sale of the company's assets in June 1885 [8], but does not seem to have reopened.

Birkett Bank Colliery was never connected to the main line railway system, and, being close to the canal, had no need of any lengthy tramroad system.

The Early Ince Collieries

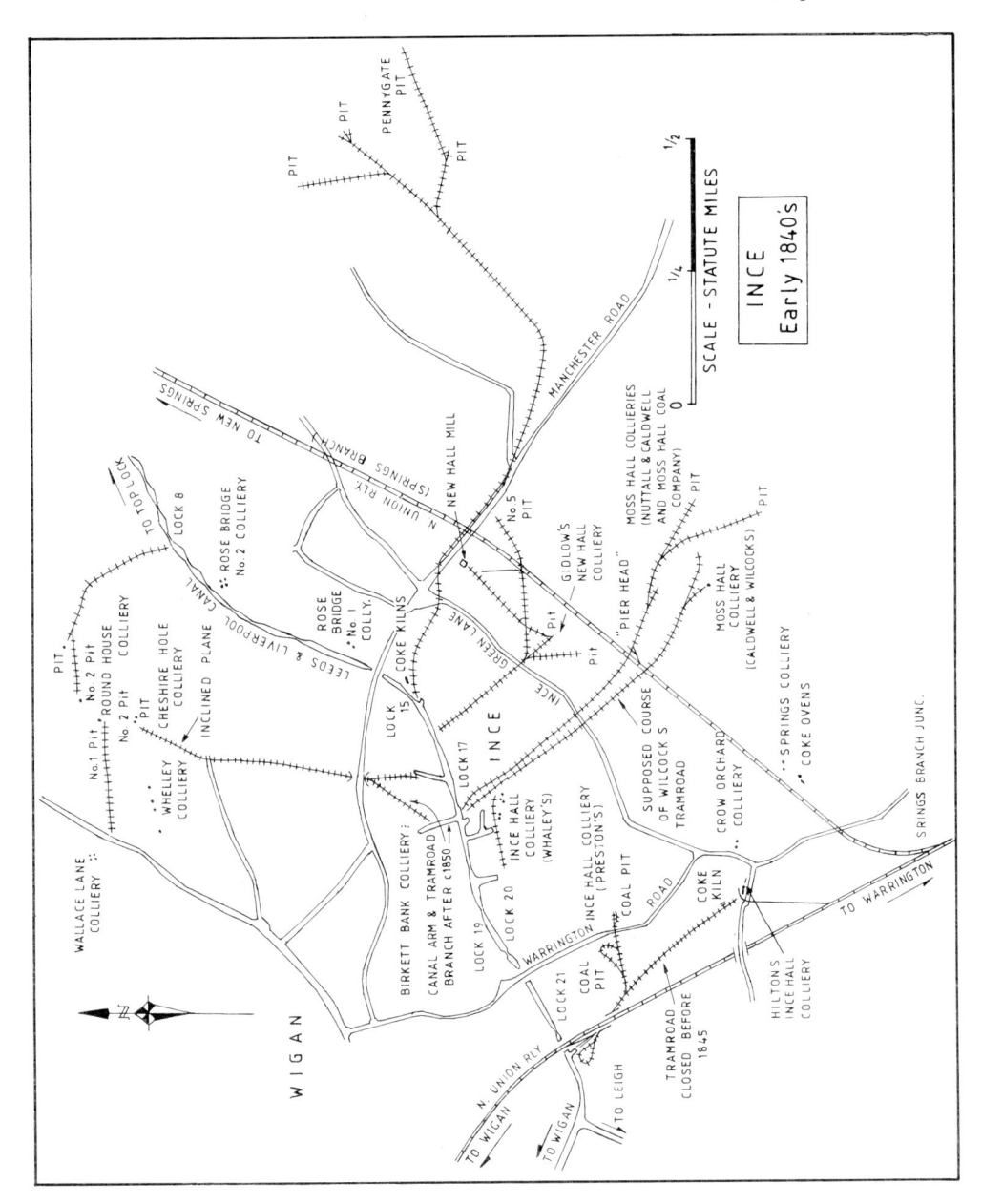

The Early Ince Collieries

Cheshire Hole, Round House and Platt Lane Collieries

Stanley's map of 1833 [9] shows a tramroad running from Cheshire Hole Colliery to the Leeds and Liverpool Canal. The 1/1056 Town Plan of Wigan, surveyed in 1847, shows the line terminating at a canal basin between Lock 16 and Lock 17, with an inclined plane between the colliery and the level crossing over Platt Lane. From the information given on Stanley's map we know that the colliery was worked by Thomas Ashall in the early 1830s. It later passed into the hands of Henry Wright and Henry Taylor, probably at the time they acquired the Round House Colliery in 1848.

The 1st edition of the 6" map, surveyed in 1845 and 1846, also shows two short tramroads from Round House Colliery, which was situated a little to the north of Cheshire Hole. One ran to the main Wigan to Blackrod road, the other to a canal basin below Lock 8. Thomas Ashall, with other partners, leased mineral rights in this area from John Walmesley on 30th October 1837, for a period of 21 years [10], and we believe that the development of Round House Colliery and its tramroads dates from this period. It is significant that, in August 1838, there was a request by the Leeds and Liverpool Canal Company to Mr Ashurst (sic) to pay rent for a canal basin he had constructed near Lock No 8 [11].

The lease from John Walmesley was transferred to the Wright and Taylor partnership on 2nd October 1848 [10] and other leases were obtained from Ralph Thicknesse on 12th November of the same year [12,13]. Subsequently Round House and Cheshire Hole appear to have been known collectively as the Platt Lane Colliery.

A revision of 1st edition of the 6" map, published about 1850, shows that a branch tramroad had been built, leaving the original Cheshire Hole line at the tunnel under the Wigan to Hindley road and leading to a basin below Lock 17, adjacent to Birkett Bank Colliery. We assume that this branch was built after the Wright and Taylor partnership took over, as it terminated at what later maps describe as Wright's Basin

Henry Taylor withdrew from the partnership on 4th May 1855, [14], the firm then becoming known as Wright and Mercer. There were further changes in title, to Henry Wright and Company on 1st January 1861 [15] and to the Platt Lane Coal Company on 18th October 1865 [16].

The collieries were taken over by the Wigan and Whiston Coal Company, with Mr Fidler, one of the partners in the Platt Lane Company, as managing director. The Mines Lists record that this took place in 1865 and we shall be following the later history of the firm in Chapter 7.

As far we are aware none of the tramroad systems serving the Round House and Cheshire Hole Collieries used locomotives. They were undoubtedly narrow gauge and are therefore most likely to have employed horse traction. They were probably abandoned in the late 1860s.

Woodcock and Haliburton's Ince Hall Colliery

Stanley's map of 1833 marks a tramroad from a basin on the Leeds and Liverpool Canal, below Lock 15, south of the Wigan to Hindley road bridge, leading to pits in the vicinity of Hindley Hall, and notes that it was owned by Woodcock. The tramroad is also shown on the Deposited Plans of the Springs Branch, dated 1829 [17], so we presume that it had been constructed during the 1820s.

The pits appear to have been opened out by Thomas Woodcock in conjunction with Alexander Fowden Haliburton. The workings were evidently extended during the 1830s and

The Early Ince Collieries

1840s, as there are records of several new leases from Thomas Joseph Trafford and William Gerard Walmesley during this period [18,19]. The Ince Rates Book for 1838 refers to colliery property occupied by Woodcock and Haliburton at Cinnamon Brow.

By the mid 1840s, Woodcock appears to have dropped out of the partnership. The Book of Reference accompanying the Deposited Plans for the Bolton Wigan and Liverpool Railway, dated 1844 [20] show the occupiers as A F Haliburton and Peter Worthington. After 1st January 1845 the leases mentioned above only refer to A F Haliburton.

The tramroad, at what must have been its maximum extent, is shown on the 1st edition of the 6" map, surveyed in 1845 and 1846. By about 1850, when a revision of the 6" map was published, standard gauge sidings had also been laid in to some of the pits from the newly opened Wigan to Bolton line of the Lancashire and Yorkshire Railway.

In 1854, Haliburton sold out to the Kirkless Hall Coal Company, which continued to operate the tramroad to the canal for a short period. As we shall describe in Chapter 17, the connection to the main line near Hindley formed the starting point for a new railway which the firm constructed to serve its Kirkless Works.

William Gidlow's New Hall Collieries

Stanley's map of 1833 shows a tramroad somewhat to the south of Woodcock's, owned by Gidlow. This ran to the canal from the site occupied from the mid 1840s by the Ince Hall Coal and Cannel Company's Middle Coal Works. It is not shown on the Deposited Plans for the Springs Branch, dated 1829 [21]. It is however recorded on the 2" drawings prepared between 1840 and 1842, which formed the basis of the 1st edition of the 1" map, where it is shown as serving the New Hall Colliery.

Most of the pits were on the west side of the Springs Branch, but one, which we can identify from the 1st edition of the 6" map as New Hall No 5 Pit, was on the east side. A branch of the tramroad crossed the Springs Branch on the level to reach this pit. There was another branch of the tramroad terminating at the New Hall Mill, which also had a siding from the Springs Branch.

We believe that the tramroad only had a life of some ten to twelve years, which is consistent with what we know about William Gidlow's colliery operations. The first reference which we have been able to find is in the Ince Rate Book for 1838 [22] where he is shown as occupier of the New Hall Colliery. He also appears as a colliery proprietor at Ince in the Commissioners Report of 1842 [23]. He paid Lord's rent of 4 shillings per year to W A Walmesley in respect of the level crossing of his tramroad over Ince Green Lane [24]. The last recorded payment was on 25th December 1842 and we conclude that the tramroad and the colliery had been closed sometime during that year.

Nuttall and Caldwell and the Moss Hall Collieries

Moving south west along the canal, we come to another early tramroad shown on Stanley's map of 1833 and serving the Moss Hall Colliery. Although Stanley records the owner as Nuttall, it was in fact operated by George Nuttall in partnership with William Caldwell. The tramroad was in existence before 1829, since it is shown on the Deposited Plans prepared in that year for the Springs Branch line [21]. The tramroad terminated at the Leeds and Liverpool

The Early Ince Collieries

Canal just below Lock 17, and there was a level crossing over the Springs Branch when this line was eventually built in 1838.

Both the Nuttall and the Caldwell families had many connections with coal mines, first in the vicinity of Ince and later at Platt Bridge. The task of interpreting the developments of the collieries is made more difficult since sometimes they were carried out as joint ventures between the two families and sometimes with other partners. The mines must, in any event, have been worked very much as a single enterprise, even if separate financial arrangements were in place. In 1848[25] John Wright was Agent for all the Nuttall's and the Caldwell's Ince operations. By 1851[26] the mines were all managed by John Christopher.

We know that George Caldwell obtained a mining lease from William Ince Anderton in 1820[27] and is shown as owning pits at Ince in 1824[5]. We think that the Moss Hall Colliery was opened out at a later date. It was certainly in operation by 1838, as the Ince Rate Book for April of that year[22] shows that George Nuttall and William Caldwell were the occupiers. The Rates Book also records that the same partners had pits near Belle Green Lane. In addition, George Nuttall occupied a wharf, crane and pier head at Rose Bridge, while John and William Caldwell had lime kilns in the vicinity.

In April 1846[28], permission was granted to the Nuttall and Caldwell partnership to construct a side-basin near Lock 15 at a colliery that had recently been opened. We believe that this basin is the one marked on the 1st edition of the 6" map below Lock 15, just to the south west of Woodcock and Haliburton's pier head. This colliery, unlike those at Moss Hall, does not seem to have been connected to the main line railway system, nor to have had tramroads of any significant length.

By the the late 1830s or early 1840s, George and William Caldwell, with other partners, trading as the Moss Hall Coal Company, had sunk new pits adjacent to those of the Nuttall and Caldwell partnership. To confuse matters, both were usually referred to as the Moss Hall Colliery, although one was also described as Amberswood Colliery on the Deposited Plans for the Bolton Wigan and Liverpool Railway dated November 1844[20].

The new colliery seems to have been served by a short branch from Nuttall and Caldwell's tramroad, which appears to have conveyed coal from both concerns to the canal. We think that these developments needed additional loading facilities at the canal, as, on 23rd February 1836, Nuttall and Caldwell were granted permission to construct a side basin near Lock 17[29].

New pits were also opened out a little to the south west of those of the Nuttall and Caldwell and the Moss Hall Coal Company at a date we have not been able to determine. The Deposited Plans for the Manchester and Southport Railway, dated November 1845[30], show that this third colliery had its own separate tramroad to the Leeds and Liverpool Canal. This ran generally parallel to Nuttall and Caldwell's line, but a hundred yards or so to the west of it. There was a separate level crossing over the Springs Branch. Although the extremity of the line is not shown on the Deposited Plan, the canal wharf must have been below Lock 17, but well above Lock 18.

The Book of Reference accompanying the 1844 Deposited Plans of the Bolton Wigan and Liverpool Railway[20] shows that the lessees of the third Moss Hall Colliery were William Caldwell and Thomas Wilcocks. Thomas Wilcocks was shown as the occupier. This is clearly the colliery near Amberswood Common which Mr Wilcocks advertised for sale in December 1845 [31]. The sales notice stated that the colliery was connected to the Leeds and Liverpool Canal by a tramroad, and that the New Springs Branch and the intended Liverpool and Bury and the intended Manchester and Wigan Railways ran over the land. The inference is that the colliery was at this time served only by a narrow gauge tramroad, unconnected with the main line system.

The Early Ince Collieries

We think that, following the sale, the colliery was absorbed into the workings of one or other of the adjacent Moss Hall Collieries, and that the independent tramroad to the canal was closed. Concurrently changes were taking place to the original Nuttall and Caldwell tramroad.

By 1845 a short standard gauge siding had been laid in on the east side of the Springs Branch to a point on the Nuttall and Caldwell/ Moss Hall tramroad. This shown as a "pier head" on the Deposited Plans of the Manchester and Southport Railway of 1845 and 1846 [30,32], and was clearly a transhipment point for coal from narrow gauge to standard gauge wagons.

The Deposited Plans of the Manchester and Southport Railway also show that other developments were taking place, occasioned by the construction of the private canal to serve the Ince Hall Coal and Cannel Company's Middle Works. There is no trace of this canal on the 1845 Deposited Plan, but in November 1846, when the second of the plans was issued, it had already been dug from the main Leeds and Liverpool Canal as far as Ince Green Lane. Excavation was in progress between there and the Middle Coal Works which would cut through the Moss Hall tramroad leading to the Leeds and Liverpool Canal below Lock 17.

The narrow gauge tramroad system serving the Moss Hall Collieries seems to have been abandoned at this time and replaced by a standard gauge line. This followed the course of the original line until it approached the Springs Branch. It then turned south west to cross the Springs Branch on the level about 50 yards to the south of the original Moss Hall tramroad crossing. The new standard gauge line then swung round to follow the course of Willcock's tramroad as far as the new Wigan and Bolton line of the Lancashire and Yorkshire Railway, where a siding connection was provided. A tip to load barges was provided where the colliery railway ran alongside the Ince Hall company's private canal.

The 1/1056 Town Plan of Wigan, surveyed in 1847, shows what must have been an interim arrangement until the new standard gauge line had been completed. Both the tramroad and the new canal are shown. The pier head of the tramroad occupies a small piece of land between the entrance to the branch canal and Lock 17. Unfortunately the Town Plan does not extend sufficiently far to show the tramroad in its entirety. We presume that there must have been a bridge or a temporary embankment to carry the tramroad over the canal excavations.

We think that the standard gauge lines came into use in the first half of 1848. Lord's Rent of one shilling per year was charged by William Walmesley to George Nuttall in respect of the tramroad crossing over Ince Lane and the last payment was for the period up to 9th May 1848 [24]. The standard gauge system is shown on a revision to the 1st edition of the 6" map, published around 1850. The map was originally surveyed in 1845 and 1846, but contains alterations in the vicinity of the Lancashire and Yorkshire Railway, opened in 1848. A portion of the Nuttall and Caldwell tramroad is shown on its original site, to the north of the private canal, but access to the original pier head is blocked by Swindell's chemical works.

We have been unable to trace whether the new standard gauge lines were built by the Moss Hall Coal Company or by the Nuttall and Caldwell partnership. We think that it must have been the former and that this firm conveyed traffic on behalf of Nuttall and Caldwell to the main line railways and to the canal.

The two separate Moss Hall collieries survived until 1864, when that worked by Nuttall and Caldwell appears to have closed, notwithstanding the fact that it continues to be shown in the Mines Lists up to and including 1867. The plant at Nuttall and Caldwell's colliery was offered for sale on 27th April 1864 [33]. There was a further sale on 1st June, which included 35 5-ton railway wagons and an unspecified number of canal boats [34].

The Early Ince Collieries

The Moss Hall Coal Company, on the other hand, continued in existence. It expanded its operations by opening out new collieries near Platt Bridge and its railway was extended across Amberswood Common to serve them. We must however leave the later history of the company until a later chapter.

Swarbrick's Ince Hall Collieries

On 1st January 1823 Richard Swarbrick leased mining rights from William Ince Anderton over a large area of ground lying east of Warrington Road, between the canal and Ince Green Lane[35]. On 12th April 1826 Thomas Swarbrick and James Berry were taken into partnership[36].

The partners commenced operations by opening out a colliery near the canal, below Lock 17. The lease included the right to build a side basin from the canal, not exceeding 300 yards in length and not exceeding 20 yards in width. The work on the basin seems to have been completed towards the end of 1823, as, on 17th September of that year, the firm was authorised to make a junction with the main line of the Leeds and Liverpool Canal near Lock 18[37].

Financial difficulties soon overtook the enterprise and these seem to have to have prevented the partners from developing the mines to the full. Their property was mortgaged to Humphrey Nicholls in October 1826 and, in attempt to reduce their losses, some parts of their lease were transferred to George Caldwell and to John Lord on 20th January 1830[36].

Either the Swarbrick partnership or one of the new lessees was apparently opening out a new colliery in 1832. The Leeds and Liverpool Canal Company's Minutes record that on 20th September an application was received from the Ince Hall Colliery, relating to a tramroad from pits which were being sunk on Mr Anderton's estate, adjacent to the Leigh Branch of the canal. The colliery company proposed to extend its existing light tramroad over a drawbridge on the Leigh Branch to reach the highway, replacing the horses and carts then in use. Although permission was granted to do this on 9th November[38], it is by no means clear that either the colliery itself or the tramroad were ever completed. There is no trace of either on the 2" drawings prepared in 1840 to 1842 for the first edition of the 1" map.

Despite, or perhaps because of, these developments, Swarbrick's financial problems continued. A letter dated 18th February 1835, from John Lord to W I Anderton, noted that Swarbrick was still in arrears with his rent, but advised against foreclosing as this could result in all the mines being drowned out[39]. Presumably the pumping engine was at Swarbrick's colliery.

On 5th February 1838[40], Richard Swarbrick retired from the partnership, which then included Thomas Swarbrick and T G Bennet, the firm subsequently being known as T G Bennet and Company[41,42]. Shortly afterwards the new partnership seems to have withdrawn entirely from the coal mining business, and the last remaining parts of the lease were taken up by other colliery proprietors.

Whaley's Ince Hall Colliery

One portion of the original Swarbrick lease had already been transferred on 22nd April 1835 to a partnership including James Whaley and Frederick Gerard[36]. We think it likely that Whaley and Gerard sank new pits near to the canal and then later took over the adjacent colliery belonging to the Swarbrick partnership.

The Early Ince Collieries

We know that, on 17th February 1837, Whaley and Gerard were granted permission to construct another side basin[43], between Locks 17 and 18. We also know that they took over the basin constructed in 1823 by Swarbrick.

Sometime after 1842[23,25], the partnership had become known as Whaley, Gerard and Westall. Westall retired from partnership on 6th May 1847[44], James Whaley died on 26th December 1847[45,46] and, in 1851, Gerard withdrew[47]. Charles and Thomas Whaley, as executors of James Whaley's will, continued in control until the death of Charles Whaley on 14th August 1861. Thereafter the colliery was worked by Thomas Whaley until it was abandoned in March 1864[48]. The lease was surrendered on 26th February 1866.

Two sales of plant took place, on 12th March 1863[49] and a year later, on 27th April 1864[50]. That in March 1863 included, according to the sales notice[51], a high pressure beam engine about 10" dia by 3ft stroke and a cylindrical boiler 14ft long by 4'6" dia, nearly 500 yards of wagon rails weighing 60 lbs per yard, a large quantity of grooved wrought iron bar for a tramway, coal trams and three pairs of narrow boats which were capable of passing any of the locks in the Wigan, Manchester and Runcorn districts.

These boats, all in good working condition, comprised "the Ann and the Mersey, which have worked together and carry 55 tons, the Irwel (sic) and the Mary, which carry the same weight, and the Margaret and the Alfred, the latter being an iron boat, the pair carry about 50 tons".

No connection was ever made with any of the main line railways, the whole of the output, other than that sold locally, being sent away by canal. A few short sections of tramroad sufficed to link the pits with loading places at the two basins referred to earlier.

Preston's Ince Hall Colliery

Richard Preston appears to have opened up his Ince Hall Colliery in the late 1830s, and is recorded as occupier in the Ince Rates Book for April 1838[22]. The mining leases do not seem to have been formally assigned to him by Swarbrick until 12th October of that year[52].

The pits were located on both sides of Warrington Road, in the vicinity of Rock House. By the time that the surveys were made in 1840 to 1842 for the 1st edition of the 1" map, a tramroad had been built to serve them. This joined the line leading from Hilton's colliery to the canal below Lock 21, which we describe later. It seems that both firms shared the same pier head.

Preston's Ince Hall Colliery appears to have closed in the late 1840s, since the 1850 Ince Rate Book[53] implies that it was then out of use. Preston certainly does not appear in the Lists of Mines which were published from 1853/4 onwards, but the tramroad from the pits near Rock House to the canal was still in place in 1864, when it appears on the North Union Railway Line Plan[54]. By 1874, when the Deposited Plans were prepared for a proposed widening of the North Union Railway between Bamfurlong and Boars Head, all trace of the tramroad had disappeared[55].

We think it likely that Preston's pits were taken over by James Kay, who is shown as occupier of an Ince Hall Colliery in the Ince Rates Book for 1850[53] and in the Mines Lists between 1853/4 and 1857. This belief is strengthened by the fact that he is also shown as working collieries nearby, at Little Westwood and Westwood Hall, in the period up to 1856. The property passed to Robert James in 1858. It was probably Robert James who went on to sink the Welch Pits alongside the Springs Branch, which we shall describe in the next chapter. The Welch Pits were also known as the Ince Hall Colliery, and from the information given in the Mines Lists it is not possible to be precise about the dates for these events.

The Early Ince Collieries

Meanwhile, the Preston family had turned to other interests. The Ince Directory for 1853 [56] lists John and Richard Preston as brickmakers and railway contractors. The Line Plan for the North Union Railway, dated 1864 [54] shows a siding south of Springs Branch Junction leading to property owned by J Preston and R Hilton, later altered to J Preston and others. We are not sure which of the various Preston enterprises this served.

We believe that the brickworks was the one shown on the 1st edition of the 25" map, out of use, and located to the south west of the Ince Waggon and Iron Company's works. The firm was probably wound up in 1871, as there was a sale of the property of the late Richard Preston in October of that year. This included 42 6- and 8-ton railway wagons, which were stated to be lying at the Ince Hall sidings near Ince Wagon Works [57].

H and E Hilton's Ince Hall Colliery

There was yet another Ince Hall Colliery on the west side of Warrington Road, near Ince Old Hall, on land owned by John Walmesley. The colliery seems to have been sunk in the mid 1820s, if not earlier, and was joined to the Leeds and Liverpool Canal below Lock 21 by a tramroad some half a mile in length. The tramroad is shown on the 1829 Plan of the Wigan Branch Railway [21] and on Stanley's 1833 map [9], where the owners are given as Swarbrick. We assume from this that the Swarbrick partnership had leased mineral rights from John Walmesley as well as W I Anderton, although we have been unable to find any documentary proof.

By 1838 the colliery had been taken over by Henry and Edward Hilton, who are shown as occupiers in the Ince Rates Book for that year [22]. The Hiltons, in addition to their coal mining activities here and and at Platt Bridge, also had a textile finishing business and owned a paper mill at Darwen.

In April 1841 the firm was granted permission to make a side basin at the 21st Lock [58], which suggests that the new owners were intending to extend Swarbrick's original pier head. The 1st edition of the 1" map, surveyed in 1840 to 1842, shows that a standard gauge siding had also been constructed from the colliery to the North Union line north of Springs Branch Junction.

In 1841, H and E Hilton placed an order, from their Darwen address, for two tender locomotives from Nasmyth, Gaskell and Company of Patricroft, at a cost of £2440 [59], The obvious intention was to work their own coal traffic to Preston and elsewhere and this is confirmed by entries in the Nasmyth, Gaskell records. Over the period from October 1841 to March 1842 H and E Hilton were charged £ 162-8-8d for spare parts, for repairs and for 49¼ days of mechanics' time with the locomotives on trial on the North Union Railway [60].

There is also a suggestion by Arbuthnot [61], who had access to records now destroyed, that the engines were intended to work at Coppull Colliery. As we shall describe in Part 2, Chapters 24 and 25, there is evidence to show that Edward Hilton was associated with Burgh Colliery and also, by inference, with Coppull Colliery before John Hargreaves took over. Possibly the two locomotives worked coal traffic from both Ince Hall and Coppull Collieries.

The Nasmyth, Gaskell Locomotive Specification Book [62] suggests that the engines were of the 2-2-2 wheel arrangement, but this seems doubtful in view of the duties on which they were employed. It must be borne in mind that the Specification Book itself dates only from the 1850s and information relating to locomotives prior to that time had been reassembled from earlier records, not always correctly.

The Early Ince Collieries

It appears that the Hiltons had overstretched themselves financially in their various ventures. Edward Hilton was declared bankrupt on 16th June 1842[63] and Henry Hilton on 28th July of the same year[64]. By the time that the 1st edition of the 6" Map was surveyed in 1845 and 1846, the Ince Hall Colliery and the adjacent coke ovens were out of use. With the demise of the Hilton partnership in 1842, the tramroad south of the junction with Preston's line was abandoned. Both the 1st edition of the 6" map, surveyed in 1845 and 1846, and the 1/1056 Town Plan, surveyed in 1847, indicate that the tracks had been lifted.

The pits were subsequently reopened by Thomas Pearson and we shall be following their later history in Chapter 9. We have been unable to trace what happened to the locomotives. As they were almost new they undoubtedly saw further use. It is tempting to think that they were taken over by Thomas Pearson, or possibly by the Ince Hall Coal and Cannel Company which was starting its operations at the time. Unfortunately we have no real evidence.

LOCOMOTIVE SUMMARY

Ince Hall Colliery
(later known as Crow Orchard)

c1820 to c1838	Various Swarbrick partnerships
c1838 to c 1842	H and E Hilton
c1842	Taken over by Thomas Pearson

	2-2-2(?)	NG	9	1841	14"x18"	5'0"
		(Tender	14	1841)		

New
Unknown history after bankruptcy of H and E Hilton in 1842

	2-2-2(?)	NG	10	1841	14"x18"	5'0"
		(Tender	15	1841)		

New
Unknown history after bankruptcy of H and E Hilton in 1842

References to Chapter 6

1. WRO DD An 4/20
2. WRO DD An 1/1
3. WRO DD An 6/2
4. WRO DD An 5/2
5. *History, Directory and Gazeteer of the County Palatine of Lancashire* – Edward Baines – Liverpool 1824–5
6. WRO DDX Ap 94/9
7. WO 25-4-1862
8. WO 3-6-1885
9. "Plan Showing the Situation of Collieries Communicating with the Canals and Railways in Lancashire" – W Stanley – 1833 – Liverpool Library – Binns Collection Vol 28, item 68
10. WRO DDX Ta 38/6
11. Leeds and Liverpool Canal Company's Minutes, dated 17-8-1838
12. WRO DDX Ap 94/18
13. WRO DDX Ta 38/6
14. LG 29-1-1856
15. LG 18-1-1861
16. LG 24-10-1865
17. LRO PDR 186
18. LRO DDX Tr Box 84
19. WRO DDX EL 1/8
20. LRO PDR 411
21. LRO PDR 186
22. Formerly in Ince UDC Offices
23. *Reports to the Commissioners on the Employment of Children* – 1842 – Appendix A

107

The Early Ince Collieries

24 WRO DD Wa Walmesley Ledgers
25 *Royal National Commercial Directory and Topography of the County of Lancaster* – Isaac Slater – Manchester, 1848
26 *Royal National Commercial Directory and Topography of the County of Lancaster* – Isaac Slater – Manchester, 1851
27 WRO DD An 49/515
28 Leeds and Liverpool Canal Company's Minutes, 9-4-1846
28 Leeds and Liverpool Canal Company's Minutes, 23-2-1836
30 LRO PDR 502   31 PG 20-12-1845
32 LRO PDR 539   33 BC 16-4-1864
34 WO 28-5-1864   35 WRO DD An 49/516
36 WRO DD An 50/527
37 Leeds and Liverpool Canal Specification Book at Skipton Museum
38 Leeds and Liverpool Canal Company's Minutes, 9-11-1832
39 WRO DD An 9/15   40 LG 1838, p 443
41 BC7-2-1839   42 BC 16-2-1839
43 Leeds and Liverpool Canal Company's Minutes, 17-2-1837
44 LG 1848, p 579   45 WO 1-1-1848 46 PG 1-1-1848
47 LG 4-3-1851   48 WRO DD An 55/570
49 WO 27-2-1863   50 BC 16-4-1864
51 Copy in authors' possession   52 WRO DDAn 50/530
53 Formerly at Ince UDC Offices
54 Line Plan of North Union Railway – LNWR, 1864 – 2 chains to 1 inch – at GMRO
55 LRO PDR 994
56 *A New Alphabetical and Classified Directory of the Boroughs of Bolton, Bury and Wigan, with the Parishes of Dean and Leigh* – Wm Whellan and Co Manchester, 1853
57 WEx 29-10-1871
58 Leeds and Liverpool Canal Company's Minutes, 2-4-1841
59 Nasmyth Documents at Salford Library – Sales Book A
60 Nasmyth Documents at Salford Library – Order Book
61 Nasmyth Documents at Salford Library – Manuscript List compiled by R Arbuthnot, May 1933
62 Nasmyth Documents at Salford Library – Specification Book
63 LG Nov to Dec 1843   64 LG 1843, p 2825

CHAPTER 7

DEVELOPMENTS AT INCE – 1845 TO 1900

So far we have been dealing with mines and railways which had their origins in the 1820s and 1830s. We now move on to a group of collieries which date from the mid 1840s and which, for the best part of fifty years, made Ince one of the most prolific areas in the country for coal production.

Ince Hall Coal and Cannel Company's Collieries

John Lancaster, later to become one of the great Victorian mining entrepreneurs and whom we shall meet in connection with the Wigan Coal and Iron Company, had started his coal mining career with a colliery which he had sunk at Patricroft, near Eccles. In the early 1840s he turned his attention to the Wigan area, and on 12th May 1843, in partnership with James Hodgkinson and James King, obtained a lease from William Ince Anderton[1]. This gave mining rights in an area between the Leeds and Liverpool Canal and Ince Green Lane, which we believe had previously been leased to Richard Swarbrick.

The partnership, which also seems to have been known as James King and Company and the Ince Hall Coal and Cannel Company, sank two pits adjacent to the canal near Lock 19. The firm was granted permission to build a side basin above Lock 19[2]. It also constructed a private railway to connect with the Springs Branch. Both railway and canal basin were completed by the time the 1st edition of the 6" map was surveyed in 1845 and 1846.

At about the same time a partnership, consisting of William Lancaster (John's brother), Samuel Blackburn and John Swindells, was developing in an area to the east. The firm, which was variously known as John Swindells and Company and the Ince Union Coal and Cannel Company, seems to have taken over William Gidlow's New Hall Colliery about 1845. Mining rights in adjacent areas were obtained from William Ince Anderton on 12th May 1846[3] and on 8th July 1846[4]. There was also a lease from W G Walmesley on 1st January 1847[5].

On 1st January 1847 Swindells and Company took over James King and Company's colliery[6,7]. The original James King site became known as the Lower Patricroft Colliery, or the Lower Coal Works, or the Bottom Place. The Swindells site was known as the Middle Patricroft Colliery, or the Middle Coal Works, or simply as the Middle Place. A Joint Stock Company was formed on 8th January 1848, under the title of the Ince Hall Coal and Cannel Company, to take over the operation of the two collieries. It is of interest to note that the seal adopted by the Company featured a 2-2-2 tender locomotive, perhaps to emphasise its railway operations.

As we have noted in the previous chapter, a private branch canal was constructed to serve the Middle Coal Works. This was a little over three quarters of a mile in length and led from the main line of the Leeds and Liverpool Canal below Lock 17. For the first half mile it ran in a

Developments at Ince – 1845 to 1900

south-easterly direction until it neared the Springs Branch railway. It then turned north east, parallel to the Springs Branch, to reach the colliery. A rail connection was also provided between the Middle Coal works and the Springs Branch, which must have crossed the canal on a movable bridge.

We are not sure whether the canal was started during Thomas Gidlow's occupancy of the New Hall Colliery, or whether it was part of the development undertaken by Swindells and Company. It does not seem to have been completed until after the formation of the Ince Hall Coal and Cannel Company.

The canal is only shown in a rudimentary form on the Deposited Plans [8] for the Manchester Wigan and Southport Railway prepared in 1845, and the siding connection with the Springs Branch does not appear at all. The Deposited Plans [9] for the same railway, dated November 1846, show the excavation of the canal well under way, with the railway connection already completed.

The 1st edition of the 6" map, surveyed in 1845 and 1846, shows the canal almost finished, but with the connection from the Springs Branch and the Moss Hall tramroad carried over the canal on what appear to be embankments. New Hall No 5 Pit is connected to the main colliery workings by a railway or tramway which runs across the Springs Branch. Gidlow's tramroad to the main line of the Leeds and Liverpool canal has disappeared.

A revision of the 6" map, published around 1850, shows the canal completed, with the Moss Hall tramroad replaced by a new standard gauge line which keeps clear of the canal. New Hall No 5 Pit is now served by a spur from the Springs Branch, and the earlier level crossing has apparently been taken out.

The revised 6" Map, but not the original printing, shows that the Ince Hall Coal and Cannel Company's engine shed was at the Middle Coal Works. The 1864 Line Plan of the North Union Railway [10] makes it clear that the colliery company's locomotives must have used the London and North Western Railway's tracks when travelling between the Middle and Lower Coal Works. At this time, there was no independent private line linking them together, although one seems to have been provided later. The 1st edition of the 25" map, surveyed in 1888 to 1892, shows a line running from the Middle Coal Works parallel to the Springs Branch and then swinging away through the Ince Waggon Works to join the branch to the Lower Coal Works.

At the Lower Works the first sod for two further pits was cut on 7th August 1847 and Arley seam was reached in October 1849 [11]. The Lancashire and Yorkshire Railway's Wigan to Bolton line, which was opened in 1848, passed near to the Lower Works and connections were put in to serve the original pair of pits. When the new pits were eventually completed in 1850, after delays due to flooding, they too were connected to the Lancashire and Yorkshire Railway and to the private line leading to the Springs Branch.

The Ince Rate Book for 1850 [12] shows the Ince Hall Coal and Cannel Company in occupation of what is still described as the New Hall Colliery and a new mine, in addition to the Pemberton Pits at Middle Place and the King Coal and Cannel Pits at Bottom Place. We think that the new mine was on the east side of the Springs Branch, near to the site of the earlier New Hall No 5 Pit. It was probably later known as Gravel Hole Pit or alternatively No 2 Pit.

There were further developments, again we believe on the east side of the Springs Branch and adjacent to Manchester Road. The Springs Branch Pit, which we think is the same as that later known as the Laneside Pit, was described in November 1861 as recently sunk [13,14].

Developments at Ince – 1845 to 1900

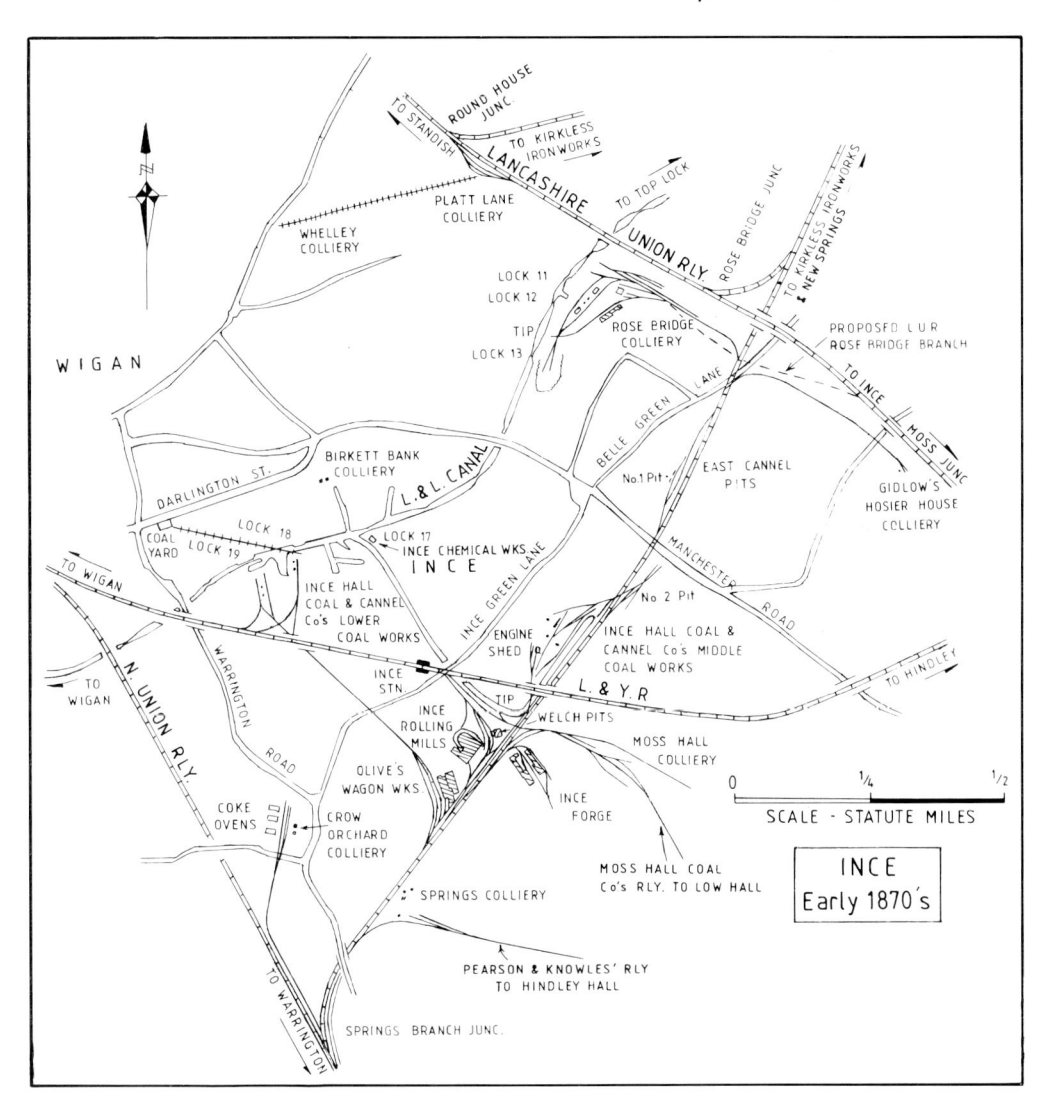

The North Union Railway Line Plan of 1864[10] shows that the Ince Hall Coal and Cannel Company's sidings at the Middle Coal Works had, by this date, been extended along the north bank of the private canal. They then continued round the end of the basin and over the site of the earlier level crossing to gain access to what the Line Plan describes as Gravel Hole Sidings and Ince Hall No 2 pit, on the east side of the Springs Branch. A connection was provided to the Springs Branch at essentially the same point as that previously serving New Hall No 5 Pit. We think that the Sidings Agreement dated 25th June 1862 probably refers to these sidings and the level crossing. The Line Plan also shows a siding, on colliery company land between the Springs Branch and the Ince Hall Canal, apparently to load barges from coal wagons which had come across the Springs Branch from the pits on the east side.

111

Developments at Ince – 1845 to 1900

In October 1861 it was recorded that the Ince Hall Coal and Cannel Company was opening the new East Cannel Pits, and that they had been sinking for 18 months [15]. These were on a site to the west of the Springs Branch, north of Manchester Road Level Crossing. The Sidings Schedules show that two connections were provided with the Springs Branch, one at the north end of the colliery yard, the other at the south. It seems likely that the colliery company's locomotives worked over the Springs Branch to reach the new pits.

Further developments took place at the Middle Coal Works shortly afterwards. In 1869 the two Saw Mill Pits were sinking [16]. These, if we can believe the 1930 6" Geological Map, were on the west of the Springs Branch, to the north of the earlier Pemberton Pits, and required an extension of the internal railway system.

In 1873 the Ince Hall Coal and Cannel Company were stated to be sinking a new pit at Amberswood [17,18]. We have been unable to locate this, but we think that it was probably near to the later Moss Colliery of Crompton and Shawcross and that it had a connection to this firm's railway system.

From the early 1870s coal wound at the East Cannel Pits was screened at the Middle Coal Works and a tubway was built between the two sites. This ran parallel to the Springs Branch, passing under Manchester Road by a bridge which had been authorised by the Ince Local Board on 7th August 1872 [19]. Following these developments all coal was despatched from the Middle Coal Works, and a note of 12th August 1878 in the Sidings Schedules recorded that the connections with the Springs Branch at the East Cannel Pits were then no longer in use.

Meanwhile, at the Lower Coal Works, new wagon shops had been constructed after a serious fire, on 20th September 1861, had destroyed the original buildings [20]. The new shops, which were stated to occupy a central position in Ince Green Lane, came into use at the end of 1863 or the beginning of 1864 [21,22].

New coke ovens were erected at the Lower Works in the early 1870s. They were brought into use at the end of 1871 and, by October 1873, 76 ovens were in operation [23].

At the same period, or perhaps slightly earlier, a tramway was built from the Lower Coal Works to a landsale yard in Darlington Street. It was certainly in use by 1874, as the coal yard is shown on the Deposited Plans of the Wigan Junction Railway submitted to Parliament in November of that year [24] and on the Line Plan of the Wigan Junction Railway, dated 1883 [25]. The 1876 Town Plan of Wigan [26] shows the tramroad crossing the Clarington Brook and the Leeds and Liverpool Canal.

In the late 1870s, the sidings from the Lower Coal Works to the Lancashire and Yorkshire Railway had to be moved nearer to Ince Station, to make way for the new line which the Wigan Junction Railway was constructing between Strangeways and Darlington Street. Section 33 of the Wigan Junction Railway Act of 1875 [27] protected the interests of the Ince Hall Coal and Cannel Co Ltd, requiring that a connection with the Lancashire and Yorkshire be maintained and that the colliery company receive monetary compensation for the inconvenience suffered.

The Sidings Schedules state that the Ince Hall Company obtained £15,000 in compensation from the Wigan Junction Railway and in addition a connection was provided between the Ince Hall Company's private line to the Lower Coal Works and the Wigan Junction Railway. This connection seems to have been covered by agreements dated 29th December 1880 and 11th May 1881 which are referred to in the Sidings Schedules.

When an extension of the Wigan Junction Railway from Darlington Street northwards was actively being pursued around 1880, progress was blocked by the Ince Hall Coal and Cannel Company's coal yard. The Sidings Schedules record that the Ince Hall Company's leasehold interest in the yard was purchased by the railway company under an agreement dated 29th December 1880. The yard and its associated tramway from the Lower Coal Works seems to have disappeared shortly afterwards.

On 10th May 1871, the firm changed its status from a Joint Stock Company to a Limited Liability Company[28]. It appears to have continued to prosper for another decade or so. Then, in 1884, the Company was declared bankrupt, on a petition from one of the lessors, H J Walmesley[29]. The collieries seem to have closed almost immediately. The Company was being wound up in July 1885[30], the process being completed in July 1888[31].

Charles Gidlow Jackson, Thomas Gidlow's nephew[32] and lessor of the mining rights for a large part of the Company's property, took over the Middle Coal Works and East Cannel Pits in June 1884[33,34]. We shall be following the subsequent course of events below in the section dealing with the Ince Coal and Cannel Company.

The rest of the property was sold at a series of auctions which took place over a twelve month period from October 1884 to September 1885. Included in that at the Bottom Place held on 20th October 1884 were 160 8-ton coal wagons[35]. The locomotive COLONEL and 200 8-ton and 6-ton wagons were for sale on 24th November 1884, again at the Bottom Place[36]. There must have been no worthwhile bid for COLONEL, for it was readvertised for sale on 2nd February 1885, along with its sister engine BLACK DIAMOND and 100 coal wagons[37].

There were further sales at the Britannia Pit, the Old Yard Pit and Birkett Bank Colliery on 3rd June 1885, at the Arley Mine on 17th June 1885 and at the Cannel Pits and Yard Mine on 1st July 1885[38]. There was a concluding sale later in July[39] and a final clearance sale in September[40].

The Arley Pits at the Bottom Place were reopened by William Crompton in August 1885[41] and again we shall be following these developments below, in the section dealing with the Welch Pits Colliery.

The two locomotives offered for sale in 1884 and 1885 are the only ones which we have able to trace in connection with the Ince Hall Coal and Cannel Company and perhaps were the only ones that the firm ever owned. The sales notices[36,37] describe COLONEL as a four wheels coupled tender engine, with driving and trailing wheels 5ft in diameter, and leading wheels 3'2" diameter. The cylinders, which were outside the frames, were 15½"bore and 24" stroke. BLACK DIAMOND was stated to be of the same type and make.

BLACK DIAMOND had suffered a serious boiler explosion on the morning of Saturday 19th October 1878, when standing under the Lancashire and Yorkshire bridge at the Bottom Coal Works[42]. The whole of the upper part of the boiler and a good deal of the lower part were blown away, a driving wheel was cut off and the name plate was blown over the nearby coke ovens. The cause of the explosion was put down to thinning of the plates[43].

Evidence given at the inquest on the brakesman, who was killed by the explosion, suggests that the company only had two locomotives, both almost identical. It appears that they had then been in use for upwards of thirty years and had been reboilered several times.

From their age, and from the fact that they were tender engines, we think that they must originally have been purchased for working the Ince Hall Company's coal trains over the main lines. By 1878, the engines were only working ten miles a day[43]. The earliest reference which we have found to these main line workings is in the Grand Junction Railway Minutes for March 1848[44]. Trevithick, the GJR Engineer, reported that the Ince Hall Coal and Cannel Company was not delivering coal to Crewe using its own locomotives, as it had contracted to do. Whether it did so afterwards, we do not know.

Developments at Ince – 1845 to 1900

The Ince Hall Coal and Cannel Company, in common with other colliery concerns in and around Wigan, ran its own trains to Preston for many years. The firm, or more precisely Mr Lancaster, was fined £20 in March 1849, because one of the locomotives had set fire to a haystack near Euxton[45]. The trains were still operating in January 1857, as indicated in the London and North Western Railway's Working Time Table of that date[46].

The firm also seems to have worked its own coal traffic to Liverpool, via Parkside Junction and the Liverpool and Manchester line. In 1852 a locomotive driver employed by the Ince Hall Coal and Cannel Company was killed when uncoupling his engine on Sutton Bank, near St Helens Junction[47].

114

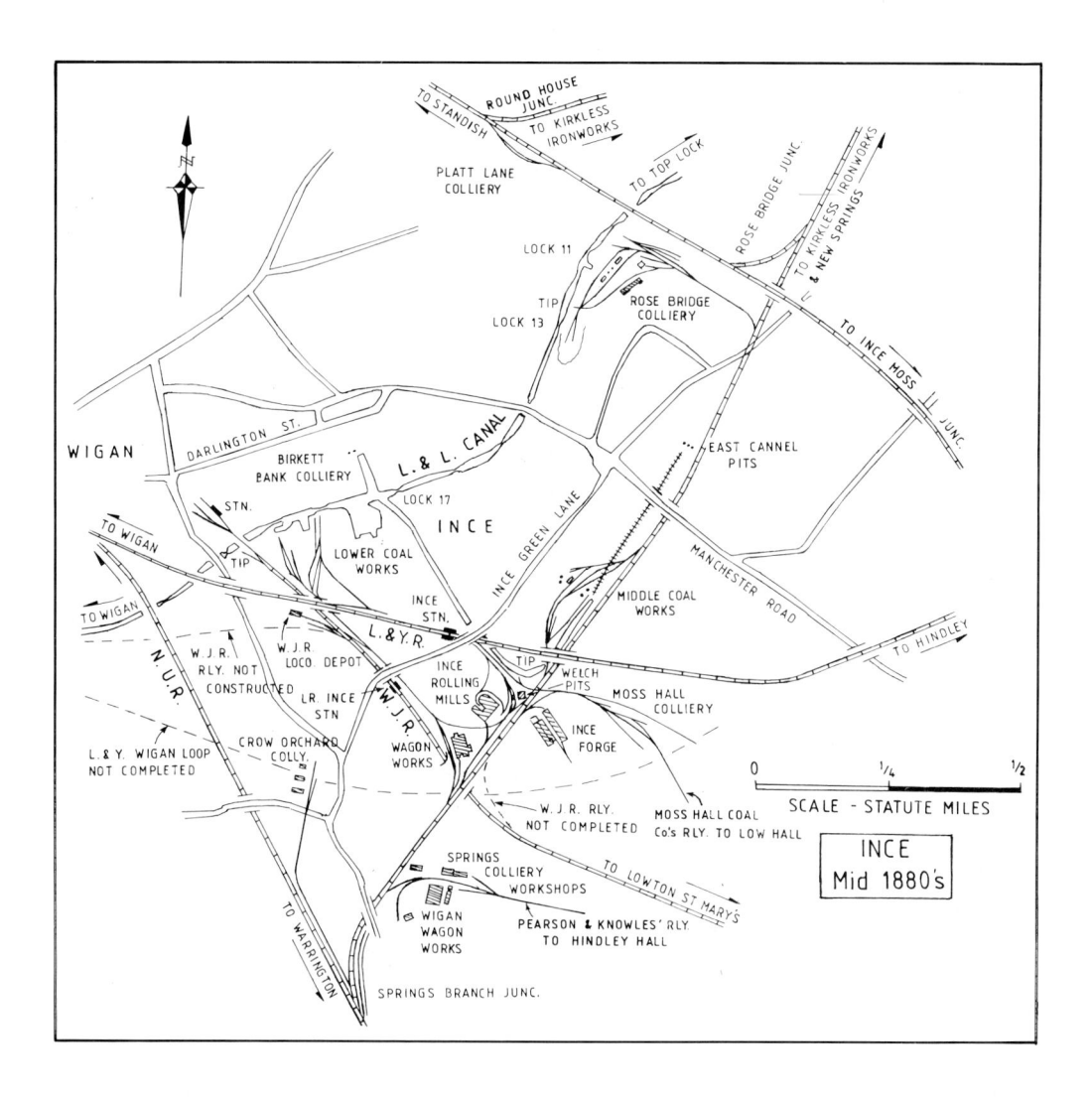

Ince Chemical Works

We must now return to another early enterprise associated with John Swindells and Company, the founders of the Ince Hall Coal and Cannel Company.

The Ince Chemical Works was located near the Leeds and Liverpool Canal at Lock 17. The land it occupied was leased to Swindells and Williams by William Ince Anderton on 13th November 1850 [48]. It is shown in the Ince rate book for 1850 [12] in the occupation of John Swindells and Company.

The works does not appear on the 1st edition of the 6" map, surveyed in 1845 and 1846. It is, however, shown on the revised map, published about 1850, occupying a site across the trackbed of the original Moss Hall tramroad near the canal. The section of tramroad between the chemical works and the Middle Coal works is still in situ. We think that it may have remained in use to convey coal to the chemical works from Swindell's collieries.

The works was mortgaged to Sir John Bickerson Williams on 26th March 1851 [49]. The lease was transferred to John Swindells Marsden on 29th November 1851 [50] and the works was up for sale on 2nd November 1852 [51]. It was purchased by Messrs Laing and Dale, to whom the lease was transferred on 2nd December 1851 [52].

Laing died on 29th December 1861 and the business was carried on for a time by his representatives [53]. It was taken over by John Garrett and Thomas Garrett, to whom the lease was transferred on 31st March 1853 [54]. The Garretts were indicted for nuisance in May of that year [55].

The works was transferred by the Garretts' mortgagees to a Miss Ann Pratt on 12th December 1866 [56] and was advertised for sale on 9th and 10th May 1867 [57]. The Garretts were declared bankrupt on 18th October 1869 [58].

The works was reopened in 1872 by the Wigan Alkali Company and converted to the manufacture of caustic soda. It had closed again in 1873 and there was further sale at the end of 1874 [59]. By February 1875 the works was said to be in a ruinous state [60].

The lessor, William Ince Anderton, started proceedings in the Chancery Court against Ann Pratt. From the evidence which was presented it was clear that works had never been successful financially and was never likely to be [60]. Miss Pratt was left to pay the outstanding rent and other costs [61].

Gidlow Jackson's Ince Coal and Cannel Company

The collieries which Charles Gidlow Jackson took over on the bankruptcy of the Ince Hall Coal and Cannel Company in 1884 comprised the East Cannel, Lane End, Pemberton, Saw Mill and Gravel Hole Pits, employing about 900 men [62,63].

Gidlow Jackson was quick to put some of the pits back into back into production. In December 1884 he announced that he was trading as the Ince Coal and Cannel Company [64]. He was also quick to build a new office block off Ince Green Lane, for which he submitted a plan to the Ince Local Board in September 1884 [65].

The pits on the east side of the Springs Branch, adjacent to Manchester Road, seem to have been dismantled soon afterwards, apart from one which was retained as a pumping station. The sidings which served them had all been lifted by the time the 1st edition of the 25" map was surveyed in 1892. According to Sidings Schedules the connection here with the Springs Branch had been taken out in 1887.

Developments at Ince – 1845 to 1900

The East Cannel Pits and the part of the Middle Coal Works to the west of the Springs Branch continued in operation until the end of the century. The tubway connecting the two sites had been abandoned. According to Traffic Committee Minute 42304, quoted in the Sidings Schedules, the southern connection between the East Cannel Pits and the Springs Branch was reinstated in 1889.

The northern connection seems to have been restored in 1893, although this is not completely certain, as the compiler of the Sidings Schedules obviously had difficulty in identifying the multiplicity of sidings which were served by the Springs Branch. The connection on the east side of the Springs Branch south of Manchester Road Crossing also seems to have been restored at the same time.

Goods Traffic Committee Minute 1114 of 9th August 1893, quoted in the Sidings Schedules, stated that Gidlow Jackson was given permission to operate his own locomotive from the East Cannel Pits to the Middle Coal Works free of charge. This was for a period of 12 months and was to enable him to convey spoil to fill low lying ground on the east side of the line. We presume that this was concerned with the restoration of the site of the Gravel Hole and Lane Side Pits. A new connection was provided at a point 1643 yards from Springs Branch Junction.

The Ince Coal and Cannel Company's collieries closed in 1899 and the whole of the equipment was put up for sale in October of that year [66]. The advertisement mentions plant at the East Cannel, Lane Side, Pemberton, Saw Mill and Gravel Hole Pits.

The pits in the main part of the Middle Coal Works, to the west of the Springs Branch, never seem to have worked again. The area was later developed as a wagon works. The East Cannel Pits were taken over by the brothers Thomas and William Latham, who had acquired Rose Bridge Colliery a few years earlier. We shall be dealing with the later history of both these sites in the next chapter.

The portion of the Middle Coal Works on the east side of the Springs Branch was taken over for a few years by a machinery merchant named Henry Mitchell. His premises at Gravel Hole Siding, Ince Bar, and Lane Side Pit, Ince, together with a quantity of mining equipment and a locomotive, were advertised for sale in September 1907 [67]. As will be described in the next chapter, the yard was sold for use as a wagon works.

Correspondence between Alexander Bertram, of the Wigan Coal and Iron Company, and Mr Cookson of the Ince Hall Coal and Cannel Company [68] suggests that Gidlow Jackson was using a locomotive of his own from the time he took over the collieries. One was certainly there in February 1885 and is referred to in a letter dated 5th February 1885 from Bertram to Cookson. We have no further information about this engine, other than it had 12" cylinders. It was probably acquired second hand, since it needed extensive repairs when Mr Bertram reported on its condition in December 1885.

The colliery company must have decided to replace it, as in February 1886 Mr Bertram helped to prepare the specification for a new locomotive. Tenders were received from Black, Hawthorn and Company of Gateshead, from Peckett and Sons of Bristol and from Nasmyth, Wilson and Company of Patricroft, which were then assessed by Mr Bertram. We know that it was Nasmyth, Wilson and Company which was successful, for we have it on record that they supplied a six coupled side tank later in the same year, which carried the name GIDLOW.

Following the sale of Gidlow Jackson's Ince Hall Collieries in 1899, GIDLOW went to Thomas W Ward Ltd, the Sheffield machinery dealers. The records of this firm show that it was resold to Chatterley-Whitfield Collieries Ltd, of Stoke-on-Trent, in 1905 for £535, where it was renamed ROGER. It survived there until December 1965, when it was broken up.

Developments at Ince – 1845 to 1900

The Nasmyth, Wilson locomotive GIDLOW in later years. It was named ROGER while it was with the Chatterley-Whitfield Collieries Ltd.
Industrial Railway Society, Ken Cooper Collection

The Welch Pits

The Welch Pits were located on the west side of the Springs Branch to the south of the Moss Hall level crossing, and also went under the name of Ince Hall Colliery.

As we have already noted, in Chapter 6, it seems likely that the Welch Pits were opened out by Robert James a little after 1860, to replace earlier workings, also known as the Ince Hall Colliery, a little further west. Robert James' concern seems to have traded from time to time as the Ince Hall Coal Company and the Ince Hall Colliery Company.

A short private railway was built from the colliery to the Lancashire and Yorkshire Railway near Ince Station. The siding connection here, adjacent to that of the Moss Hall Coal Company, was provided under an agreement of 4th April 1862[69]. The Sidings Schedules show that there were two connections with the Springs Branch, at 743 yards and 1236 yards from Springs Branch Junction, which were put in under an agreement dated 29th November 1864.

Robert James failed in 1866 and a note in the Sidings Schedules records that there were unpaid bills due to the London and North Western Railway of £191-0-7d in respect of the sidings and £22-10-3d for the carriage of goods. The colliery was taken over by Crompton and Shawcross in the same year.

As we shall see in Chapter 10, Crompton and Shawcross's main sphere of activity was at Amberswood and Strangeways. We presume that one of the locomotives from there was outstationed at the Welch Pits.

117

Developments at Ince – 1845 to 1900

There were further developments at Ince in August 1885, when Crompton and Shawcross took over the Arley Pits at the Bottom Place [41], following the demise of the Ince Hall Coal and Cannel Co Ltd. At the same time, they took over operation of that company's railways linking the Lower Coal Works with the Springs Branch, the Lancashire and Yorkshire and the Wigan Junction.

The 1st edition of the 25" map, surveyed in 1888 to 1892, shows a branch leading from the private line to the Lower Coal Works which gave direct access to the Welch Pits and to the Middle Coal Works. We are not sure whether this was put in by Crompton and Shawcross after 1885 or whether it had been provided earlier by the Ince Hall Coal and Cannel Company to give through running between their two sites.

Be that as it may, the Sidings Schedules, although not explicit on the point, suggest after 1885 Crompton and Shawcross exchanged traffic with the LNWR only over the ex-James's connections at 743 yards and 1236 yards from Springs Branch Junction and that the former Ince Hall Coal and Cannel Company's connection at 685 yards was used only by Olive and Sons.

The Welch Pits, which had simply been known as Crompton and Shawcross's Ince Hall Colliery up to 1885, were subsequently referred to as Ince Hall Pemberton Pits. The former Ince Hall Coal and Cannel Company's pits at the Lower Coal works were referred to as Ince Hall Arley Pits.

The Arley Pits closed in 1892 and were then dismantled. A sale of plant, held on 13th October 1892, included a six wheeled, four coupled tank locomotive with 11" x 22" cylinders [70,71,72].

The Pemberton Pits do not appear in the Mines Lists after 1888, although we think that the Seven Foot Mine, which is shown under Crompton and Shawcross ownership between 1895 and 1901, may represent a temporary reopening of the Welch Pits. The sidings Schedules note that the connection at 743 yards from Springs Branch Junction was removed in October 1903, that at 1236 yards being retained for the use of the Church Iron Works. The connection with the Lancashire and Yorkshire Railway, which also served the Ince Hall Rolling Mills, was taken up in 1900.

To maintain deliveries of coal to customers at Ince, Crompton and Shawcross opened a new landsale depot in the goods yard of the former Wigan Junction station, by now Great Central Railway. The Sidings Schedules record that the facilities here were provided under an agreement dated 4th October 1904. Coal was conveyed at special rates from the Victoria, Grange and Strangeways Hall Collieries.

The coal yard at Ince lasted well into the twentieth century. It became the property of Lancashire Associated Collieries Ltd, which was formed on 1st July 1935. It was taken over by the National Coal Board on 1st January 1947 and closed shortly afterwards. The agreement with what was now British Railways was terminated on 31st March 1948.

Ince Wagon Works

The earliest reference which we have been able to find to a wagon works at Ince is in an 1858 directory [73]. This shows Richard Preston at what is described as the Ince Railway Waggon Works. John and Richard Preston also appear in an 1853 Directory [74] as brickmakers and railway contractors. We presume that their brickworks is the one shown, apparently not then in use, on the 1st edition of the 25" map, in a position between Ince Old Hall and the Ince Waggon and Ironworks Company's premises.

We have a record that the partnership between Peter Johnson, John Preston and Richard Preston was dissolved on 17th May 1862, leaving Richard Preston to carry on the business alone [75].

There was a sale of plant of the late Richard Preston at the end of 1871 [76] which is the last we hear of the family in the area. Included in the sale were 42 6- and 8-ton railway wagons lying at the Ince Hall sidings near the Ince Wagon Works.

We know that Olive and Sons had a wagon works in the same neighbourhood in the 1870s and we think it likely that they took over the premises previously occupied by the Prestons. Olive and Sons' works was situated immediately to the south of the Welch Pits and adjacent to the Ince Hall Coal and Cannel Company's line from the Lower Coal Works to the Springs Branch. A note in the Sidings Lists, dated 1st December 1878, records that Olive's works was reached over the Ince Hall Coal and Cannel Company's connection with the Springs Branch. It seems that the Ince Hall company's railway also provided a route for Olive and Company's traffic to and from the Wigan Junction Railway.

By June 1881, Richard Olive had been declared bankrupt [77]. He had recently opened the Springside Wagon Works at Summerseat, near Bury, and also had a works at Hexthorpe, near Doncaster. The Springside works was put up for sale in July 1882 [78].

The Springside Works apparently passed into the hands of J Olive and Company. It was up for sale again on 12th February 1894, following the bankruptcy of this firm [79]. The Ince works was taken over by the Ince Waggon and Ironworks Co Ltd, which was formed on 12th February 1883 [80]. The Managing Director was Mr T D Swift and Richard Brancker, Robert Kay and Charles Gidlow Jackson were among the principal shareholders.

When the Crompton and Shawcross collieries at the Bottom Place closed in 1892, the wagon company took over the railway from the Springs Branch to the Lower Coal Works so as to maintain their connection with the Wigan Junction line. The Sidings Schedules show that the new arrangements in respect of this connection were ratified under an agreement of 17th January 1898. We deal with the later history of the site in Chapter 8.

We presume that, up to the closure of the pits at the Bottom Place, shunting at the wagon works had been performed by the Ince Hall Coal and Cannel Company and later by Crompton and Shawcross. The first locomotive owned by the Ince Waggon and Ironworks Company for which we have firm information was a six coupled saddle tank which had been built in 1868 by the Hunslet Engine Company of Leeds for the public works contractors, Leather and Smith. The Hunslet records show that by 1873 it had been acquired by C. Chambers, another contractor and that by March 1895 spares were being ordered from the wagon works.

There must have been at least two locomotives here before this. On 1st August 1895, the Ince Waggon and Ironworks Company advertised for sale a four coupled saddle tank, built by Manning, Wardle and Company, which was stated to have 12" cylinders and 3'0" diameter driving wheels [81]. On 1st November of the same year they advertised a four coupled saddle tank built by Black, Hawthorn and Company of Gateshead, with 12" x 18" cylinders and 3'2" wheels [82]. We cannot be sure whether these engines had actually been in use at the works or whether the firm was merely engaged in some speculative second hand trading.

Ince Hall Rolling Mills

The Ince Hall Rolling Mills occupied a site alongside the Springs Branch, between Olive's Wagon works and the Welch Pits. The works opened on 1st January 1872 [83,84], the Ince Hall

Developments at Ince – 1845 to 1900

Rolling Mills Co Ltd having been incorporated on 1st August 1871[85]. William Crompton seems to have been the prime mover and was recorded as chairman of the company in 1873[86]. At that time, 20 puddling furnaces were in operation making wrought iron, together with forges and rolling mills manufacturing finished products. The Mineral Statistics show that by 1878 the works comprised 24 furnaces and 4 rolling mills.

A report of 11th December 1878, noted in the Siding Schedules, records that the Ironworks used the same connection to the Springs Branch as the Welch Pits. The Line Plan of the Liverpool, Bolton and Bury Railway shows that the Ironworks had a separate connection to the Lancashire and Yorkshire Railway, adjacent to that which served the Welch Pits, provided under an agreement dated 18th September 1876[87].

In 1880 the Ince Hall Rolling Mills Company was in financial trouble and a petition for winding it up was made by the Wigan Coal and Iron Co Ltd on 4th December[88,89]. A liquidator was appointed in an attempt to carry on the works, which was put up for sale as a going concern on 23rd August 1881. No satisfactory offer was received at the time[90] and the works was eventually purchased on 31st October 1881 by the proprietors of the Wigan Rolling Mills Company[91]. A new agreement relating to the Lancashire and Yorkshire sidings was signed with this firm on 3rd March 1882.

The Ince works closed again in the 1890s and we shall be following the subsequent history of the site in Chapter 8.

The Sidings Schedules record that the connection with the Lancashire and Yorkshire Railway was taken up in 1900. Latterly it had served the Welch Pits as well, as shown on the 1st edition of the 25" map.

Ince Forge

The Ince Forge Company was founded in 1856 by William Melling Senior, in partnership with his son, William Melling Junior and John Burrows[92]. All had previous connections with the Haigh Foundry. The site chosen for the works was adjacent to the Springs Branch, just to the south of the level crossing with the Moss Hall Coal Company's railway. The land was leased by Melling and Burrows from William Ince Anderton on 12th September 1856[93]. A steam hammer was ordered from James Nasmyth in April of that year and was apparently delivered in December[94].

Ince Forge specialised in the manufacture of heavy equipment for a wide variety of industrial uses. As might be expected, a large part of its output went to the coal mines. From around 1860, the firm added locomotives to its range of products. In the absence of written records we shall probably never discover how many engines were constructed, although this side of the business always seems to have been a minor part of the firm's activities.

There was a strong tradition that the Ince Forge Company had built a number of locomotives for local collieries. The general arrangement drawing, reproduced here and which carries the date 1867, was acquired by the authors in the early 1950s. At that time, Mr William Melling told us that this engine had been supplied to the Moss Hall Coal Company. He was obviously relying on the memory of what his predecessors had told him, but the story is to some extent confirmed by what we learned from old employees of the Moss Hall company.

We know that a broad gauge 2-4-0 saddle tank was built in 1871 for the South Devon Railway, where it was named PRINCE[95]. It was taken over by the Great Western Railway in

1876 and became No 2137. It was subsequently converted to standard gauge and finally taken out of service in 1899. It is reputed have been No 14 in the Ince Forge maker's list, so thirteen other engines may have been turned out by the firm before this.

We also know that, in 1875, the Ince Forge supplied the South Devon Railway with most of the parts, including the boilers, for three more locomotives [96]. The intention was that they should have been put together at the South Devon's Newton Abbot workshops. The amalgamation with the Great Western Railway intervened and the parts were taken to Swindon. There they were assembled in the form of standard gauge 2-4-0 Tanks, and were turned out in December 1878 carrying Great Western numbers 1298, 1299 and 1300. No 1299 was later fitted with a crane. All were taken out service between 1926 and 1936.

The last reference to locomotive building at the Ince Forge is in 1883. An advertisement appeared in April that year, offering for sale two new six coupled tank locomotives. One, with 11" cylinders, was priced at £500, the other, with 12" cylinders, at £530 [97]. We cannot say whether these engines were in stock or whether the firm was waiting for an order before it started manufacture. Certainly no locomotive answering to this description is known to have been purchased locally.

It seems that the Ince Forge also dealt in second hand locomotives from time to time. In 1866, two second hand engines, said to suit a contractor or a colliery, were offered for sale [98].

Ince Forge Co Ltd, a firm in which the Melling family held a controlling interest, was registered on 20th December 1900 to acquire the works [99]. We shall follow its subsequent history in Chapter 8.

General arrangement drawing of locomotive built by the Ince Forge Company. Copied from original drawing in authors' possession

Developments at Ince – 1845 to 1900

Thomas Gidlow's Hosier House Colliery and Iron Works

Charles Gidlow Jackson's uncle, Thomas Gidlow, opened up the Hosier House Colliery in the early 1850s. This was situated to the east of Petticoat Lane and was served by a private line which left the Springs Branch immediately south of Belle Green Lane level crossing.

A few years later Thomas Gidlow sank the Ladies Lane Colliery, at Hindley on the south side of the Lancashire and Yorkshire Railway's Wigan to Bolton line. Ladies Lane is first shown in the Mines Lists for 1859 and was sold to the Wigan Coal and Iron Co Ltd in 1870, presumably to raise capital for a more ambitious venture.

In November 1871 it was reported that Mr Gidlow was making preparations for the erection of a large ironworks near Hindley station, and that this would be the third in the area to be started in the last few months [100]. If this implies that the original intention had been to site the works at Ladies Lane, then plans must have been changed. In the event, the works was built near the Hosier House Colliery.

In November 1875 a prospectus was issued for the Lancashire Iron and Steel Co Ltd, which intended to take over the iron works as from 1st January 1876. The prospectus [101,102] stated that the sidings had been cut to the works, but that the track had still to be laid. Presumably the works was not yet in production. The flotation seems to have fallen through. The next we hear is that the Gidlow Coal and Iron Co Ltd had been registered on 19th November 1881 to acquire the Hosier House Colliery and the iron works [103,104,105].

The new company was soon in financial difficulty, and, according to the Ince Local Board Minutes for 5th November 1884, the works closed on 1st September 1882 [106]. The firm was in liquidation by October of the same year [107] and a winding up order was made on 7th November [105].

A sale of plant at the works took place on 4th April 1883, which included 8 6-ton wagons [108]. The Hosier House Colliery, described as adjoining Gidlow Ironworks, was up for sale on 11th July 1884 [109]. There were further sales here on 2nd September [110] and 30th October 1885 [111], the latter organised by Thomas Johnson, a machinery dealer, who had evidently purchased some of the equipment. A note, dated July 1886, in the Sidings Schedules records that the line between the colliery and the railway company's boundary had been taken up.

Rose Bridge Colliery

Rose Bridge Colliery was situated on the east side of the canal, north of Manchester Road, and was connected with the Springs Branch by a private railway some 600 yards in length.

We believe that the colliery had originally been sunk in the 1830s by Thomas Case and Company, a firm which had associations with Douglas Bank Colliery, which we describe in Part 2, Chapter 21. The 1st edition of the 6" map, surveyed in 1845 and 1846, shows Rose Bridge No 1 Pit adjacent to the Leeds and Liverpool Canal, between Locks 13 and 14, and No 2 Pit between Locks 10 and 11. There is no rail connection to the colliery. It is clear that coal was shipped direct from pits to the canal, as the Ince Rate book for 1838 [112] records that Messrs Thomas Case and Co were assessed on their canal basin.

In the early 1850s John Grant Morris joined the firm, which then became known as Case and Morris. There were further changes following the dissolution of this partnership on 31st March 1863. The firm continued to trade as Case and Morris, the new partners being John Grant Morris, Henry Frederick Walker and Arthur le Blanc. The Mines Lists suggest that John

Grant Morris assumed sole control in 1873. On 10th July 1875, Rose Bridge and Douglas Bank Collieries Ltd was formed [113].

Soon after John Grant Morris joined the firm, steps were taken to modernise both the Rose Bridge and Douglas Bank Collieries. In 1858 new pits were sunk at Rose Bridge which were then the deepest in the country at 600 yards. We think that the railway connection with the Springs Branch dates from this period.

In the early 1860s the Lancashire Union Railway was being promoted and it was intended that the main line would pass close to Rose Bridge Colliery. Case and Morris opposed the Bill which was submitted to Parliament in 1864. Following negotiations, an agreement was signed on 3rd May 1864 under which Case and Morris withdrew their objection. In return, the London and North Western Railway were to provide a connection to the colliery from the new line and to convey coal to Garston, Widnes and Runcorn at 1s 2d per ton [114].

The main line of the Lancashire Union was authorised by an Act of 1864 [115]. The branch to Rose Bridge, which would have joined the existing colliery line some 200 yards from the connection with the Springs Branch, was included in the Lancashire Union Bill of 1865. It appears as Railway No 7 on the Deposited Plans of November 1864 [116].

In the event, the link to the Lancashire Union was never constructed. However, tolls on traffic from the colliery were reduced to those which would have applied if it had been built. This was confirmed by Goods Rates Sub-Committee Minute 636, quoted in the Sidings Schedules. These also note that the idea of connection with the Lancashire Union line was revived in 1901, although again this came to nothing.

INCE photographed at Douglas Bank. The engine was transferred here after Rose Bridge Colliery closed in 1894.
J.A. Peden Collection

Developments at Ince – 1845 to 1900

We know of only one locomotive used at Rose Bridge Colliery during this period. According to an old employee whom we interviewed, a small four coupled, inside cylinder saddle tank named INCE worked here. We have been unable to establish who built it.

Towards the end of the nineteenth century the readily workable coal reserves were becoming exhausted and the Rose Bridge Colliery was closed in 1894. There was an auction sale on 18th September of that year [117] and the colliery passed into the hands of the brothers Thomas and William Latham. We shall be following its later history in Chapter 8.

The locomotive INCE was transferred to Douglas Bank Colliery, where it was finally broken up about 1921. INCE is said to have made the journey from Rose Bridge through the streets. The engine was driven in steam over short lengths of track which were moved forwards as soon it had passed over. Presumably it was not in a fit state to travel over the main line companies' tracks.

Platt Lane Colliery

As we have seen in Chapter 6, the original Platt Lane collieries were taken over by the Wigan and Whiston Coal Company, which, as the name implies, also owned a colliery at Whiston, near Rainhill. Mr Fidler, one of the partners in the Platt Lane Company, was managing director.

The Wigan and Whiston Company appears to have started sinking a new Platt Lane Colliery in the late 1860s, on a site near the old Round House Colliery. It was served by a bank of sidings from the adjacent Lancashire Union Railway. According to the Sidings Schedules, these were provided under an agreement dated 4th November 1869 and were opened for traffic in January 1870.

The older Round House and Cheshire Hole colliery workings, together with their tramroads to the canal, appear to have been closed when these new developments had been completed. This is confirmed by examination of the 1876 Map of the Borough of Wigan [26]. Only one tramroad is now shown, and that apparently out of use, running from Whelley Colliery, near the main road, to the new Platt Lane Colliery.

Platt Lane Colliery was leased by the Wigan and Whiston Coal Company in 1888 to the brothers William and James Latham [118], who worked it until the mid 1890s. It is shown on the 1st edition of the 25" map, surveyed in 1889 to 1892, with a reduced siding layout. It is given the name Cheshire Holes Colliery, apparently in error.

The Wigan and Whiston Coal Co Ltd, which had been registered as a limited company on 21st December 1895, was in liquidation in January 1896 [119]. A new company, Whiston Collieries Ltd was formed to take over the Whiston mines [120], the Platt Lane operations apparently being abandoned at this time.

According to a Goods Traffic Committee Minute of 16th May 1900, quoted in the Sidings Schedules, the sidings were by then disused and had been taken up.

Some small scale mining operations were carried on in the early years of the twentieth century, none large enough to warrant rail connections.

The 2nd edition of the 25" map, surveyed in 1907, marks Round House Colliery a little to the south west of the now disused Platt Lane pits. We believe that this was the colliery operated by Thomas Marsden under a lease dated 10th November 1903, and from 1st January 1907 by Grady, Sherrington and Ramsay, trading as the Whelley Colliery Company. The firm was in liquidation 1909, and the property put up for sale in July of that year [121]. The Mines Lists show

Developments at Ince – 1845 to 1900

that the colliery was formally abandoned in 1910 and the lease was terminated on 7th June 1910. There was a further sale at the Whelley Colliery, described as being behind Thompson Street, on 24th May 1910, but there was no satisfactory bid [122]. It was later reported that the colliery had been sold piecemeal on 7th June [123].

LOCOMOTIVE SUMMARY

Ince Hall Coal and Cannel Company's Pits

1843 to 1845	Lower Coal Works – James King & Co
1845 to 1848	Lower Coal Works – Swindells & Co
1847 to 1848	Middle Coal Works – Swindells & Co
1848 to 1871	Lower and Middle Coal Works – Ince Hall Coal and Cannel Company
1871 to 1884	Lower and Middle Coal Works – Ince Hall Coal and Cannel Co Ltd (Also East Cannel Pits after 1861)
1884	Middle Coal Works and East Cannel Pits taken over by Ince Coal and Cannel Co Ltd
1885	Lower Coal Works sold to Crompton and Shawcross

COLONEL		2-4-0	OC			15½"x24"	5'0"
For sale Nov 1884							
BLACK DIAMOND		2-4-0	OC			15½"x24"	5'0"
For sale Nov 1884							

Middle Coal Works and East Cannel Pits

1884 to 1899   Ince Coal and Cannel Co Ltd
For later history see Chapter 8

		loco				12"	
Reported to be in bad state of repair in 1885							
GIDLOW		0-6-0T	OC	NW	304	1886	14"x22"	3'5"
New							
To Thomas W Ward of Sheffield and resold to Chatterley-Whitfield Collieries Ltd, Stoke on Trent							

Lower Coal Works

1885 to 1892   Crompton and Shawcross

	0-4-2Tk or 2-4-0Tk		11"x22"
For sale October 1892			

Welch Pits

c1860 to 1866	James Kay
1866 to c1900	Crompton and Shawcross

No record of locomotives used here

125

Developments at Ince – 1845 to 1900

Ince Hall Rolling Mills

1872 to 1881   Ince Hall Rolling Mills Co Ltd
1881 to c1895   Wigan and Ince Rolling Mills Co Ltd
For later history see Chapter 8

No record of locomotives used here

Ince Hall Waggon Works

c1855 to c1870   John and Richard Preston
c1870 to 1883   Richard Olive and Sons
After 1883   Ince Waggon and Ironworks Co Ltd

For locomotives see chapter 8

Rose Bridge Colliery

Before c1850   Thomas Case
c1850 to 1875   Various Case and Morris partnerships
1875 to 1894   Rose Bridge and Douglas Bank Collieries Ltd
For later history see Chapter 8

INCE   0-4-0ST   IC
  To Douglas Bank Colliery in 1894

References to Chapter 7

1	WRO DD An 53/547		
2	Leeds and Liverpool Canal Company's Minutes 14-4-1845		
3	WRO DD An 53/542	4	WRO DD An 53/543
5	LRO DD Wa	6	WRO DD An 53/544
7	WRO DD An 53/545	8	LRO PDR 502
9	LRO PDR 539		
10	Line Plan of North Union Railway – LNWR, 1864 – 2 chains to 1 inch – at GMRO		
11	MJ 20-10-1849	12	Formerly in Ince UDC Offices
13	WO 8-11-1861	14	WEx 9-11-1861
15	WO 21-3-1862	16	WO 24-7-1874
17	*Iron* 28-6-1873	18	*Iron* 25-7-1874
19	WRO DD IN 1/3	20	WO 20-9-1861
21	WO 5-1-1866	22	WEx 6-1-1866
23	WRO DD IN 1/4	24	LRO PDR 990
25	Line Plan of Wigan Junction Railway – Henry Fowler, Surveyor, 1883 – 2 chains to 1 inch – at BRPB, Manchester Office		
26	*"Plan of Borough of Wigan, surveyed and corrected up to 1st January 1875 with corrections to up to December 1876"* – 220ft to 1 inch – J. Hunter Borough Surveyor		
27	38 & 39 Vic cap clxxxix; 2-8-1875	28	WO 9-5-1884
29	LRO DD WA	30	LG 25-7-1885
31	LG 15-6-1888	32	WEx 5-4-1905
33	WO 27-6-1884	34	WO 4-7-1884
35	WO 11-10-1884	36	WO 5-11-1884
37	WO 14-1-1885	38	WO 15-4-1885

39	WO 15-7-1885	40	WO 9-9-1885
41	WO 8-8-1885	42	WO 26-10-1878
43	WO 2-11-1878		
44	Quoted in *"Locomotives of the Grand Junction Railway"* by E Craven, in *Mancunian* No 143, Journal of Manchester Locomotive Society, March 1988		
45	BC 31-3-1849	46	PRO Rail 946/1
47	PC 17-4-1852	48	WRO DD An 54/550
49	WRO DD An 54/552	50	WRO DD An 54/554
51	WT Oct 1852	52	WRO DD An 54/555
53	WEx 4-1-1862	54	WRO DD An 55/557
55	WEx 29-5-1863	56	WRO DD An 55/572
57	LC 4-5-1867	58	WRO DDAn 74/9
59	BC 29-8-1874	60	WRO DD An 74/8
61	WRO DD An 74/6	62	WO 27-6-1884
63	WO 4-7-1884	64	WO 20-12-1884
65	WRO DD IN 1/5	66	WO 7-10-1899
67	WO 7-9-1907	68	WRO DDZ A13 Misc 40
69	Line Plan of Liverpool, Bolton and Bury Railway – LMSR Euston, 1940 to1942 – 2 chains to 1 inch at BRPB, Manchester Office		
70	WO 24-9-1892	71	BC 24-9-1892
72	CG 7-10-1892		
73	*Royal National Commercial Directory of Manchester and Liverpool and the Principal Manufacturing Towns of Lancashire* – Isaac Slater, Manchester, 1858		
74	*A New Alphabetical and Classified Directory of the Boroughs of Bolton, Bury and Wigan with the Parishes of Dean and Leigh* – William Whellan & Co, Manchester, 1853		
75	LG 30-5-1862	76	WEx 29-10-1871
77	BC 25-6-1881	78	BC 14-1-1882
79	BC 2-1-1894	80	Information supplied by Mr Tony Watts
81	MM 1-8-1895	82	MM 1-11-1895
83	WO 5-1-1872	84	MJ 6-1-1872
85	MJ 12-8-1871	86	WO 1-7-1873
87	Line Plan of Liverpool, Bolton and Bury Railway, 17 mp to 16 mp, and Pemberton Loop – LMSR Euston, 1940–2 – 2 chains to 1 inch at BRPB, Manchester Office		
88	WEx 27-11-1880	89	WO 26-11-1880
90	WO 26-8-1881	91	Iron 7-10-1881
92	WO 9-9-1881	93	WRO DD An 57/602
94	Nasmyth Documents at Salford Library – Order Books		
95	*The Locomotives of the Great Western Railway, Part Two* – Railway Correspondence and Travel Society, 1952		
96	*The Locomotives of the Great Western Railway, Part Three* – Railway Correspondence and Travel Society, 1956		
97	MM 4-4-1883	98	Engineer 23-11-1866
99	WO 12-1-1901	100	MJ 11-11-1871
101	BC 11-12-1875	102	CG 17-12-1875
103	MJ 26-11-1881	104	WO 9-12-1881
105	PRO 31/2895/16076 X/L 05835	106	WRO DD IN 1/5
107	WO 27-10-1882	108	WO 17-3-1883
109	WO 21-6-1884	110	WO 12-8-1885
111	WO 30-10-1885	112	Formerly in Ince UDC Offices
113	WO 18-7-1875	114	WRO DDX El 76/2
115	27 & 28 Vic cap cclxxiii; 25-7-1864	116	LRO PDR 797
117	WO 1-9-1894	118	WO 18-11-1893
119	WEx 4-1-1896	120	WO 4-1-1896
121	WO 17-7-1909	122	WO 28-5-1910
123	WO 10-6-1910		

CHAPTER 8

INCE IN THE TWENTIETH CENTURY

By the turn of the century most of the larger collieries had closed and the readily available good quality coal had been exhausted. A few small pits remained, which were worked in a sporadic fashion up to the outbreak of the second world war. With the demolition of the earlier collieries, large areas of land, with good rail connections, were available for redevelopment. Ince became one of the main centres in Lancashire for the construction and repair of railway wagons. Machinery merchants and other firms which were dependent on the coal trade also moved in.

Rose Bridge Colliery and the East Cannel Pits up to 1914

Rose Bridge Colliery was reopened by the brothers Thomas and William Latham, following the sale by the Rose Bridge and Douglas Bank Colliery Co Ltd in July 1894. Five years later, in 1899, the Latham Brothers acquired the East Cannel Pits, when these were put on the market by Charles Gidlow Jackson. At this time they were also working a colliery at Eccleston Hall, near St Helens.

To operate the railway system at Rose Bridge, the Latham Brothers are recorded as having acquired a second hand six coupled saddle tank from the Tawd Vale Coal Co Ltd at Skelmersdale in 1899. Named ENTERPRISE, this engine had originally been built by the Leeds firm of Manning, Wardle and Company in 1863.

Latham Brothers seem to have purchased a second locomotive to cater for the additional traffic arising at the East Cannel Pits. This was a four coupled saddle tank, built by Peckett and Sons of Bristol in 1901, which came second hand from the Whitecross Company of Warrington.

One of these engines, we are not sure which, featured in a court case at Wigan on 19th March 1905 [1]. The driver and the brakesman were found guilty of being drunk in charge of a locomotive at Rose Bridge on 27th February. They were fined 1/– each and lost their jobs.

Goods Traffic Committee Minute 4208 of 13th December 1899, quoted in the Sidings Schedules, records that Latham Brothers were granted permission to run their engine over the Springs Branch between the junction with their Rose Bridge sidings and the northern connection to the East Cannel Pits, on payment of £5 per annum toll. Under an agreement dated 12th April 1904 they were authorised to work over the southern connection to the East Cannel Pits as well, on payment of an additional £5 per annum toll.

The working was discontinued in March 1911, but tolls for the use of the Springs Branch were not paid after April 1909 on the advice of Latham Brothers' solicitor. The Sidings Schedules note that they claimed that such use of the Springs Branch by private engines was free of toll under Section 96 of the North Union Act of 1834. The matter was not pursued as William Latham died on 12th November 1910 [2] and Thomas on 26th November 1911 [3].

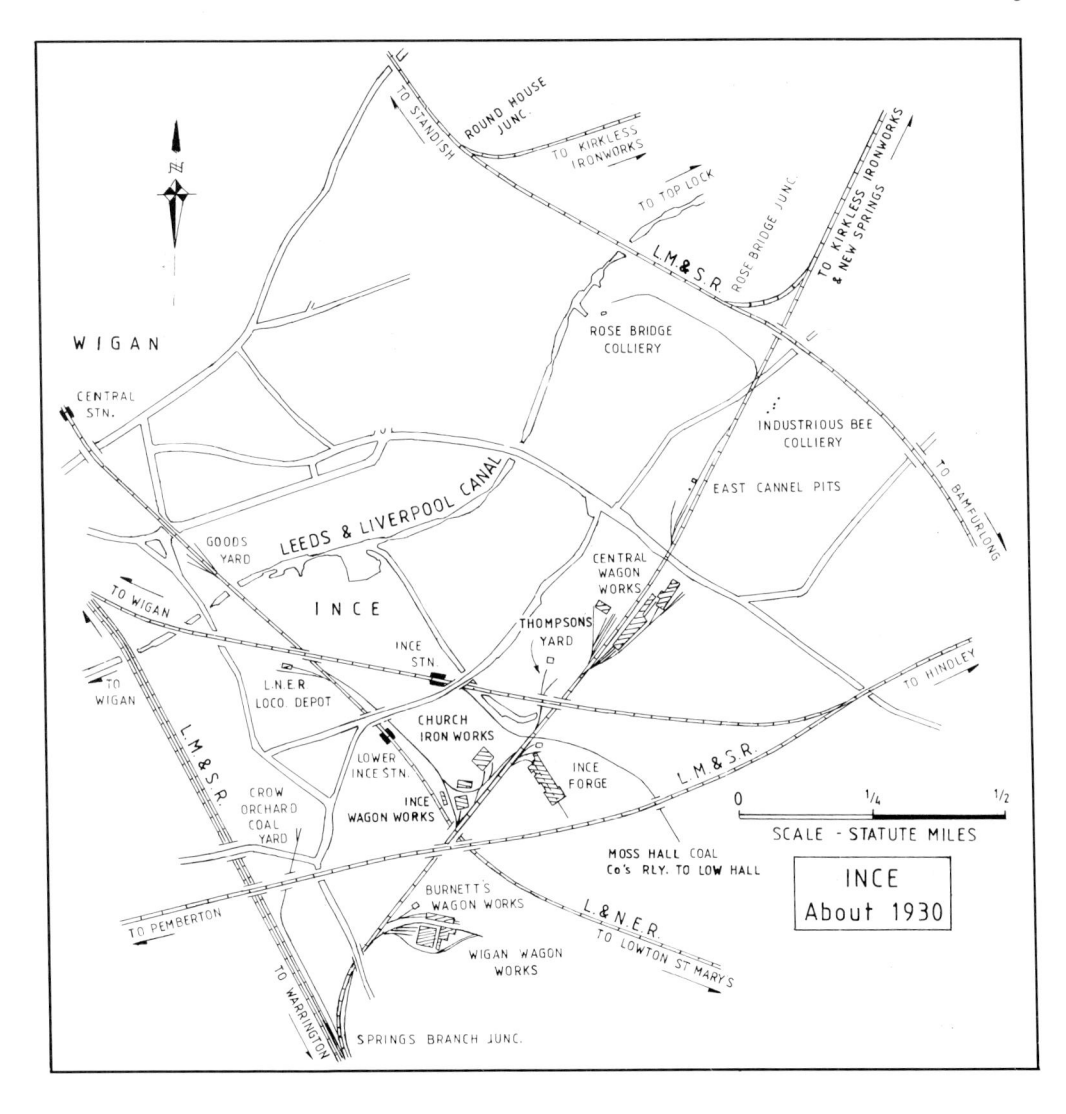

Ince in the Twentieth Century

Ince in the Twentieth Century

Rose Bridge Colliery and the East Cannel Pits, as well as the Eccleston Hall Colliery, were closed in 1910. The auction of the Eccleston Hall Colliery, which took place in August, attracted a large attendance [4]. It was stated that the items for sale included three locomotives and two miles of railway track [5].

A dismantling sale at Rose Bridge took place on 2nd to 4th November 1910 [6,7], an unspecified locomotive being included. In June 1911, a six coupled locomotive with 13" cylinders was offered for sale [8]. We identify this as ENTERPRISE, which later went to Sanquahar and Kirkconnel Collieries Ltd, in Dumfriesshire.

There was a sale of surplus plant at East Pits in November 1911, which included a saddle tank loco rebuilt in 1904 [9,10]. We presume that this was the Peckett locomotive, which was sold to Thompson and Company, the Ince machinery merchants. It was later resold to Francis Morton and Co Ltd, at Garston.

The East Cannel Pits after 1914

The East Cannel Pits were reopened by Ince Hall Collieries Ltd, a firm incorporated by the sons of the Latham brothers on 24th March 1914 [11]. The Mines Lists show that the colliery was abandoned in May 1933. The company went into voluntary receivership on 1st May of that year and was finally dissolved on 5th January 1945 [12]. The Sidings Schedules state that work to remove the connections was reported to be complete on 8th September 1936.

We learn from the Sidings Schedules that, for a period from 1921, perhaps up to the closure of the colliery, Shell-Mex Ltd had permission to use one of the East Pit sidings for discharging tank wagons.

Rose Bridge Colliery after 1914

According to the Sidings Schedules dismantling of Rose Bridge Colliery had been completed by February 1914. This, however, was not the end of the story as far the railway system there was concerned.

Mr Albert Longworth took over one of the sidings under an agreement with the London and North Western Railway dated 14th November 1914. We think that this was in connection with his scrap metal and machinery business, which the Sidings Schedules state provided some of the traffic.

In 1921, Longworth went in for coal mining as well. He opened up a small colliery on the opposite side of the Springs Branch, named the Industrious Bee after the nearby public house. A note in the Sidings Schedules, dated November 1921, records that there had been discussions between Albert Longworth and the railway company, about a direct connection to his colliery. Nothing came of this and instead he was given permission to use the Rose Bridge siding to load coal brought from the Industrious Bee by road. These arrangements seem to have come into effect in 1920 or 1921 and we believe that Longworth vacated his Rose Bridge siding when the Industrious Bee Colliery closed in 1939.

Meanwhile mining had been resumed on the Rose Bridge site after the first world war by William Latham in partnership with James Gaskill, but on too small a scale to need rail transport. The Mines Lists for 1920 record that only 11 men were employed underground. Gaskill retired from the business in 1923 or 1924, leaving Latham to carry on until the pit was closed in February 1926.

In 1922 Sydney and Geoffrey Rayner started to dewater the earlier Rose Bridge Colliery with a view to reopening it. The Rayners formed the Rose Bridge Colliery Co Ltd, which was registered on 18th June 1923 [13]. Work was suspended in April 1926 and the colliery formally abandoned on 24th September 1927. However, pumping recommenced in 1929 and the Mines Lists show that the colliery came into production in 1930.

The Sidings Schedules record that an agreement was signed by the Rose Bridge Colliery Company on 27th August 1923 in respect of a rail connection with the Springs Branch. In view of the lack of progress in reopening the colliery the matter was allowed to lapse. The Sidings Schedules, in a note dated July 1930, state that the company had applied again for a connection. A new agreement was signed on 4th December 1930. The single lead from the Springs Branch, already provided for Albert Longworth, was converted to a double lead to accommodate the Rose Bridge Colliery Company.

To work the Rose Bridge Colliery Company's traffic, locomotives were transferred from other collieries in which the Rayners had an interest. ALICE and EDWARD, two six coupled saddle tanks, built by Manning, Wardle and Company in 1905 for John Scowcroft's Hindley Green Colliery, are reputed to have arrived in the early 1930s. EDWARD does not seem to have lasted very long at Rose Bridge and had been broken up by December 1938.

According to the Sidings Schedules, coal production ceased at Rose Bridge on 24th July 1941. However, the Rose Bridge Colliery Company continued to use the premises for wagon repairs until 1952 or 1953. ALICE was still here in June 1948 but was scrapped shortly afterwards. It had been replaced by small 48 HP diesel locomotive, purchased from Ruston and Hornsby of Lincoln in 1946.

ALICE at Rose Bridge Colliery on 27th June 1948. Out of use and awaiting scrapping. George Shuttleworth

Ince in the Twentieth Century

One of the sidings at Rose Bridge was used by Hough and Sons Ltd for the repair of locomotives. As we shall see later, Houghs had previously used part of the premises of the Ince Wagon Works for these activities, but seem to have moved to Rose Bridge around 1938.

We believe that the four coupled saddle tank, built in 1916 by Andrew Barclay Sons and Company of Kilmarnock and reported at Rose Bridge in 1938, was actually the property of Hough and Sons. It had been built for the Winstanley Colliery Company and had been acquired by Houghs following the closure of the colliery.

KENYON, a four coupled saddle tank built by Black, Hawthorn and Company in 1875, was noted at Rose Bridge in January 1946. It was owned by William Evans and Company of Widnes and was being repaired by Houghs. ASBESTOS, a four coupled saddle tank built by Hawthorn, Leslie in 1901 and owned by Turners Asbestos Cement Co Ltd, of Trafford Park, was here at the end of 1947.

Wagon repairing activities ceased in 1952 or 1953 and Rose Bridge Colliery Co Ltd went into voluntary liquidation. The Sidings Schedules state that notice to terminate the private sidings agreement was given by letter dated 17th August 1953. The diesel locomotive was sold for use at the Ince Forge at about this time.

Ince Forge 1900 to 1943

As we have seen in Chapter 7, the Ince Forge had been established in 1856 and, in 1900, had been transferred to a Limited Liability Company formed by the Melling family.

Ince Forge had a direct connection with the Springs Branch and there was also a connection with the Moss Hall Coal Company's railway. According to a note in the Sidings Schedules, dated June 1905, traffic to and from the Lancashire and Yorkshire Railway was worked by the Moss Hall Coal Company. This must have ceased in the 1920s, as a further note, dated October 1929, states that all the Ince Forge Company's traffic was now dealt with over the their Springs Branch connection. The Ince Forge Company had at one time claimed the right to work their own engine over the Moss Hall Company's line crossing the Springs Branch. The Sidings Schedules record that they did so on at least one occasion, despite protests from the London and North Western Company.

We have no record of the engines used for shunting at the Ince Forge during the early part of its history. As we have described in Chapter 7, the firm built several small locomotives in the 1860s for use in the local collieries and it is quite likely that they built one for their own purposes at the same time. However, we lack any real proof that this was so.

In 1905, three steam tram locomotives, redundant following the electrification of the system, were purchased from the Bury, Rochdale and Oldham Tramways Company. They were from a batch of four engines which had been built by Beyer, Peacock and Company in 1886. The running numbers cannot now be established with certainty, although one is believed to have been 84 in the BR&OTC list [14,15]. At the Ince Forge they were named ANT, BEE and BUG [16].

According to old employees whom we interviewed in the late 1940s, one of the tram engines was later used at the Withnell Brick and Terra Cotta Works near Chorley. We have been unable to confirm this, although we know that in June 1907 the Ince Forge Company was advertising for sale what was described as a geared contractors shunting locomotive with 8" cylinders [17]. By the 1930s only one of the three engines remained at Ince Forge. This continued in service until 1953, an object of great interest to the railway enthusiasts of the period.

ANT, one of the three tram engines purchased by the Ince Forge from the Bury, Rochdale and Oldham Tramways Company. Note, in the background, the signal box controlling the level crossing between the Moss Hall colliery railway and the Springs Branch.   J.A. Peden Collection

The Later History of Ince Forge

The Ince Forge continued to be managed by successive generations of the Melling family until 1943[18,19], when it became a subsidiary of William Park (Forgemasters) Ltd.

This was an old established company, which could trace its origins to 1790, when William Park and James Diggle set up in partnership at the Wigan Forge at School Common. In 1842, the firm, now known as William Park and Sons, moved to new premises in the Wiend[20]. It remained here until about 1890 when Henry Park purchased the Clarington Brook Forge, which in the 1850s had been owned by James Bimson[21] and in the 1870s by James Whitfield[22]. The Ince Local Board Minutes for 9th April 1890[23] record that Park submitted plans to extend the forge and applied to remove "the sewer pipe running through the old tramway tunnel near the Bay Horse Inn".

William Park (Forgemasters) Ltd became a holding company in 1957, following the absorption of Gullick Ltd and Webb's forge at Bury[24]. The Ince Forge Co Ltd continued to operate under its own name for a few years, until the works was redeveloped. The premises are now occupied by Gullick Dobson Ltd, the mining equipment division of the Dobson Parks Industries group.

The tram engine passed into the ownership of William Park (Forgemasters) Ltd and was used by the firm until 1953. It was replaced by the Ruston and Hornsby diesel locomotive which had been purchased from the Rose Bridge Colliery Co Ltd when the wagon shops closed.

Ince in the Twentieth Century

The tram engine, by now something of a historical curiosity, was presented to the British Transport Commission and was sent to Crewe Works in October 1954. It subsequently became part of the collection of the National Railway Museum and was on loan to the Dinting Railway Centre up to the time this closed.

Rail traffic ceased at the Ince Forge in the early 1970s and the siding connection with the Springs Branch was removed. The diesel locomotive was noted at the works in November 1973, but by that date had been presented to the Live Steam Preservation Group. It is now at the Mining Museum at Astley Green.

Church Iron Works

The Ince Hall Iron Works premises, which seem to have been derelict since about 1890, were taken over around 1900 by W and J Ellison, described in the Sidings Schedules as nail manufacturers of Salford. It appears that during Ellisons' period of occupation the name was changed to the Church Iron Works.

Ellison's company was in liquidation in June 1906[25]. The works was offered for sale as a going concern on 14th December 1906 but there was no purchaser[26]. In 1909 the Church Ironworks Co Ltd was registered to take over the premises and the business recently carried on by J. Wood[27].

The Sidings Schedules show that there was a new agreement with the London and North Western Railway, dated 30th June 1915, in respect of the connection with their line at 1238 yards from Springs Branch Junction. The 2nd edition of the 25" map, surveyed in 1907, shows that the internal lines between Church Iron Works and the Ince Waggon and Iron Company's yard were retained. As far as we are aware the connection with the Lancashire and Yorkshire railway, which had been removed in 1900, was not reinstated. It does not appear on the 2nd and subsequent editions of the 25" map.

The Church Iron Works was sold on 5th July 1920 to William Fairclough of Ince for a sum of £7,500[28]. We believe that it was after this that the works came under the control of Monks, Hall and Co Ltd of Warrington, which itself became a subsidiary of Richard Thomas and Co Ltd.

The Church Iron Works Co Ltd went into voluntary liquidation on 24th January 1936[29]. The Sidings Schedules state that the works finally closed about 1937. The site was taken over by the Ince in Makerfield Urban District Council for a housing development, in accordance with a conveyance dated 13th November 1937. The siding connection with the Springs Branch was retained for the delivery of building materials and the Ince UDC agreed to honour the previous agreement on 17th January 1938. The first five wagons loaded with paving slabs from Shap arrived on 9th May 1938.

We have virtually no information about the locomotives used at the Church Ironworks either before or after its reopening in 1909. It seems that engines were moved between various works in the Monks, Hall group from time to time, and it has proved difficult to deduce which locomotives were at each of the works at any one period.

According to one of the old employees of the Ince Wagon Works that we interviewed in the early 1950s, BLANCHE was employed at Church Ironworks after the first world war. This was a four coupled saddle tank, built by Peckett and Sons of Bristol in 1893. It had been delivered to W T Jinkin for use on a contract in Cornwall. After passing through the hands of R T Relf and Sons, another contracting firm, it came to Wigan possibly around 1914. According to our informant, it had been at the Albion Ironworks at Aspull before being transferred to Church Ironworks.

Ince Waggon and Ironworks

We have already described, in Chapter 7, how the Ince Waggon and Ironworks Co Ltd took over from Olive and Sons in the 1880s. We have also recorded such information as we have about the locomotives which were used up to the end of the century.

We know from the records of Thomas Mitchell and Sons [30], the Bolton machinery dealers, that the wagon works obtained a second hand four coupled saddle tank in January 1901. This had been purchased by Mitchells from Shakerley Colliery, near Tyldesley. We presume that it was the H class engine with 12" cylinders, which had been built by Manning, Wardle and Company in 1873 for W Ramsden at Shakerley.

The Ince Waggon and Ironworks Company advertised that it had a locomotive for sale in September 1906 [31]. This could have been the six coupled saddle tank, built by the Hunslet Engine Company in 1868, which had been acquired about 1895.

Another second hand locomotive, JOHN BULL, was purchased a few years later, from Holme and King, the Wigan based contractors. A four coupled saddle tank, this engine had been built by Manning, Wardle and Company in 1875 for Scott and Edwards and was delivered to Melmerby, in North Yorkshire, for use on one of their contracts. It had later seen service with Dransfield and Company, another contracting firm, before being bought by Holme and King in 1896.

JOHN BULL and the Manning, Wardle four wheeler which came from Thomas Mitchell seem to have lasted until after the first world war. Information from old employees suggests that they were scrapped around 1922 and around 1929 respectively.

The last steam locomotive to be used by the wagon works arrived about 1926. Named FRENCH, it was another four coupled saddle tank, built by Manning, Wardle, but of the rather smaller E Class design. It had been supplied in 1902 to the Derwent Valley Water Board for use on the construction of a reservoir in the Peak District. It had later been used by Albright and Wilson at their Oldbury chemical works. FRENCH was in use at the wagon works until the middle of the second world war, the manufacturer's records showing that spare parts were supplied up to January 1942.

W R Davies, the proprietor of several wagon works in other parts of the country, acquired a controlling interest in the Ince Waggon and Ironworks Co Ltd in December 1919. The works does not seem to have prospered under the new management and was reported to be in a run down state when Davies went bankrupt in 1932.

The Ince Waggon and Ironworks Co Ltd was taken over by the Central Wagon Co Ltd in December 1933, although it continued to trade under its own name. The new owners carried out a considerable amount of modernisation and alteration [32]. New agreements were negotiated in respect of the siding connection at Lower Ince, with the London and North Eastern Railway on 25th December 1943 and with the British Transport Commission on 22nd March 1948.

With the reduction in British Railways freight services in the 1960s, the wagon repairing business went into decline. Some diversification took place and the Central Pallet Company was set up to utilise part of the premises. The works finally closed around 1980 and remains derelict at the time of writing. However, moves are afoot to demolish it and build a housing estate. In June 1989 Messrs Bennett were granted planning permission by the Wigan Metropolitan Borough to redevelop the site, stated to contain 4 hectares of land [33].

Ince in the Twentieth Century

Central Wagon Company's Ince Works

The first steps to develop wagon building and repair works on the former Ince Hall Coal and Cannel Company's colliery sites seem to have been taken in the early years of the present century. In 1907, Henry Mitchell's yard at Gravel Hole Siding, on the east side of the Springs Branch, was sold for use as a wagon works. Henry Mitchell was evidently a machinery merchant and the sale, which took place on 17th September of that year, included a four coupled tank locomotive with 10¼" x 20" cylinders and 3'0" diameter wheels [34].

Workshops were erected by the Chorley Wagon Co Ltd and the Sidings Schedules record that the connection with the London and North Western line at 1643 yards from Springs Branch Junction was used by the firm. This connection had originally been provided for Gidlow Jackson's Ince Coal and Cannel Company. The 2nd edition of the 25" map suggests that it had latterly also given access to Mitchell's Gravel Hole yard.

The Central Wagon Co Ltd was registered in 1911 to acquire the business at Springs Branch of the Chorley Wagon Co Ltd. Within a few years two new shops had been built and the works had been extended almost as far as Manchester Road. An additional connection with the Springs Branch, at 1479 yards from the junction, was provided under an agreement dated 30th October 1913. Some alteration to the siding layout took place when the Springs Branch was converted to single track. The Sidings Schedules note that the work to do this was ordered on 1st April 1943.

There was also development on the west side of the Springs Branch. Towards the end of the first world war the Central Wagon Company leased land from Gidlow Jackson for the construction of another works. However the 6" maps for 1928 and 1938 suggest that little actually happened until the 1930s, when new wagon repair shops were erected.

Under an agreement of 2nd March 1917 the company were permitted to use a siding connection at 1456 yards from Springs Branch Junction. This appears originally to have been laid in for the Ince Hall Coal and Cannel Company as alternative access to their Middle Coal Works and was presumably used later by the Ince Coal and Cannel Company. According to a note dated June 1900, quoted in the Sidings Schedules, the points had been spiked out of use and the track outside the railway company's boundary had been taken up. In 1911 there was discussion about removing the connection, but it was left in place.

It appears that John Heaton Senior and John Heaton Junior also entered into a lease for land on the west side of the Springs Branch. As the Sidings Schedules put it, the Heatons acquired the interest of the Central Wagon Company in the siding, subject to certain agreements as to user with the Wagon Company. There was a supplemental agreement with the Heatons relating to the siding dated 18th July 1918.

There was a dispute between the Central Wagon Company and the Heatons which related to the use of the siding. This is mentioned in a note in the Sidings Schedules dated February 1917. In July 1920, the railway company's solicitor had been asked to give the Heatons notice to quit. The private sidings agreement with them was terminated after the expiry of twelve months notice from 6th August 1920. A new agreement was made between the Central Wagon Company and the recently formed London Midland and Scottish Railway dated 6th June 1923. The agreement, operational from 1st November 1922, was ratified by Traffic Committee Minute No 35 of 1st March 1923.

In the 1920s and 1930s the Central Wagon Company went through a period of rapid expansion. Through the construction of new works and through the take-over of existing firms, it established itself country-wide. According to a letterhead of 1954, the Central Wagon Group then consisted of :–

Central Wagon Co Ltd,with works at Wigan, Stoke, Wednesbury and Barrow-in-Furness.
Doncaster Wagon Co Ltd, with works at Doncaster, Clay Cross, and Rotherham.
Ince Waggon and Ironworks Co Ltd, with works at Wigan.
Preston Wagon Co Ltd, with works at Preston.
Moys Wagon Co Ltd, with works at Peterborough.
Roger Bolton and Sons Ltd, with works at Wigan.
Lancashire Wagon Co Ltd, with works at Wigan.

The works on both sides of the Springs Branch were reconstructed after the end of the second world war. Many of the old buildings were demolished and replaced by new. Land made redundant by the closure of the Springs Branch through the site was purchased from British Railways on 4th September 1962 [35]. Further land became available in the second half of 1968 when part of Thompson and Company's scrap yard was cleared away.

Some ventures, such as the factory for the construction of containers, never really got off the ground, while other wagon building activities prospered for a time. With the declining demand for new freight rolling stock, trade began to die away in the 1970s. Rail traffic ceased around 1973. Final closure came around 1980.

Some of the buildings are now occupied by firms such as Collins Reinforcements Ltd. Others have been demolished to make way for new factory units to accommodate light industry.

The first reference we have to locomotives is in January 1925, when the Central Wagon Company at Wigan was advertising two six coupled engines for sale [36]. We think that they had not actually been used at the Ince works but probably were engines which had been hired out by the firm.

It seems likely that, in common with many other similar works, wagons were moved by means of tractors running on road wheels and by capstans. The first internal combustion locomotive appears to have been purchased in connection with the post war expansion of the works.

A four wheeled diesel, built by Ruston and Hornsby in 1937, came second hand in 1958. This was followed by two four coupled diesel locomotives, built by John Fowler and Company of Leeds, also second hand. One arrived about 1959 and the other in 1964. These three engines were sold about 1969 and replaced by a second hand four wheeled diesel hydraulic locomotive, built by Thomas Hill of Rotherham in 1964. This lasted until 1973, when it was sold to the National Coal Board for use at Welbeck Colliery, in Nottinghamshire.

West Lancashire Wagon Co Ltd

This firm was founded in 1874 [37] to lease wagons to colliery companies and other similar users. It also had a side-line in hiring out locomotives. As far as we have able to trace, the company did not engage in wagon manufacture itself, simply purchasing what it needed from established builders, and making its profits from hire and hire-purchase arrangements. We have included a brief description of the firm's activities as an example of one of the less well known aspects of colliery railway operations.

Ince in the Twentieth Century

The Ruston and Hornsby diesel locomotive at the Central Wagon Company's works. Taken on 19th September 1964.
P G Hindley

An 1881 list of directors [38] includes many prominent colliery owners, such as W J Lamb, George Caldwell, Horace Mayhew, J H Johnson, Thomas and John Stone. We presume that they regarded the company as a profitable investment as well as an adjunct to their colliery enterprises.

The following table, based on the annual Directors' reports [38], gives an indication of the scope of the firm's activities:

As at	Wagons owned	Locos owned
Dec 1875	862	1
Dec 1876	1297	1
Dec 1877	1599	2
June 1879	2303	4
Dec 1880	2088	4
June 1881	2411	3

In the absence of any records of the company, we have been unable to discover any details of the locomotives which appear in the above list, or to whom they were hired. There were clearly some changes to the locomotive stock through the years. At the end of 1879 the company was advertising a locomotive with 10"x16" cylinders for sale [39,40,41]. In 1888 it was advertising a locomotive with 10½" cylinders "for sale or hire, extra heavy, recently overhauled" [42].

138

Calderbank's Scrap Yard

Elias Calderbank, popularly known as "Spot Cash" Calderbank, started business as a scrap dealer in premises at Orchard Street in 1907. He opened another yard near Britannia Bridge soon afterwards and, in April 1924, the firm was turned into a limited company.

According to the Sidings Schedules, Mr Calderbank, whose address was given as Orchard Street, Wigan was granted permission to use one of the sidings at the Church Iron Works. Letters dated 18th November 1919 and 17th January 1920 are quoted. The main business conducted here was cutting up old machinery for scrap metal. The firm is credited with dismantling world war one field guns and tanks; presumably these were delivered by rail to the Church Iron Works site.

We think that the operations at Ince came to an end before 1930. The firm, however, continued in business at Orchard Street until 1985 and at Britannia Bridge until 1987. Members of the family still operate a scrap yard at the Bradley Hall Trading Estate [43].

Thompson and Co (Wigan) Ltd

Thompson and Company was an old established firm of general dealers to the engineering and mining industries. In 1869, the partners were described as iron and steel merchants who also dealt in blasting powder and fuse and heavy and light rails and fittings for collieries and contractors [44].

In order to expand its business, Thompson and Company leased the south western part of the Middle Coal Works site from Gidlow Jackson and, according to the Sidings Schedules, were established here by February 1902. The firm took over what had originally been the Ince Coal and Cannel Company's No 1, or southern connection, with the Springs Branch. The premises which were taken over included the old Ince Hall Coal and Cannel Company's locomotive shed, which was still in existence in 1968, and the office block which had been built for Gidlow Jackson's Ince Coal and Cannel Company in 1884.

At the Ince yard, Thompson and Company moved into the scrap metal and second hand machinery business. Part of the firm's trade was in locomotives which were purchased from local collieries. In many cases the engines were only fit for scrap but some were repaired and either hired out or resold. Such details of these activities as we have been able to gather together are recorded at the end of the chapter. We must point out that we cannot vouch for their reliability, as most of the information has come from old employees at various collieries.

When steam locomotives were being withdrawn from service in large numbers by British Railways in the 1960s, many were purchased by Thompson and Company and cut up for scrap. Around 200 from the Eastern, Western and London Midland Regions passed through the firm's hands between July 1960 and September 1966.

The subsequent history of the premises has not been fully recorded. The firm was latterly a subsidiary of the the Central Wagon Co Ltd. As mentioned earlier, part of the site was cleared during the second half of 1968 and new workshops were erected to provide additional wagon building capacity. A small diesel locomotive was purchased in 1967, from the North Wales Wagon Co Ltd at Queensferry, near Chester. It had originally been constructed by Ruston and Hornsby of Lincoln in 1953. As well as shunting at Thompson and Company's premises, the locomotive also seems to have been used at neighbouring works of the Central Wagon Company. Its ownership in later years is not entirely clear.

Ince in the Twentieth Century

The yard had closed by May 1983, when the locomotive was noted to be out of use. By July 1985, the premises were up for sale and the locomotive had been sent away.

Holme and King Ltd

The partnership of Holme and King was established in the 1880s to carry on business as public works contractors. A limited company was formed on 11th July 1900[45] and at about this date a plant yard was set up near to Britannia Bridge at Lower Ince.

We have been unable to locate these premises with certainty. We think that they were probably on the site of the Ince Hall Coal and Cannel Company's Lower Coal Works, which had been taken over by Crompton and Shawcross and finally closed in 1892. The 2nd edition of the 25" map, surveyed in 1907, shows an enclosed compound here with scattered buildings and railway tracks. The tracks link up with the private line to the Springs Branch, by now operated by the Ince Waggon and Iron Company.

Holme and King were in financial difficulty by 1913 and the firm was wound up on 24th April 1914[45]. The plant at the Britannia Bridge yard was sold by order of the receiver on 14th March 1913 and included a six coupled locomotive with 12" cylinders[46].

Hough and Sons Ltd

The boilermaking firm of Hough and Tarbuck was established under a partnership agreement dated 11th May 1868[47]. Tarbuck left the partnership on 10th March 1869, the firm subsequently becoming known as John Hough and Son[48] and later Hough and Sons[47]. The partnership was dissolved on 15th December 1922[47] and a limited liability company formed under the same title.

The headquarters of the firm was at the Newtown Boiler Works, on the Pemberton side of Adams Bridge, on a site now occupied by Smiths Shearings Coach Depot. Although the works adjoined the Lancashire and Yorkshire Railway, no siding was provided because of the difference in levels. To handle the heavier plant, Houghs acquired additional premises at Ince.

The Sidings Schedules record that Mr R Hough, about 1913, purchased from Holme and King a siding which had a connection with the Ince Waggon and Iron Company's line. We infer from this that, assuming our previous interpretation is correct, Hough and Sons took over the yard at the Lower Coal Works site. The Sidings Schedules, in a note dated April 1923, record that Mr Hough's traffic chiefly consisted of boilers and dead locomotives which were placed in the Iron Works siding and afterwards hauled by a private engine to Mr Hough's premises.

As well as repairing boilers and locomotives on behalf of local industrial concerns, Hough and Sons were also second hand dealers and hirers of machinery. A list of locomotives which are believed to have passed through their hands is given at the end of the chapter. Prior to 1938, this is based on unconfirmed information from old employees at a number of different collieries. The later information comes from personal observations of the authors and their colleagues.

From the 1930s, if not earlier, Hough and Sons were carrying out locomotive repairs in a building within the Ince Waggon Works boundary. Before and after the second world war, the firm also made use of premises in the pit yard at Rose Bridge Colliery. One locomotive, SCOBRIT, was repaired at the Ravenhead Brickworks at Upholland in 1948 and 1949.

LOCOMOTIVE SUMMARY

Rose Bridge Colliery and East Cannel Pits

1894 to 1910   Thomas and William Latham (Rose Bridge)
1899 to 1910   Thomas and William Latham (East Cannel Pits)

ENTERPRISE   0-6-0ST   IC   MW   91   1863   12"x17"
  Ex Tawd Vale Coal Co Ltd, 1899
  To Sanquahar and Kirkconnel Collieries Ltd, 1910

                                        0-4-0ST   OC   P   895   1901   14"x20"
  Ex Whitecross Co Ltd
  To Francis Morton and Co Ltd, Garston, reputedly via Thompson, Ince, between July 1911 and February 1912

East Cannel Pits

1914 to 1933   Ince Hall Collieries Ltd

No information about locomotives used

Rose Bridge Colliery

1922   Sydney and Geoffrey Rayner
1923 to 1953   Rose Bridge Colliery Co Ltd (Colliery closed 1941, wagon shops only after this date)

ALICE   0-6-0ST   IC   MW   1651   1905   15½"x22"
  Ex J Scowcroft and Co Ltd
  Scrapped after June 1948

EDWARD   0-6-0ST   IC   MW   1652   1905   15½"x22"
  Ex J Scowcroft and Co Ltd
  Scrapped by 1938

                                          4wDM   RH   244580 1946   48DS Class
  New
  To Ince Forge 1953

Ince Forge

Before 1943   Ince Forge Co Ltd
1943 to c1960   Ince Forge Co Ltd (subsidiary of William Parks (Forgemasters) Ltd)
Later   Parks Forge Ltd
Later   Gullick Dobson Ltd
Rail traffic ceased c1972

Two second hand locomotives for sale, November 1866 (Engineer 23-11-1866)

                                    0-6-0 tank loco   12"
  For sale new, April 1883, £530 (MM 2-4-1883)

Ince in the Twentieth Century

                                    0-6-0 tank loco   11"
For sale new, April 1883, £500 (MM 3-4-1883)

                                    0-4-0TGV   BP   1886   (2) 7¾"x11" 2'6"
Ex Bury, Rochdale and Oldham Tramways Company in 1905
To Wm Park (Forgemasters) Ltd with site
To British Transport Commission, Crewe by Nov 1954

                                    0-4-0TGV   BP   1886   (2) 7¾"x11" 2'6"
Ex Bury, Rochdale and Oldham Tramways Company in 1905

                                    0-4-0TGV   BP   1886   (2) 7¾"x11" 2'6"
Ex Bury, Rochdale and Oldham Tramways Company in 1905

The above three locos were numbered by BR&OTC in the series from 83 to 86 and had Beyer, Peacock works numbers between 2733 and 2736. They were given the names ANT, BEE and BUG at Ince Forge, although not necessarily in that order
One of these locomotives was offered for sale by the Ince Forge Co Ltd in June 1907

                                    4wDM   RH   244580   1946   48DS Class
Ex Rose Bridge Collieries Ltd in 1953
To Live Steam Preservation Group, about 1973

Church Iron Works

c1900 to 1906   W and J Ellison
1909 to 1936   Church Iron Works Co Ltd

BLANCHE   0-4-0ST   OC   P   505   1893   10"x14"
Believed to have been transferred from Albion Ironworks for use at Church Ironworks, probably after 1920

Ince Waggon Works

From 1883   Ince Waggon and Ironworks Co Ltd
  Subsidiary of Central Wagon Co Ltd from 1933
  Works closed c 1980

                                    0-4-0ST   OC   MW   12"   3'0"
For Sale August 1895 (MM 1-8-1895)

                                    0-4-0ST   OC   BH   12"x18"   3'2"
For Sale November 1895 (MM 1-11-1895)

                                    0-6-0ST   IC   HE   32   1868   13"x18"   3'1"
New to Leather, Smith and Company, Portsmouth
Ex C Chambers, contractor, by March 1895
Possibly the locomotive for sale September 1906 (MG 1-9-1906)

                                    0-4-0ST   MW   469   1873   12"x18"
New to W Ramsden, Shakerley Colliery
Ex Thomas Mitchell and Sons, Bolton, January 1901
Believed scrapped about 1922

Ince in the Twentieth Century

JOHN BULL 0-6-0ST IC MW 516 1875 13"x18" 3'6"
   New to Scott and Edwards, Melmerby
   Ex Holme and King
   Believed scrapped about 1929

FRENCH 0-4-0ST OC MW 1582 1902 9½"x14" 2'9¾"
   New to Derwent Valley Water Board
   Ex Albright and Wilson,Oldbury,
   Scrapped about 1943

Central Wagon Works

1907 to 1911   Chorley Wagon Co Ltd
1911 to c1980   Central Wagon Co Ltd

Two six-wheeled coupled locos for sale, January 1925 (CG 30-1-1925)

   4wDM RH 183764 1937 44/48HP Class
   Ex G E Simm (Machinery) Ltd, Sheffield,1958, previously Harrison Brothers (England) Ltd, Middlesbrough.
   Disposed of about 1969

   0-4-0DM JF 22061 1938 40HP
   Ex Ministry of Supply, Eskmeals, about 1959
   Disposed of about 1969

   0-4-0DM JF 22991 1942 150HP
   Ex F Watkins (Boilers) Ltd,1964, originally R O F, Rotherwas
   Disposed of about 1969

18458 4wDH TH 140v 1964
   Ex Osborne-Hadfield Steel Founders Ltd, East Hecla Works, Sheffield, about May 1969
   To National Coal Board, Welbeck Colliery, August 1973

Thompson and Company

Most of the information given below comes from lists compiled by the Industrial Locomotive Society and the Industrial Railway Society. Except in the case of locomotives marked with a double asterisk (**), we have been unable to obtain independent evidence that the locomotives at any time passed through the hands of Thompson and Company

   0-4-0ST OC P 895 1901 14"x20"
   Ex Thomas and William Latham, Rose Bridge Colliery, between July 1911 and February 1912
   To Francis Morton and Co Ltd, Garston, between February 1913 and July 1913.

JANE 0-4-0ST OC MW 702 1878 14"x18" 3'0"
   Ex Worsley Mesnes Colliery Co Ltd, 1930
   Hired to Blainscough Colliery Co Ltd, Coppull 1934

GLADYS 0-6-0ST OC FW 342 1877 13"x20" 3'6"
   Ex Scot Lane Coal Co Ltd
   Hired to Bickerstaffe Collieries Ltd,1934,
   Hired to Blainscough Colliery Co Ltd, 1934
   Hired to Ince Waggon and Ironworks Co Ltd, 1934

Ince in the Twentieth Century

                        0-6-0T   IC   HE   1151   1914   15½"x20"   3'4"
    Ex J Roscoe and Sons, Peel Hall Colliery, KING GEORGE V, 1948
    Another version is that this locomotive was HE 953 of 1907, ex Peel Hall Colliery EDWARD VII

**   4wDM   RH   349032   1953   48DS Class
    Ex North Wales Wagon Co Ltd, Queensferry, Flints, October 1967
    Used as yard shunter and sold or scrapped between May 1983 and July 1985

Hough and Sons Ltd, Boilermakers and Machinery Merchants

Most of the information given below comes from lists compiled by the Industrial Locomotive Society and the Industrial Railway Society. Except in the case of locomotives marked with a double asterisk (**), we have been unable to obtain independent evidence that the locomotives at any time passed through the hands of Hough and Sons Ltd.

    GLADYS   0-6-0ST   OC   FW   342   1877   13"x20"   3'6"
      Ex Holme and King
      To Scot Lane Colliery Co Ltd, 1914

    FRECKLETON   0-6-0ST   IC   MW   1155   1890   14"x20"   3'6"
                                Rbt 1921
      Ex Holme and King
      Reputed to have been sold to White Moss Coal Co Ltd

    PRINCE   0-6-0ST   IC   P   876   1900   16"x22"
      Ex Pemberton Colliery Co Ltd, Pemberton 1929

    KING   0-4-0ST   OC   AB   1448   1919   14"x22"   3'5"
      Ex Bromilow, Foster and Co Ltd, Ashtons Green, 1930
      Hired to Blainscough Colliery Co Ltd, Coppull, 1933
      Hired to Ince Waggon and Ironworks Co Ltd, Ince, 1933 to 1934
      To Chamber Colliery Co Ltd, Audenshaw, 1934

    QUEEN   0-4-0ST   OC   AB   1784   1923   14"x22"   3'5"
      Ex Bromilow, Foster and Co Ltd, Ashtons Green, 1930
      To Digby Colliery Co Ltd 1932

    ** WINSTANLEY   0-4-0ST   OC   AB   1465   1916   14"x22"   3'5"
      Ex Winstanley Collieries Ltd
      Repaired at Rose Bridge Colliery and subsequently stored there

    TOMLINSON   0-6-0ST   OC   AB   1088   1906   15"x22"   3'5"
      Ex Ellerbeck Collieries Ltd 1933
      Reputedly to West Leigh Colliery Co Ltd, 1933, possibly on hire

    JAMES   0-6-0ST   OC   HL   2285   1895   14"x20"   3'6"
      Ex Blainscough Colliery Co Ltd
      Reputedly to West Leigh Colliery Co Ltd, 1931, possibly on hire

    VULCAN   0-4-0ST
      Reputed to have been repaired at Ince Waggon and Ironworks premises

    MARION   0-4-0ST
      Reputed to have been repaired at Ince Waggon and Ironworks premises

LEIGH
Reputed to have been repaired at Ince Waggon and Ironworks premises

** BAGHDAD   0-4-0ST   OC   P   914   1901   10"x14"   2'6"
Ex Forsters Glass Co Ltd, St Helens,
Repaired at Ince Waggon and Ironworks premises and subsequently stored there. Noted there March 1940

BESS   0-4-0ST   OC   HL   3933   1937   14"x22"   3'6"
Ex Pemberton Colliery Co Ltd, about 1946
To Pilkington Bros Ltd, St Helens

** KENYON   0-4-0ST   OC   BH   296   1875   12"x19"   3'2"
                   Rbt VF 1936
Repaired at Rose Bridge Colliery site during 1945 on behalf of the owners, William Evans and Co (Manchester) Ltd, Widnes

** ASBESTOS   0-4-0ST   OC   HL   2780   1909   14"x22"   3'6"
Repaired at Rose Bridge Colliery site during 1947 on behalf of the owners, Turners Asbestos Cement Co Ltd, Trafford Park

** SCOBRIT   0-4-0ST   OC   HL   3491   1921   14"x22"   3'6"
Ex Southern Oil Co Ltd, Trafford Park, SCOBRIT, 1948
Repaired at Ravenhead Brickworks, Upholland
To Forsters Glass Co Ltd, St Helens, 1949

References to Chapter 8

1	WO 11-3-1905	2	WO 17-12-1910
3	WO 2-12-1911	4	WO 20-8-1910
5	CG 29-7-1910	6	WO 22-10-1910
7	CG 28-10-1910	8	CG 16-6-1911
9	WO 4-11-1911	10	WO 11-11-1911
11	WO 4-4-1914	12	Companies House Records
13	WO 30-6-1923		

14   "The Wigan Steam Tram Engine" – Charles W Reed – *Journal of Stephenson Locomotive Society* October 1958
15   *The Manchester Bury Rochdale and Oldham Steam Tramway* – W G S Hyde – The Transport Publishing Company, Glossop n.d. about 1980
16   "The Wigan Steam Tram Engine" – Charles W Reed – *Journal of Stephenson Locomotive Society*, October 1958

17	MM 28-6-1907	18	WEx 28-1-1949
19	WEx 4-2-1949	20	WEx 13-11-1886

21   *A New Alphabetical and Classified Directory of the Boroughs of Bolton, Bury and Wigan, with the Parishes of Dean and Leigh* – William Whellan and Company, Manchester, 1853
22   *Royal National Commercial Directory and Topography of the County of Lancaster* – Isaac Slater, Manchester, 1871
23   WRO DD IN 1/7
24   *Wigan* – published by County Borough of Wigan – n.d. about 1970

25	WO 9-6-1906	26	WO 22-12-1906
27	WO 10-7-1909	28	WRO DDX E1 169/17

29   *Register of Defunct and Other Companies Removed from the Stock Exchange Year Book* – Stock Exchange Year Book Publishing Co Ltd, 1959

30	Abstract in authors' possession	31	MG 1-9-1906
32	Information supplied by Mr Tony Watts	33	WO 15-6-1989
34	WO 7-9-1907		

35   Line Plan of Springs Branch Railway LNWR, 1915 – 2 chains to 1 inch – at BRPB, Manchester Office

Ince in the Twentieth Century

36	CG 30-1-1925	37	WO 9-2-1877
38	West Lancashire Wagon Co Ltd Directors' Reports for period 1875 to 1881 – copies in authors' possession		
39	WO 31-10-1879	40	WO 7-11-1879
41	WO 26-11-1879	42	WO 7-11-1888
43	Information supplied by Mr Ted Cheetham, following discussions with Mr Alan Calderbank on 7-2-1990 and 14-2 1990		
44	*The Wigan Directory* – John Worrall, Blackburn 1869		
45	Companies House Records	46	MG 5-3-1913
47	WRO DDX El 211/1	48	WO 13-6-1869

CHAPTER 9

PEARSON AND KNOWLES INCE COLLIERIES

The previous three chapters have studied the growth and decline of the coal mines and other industries in Higher and Lower Ince. We now move a little further south, to look at a group of collieries, still mostly within the Ince boundary, which are associated with the firm of Pearson and Knowles. We shall also deal with the various works set up in in this area by the wagon building and repairing industry.

Pearson and Knowles' Ince Collieries up to 1860

Thomas Pearson, a Liverpool millwright and engineer, for several years followed the business of general merchant at Dale Street in Liverpool. He subsequently became a member of his father's firm – Thomas Pearson and Company, Engineers and Boiler Makers, Boundary Street, Liverpool. His first ventures into coal mining appear to have been at Barley Brook, on the north-western outskirts of Wigan and at Stone Lane in Hindley[1].

His connections with Ince commenced in the early 1840s when he sank the Springs Pit, alongside the Springs Branch. He also built coke ovens on an adjacent site. At about the same time he took over the colliery near Ince Old Hall that had previously been worked by H and E Hilton and which we have already referred to in Chapter 6. Known as the Ince Hall Colliery in Hilton's time, it was later referred to as the Crow Orchard Colliery, or sometimes as Pearson and Knowles' Arley Colliery.

A siding from Crow Orchard to the North Union main line had already been provided during Hilton's period of ownership. It appears that Pearson was also planning a line of his own which would provide an independent outlet to the Leeds and Liverpool Canal. Early in 1845, he applied to the canal company to erect a pier head near Britannia Bridge. The request was refused on the grounds that it would interfere with the towpath and the scheme seems to have been dropped[2].

By 1864, the connection with the North Union had been extended as an independent track, parallel to the main running lines, giving access to the sidings at Springs Branch Junction[3]. Further details of the railway layout at Crow Orchard are shown on the Deposited Plans for the L&Y Wigan Loop Line, dated November 1861[4], and for the LNWR Bamfurlong to Boars Head Diversion and Widening[5], dated of November 1874.

Thomas Knowles, who had been appointed overlooker at the collieries in 1848, was taken into partnership in 1854[6,7]. Hindley Hall Colliery was opened by the new partnership in the late 1850s. It first appears in the Mines List in 1857 as being worked by Blackie and Knowles. From 1859 onwards it is shown in the occupation of Pearson and Knowles. A mining lease, commencing on 1st May 1858, associated with this colliery, was granted by John de Trafford to John Pearson and others[8].

Pearson and Knowles Ince Collieries

A private railway was constructed across Amberswood Common to link up with Springs Colliery and the London and North Western Railway system. This new line crossed the Moss Hall Coal Company's railway to Low Hall on the level on Amberswood Common.

Thomas Pearson is known to have been working his own coal trains over the North Union Railway to Preston, and possibly elsewhere, from the early 1840s. There is a record that in March 1841 he purchased a Planet Class 2-2-0 from the Liverpool and Manchester Railway[9]. Built by Fenton, Murray and Company in 1831, it had been No 19 VULCAN on the Liverpool and Manchester.

On 7th September 1841, Mr Pearson's locomotive ASA collided with a stage coach on a level crossing at Euxton. The engine was running tender first and hauling a train of seven empty wagons from Preston to Springs Colliery[10,11]. In the subsequent official report on the accident[12], ASA was described as a six wheeled engine, so it was clearly not the one which had come from the Liverpool and Manchester Railway. ASA was stated to be limited to 15 mph. The weights were given as locomotive 13 tons, tender, half full, 5 tons and empty wagons 43 to 44 cwt each.

There was another accident to one of Mr Pearson's trains on 27th February 1844. As it was proceeding up Coppull Bank with empty wagons from Preston, it was run into from behind by a train belonging to Richard Hollinshead Blundell, headed by his locomotive ACE OF TRUMPS[13]. The brakesman on one of the trains was fatally injured and he was conveyed to his home at Golborne on Pearson's engine.

In addition to his colliery interests, Thomas Pearson had continued in business at the Liver Foundry in Parliament Street Liverpool. It was here that he turned his hand to locomotive building, LIVER being completed in 1844 to work the coal trains from his collieries. Before being put into traffic, it was tested on the 1 in 100 incline between Wigan and Boars Head. With a boiler pressure of 70 psi, it successfully hauled a train of 31 wagons weighing 6 tons each[14].

It was given a further trial on 7th October 1844 when it left for Preston with 40 empty wagons weighing 240 tons. It climbed Boars Head incline with great ease and at Coppull 11 more wagons were attached to give a total weight of 306 tons. It was stopped and started on the incline beyond Coppull without difficulty. LIVER was stated to have six coupled wheels 4'7" diameter, 14" x 20" cylinders and a working pressure of 60 psi. It weighed, with water, 14 tons 16 cwt[15].

On Monday, 3rd February 1845, the locomotive men employed in working the trains from Springs Colliery were given a supper at the Victoria Hotel at Wigan. During the proceedings it was stated that LIVER had been most successful and, with Driver William Smith in charge, it had taken a train of forty wagons, weighing 260 tons, up Boars Head incline. It was also stated that the locomotive DAVID, which had just been given thorough repairs and alterations, would be likely to realise the expectations that had been formed on her trials that Monday[16]. Apart from this tantalising reference, we have no information about DAVID.

The next we hear of LIVER is at Preston in 1846. On 17th August a train of 32 coal wagons, headed by Mr Pearson's locomotive LIVER, was run into by a train from Fleetwood[17].

In 1847, Thomas Pearson was trying to sell some of his engines. On 12th January it was reported to the Northern Division Locomotive Committee[18] of the London and North Western Railway that he had offered three of his locomotives to Mr Chapman, Manager of the North Union line. Mr Trevithick was ordered to examine the locomotives and report back, but nothing seems to have materialised.

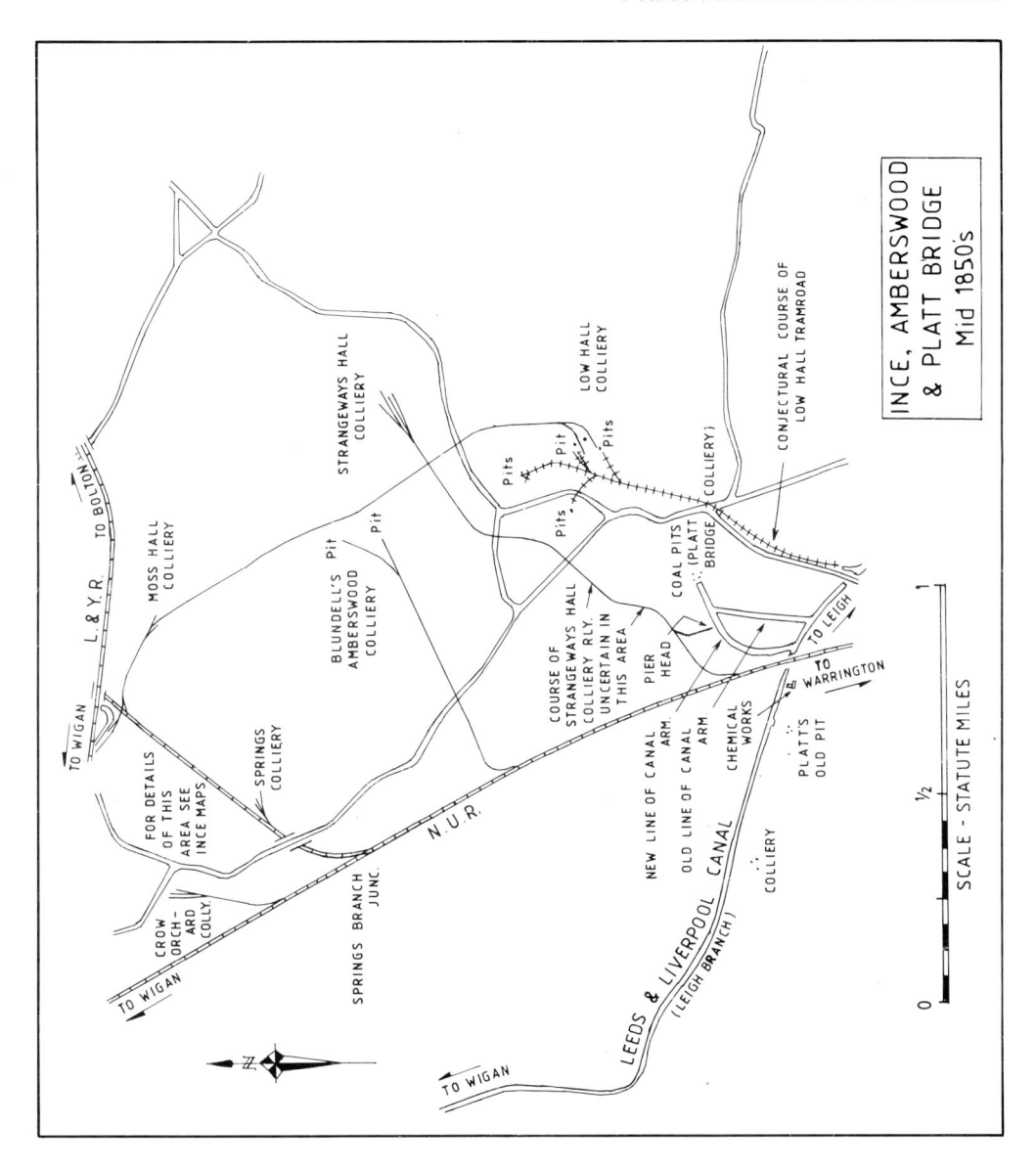

Pearson and Knowles Ince Collieries

Pearson and Knowles Ince Collieries

In August 1847 two locomotives were advertised for sale by private treaty. One was described as well adapted for luggage or heavy trains, the other for passenger work [19]. Two years later, on 25th April 1849, Pearson held a sale of surplus plant which included a four coupled, six wheeled locomotive, described as having 4'7" driving wheels and 14" x 20" cylinders [20].

Pearson and Knowles's trains continued to run over the main lines for another ten years or so. On 17th October 1850 LIVER was involved in another accident, this time near Boars Head, when working from Preston to Springs Branch [21]. The LNWR Working Timetable for January 1857 [22] records that the firm's engines were then still working between Springs Branch Junction and Preston.

Pearson and Knowles' Ince Collieries from 1860 to 1900

In 1863 Pearson and Knowles started to sink the first of the pits at the Ince Moss Colliery on the west side of the North Union line. This proved to be a most successful venture, and there were eventually six shafts at the site. The colliery was originally served by sidings from the North Union Railway main line. It also had access to the Leigh Branch of the Leeds and Liverpool Canal, where a tip for loading barges was installed at an early date.

The connection to the North Union was provided under an agreement of 23rd April 1863 [23]. The sidings do not seem to have been completed for another year or so, since they are not shown on the 1864 Line Plan of the North Union Railway [3]. Notes on the Sidings Diagram [23] and on the 1956 Line Plan of the North Union [24] suggest that the branch from the main line to the colliery had been built by the North Union company on land it had leased from W G Walmesley under a conveyance dated 30th March 1865. The leasehold interest in the branch was later sold to Pearson and Knowles.

In 1873, the Pearson and Knowles partnership amalgamated with the Dallam Forge Company and the Warrington Wire Iron Company. The Pearson and Knowles Coal and Iron Co Ltd was registered in 1874 to take over the combined business [25]. Pearson and Knowles also bought up Rylands Brothers, an old established Warrington wire manufacturing firm which had been founded in 1805. Rylands Brothers, however, continued to trade under their own name [26].

Springs Colliery appears to have closed around 1870 and is not shown in the Mines Lists after 1872. The central workshops, which Pearson and Knowles had established here, were retained until about 1905. They were then replaced by new facilities at Ince Moss. In 1892 [27], there were blacksmiths shops, machine and fitting shops, joiners shops and a wagon repair shop on the Springs Colliery site. At that date Pearson and Knowles were stated to own 5 locomotives and 1275 wagons.

Developments at Ince Moss Colliery continued during the latter part of the nineteenth century. An alternative rail outlet was provided when the Lancashire and Yorkshire Company's Pemberton Loop line was constructed. Pearson and Knowles built a railway half mile in length, northwards from the colliery to Westwood Park Sidings. The connection here was provided under an agreement dated 19th October 1887. Originally single, the colliery company's line was doubled, according to the Sidings Schedules, in 1898.

Sinking of a sixth pit, Daisy Pit, was started in 1892 and coal was first wound in July 1896 [28]. There were alterations to the railway system as a consequence. The internal siding accommodation was extended and a new connection was made with the Lancashire Union line at Ince Moss Junction, under an agreement of 31st March 1896 [29].

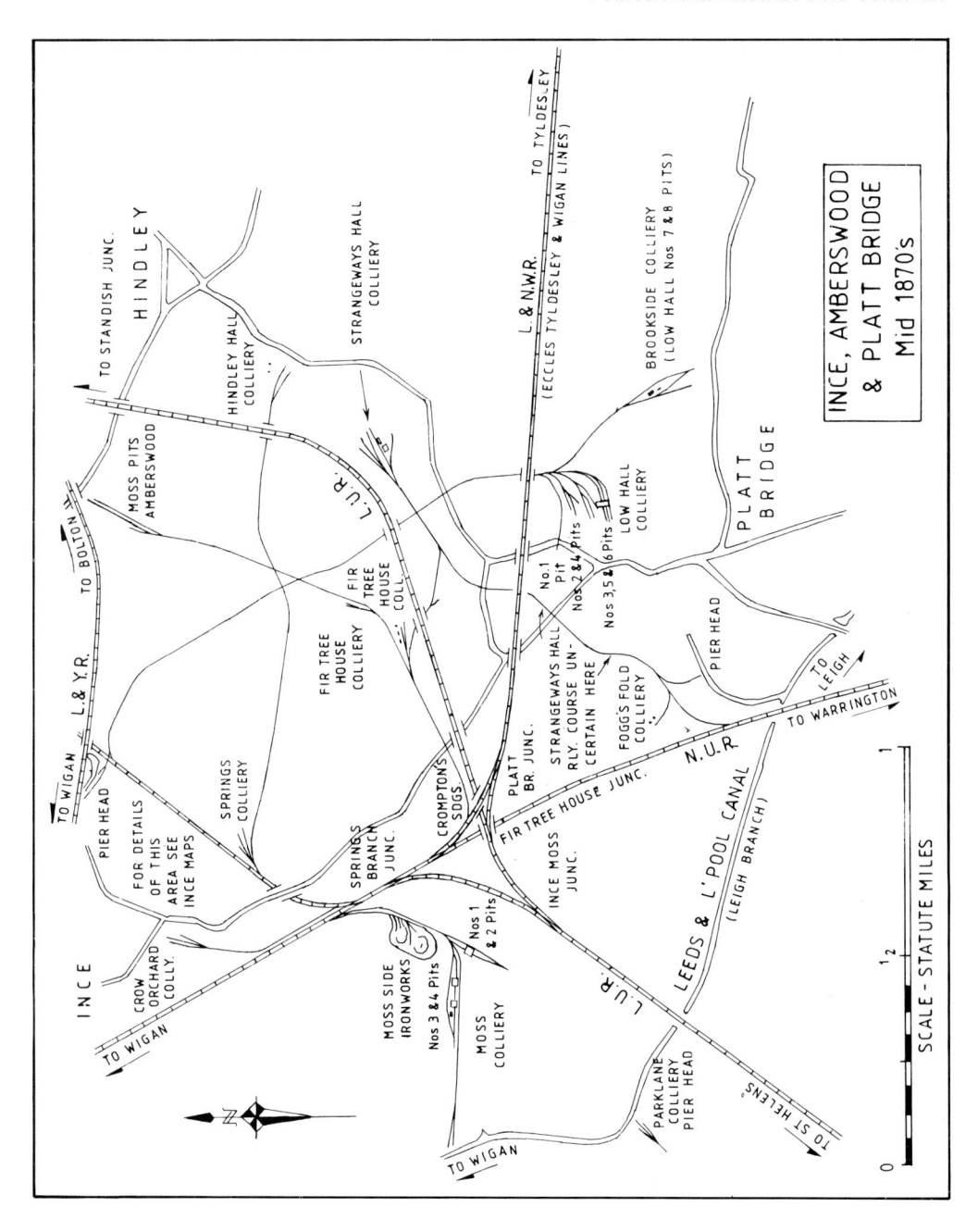

Pearson and Knowles Ince Collieries

INCE, AMBERSWOOD & PLATT BRIDGE
Mid 1870's

Pearson and Knowles Ince Collieries

Crow Orchard Colliery closed in the late 1890s, the Mines Lists for 1898 recording that Pearson and Knowles' Ince Hall Nos 1 and 2 Pits had been abandoned. By 1907, when the 2nd Edition of the 25" Map was surveyed, both colliery and adjacent coke ovens were derelict. The branch from the North Union line continued in use, serving a landsale coal depot.

Prior to this, the Crow Orchard dirt heap had been at least partially removed to provide fill for the construction of the Lancashire and Yorkshire Railway Company's Pemberton Loop Line. The contractors, Monk and Newell, were granted permission by the Ince Local Board on 2nd April 1888 to lay a level crossing over Warrington Road between Pearson and Knowles Arley Pits (alias Crow Orchard) and the construction site [30].

With the opening of the new pits at Ince Moss and Hindley Hall, engines were needed for shunting on the internal railway system. The first of these was a 2-4-0 tank locomotive, with the water tank between the frames, supplied by the Whitehaven firm of Fletcher, Jennings and Company in 1861. A more conventional six coupled side tank came from the same manufacturers in 1867. The 1861 engine carried the name LIVER, so we surmise that the old tender engine built at the Pearson's Liverpool works had been disposed of by this date.

The next locomotive which we have on record was delivered in 1875 from Sharp, Stewart and Company of Manchester. It was a four coupled saddle tank and was numbered 2 in the Pearson and Knowles list. No 3 came in 1888 from the Vulcan Foundry, of Newton le Willows. Originally a six coupled side tank locomotive, it subsequently seems to have been rebuilt with saddle tanks.

LIVER, the second locomotive to bear this name. Built by Fletcher, Jennings and Company, of Whitehaven, in 1861.
Frank Jones Collection

With the expansion of Ince Moss Colliery towards the end of the century, further motive power was required. Two identical six coupled saddle tanks were purchased from Hudswell, Clarke and Company of Leeds, one in 1894 and the other in 1895. They were numbered 5 and 6 respectively. We deduce that there must also have been a locomotive No 4 in the Pearson and Knowles list, but we have no record of what it was.

The final locomotives to come new to Ince Moss were three six coupled saddle tanks from Robert Stephenson and Company. They arrived in 1897, 1900 and 1901, and carried the numbers 7, 1 and 2 respectively. The last two presumably replaced the earlier engines with the same numbers.

Ince Moss Iron Works

Thomas Pearson was one of the proprietors of the Dallam Forge Company, which was formed in the mid 1860s to build puddling furnaces and rolling mills at Warrington. The Dallam Forge Company constructed a second ironworks on a site adjacent to the Ince Moss Colliery and this was opened on 16th January 1872[31]. A separate siding connection was provided with the North Union line, immediately to to the north of that serving the Ince Moss Colliery complex.

As noted earlier, the Dallam Forge Company was absorbed into the Pearson and Knowles Coal and Iron Co Ltd in 1874 and both the Warrington and Ince works passed to the new firm. Unlike the Dallam Forge at Warrington, the Ince ironworks does not seem to have been a success. After a series of temporary closures towards the end of the century[32,33,34] it finally closed in March 1901[35]. The site was subsequently absorbed into that of Ince Moss Colliery.

We do not know whether the iron works had its own locomotive or whether the colliery engines did the shunting.

Pearson and Knowles' Ince Collieries in the Twentieth Century

By the beginning of the century only the Moss Pits were in full operation. The Springs Pit and the Crow Orchard Pits had already ceased production. Hindley Hall Colliery closed in February 1904[36] and the railway linking it with the Springs Branch was abandoned.

Pearson and Knowles had already started to look elsewhere to expand their mining activities. Sinking started at the Chisnall Hall Colliery, near Coppull, in June 1891[37] and coal was first produced in January 1900[38]. In 1907 a controlling interest was acquired in the Moss Hall Coal Co Ltd and the Wigan Junction Colliery Co Ltd[39].

Chisnall Hall Colliery appears in Chapter 24. We shall be dealing with later history of the Moss Hall Coal Company and the Wigan Junction Colliery in Chapter 12.

In 1910, the Partington Steel and Iron Co Ltd was formed[40], with Pearson and Knowles as major shareholders. The new iron and steelworks which the company built alongside the Manchester Ship Canal near Irlam was opened in 1912[41].

At the Ince Moss Colliery, No 1 Pit closed about 1920 and No 2 Pit in 1927 or 1928. From the first world period onwards, only three locomotives seem to have been required for shunting here. According to old employees, No 2 and No 7 were sent to the former Moss Hall Company's railway system and based at the engine shed at Low Hall.

Pearson and Knowles Ince Collieries

One of the two large Hudswell, Clarke locomotives supplied for use at Ince Moss Colliery. Here seen at Low Hall shed on 20th April 1952, during a visit by a group of industrial railway enthusiasts.

Industrial Railway Society, Ken Cooper Collection

In 1930 there was a wide ranging amalgamation of coal and iron interests in South Lancashire, involving the Pearson and Knowles Coal and Iron Co Ltd and its subsidiary colliery concerns, the Wigan Coal and Iron Co Ltd and the Partington Steel and Iron Co Ltd. The iron and steelworks at Kirkless, Partington and Warrington were taken over by the Lancashire Steel Corporation Ltd, while the collieries became the property of the Wigan Coal Corporation Ltd. The new companies were registered on 1st August 1930.

Following the formation of the Wigan Coal Corporation, there were a several transfers of engines between Ince Moss and Low Hall. Such information as we have is given in the summary at the end of the chapter, based on lists compiled by the Wigan Coal Corporation at the beginning and the end of 1932, about 1941 and in April 1943.

The Vulcan Foundry engine, No 3, was taken out of service before 1932 and does not appear in the list dated 21st January 1932. The Hudswell, Clarke and Robert Stephenson engines remained in operation, either at Ince Moss or Low Hall.

The Westwood Park Sidings, on the former Lancashire and Yorkshire Railway's Pemberton Loop line, were closed towards the end of 1944. Thereafter, all coal was sent out over the former London and North Western Railway. According to the Sidings Schedules, the connections at Westwood Park were not finally removed until 31st August 1952.

The coal yard on the old Crow Orchard site survived to be taken over by Lancashire Associated Collieries Ltd on 1st July 1935 and became the property of the National Coal Board on 1st January 1947. It closed a few years later and the lines beyond the railway company's

Pearson and Knowles Ince Collieries

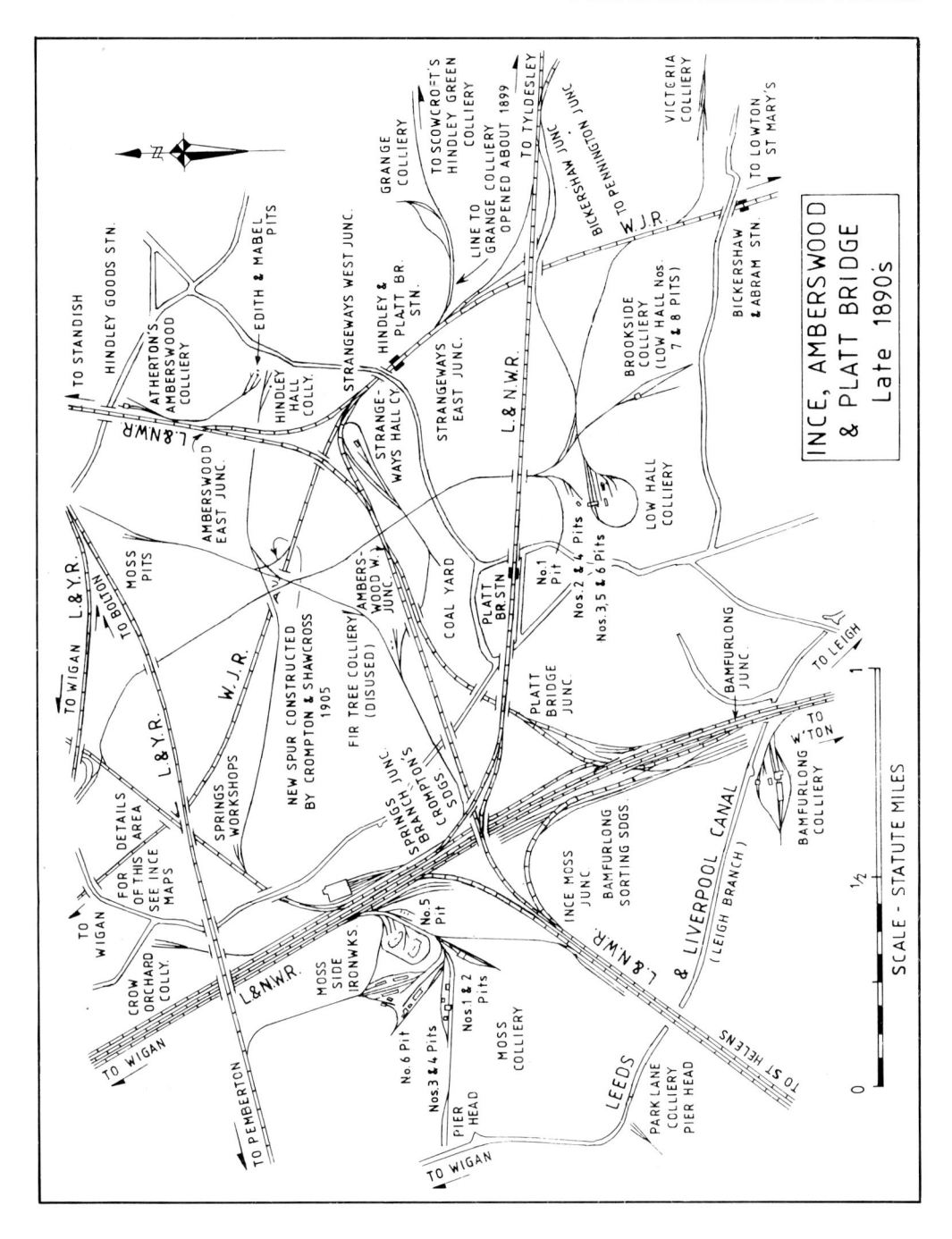

Pearson and Knowles Ince Collieries

One of the three locomotives supplied by Robert Stephenson and Co Ltd for use at Ince Moss. At work on 10th April 1956. D.L. Chatfield

boundary had been lifted by 1956[24]. Latterly, the railway company's locomotives worked the traffic over the sidings from the main line to the coal yard.

On Vesting Day, the Ince Moss locomotive stock comprised the Hudswell, Clarke engine, No 5, and the Robert Stephenson engines Nos 2 and 7. The last mentioned was actually at John Pit at the time, deputising for another engine which was under repair.

Following nationalisation, locomotive transfers between collieries in the Wigan Area took place at frequent intervals and we have provided such information as we have available about these movements in the summary at the end of the chapter.

Ince Moss Colliery was closed in November 1962. By this date a number of locomotives from other collieries in the Wigan Area had been sent there and were stored out of use. The intention seems to have been to set up a locomotive repair shop, replacing that at Kirkless[42]. The project was dropped and the majority of the engines were broken up in the period up to February 1966.

A note added to the 1956 Line Plan[24] states that the siding agreement in respect of the connection with the Lancashire Union line at Ince Moss Junction was terminated on 31st October 1966. We believe that the agreement relating to the connection with the North Union line at Springs Branch Junction was terminated at the same time.

Wigan Wagon Co Ltd

The Wigan Wagon Company was formed in 1873 or 1874 and set up a works, near to the

Springs Colliery site, alongside Pearson and Knowles railway to the Hindley Hall Colliery. In May 1874 it was reported that one shed had been erected, 186 ft. long and 20 ft. wide, to hold ten wagons, and that another was to be built [43].

The original shops seem to have been on the south side of Pearson and Knowles' line. There were extensions in 1884, again on the south side of the line, and the new railway system in the works was reported complete on 2nd December of that year [44].

The first directors included Mr Walker, Mr Israel Knowles, Mr William Crompton [45], Mr John Seddon [46]. Mr William Lamb [47] and Mr George Caldwell [48] appear to have joined later.

The 1st edition of the 25" map, surveyed in 1888 to 1892, shows that the Wigan Wagon Company's traffic was conveyed over Pearson and Knowles' railway to reach the Springs Branch. In the late 1890s an independent line was constructed, the new connection with the Springs Branch being covered by an agreement dated 28th August 1896 [49].

The Wigan Wagon Company was taken over by Wagon Repairs Ltd, a firm with branches throughout the country, although in September 1945 [50] the Wigan Wagon Company was still trading under its own name. The works survived until about 1960, when it closed as a result of the severely curtailed carriage of freight by British Rail.

A note added to the 1915 Line Plan of the Springs Branch [49] states that the private sidings agreement was terminated on 31st December 1965. The works was subsequently demolished.

In the late 1930s a small four wheeled internal combustion locomotive was used here. It was replaced at the end of the second world war by a four wheeled diesel locomotive. This came new from Ruston and Hornsby of Lincoln, from where it was despatched 20th September 1945. It had the name LITTLE AUDREY painted on.

One locomotive list which we have seen suggests that previously the wagon works had used a small four coupled saddle tank named EDITH. Built by Hawthorn, Leslie and Company of Newcastle in 1886, this engine had been supplied to the Ansley Hall Coal and Iron Co Ltd, in Warwickshire. It was reputed to have been sold by this firm to the Wigan Wagon Co Ltd, but we have been unable to obtain confirmation that the locomotive actually worked at Ince.

T Burnett and Co Ltd

In the early years of the present century, Pearson and Knowles vacated their central workshops at the old Springs Colliery. T Burnett and Co Ltd, a firm with head offices in Doncaster, then leased part of the site from the Walmesley Estate for a wagon works and probably took over some of the existing buildings. Pearson and Knowles' original connection with the Springs Branch was retained, a new agreement between the London and North Western Railway and T Burnett and Co Ltd being signed on 28th December 1905 [51].

According to the Sidings Schedules, Burnett's tenancy was terminated by the Walmesley Estate in 1937. The District Goods Manager at Warrington gave the firm notice to quit the land they leased from the railway company and to terminate the private sidings agreement. A note dated 1939 recorded that all the internal sidings had been removed. The works seems to have been demolished shortly afterwards and does not appear on 1948 revision of the 6" map.

Pearson and Knowles Ince Collieries

W R Davies and Co Ltd

The Sidings Schedules record that Messrs W R Davies, in November 1906, rented some of the old colliery buildings, which we believe were situated alongside the Springs Branch, for wagon repairs. W R Davies and Co Ltd and T Burnett and Co Ltd shared the same connection with the Springs Branch and there seems to have been no separate agreement between Davies and the railway company.

A note in the Sidings Schedules, dated December 1932, stated that W R Davies and Co Ltd were in liquidation. The works seems later to have been taken over by Wagon Repairs Ltd, as there is reference to a letter of 21st December 1934 from Burnett and Co Ltd to the LMS Railway Agent at Wigan. This asked for instructions to be given that no further wagons should be placed in their sidings for any other people. The lease with Wagon Repairs had been finished with and if anybody went over their sidings it would be treated as trespass. The Goods Agent issued instructions accordingly and we hear no more of either W R Davies or Wagon Repairs on this site.

LOCOMOTIVE SUMMARY

Pearson and Knowles Ince Collieries

c1845 to 1854	Thomas Pearson
1854 to 1874	Pearson and Knowles partnership
1874 to 1930	Pearson and Knowles Coal and Iron Co Ltd
1930 to 1946	Wigan Coal Corporation Ltd
After 1-1-1947	National Coal Board

                                         2-2-0   FM   1831
Ex Liverpool and Manchester Railway, 19 VULCAN, in March 1841

ASA   6 wheeled
  In accident on North Union Railway 7-9-1841

LIVER	0-6-0	Thos Pearson, Liver Foundry					
		Liverpool			1844	14"x20"	4'7"
DAVID	0-6-0 ?						
LIVER	2-4-0WT	OC	FJ	22	1861	15"x22"	4'8"
New							
Scrapped or sold							
	0-6-0T	OC	FJ	74	1867	14"x20"	4'0"
New							
Scrapped or sold							
No 2	0-4-0ST	OC	SS	2472	1875	12"x20"	
New							
Scrapped or sold							

3		0-6-0T	IC	VF	1237	1888	15"x22"	4'0"

New
Converted to 0-6-0ST
Scrapped or sold before 1932

No 5		0-6-0ST	IC	HC	422	1894	16"x22"	3'10"

New
To Wigan Coal Corporation Ltd 1930
To Low Hall before January 1932, returned after April 1943
To NCB at Ince Moss 1-1-1947

No 6		0-6-0ST	IC	HC	449	1895	16"x22"	3'11"

New
To Wigan Coal Corporation Ltd 1930 at Ince Moss
To Low Hall after 1943 and before April 1946
To NCB at Low Hall 1-1-1947

No 7		0-6-0ST	IC	RS	2848	1897	15"x20"	3'7"

New
Reputed to have gone to Low Hall during first World War
To Wigan Coal Corporation Ltd 1930
At Ince Moss in January 1932
To Low Hall before 1941
To John Pit before 1-1-1947
To NCB 1-1-1947, at John Pit, Standish

No 1		0-6-0ST	IC	RS	2880	1900	15"x20"	3'7"

New
To Wigan Coal Corporation Ltd 1930 at Ince Moss
To Low Hall between 1941 and 1943
To N C B at Low Hall 1-1-1947

No 2		0-6-0ST	IC	RS	2992	1901	15"x20"	3'7"

New
Reputed to have gone to Low Hall during first World War
To Wigan Coal Corporation Ltd 1930, probably at Low Hall
To Ince Moss before March 1940
To NCB 1-1-1947 at Ince Moss

SOL		0-6-0ST	IC	WCI		1878	16"x20"	4'3"

Temporarily here in 1943 (At Clock Face in 1941 and on 1-1-1947)

JOHN		0-6-0ST	IC	PK		1911	16"x22"	4'0"

Temporarily here in 1946 (At Chisnall Hall in April 1943 and 1-1-1947)

Wigan Wagon Works

1874 to c1960   Wigan Wagon Co Ltd
   Latterly a subsidiary of Wagon Repairs Ltd

4wDM

LITTLE AUDREY		4wDM		RH	235515	1945	48DS Class

New, despatched from maker's works on 20-9-1945
To Wagon Repairs, Long Eaton Works, Derbyshire, about January 1964

Pearson and Knowles Ince Collieries

National Coal Board, Ince Moss Colliery

1947 to 1960   North Western Division, Wigan Area
1961 to 1965   North Western Division, West Lancashire Area
Ince Moss Colliery closed 1962, but premises retained as store until 1965

No 5   0-6-0ST   IC   HC   422   1894   16"x22"   3'10"
  To NCB at Ince Moss 1-1-1947
  To Low Hall by 4-1-1948
  Temporarily returned to Ince Moss mid 1952
  Scrapped at Low Hall 6-1959

No 6   0-6-0ST   IC   HC   449   1895   16"x22"   3'11"
  To NCB at Low Hall 1-1-1947
  Temporarily here from Low Hall during 1949

No 7   0-6-0ST   IC   RS   2848   1897   15"x20"   3'7"
  To NCB 1-1-1947, at John Pit, Standish
  Transferred from Standish to Ince Moss, after temporary work at Clock Face, by 18-6-1947
  To Kirkless Workshops during 1955 and scrapped there 11-1955

No 1   0-6-0ST   IC   RS   2880   1900   15"x20"   3'7"
  To NCB at Low Hall 1-1-1947
  To Ince Moss, from Dallam Forge, by 2-1952
  To Kirkless Workshops 18-4-1955, returned 14-12-1955
  To Kirkless Workshops 22-12-1958, returned 11-5-1959
  To Walkden Yard 11-1961 and scrapped there 3-1963

No 2   0-6-0ST   IC   RS   2992   1901   15"x20"   3'7"
  To NCB 1-1-1947 at Ince Moss
  To Kirkless Workshops 17-10-1953, returned 2-9-1954
  To Kirkless Workshops 14-2-1958 and scrapped there by 2-1959

PEMBERTON   0-4-0ST   OC   HL   3878   1936   14"x22"   3'6"
  From Pemberton 12-1947
  To Chisnall Hall end of 1950
  From Welch Whittle for store before 2-1960
  To East Lancashire Area 1-1961 and scrapped at William Pit, Whitehaven, 4-1969

No 2   0-6-0ST   IC   MW   1925   1917   14"x20"
  Temporarily here from Mains during 1951
  From Mains to Ince Moss by 4-1961
To Kirkless Workshops 29-8-1961 and then Standish. Sold from John Pit to Jose K Holt and Gordon 6-1965 and
  scrapped at their Chequerbent Yard 8-1965

No 1   0-6-0ST   IC   RS   2991   1900   15"x20"   3'7"
  Temporarily here from Mains during 1952 and 1953

ACHILLES   0-6-0ST   IC   HCR   217   1880   14"x20"   3'10½"
  From Kirkless Workshops 2-1955
  To Low Hall by 16-4-1955

WANTAGE   0-6-0ST   IC   NW   548   1898   16"x20"   4'3"
  From Standish at end of 1958
  Scrapped at Ince Moss 3-1963

Pearson and Knowles Ince Collieries

	4WDM		RH	338418	1953	88DS Class	

    From Alexandra by 11-1962
    Scrapped at Ince Moss 9-1965

11456	0-6-0ST	IC	BP	1989	1891	17½"x26"	4'6"

    Reb Hor 1896 from tender loco
    From Kirkless Workshops 1-4-1960
    To Parsonage 10-1961

BILL	0-6-0ST	IC	HE	1901	1938	15"x20"	3'7"

    From Low Hall February 1958
    To Walkden Yard 11-1961 and scrapped there 3-1963

LINDSAY	0-6-0ST	IC	WCI		1887	16"x20"	4'3"

    Temporarily here from Standish mid 1966

FAIRFIELD	0-4-0ST	OC	KS	4025	1919	15"x20"	3'6"

    From Haydock between 2-1961 and 12-1961
    To Ravenhead by 3-1962

LYON	0-6-0ST	IC	HE	1809	1936	15"x20"	3'7"

    From Parsonage 9 or 10-1961
    Scrapped at Ince Moss 2-1966

3'6" Gauge

	4wDM		RH	279629	1949	48DS Class

    Transferred from Kirkless Store to Ince Moss after 29-9-1963 and before 1964
    Scrapped or sold about 1965

References to Chapter 9

1. *Colliery Manager and Journal of Mining Engineering* 24-6-1887
2. Leeds and Liverpool Canal Company's Minutes 14-4-1845
3. Line Plan of North Union Railway, including Springs Branch – LNWR, 1864 – 2 chains to 1 inch –at BRPB, Manchester Office
4. LRO PDR 728
5. LRO PDR 994
6. BC 3-12-1883
7. WO 9-12-1883
8. LRO DDX Tr Box 84
9. *British Locomotive Catalogue 1825–1923, Vol 2A* – compiled by late Bertram Baxter – Moorland Publishing Co, Ashbourne, 1978
10. *Manc Courier* 11-9-1841
11. PP 11-9-1841
12. Parly Papers Vol XLIL p55
13. Parly Papers 1846 Vol XXXIV p8
14. MJ 5-10-1844
15. MJ 12-10-1844
16. PG 8-2-1845
17. PG 22-8-46
18. LNWR Northern Division Locomotive Committee Minutes 12-1-1847
19. Herepath 14-8-1847
20. PC 21-4-1849
21. BC 19-10-1850
22. PRO Rail 946/1
23. LNW Sdgs Diag No 93, dated December 1916
24. Line Plan of North Union Railway, Bamfurlong 4¼ mp to Boars Head 9 mp 1/1250 – British Railways, Euston, 1956 – at BRPB, Manchester Office
25. WO 15-5-1874
26. WO 5-10-1907
27. CG 16-12-1892
28. WO 25-7-96
29. LNW Sdgs Diag No 110, dated December 1916

Pearson and Knowles Ince Collieries

30	WRO DD IN 1/5	31	WO 22-1-1872
32	WO 15-6-1895	33	BJ 2-10-1895
34	WO 15-10-1898	35	WO 23-3-1901
36	WO 20-2-1904	37	WO 6-6-1891
38	WO 27-1-1900	39	WO 14-9-1907

40 *Register of Defunct and Other Companies Removed from the Stock Exchange Year Book* – Stock Exchange Year Book Publishing Co Ltd, 1959
41 WO 23-9-1912
42 *"Indian Summer at Kirkless"* by Cyril Golding – *Journal of the Industrial Locomotive Society*, Nov/Dec 1962 and Jan 1963
43 WO 29-5-1874
44 WO 26-12-1884
45 WO 29-5-1874
46 WO 10-10-1891
47 WO 11-12-1897
48 WO 27-10-1910
49 Line Plan of Springs Branch LNWR, 1915 – 2 chains to 1 inch – at BRPB Manchester Office
50 Ruston and Hornsby Ltd, documentation re new locomotive, June and Sept 1945 – copy in authors' possession
51 LNWR Sdgs Diag No 85, dated December 1916

CHAPTER 10

AMBERSWOOD AND STRANGEWAYS HALL

We continue our study of the collieries at Ince and now turn our attention to the area around Amberswood Common. Pits were sunk here in the 1840s by Richard Hollinshead Blundell, whom we have already met at Orrell and at Pemberton. The Amberswood mines were later worked by Crompton and Shawcross and we shall stray across the Hindley boundary in order to include the other collieries worked by this firm.

The maps showing the tramroads and railways serving the collieries worked by Blundell and by Crompton and Shawcross are in Chapter 9.

Blundell's Amberswood Colliery

In September 1839, Richard Hollinshead Blundell obtained a lease from William Gerrard Walmesley and, during the period up to 1842, sank a number of shallow pits which were collectively known as the Amberswood Colliery[1]. The 1st edition of the 1" map, surveyed in 1840 to 1842, shows that a private railway had been built to serve the colliery.

Originally the colliery line joined the North Union at a point about 600 yards south of Springs Branch Junction. The connection here was removed in the early 1860s, during the construction of the London and North Western Railway's Eccles, Tyldesley and Wigan line. A replacement was provided a short distance along the new line, at Fir Tree House Sidings. (Latterly, the signal box controlling the connection was known as Crompton's Sidings. The Sidings Schedules refer to the location as Fir Tree House Sidings up to the time of closure.)

In the early 1840s Blundell was working his own coal traffic to Preston over the North Union Railway. As recounted earlier, his locomotive, ACE OF TRUMPS, hauling a train of empty wagons from Preston to Ince, was involved in an accident near Coppull on 17th February 1844[2]. ACE OF TRUMPS was involved in another accident, at Preston, on 9th November 1849[3]. We think that another engine, TRIUMPH, belongs to the same period. All that we know about this was that its nameplate used to hang on the wall of the locomotive shed at Blundell's Pemberton Colliery.

The Liverpool and Manchester Railway Minutes for 2nd, 16th and 19th September 1844[4] record that Blundell was one of the colliery proprietors who were authorised to use their own locomotives between Parkside and Liverpool. The Earl of Crawford was refused similar facilities on the Liverpool and Manchester and he entered into an agreement in October 1842 whereby Blundell would haul up to 100 tons per day of the Earl's coal and cannel to Liverpool on payment of the appropriate toll[5].

It seems that Blundell's engines also worked as far south as Winsford. At a Grand Junction Railway Board Meeting in May 1844[6] the Secretary reported that "the engine and waggons of Mr Blundell would come on the line on the 6th with coal for Messrs Falks Brothers".

At the end of 1846 one of Blundell's trains returning from Preston to the collieries was in an accident at Amberswood [7]. It ran into wagons which had been left standing on the running line.

No information has survived about the earliest locomotives used on these trains. We know that in 1850 the firm purchased an 0-4-2 tender locomotive from the Liverpool, Crosby and Southport Railway [8]. This had been built by Tayleur and Company, of the Vulcan Foundry, two years earlier, and was presumably good value for money at £1650.

We assume, at least up to the early 1850s, these engines were based at the Amberswood Colliery. We presume that they also worked coal traffic from Blundell's Mesnes Colliery, which was located alongside the North Union line to the north of Wigan. It seems quite likely that, following the completion of the sidings serving Pemberton Colliery, Blundell ran coal trains from here to Preston, using the L&Y tracks as far as Wigan.

Operation of trains over the main line to Preston ceased before 1857. The LNWR Working Time Table for January of that year [9] shows that the firm was then only using the North Union tracks between Springs Branch Junction and Wigan. We infer that Blundell was now working his own coal traffic to Liverpool over the Lancashire and Yorkshire route, in the same way as the Earl of Crawford and Balcarres. Perhaps the base for the Blundell locomotives was transferred from Amberswood to Pemberton at this period. We can only conjecture.

A news item in the Wigan Observer recorded that the first train ran on the new line from Rainford Junction to St Helens on 5th December 1857 [10]. It consisted of 20 wagons of coal and an engine from the colliery of Messrs Blundell at Ince travelling to Garston Dock. It is not clear from the article whether the locomotive actually belonged to Blundell. What is also of interest is that the opening of the line had taken place well before the usually quoted date of 1st March 1858.

Crompton and Shawcross's Amberswood Pits

Richard Blundell's son, Henry, who had taken over the firm on his father's death in 1853, gave up the Amberswood workings in the early 1870s. The Ince Coal and Cannel Company then leased part of the area from Caroline Walmesley [1] and, in June 1873, started to to sink a new pit to work the Amberswood coal. Part of the area must also have been leased by Crompton and Shawcross, as the Mines List from 1873 onwards show this firm as occupiers of an Amberswood Colliery.

The Crompton and Shawcross partnership was already established nearby. The firm was reported to be sinking a pit on the moss in October 1864 [11] and coal was first wound here in April 1865 [12]. The Mines Lists between 1865 and 1868 describe these pits as Pear Tree House Colliery. From 1869 onwards they are shown as Fir Tree House Colliery.

Fir Tree House Colliery was adjacent to Blundell's railway and its seems clear that Crompton and Shawcross worked their own traffic over the line, at least as far as the North Union sidings.

Fletcher, Jennings and Company of Whitehaven supplied two small four coupled side tank engines in 1867 and 1871, named VENTURE and PROGRESS respectively. There must have been at least one earlier locomotive, as the Fletcher, Jennings records note that an old PROGRESS was taken in part exchange for the the engine supplied in 1871.

Sometime before 1873 the private railway had been extended to serve pits near Manchester Road, crossing the Moss Hall Coal Company and the Pearson and Knowles lines on the level.

Amberswood and Strangeways Hall

In the absence of firm information, we cannot say whether this extension was built by Blundell or by Crompton and Shawcross. We consider it possible that Blundell sank the pits here as his Amberswood Colliery expanded and that they were taken over by Crompton and Shawcross when Blundell moved out. Whatever its origins, we know that by November 1873, Crompton and Shawcross had taken over the operation of the line. The Deposited Plans for the Wigan Junction Railway [13] prepared at that date record the firm as occupiers.

We think that the extension over the moss also served the pits which the Ince Hall Coal and Cannel Company sank at Amberswood. These, we believe, were in the vicinity of Moss Hall Farm and it seems likely that Crompton and Shawcross worked the coal traffic from them to the main line sidings.

The increased scale of railway operations required more motive power. In 1873, Crompton and Shawcross purchased an 0-4-2 saddle tank second hand from the North London Railway [14]. This was one of a batch of five engines built by Beyer, Peacock and Company of Manchester in 1860, carrying North London Railway numbers 38 to 42. Crompton and Shawcross resold the locomotive to Fletcher, Jennings and Company as it was too heavy for their tracks. The Fletcher, Jennings records show that it was rebuilt or reconditioned by them, under their works number 154, and was later used at a Whitehaven colliery.

In 1874, Fletcher, Jennings and Company supplied two more four coupled side tank engines, similar to those purchased by Crompton and Shawcross a few years earlier. The manufacturer's records show that one of the new locomotives carried the name SUCCESS.

Before continuing the Crompton and Shawcross story, we need to look at another colliery with which the firm was associated, a little to the south.

Strangeways Hall Colliery

Strangeways Hall Colliery was situated to the north west of the Platt Bridge to Hindley road, not far from Strangeways House. The 1st edition of the 6" map, surveyed in 1846 and 1847, marks two coal pits here, but it is evident that these were only in a small way of business. The Hindley Tithe Map [15], undated but drawn around 1840, shows that the pits were then being worked by H and E Hilton on land owned by T J Trafford. There is no sign of any tramroad on the maps and we assume that the Hiltons transported the coal by horse and cart to the canal. They presumably used the pier head at Platt Bridge which the Ince Rate Book of April 1838 [16] shows in their occupation.

The Byrom, Taylor and Byrom partnership took over after the failure of the Hiltons, with a view to further development. There is reference in June 1848 to this partnership's Ince Colliery [17], which cannot be strictly correct as the pits were actually over the boundary, in Hindley Township. Slater's directory of 1851 [18] more accurately, lists Byrom, Taylor and Byrom at Strangeways Colliery.

The partners must have become bankrupt shortly afterwards, as the Wigan Observer in January 1853 reports that the colliery, closed since their failure, had recently been purchased. A little later, in July 1853, we learn from the Wigan Times that one of the three pits at Strangeways Hall had been taken over by Henry Taylor. Taylor and his partners, Hayes and Whittle, traded as the Strangeways Hall Coal Company and the colliery is shown under this ownership in the Mines Lists from 1853/4 onwards. William Hayes had apparently become sole proprietor on 11th September 1860, but the change is not recorded in the Mines Lists until 1873.

Amberswood and Strangeways Hall

Following the redevelopment of late 1840s, Byrom, Taylor and Byrom constructed a tramroad to the Leigh Branch of the Leeds and Liverpool Canal. A lease relating to part of the land needed for its construction was granted as from 16th October 1848 [19] and the line must have been completed by 1850, as the Ince Rate Book [20] shows that the firm was assessed for rates on it in that year. We have been unable to trace the course of this line. We think that it probably followed a similar route to the later standard gauge railway, which dates from the take over of the colliery by the Taylor, Hayes and Whittle partnership.

The Sidings Schedules make reference to a letter from Crompton and Shawcross to the London and North Western Railway, dated 11th November 1880, regarding the standard gauge line. This stated that it had been constructed under the terms of a lease, for a 30 year period starting on 30th June 1853, granted by Bartholomew Bretherton to William Hayes. There is also record of another lease, from Mrs Kay and Mrs Harwood to William Hayes, dated 14th November 1853 [21].

The railway connected with the North Union line north of Bamfurlong Bridge and, as we understand it, also served a pier head on the arm of the canal which led to Fogg's Fold. There was a level crossing with the Moss Hall Coal Company's railway a short distance west of Strangeways Hall Colliery.

Locomotives seem to have been employed on the line from its opening, as there is reference to a fatal accident involving an engine and some wagons on Thursday, 8th June 1854 [22]. There was another fatal accident caused by a locomotive on 29th February 1856 [23].

No information about these early engines has survived. The only record we have is some ten years later. In January 1865 Mr Hayes purchased, for £550, a six coupled tender locomotive from the London and North Western Railway, where it carried the number 1363. It had been built by the St Helens Canal and Railway Company at their Sutton Works in 1849 and had passed into LNWR ownership when the St Helens Railway was absorbed in 1864 [14].

Crompton and Shawcross's Collieries 1875 to 1897

The Mines Lists show that Crompton and Shawcross took over the Strangeways Hall Colliery in 1875. With it, the firm took over the railway to the canal and the main line. By this date it had also assumed sole responsibility for the operation of the railway which had been built by Blundell to serve his Amberswood Colliery and which had later been extended to the pits near Moss Hall Farm.

Crompton and Shawcross immediately set about linking the two systems by means of a new line from the Fir Tree House Colliery to Low Green. Construction must have been undertaken immediately after the acquisition of Strangeways Hall Colliery, as the connection is marked on an 1875 Line Plan of the Lancashire Union Railway [24].

An alternative main line outlet was provided by the Wigan Junction Railway, which obtained its Act in 1874 [25]. Construction north of Stoney Lane Bridge, on the Platt Bridge to Hindley main road was deferred due to lack of funds. The Sidings Schedules record that the curve leading to the Lancashire Union at Amberswood West Junction, Railway No 4 of the 1874 Act, was actually built to ballast level by Crompton and Shawcross, under an agreement with the Wigan Junction Company, dated 1st October 1878. The track, at least as far as the colliery, was presumably laid by the Wigan Junction Company, whose line from Strangeways to Glazebrook was opened on the 16th October 1879. The first revenue earning train conveyed coal from the colliery [26].

166

When the junction with the Lancashire Union line was finally completed, in 1881 or 1882, the siding connection between Strangeways Hall Colliery and the Wigan Junction line was altered. It had originally been at a point south of Stoney Lane bridge and was now moved to a position on the spur, under an agreement dated 20th May 1880. The London and North Western Railway was given powers under the MS&L Act of 1879[27] to work over the portion of the Wigan Junction line between Amberswood West Junction and Strangeways Hall Colliery free of toll.

At the other end of the Strangeways Hall railway, the junction with North Union line at Bamfurlong was removed. According to the Sidings Lists, this was done during 1881, preparatory to the widening of the line from Golborne to Springs Branch Junction, which was authorised in 1883. The colliery railway west of the junction with the connecting line to Fir Tree House seems to have been taken up shortly afterwards.

Fir Tree House Colliery and Amberswood Colliery closed in the late 1880s. Both are noted as "not working" in the Mines Lists after 1886 or 1887. The track on the railway from Fir Tree House to the Amberswood pits was taken up at this time. It is shown in situ on the Line Plan of the Wigan Junction Railway,[28] dated 1887, but had been lifted by the 1888 to 1892 period, when the surveys for the 1st edition of the of the 25" map were made. The railway west of Fir Tree House was retained to provide a connection from Strangeways Hall to the London and North Western Railway.

Crompton and Shawcross's Edith Pits and Mabel Pits first appear in the Mines Lists for 1891. They were located were immediately to the north of Pearson and Knowles Hindley Hall Colliery and it was not possible, at this time, to connect them with the existing private railway system. Instead, a short branch was laid in to the Lancashire Union line near Hindley Goods Station, the Sidings Schedules showing that connection here was provided under an agreement, dated 11th May 1895, with A Lymm and J B Stuart, trading as Crompton and Shawcross.

Amberswood Colliery was reopened in 1894 by the Moss Collieries Co Ltd, evidently a creation of the Crompton and Shawcross partnership. The railway southwards from the pits was relaid as far as the Wigan Junction line. A connection at Moss Cutting Sidings was provided under an agreement with the Great Central Railway dated 10th May 1894. The first loaded coal wagons were despatched on 21st December 1896[29].

William Crompton, the last remaining partner in the firm, had died on 20th October 1892[30]. In October 1897, the concern was wound up as the result of a Chancery Court judgement and all the collieries ceased work[31]. The property was put up for sale on the 28th of that month[32,33,34]. It comprised the Strangeways Hall, Hindley and Moss Collieries, with three main lines, totalling 12 miles of track. There were 5 locomotives and 740 wagons, a large locomotive shed and a five row wagon repair shop.

For reasons which are not now apparent, the collieries were withdrawn from sale. In December 1897 they were purchased and reopened by a firm with the title of Crompton and Shawcross Ltd, in which J E Rayner was the principal shareholder[35].

We have little in the way of information about the locomotives used by Crompton and Shawcross between 1875 and 1897. We only know of one new engine which was purchased during this period. This was a four coupled saddle tank, built by Hawthorn, Leslie and Co Ltd of Newcastle in 1889, and named WILLIE.

Presumably the stock consisted mainly of engines purchased by the firm the 1860s and early 1870s, together with those taken over from the Strangeways Hall Coal Company. Perhaps BILLY, remembered by old employees, was one of the latter. It was evidently quite an old engine, a six coupled saddle tank with inside cylinders and bar frames, of the Bury type.

Amberswood and Strangeways Hall

For work at the Edith and Mabel Pits, two second hand locomotives were acquired, which Crompton and Shawcross named after the pits. According to one old employee whom we interviewed in the 1950s, these were two sister engines, thought have originated with a main line railway company and purchased from H Flint and Company of Ince. Another version was that only MABEL had main line associations and that EDITH was of a different type.

We are tempted to associate at least MABEL with a batch of locomotives which Flint is reputed to have obtained from the Cardiff Railway Company at this period[36]. These engines were six coupled saddle tanks, built by Parfitt and Jenkins of Cardiff for the Marquis of Bute's railways over a period from 1869 to 1881. The wheelbase must have been too long for use at the colliery, as our informants told us that the rear coupling rods were removed and that MABEL ran as an 0-4-2ST.

Crompton and Shawcross Collieries after 1897

At the time that J E Rayner acquired the Crompton and Shawcross property, he was engaged in buying up other neighbouring collieries. The Hindley Field and Victoria Collieries had been acquired before 1900, and the Hindley Green collieries of John Scowcroft Ltd were taken over during 1900 or 1901. We shall be dealing with the history of these concerns later. For the time being we must return to his Crompton and Shawcross subsidiary.

Amberswood Colliery was transferred from Moss Collieries Co Ltd to Crompton and Shawcross Ltd after Rayner took control. From 1907 this site went under the name of the Moss Pits, or the Gypsy Pits, to avoid confusion with another small colliery which the firm acquired. According to the Sidings Schedules, the Moss Pits were closed on 31st December 1910. They were reopened on 30th October 1922, but the coal could not be worked at a profit and they were closed permanently in October 1924.

Grange Colliery at Hindley opened early in 1900[37] and makes its first appearance in the Mines Lists for 1901 where it is shown in the occupation of Crompton and Shawcross Ltd. Sinking seems to have been started a few years earlier by John Hart, who from 1885 to 1899 had worked the Hussey House Colliery a little further to the south. The Mid Lancashire Coal and Cannel Co Ltd was registered in 1899[38] to take over Hart's collieries, and we think that this was when Rayner acquired an interest.

A short private branch was built from the Wigan Junction line near Hindley and Platt Bridge Station to serve Grange Colliery. The connection was provided under agreements dated 1st June 1894 and 18th April 1899 between John Hart and the Great Central Railway Company[39], endorsed by Crompton and Shawcross Ltd on 20th May 1902. It seems likely that the line was not opened until after the colliery had been taken over by Crompton and Shawcross. It was later extended to join up with the railway system of John Scowcroft and Co Ltd, another Rayner subsidiary.

Rayner at this time was intending to run his own coal trains between the various collieries that he owned. He negotiated an agreement with the Great Central Railway for Crompton and Shawcross locomotives to be used between Strangeways Colliery and Hindley. From here the Grange Colliery line and Scowcroft's railway led to the London and North Western's Eccles, Tyldesley and Wigan line. An agreement for Scowcroft's engines to use the LNWR Bickershaw Branch gave access to Hindley Field and Victoria Collieries. Another agreement with the London and North Western Railway authorised Crompton and Shawcross engines to run between Amberswood East and West Junctions, thus linking Strangeways Hall Colliery with the Edith and Mabel Pits.

Pearson and Knowles' Hindley Hall Colliery closed on 16th February 1904[40] and there was a dismantling sale on 27th April of the same year[41]. Crompton and Shawcross Ltd acquired the property and subsequently worked it in conjunction with their adjacent Edith and Mabel Pits. The firm also took over part of Pearson and Knowles' railway across the moss to the Springs Branch and this led to some reorganisation of its own lines.

The railway from Fir Tree House to the Amberswood colliery line at Moss Cutting was relaid. A spur was put in here to the former Pearson and Knowles line giving access to Hindley Hall Colliery, while the remainder of the Pearson and Knowles line westwards to the Springs Branch was abandoned. The work seems to have been completed by July 1905 when the *Wigan Observer*[42] made reference to Crompton and Shawcross's new line to Hindley Hall Colliery. The direct connection, linking the Edith and Mabel Pits to the Lancashire Union line at Hindley, was dismantled before the 3rd edition of the 6" map was surveyed in 1906 and 1907.

At the western end of Crompton and Shawcross's railway, alterations were made to the way in which traffic was transferred to the London and North Western Railway at Fir Tree House Sidings. Under an agreement of 6th October 1908, the railway company's engines were permitted to work over about 800 yards of colliery track, across Warrington Road into a new bank of exchange sidings[43]. Construction of these sidings was authorised by Goods Traffic Committee Minute 8087 of 19th July 1907.

In 1907 Crompton and Shawcross took over a small colliery owned by Henry Atherton, adjacent to the Lancashire Union Goods Station at Hindley. The Mines Lists for 1891 and 1892 show this as the Amberswood Colliery, which was then being sunk by the Hindley Coal, Brick and Tile Co. From the 1st edition of the 25" map, surveyed in 1892, it is obvious that this was quite a small affair. Two turntables on sidings in the goods yard gave access to a single track leading to the colliery, which is here called the Riding Mine.

The Mines Lists give the information that the colliery was "not working" in 1893 and 1894 and "discontinued" in 1896 to 1898. The 1898 list shows that it had been taken over by Henry Atherton. An agreement in respect of the sidings was made on 18th September 1899 between the LNWR and Henry Atherton.

The 2nd edition of the 25" map, surveyed in 1907, indicates that developments had taken place. A new connection gives access to a small screening plant which is joined to the pit by an inclined tubway. There is also a brickworks adjacent to the screens, with a tubway leading from opencast clay workings to the south of the coal pit. The new sidings were authorised by Goods Traffic Committee Minute 4619 of 17th October 1900 and were covered by an agreement with Henry Atherton dated 1st February 1901.

The brick works and the coal mine were bought by Crompton and Shawcross Ltd in 1907 and the Sidings Schedules show that the private sidings agreement was transferred to this firm in August 1907. The Mines Lists suggest that the colliery closed in 1910, but the siding was retained for a time, to serve Amberswood Brickworks. Permission was given in February 1914 for Messrs Kershaw and Topping to use the siding, as they intended to erect a wagon repair shop. This seems to have fallen through as removal of the siding was authorised by Goods Traffic Committee Minute 12337 of 21st February 1917.

Hindley Hall Colliery appears to have been redeveloped around 1910 and it seems likely that the branch to the Lancashire Union line was reinstated. The Sidings Schedules refer to an agreement relating to a connection at Hindley Goods Station dated 28th June 1910. The agreement was terminated on 31st December 1920 and the connection was taken out by July

1921. This would coincide with the closure of Hindley Hall Colliery, which the Mines Lists show was suspended in 1917 for the duration of the war, later reopened and finally abandoned in 1921.

Grange Colliery continued in operation until 1927, the Mines List showing that it was abandoned on 21st October. The Dukes Pit at Strangeways Hall was abandoned on 24th December 1927. The other two pits there remained at work until January 1937, when they too were closed down.

With the decline in traffic, the connection with the former Wigan Junction line at Moss Cutting Siding was discontinued. The Sidings Schedules state that the agreement was terminated on 16th October 1934 and that the junction had been removed by 31st January 1935. The agreements in respect of the connection at Strangeways and that to Grange Colliery, which gave access to the Scowcroft railway system, were terminated on 6th December 1938 [39]. The Sidings Schedules state that former had been removed by 27th July 1939. The Fir Tree House connection with what was now the London Midland and Scottish Railway was retained to serve other firms which had premises there.

The locomotive stock was renewed soon after J E Rayner took control of the company. Most of the former Crompton and Shawcross locomotives, which were by now quite old, disappeared in the first few years. Only the four coupled Hawthorn, Leslie saddle tank WILLIE seems to have been kept, and this survived until about 1930, when it was sold to the Lancashire Steel Corporation, for use at their Irlam Works.

The precise history of the replacement locomotives presents some difficulty to railway historians. Three new locomotives were ordered from Peckett and Sons of Bristol and three from Manning, Wardle of Leeds in the early years of the present century. Because of the way in which the the Rayners placed their orders, it is not always clear from the manufacturers records where the engines were intended to be allocated. However, from information given us by old employees, it seems that the Pecketts were employed initially at the Crompton and Shawcross collieries and the Manning, Wardles at Scowcroft's Hindley Green collieries. Inevitably there was some movement between one system and another to cover for repairs and changes in traffic patterns. Later, as colliery closures got under way, there were further transfers which do not always seem to have been recorded.

The Peckett locomotives which we associate with Crompton and Shawcross Ltd were all six coupled saddle tanks. SYDNEY and GEOFFREY, named after J E Rayner's sons, came in 1901 and 1904 respectively. The third engine was delivered in 1912. It never carried a name, being known by its makers number – 1269.

Several old employees we interviewed in the 1950s also remembered a large six coupled saddle tank named HENRY, reputedly built by the Pearson and Knowles Coal and Iron Co Ltd, at the Dallam Works at Warrington. It is not clear whether it had been taken over by Crompton and Shawcross when they acquired the Hindley Hall Colliery or whether it was purchased direct from the makers. There is a story that HENRY was commandeered by the government during the first world war and used at Richborough Port, in Kent. Certainly an engine of this description was repaired by John Wake and Co Ltd, of Darlington, a firm which specialised in buying up surplus military railway equipment. It was presumably the same engine which was advertised in July 1920 by F Gilman, a dealer in Birmingham, who was probably acting as a middle man [44]. It was described as having 16" cylinders and weighing 40 tons. We know that it was sold, still carrying the name HENRY, by Wakes to Wharncliffe Woodmoor Colliery, in South Yorkshire, where it survived until about 1968.

Maker's official photograph of the first of the three Peckett locomotives. It was named SYDNEY by Crompton and Shawcross.
Frank Jones Collection

Following the closure of the Strangeways Hall railway system, all three Peckett locomotives were sold. GEOFFREY and 1269 went to the Lancashire Steel Corporation Ltd, for use at their Irlam works. Both were scrapped there in October 1954. SYDNEY was purchased by the South Durham Steel and Iron Co Ltd, at Stockton. It was later used at Cargo Fleet Ironworks, at Middlesbrough, and was broken up there about 1958.

Fir Tree Wagon Works

The first reference that we have discovered to this establishment is in 1876 when the partnership between John Eatock, James Wright, Israel Knowles and Thomas Wright was dissolved on 27th January[45]. The firm, trading as Eatock Wright and Company of the Fir Tree House Wagon Works, was to be carried on by James Wright and Thomas Wright.

The Sidings Schedules suggest that the name was subsequently changed to the Fir Tree House Wagon and Iron Company and we believe that it was this firm which constructed new shops alongside Crompton and Shawcross's private line, to the east of the Warrington Road level crossing. These are shown on the 1927 revision of the 6" map, but not on the 3rd edition, surveyed in 1907.

The Sidings Schedules record an agreement with Crompton and Shawcross Ltd dated 30th November 1920 which permitted the Fir Tree Company to use the sidings. A little later, the property passed to the Chorley Wagon Repairing Company, a Goods Committee Minute of 19th October 1921 authorised this company to do the same.

Amberswood and Strangeways Hall

What a contrast! The second of Crompton and Shawcross's Pecketts after it had been sold to Lancashire Steel Corporation. Alex Appleton

Following the closure of Crompton and Shawcross's Strangeways Hall Colliery and the remaining parts of their railway system, there were new agreements in respect of the Fir Tree Sidings. The Sidings Schedules quote Traffic Committee Minute 5942 of 26th April 1939, which authorised the use of the sidings by Wagon Repairs Ltd and their sub tenants Hodgson and Company. There is also reference to an agreement with the Chorley Wagon Co Ltd dated 22nd July 1939.

Wagon repairing activities appear to have ceased here in 1946, as a note in the Sidings Schedules suggests that Hodgsons had sole use of the sidings from 31st December 1946.

Hodgson and Co (Liverpool) Ltd – Fir Tree House

The Sidings Schedules in a note, dated March 1928, indicate that Messrs Hodgson, of 34, Castle Street, Liverpool, had erected plant adjacent to Crompton and Shawcross's sidings for washing, cleaning and grading coke breeze from gas works.

The firm was allowed to use Fir Tree House Siding for their traffic and, as stated earlier, it continued do so after Crompton and Shawcross's collieries had finished. When the wagon works closed down, a new agreement was made with Hodgson in respect of the sidings, dated 25th September 1947. The plant ceased production in the early 1960s, the agreement was terminated on 30th September 1962 and the level crossing over Warrington Road was subsequently removed.

Amberswood and Strangeways Hall

LOCOMOTIVE SUMMARY

Amberswood Colliery

c1840 to c1870   Various Blundell partnerships

ACE OF TRUMPS
   Accident on North Union Railway, 27-2-1844

	0-4-2	OC	Tayleur 320?	1848	16"x18"	4'6"

   Ex Liverpool, Crosby and Southport Railway, 3 SEFTON, 30-1-1850
   Scrapped or sold

Strangeways Hall Colliery

c1842 to c1850   Byrom, Taylor and Byrom
1853 to c1875   William Hayes and partners
After c 1875   Crompton and Shawcross
Railway system amalgamated with that at Amberswood Colliery

	0-6-0		St H Rly	1849	4'6"

   Ex LNWR 1373 in January 1865, formerly St Helens Canal and Railway, 7 EDEN.

Amberswood and Strangeways Hall Collieries

c1865 to c1875   Crompton and Shawcross (Amberswood only)
c1875 to 1897   Crompton and Shawcross (Ambersood and Strangeways Hall)
1897 to 1937   Crompton and Shawcross Ltd (For detailsof collieries operated, see text)

PROGRESS
   To Fletcher, Jennings and Company, 1871

VENTURE	0-4-0T	OC	FJ	71	1867	10"x20"	

   New
   Scrapped or sold about 1906

PROGRESS	0-4-0T	OC	FJ	89	1871	10"x20"	

   New
   Scrapped or sold

SUCCESS	0-4-0T	OC	FJ	133	1874	10"x20"	

   New
   Scrapped or sold

	0-4-0T	OC	FJ	136	1874	12"x20"	

   New
   Scrapped or sold

	0-4-2ST	IC	BP	187	1860	16"x24"	5'0"

   Ex North London Railway, 1873
   To Fletcher, Jennings and Company, 1877

173

Amberswood and Strangeways Hall

WILLIE	0-4-0ST	OC	HL	2149	1889	14"x20"	3'0"

New
To Lancashire Steel Corporation Ltd, Irlam, about 1930

EDITH	0-6-0ST		P&J(?)

Possibly ex Cardiff Railway, via Flint
Scrapped or sold

MABEL	0-6-0ST		P&J(?)

Possibly ex Cardiff Railway, via Flint
Scrapped or sold

HENRY	0-6-0ST	IC	PK	

Reputed to have been commandeered for use at Richborough Port about 1917
Probably the locomotive which was repaired by John Wake and Co Ltd of Darlington about 1920 and sold to Wharncliffe Woodmoor Colliery Co Ltd

SYDNEY	0-6-0ST	IC	P	877	1901	16"x22"	

New
To South Durham Steel and Iron Co Ltd, Stockton about 1937

GEOFFREY	0-6-0ST	IC	P	1036	1904	16"x22"	3'10"

New
To Lancashire Steel Corporation Ltd, Irlam, about 1937 as No 17

	0-6-0ST	IC	P	1269	1912	16"x22"	3'10"

New
To Lancashire Steel Corporation Ltd, Irlam, about 1937 as No 16

References to Chapter 10

1. *"Blundell's Collieries, 1776–1966"* – Donald Anderson – Reprinted from the *Transactions of the Historic Society of Lancashire and Cheshire*, Vol 116; 1964 Vol 117; 1965, Vol 119; 1967
2. Parly Papers 1846 Vol XXXIV p8
3. BJ 10-11-1849
4. Liverpool and Manchester Railway Minutes, quoted by T J Donachy, in footnote on p 152 of *Liverpool and Manchester Railway Operations, 1831 to 1845* – publ David and Charles, Newton Abbot, 1972
5. Rylands Library – Earl of Crawford and Balcarres Papers – Box F
6. See *"Locomotives of the Grand Junction Railway"* – E Craven in *Mancunian*, Journal of Manchester Locomotive Society, No 143, March 1988
7. PG 2-1-1847
8. *British Locomotive Catalogue, 1825–1923 – Vol 3B – B*. Baxter Moorland Publishing Co, Ashbourne, 1982
9. PRO Rail 946/1
10. WO 11-12-1857
11. WO 9-10-1864
12. WO 7-4-1865
13. LRO PDR 970
14. *British Locomotive Catalogue 1825–1923, Vol 2A* – compiled by late Bertram Baxter – Moorland Publishing Co, Ashbourne, 1978
15. LRO DRL 1/35
16. Formerly at Ince UDC Offices
17. PG 3-6-1848
18. *Royal National Commercial Directory and Topography of the County of Lancaster* – Isaac Slater – Manchester, 1851
19. WRO DDX Ta 7/6
20. Formerly in Ince UDC Offices
21. WRO DDX Ta 7/11
22. WO 17-6-1854
23. Board of Trade Accident Reports Nos 43 and 49

24	Line Plan of Lancashire Union Railway, Gerards Bridge to Haigh and Branches – LNWR, Rugby, 1875 – 2 chains to 1 inch – at BRPB Manchester Office		
25	37 & 38 Vic cap cxvii; 16 7 1874		
26	*Great Central Vol 2* – George Dow – Locomotive Publishing Co, London 1962		
27	42 & 43 Vic cap cli; 21-7-1879		
28	Line Plan of Wigan Junction Railway – Henry Fowler, surveyor, 1883 – 2 chains to 1 inch – at BRPB, Manchester Office		
29	WO 26-12-1896	30	WO 29-10-1892
31	WO 2-10-1897	32	WO 16-10-1897
33	WEx 16-10-1897	34	WO 23-10-1897
35	WO 4-12-1897		
36	*Locomotives of the Great Western Railway, Part Ten* – Railway Correspondence and Travel Society, 1966		
37	WO 10-2-1900	38	WO 9-9-1899
39	Summary of Private Sidings Agreements, Wigan Junction Line – in possession of Mr Ken Plant		
40	WO 20-2-1904	41	MG 9-4-1904
42	WO 15-07-1905	43	LNW Sdgs Diag No 120, dated Dec 1916
44	MM 2-7-1920	45	LG 1-2-1876

CHAPTER 11

PLATT BRIDGE, BAMFURLONG AND MAINS

We now move south to consider the area around Platt Bridge. During the period 1820 to 1850 there were a number of pits here, most of which seem to have been too small to have required either tramroads or main line rail connections. Only fragmentary records have survived and there appear to be virtually no maps or plans, other than the Ordnance Survey 1"and 6" maps. Consequently we have had considerable difficulty in tracing the history of the mines during this period. What we have been able to put together is necessarily far from complete.

The later history is dominated by the firm of Cross, Tetley and Co Ltd, which, from the 1860s, was associated with pits over the Ashton boundary, in the vicinity of the Mesnes. In the early 1870s, the firm extended its operations by taking over and reopening some of the pits in the neighbourhood of Platt Bridge.

The maps relating to the collieries described here will be found in Chapters 9 and 13.

Platt's Bamfurlong Colliery

A notice of a sale on 10th February 1820[1] makes reference to a colliery which was then being opened out on an estate known as Bolton's. Mr Appleton, the owner of the estate, would alternatively enter into partnership with investors who would assist in working the mine. A steam engine had been erected on the premises and an Engine Pit had already been sunk. Another pit was sinking. The Leigh Branch of the Leeds and Liverpool Canal, then being constructed, ran along the side of the estate. A contract had been placed to build a basin and pier head to serve the colliery.

From a description of the estate, it seems clear that this was the colliery which was later shown on the 2" drawings and on the 1st edition of the 6" map on the south side of the canal, about 250 yards west of the North Union Railway bridge.

It is known that the colliery was worked for a time by Adam Platt, apparently unsuccessfully. The Ince Tithe Map of 1841[2] and the accompanying list of landowners and tenants, dated 27th June 1839, shows that the estate was then owned by John Dobbs and occupied by Adam Platt. The 2" drawings, prepared in 1840 to 1842, give the name Bamfurlong Colliery. By 1845, when the 6" map was surveyed, it was obviously no longer in use.

In the late 1840s the executors of John Dobbs leased the mines to a partnership which included John Price, William May, Henry Hull and William Andrews. The same partners also obtained a lease of nearby property from Samuel and William Parsons[3]. In 1850, these leases were assigned to Charles Pigot, who also seems to have held a lease of land owned by Richard Fogg. Henry Hull left the partnership in October 1850[4,5] and it seems likely that John Price had done so earlier.

It is not clear how seriously the partnership attempted to work the mines, although there is a report of an accident in March 1847 at a new pit which John Price and Company were sinking at Platt Bridge[6]. The Ince Rates Book for 1850[7] shows that Charles Pigot was assessed for rates on the colliery and canal basin in that year, although, again, there is no evidence that he produced any coal.

William May, Henry Hull and William Andrews must have defaulted on their payments to the lessor during the time they occupied the estate, as they were sued in the Chancery Court by John Hall and James Hall, the Dobbs trustees. As a result the colliery was put up for auction on 16th March 1855[8].

The property apparently failed to reach its reserve price and there was no sale. The colliery appears to have been out of use for the next ten years. In the late 1860s, mining rights over a large area in the neighbourhood of Bamfurlong were leased by Cross Tetley and Co Ltd and a large modern colliery was developed on the site of the early pits. We shall deal with the subsequent history later in the chapter.

Platt Bridge Colliery

There was another early colliery, to the east of the North Union Railway, near Platt Bridge Fold, on William Fosbrook's land. On 17th December 1833 Mr Fosbrook was granted permission to build a side basin on the canal "for loading coals for the Manchester and Liverpool markets"[9]. The side basin was actually a private arm which extended a little over a quarter of a mile to the colliery.

The Ince Rate Book for 1838[10] records that Hilton and Company occupied mines and a pier head on land owned by William Blount Fosbrook, which we assume refers to this colliery. Following the bankruptcy of the Hiltons, the colliery was up for auction on 27th July 1841, when it was stated that the original lease had been granted in August 1837[11]. The 1st edition of the 6" map gives the impression that the colliery is still active, so it may have reopened after the sale.

By the early 1850s ownership of the land had passed to the Walmesley family. In 1855 there were attempts, apparently unsuccessful, to lease the mines to Robert Lancaster and Robert Lancashire Chadwick, a partnership which traded under the style of Chadwick and Company[12]. The firm had gone out of business by February 1858[13].

The Mines Lists for 1853/4 and 1855 suggest that Platt Bridge Colliery was not then in use. The colliery is missing from the lists for 1856 and 1857. It reappears from 1858 to 1862 under the occupation of Heaton and Company. It must have closed before 1866, for Heaton's Platt Bridge Colliery was advertised for sale on 8th March of that year[14] because the works had been discontinued.

As we have noted in Chapter 10, the standard gauge railway, built around 1853 or 1854, from Strangeways Hall Colliery to the North Union line probably had a branch to a pier head on the private canal. We believe that the earlier narrow gauge line also had its terminus here, as the Ince Rates Book for 1850[7] show that Byrom, Taylor and Byrom were assessed for rates on a tramroad.

At some date which we have been unable to determine, but probably coincident with the developments at Strangeways Hall and Platt Bridge Collieries in the 1850s, the original canal arm was abandoned. It was replaced by a new cut, of somewhat larger dimensions, which joined the main line of the Leigh Branch near to the North Union Bridge. For most of its length, it ran about a hundred yards to the west of the old course.

Platt Bridge, Bamfurlong and Mains

Fogg's Fold Colliery

In the 1840s another small colliery started at Fogg's Fold, to the north of the canal arm. There was an auction sale of the property of Richard Joseph and Ellen Fogg on 26th March 1845, which included coal mines described as partly sunk. They were situated by the North Union Railway and 100 yards from "the Wigan and Manchester Canal"[15].

We think that the Fogg's Fold Colliery was left in its incomplete state after the sale and there is no evidence of its existence on the 1st edition of the 6" map, surveyed in 1845 and 1846. There were fresh developments here in the 1870s by Cross Tetley and Co Ltd, which we describe later.

Low Green Colliery

We have found a number of references to a colliery at Low Green, sometimes spelt Lowe Green. This was just over the township boundary in Hindley, although we have been unable to locate the precise site. We presume that it was to the north of Low Hall, adjacent to the tramroad and later railway from Strangeways Hall Colliery. There is a single small coal pit marked on the 1st edition of the 6" map in this position. The Strangeways Hall tramroad is, of course, not shown as it was not constructed until a year or two after the date of the survey.

Low Green Colliery, then occupied by Peter Johnson, was for sale on 17th July 1850[16]. On 11th September 1850, mines under the Low Green estate were leased by Bartholomew Bretherton to Messrs May and Company, presumably the successor to the May and Hull partnership which had leased Bamfurlong Colliery. In view of the Chancery action referred to earlier, it is unlikely that May and Company did much work at Low Green.

The colliery is not shown in the Mines Lists until 1859, when it reappears, now in the occupation of the Low Green Colliery Company. This was presumably the title adopted by the partnership of Yates, Caldwell and Pickering which leased mines at Low Green from Mathias Wood in February 1860[17]. The partnership was dissolved in 1862 and the colliery was put up for sale by auction on 16th May of that year[18].

A new Low Green Colliery Company must have been formed, as the Mines Lists continue to show a firm with this name as occupiers until 1867, the year in which the colliery seems to have closed. There was a sale on 29th July 1868, when Watson and Company were stated to be the owners[19].

We do not know whether the colliery was ever connected to the Strangeways Hall railway system, or whether it remained a small landsale colliery throughout its existence.

Riding Lane and the early Mains Collieries

Before proceeding further with the history of the collieries at Platt Bridge, we must turn our attention to the developments which were taking place over the Ashton boundary, in the vicinity of Mains. We have been unable to unravel completely the early history of the pits here. We are not helped by the fact that the collieries originally were described as Mesnes. The name was later changed to Mains, presumably to avoid confusion with the two Mesnes collieries north of Wigan which we describe in Part 2, Chapter 22.

Platt Bridge, Bamfurlong and Mains

It appears from the Mines Lists that Joseph Ashton had established a pit at Riding Lane, in the vicinity of Mains, before 1854. We know that on 18th May 1846 the Leeds and Liverpool Canal Company granted him permission to build a pier head on the Leigh Branch of the canal near Bamfurlong Bridge[20]. There is no record of a tramroad here and none is shown on the 1st edition of the 6" map surveyed in 1845 to 1847. We therefore assume that Ashton conveyed his coal to the canal by horse and cart.

According to the Mines Lists, Riding Lane Colliery continued in Joseph Ashton's occupation until 1867, when it was taken over by Messrs Cross and Company. Meanwhile Cross and Company seem to have sunk a pit of their own at Riding Lane in 1861, which was transferred to the firm of Cross Tetley and Co Ltd in 1866. This company had been formed about 1864 to take over the assets of Cross, Taylor and Company, which had been wound up[21].

Mains is first recorded in the 1855 Mines Lists under the ownership of Chadwick and Company. It seems to have closed by 1857. Joseph Ashton appears to have opened another pit here in 1864, which was taken over by Cross Tetley and Co Ltd in 1866. The Mines Lists show that a further Mains Colliery was opened in 1862 by the firm of Parr and Cross. These pits were not absorbed into Cross Tetley and Co Ltd's ownership until 1872.

We think it likely that Chadwick and Company were operating on too small a scale to need their own railway, and that the same probably applied to Joseph Ashton's workings at Riding Lane. Definitive information is not available until 1863 and 1864. A Line Plan of the North Union Railway[22] produced in the latter year shows a colliery adjacent to the main line, to which it is connected by a series of sidings. We associate this with Joseph Ashton's Mains Colliery, although we lack firm evidence.

The Deposited Plans for the Lancashire Union Railway[23] prepared in 1863, and submitted to Parliament in the 1864 Session, shows a railway or tramroad extending from the North Union towards the main road at Brynn Gates. The occupiers are shown as Robert Cross and Peter Parr, and we believe that the line must have served their Mains Colliery.

What seems to have happened in the late 1860s and early 1870s is that Cross, Tetley and Co Ltd built a new colliery complex alongside the North Union main line. This, we think, was on the site of the Mains Colliery which appeared on the 1864 Line Plan and presumably made use of the existing shafts and much of the equipment. Cross, Tetley's Riding Lane pits were subsequently discontinued and disappear from the Mines Lists between 1881 and 1883.

Cross, Tetley's Mains, Fogg's Fold and Bamfurlong Collieries

In the early 1870s, Cross, Tetley and Co Ltd expanded their sphere of operations to the area north of Mains. To the east of the North Union and to the north of the Leigh Branch of the Leeds and Liverpool Canal, they redeveloped the Fogg's Fold Colliery. To the west of the main line, they opened up the Bamfurlong Colliery on a site south of the canal where the previous owners had unsuccessfully attempted to work the coal.

Fogg's Fold Colliery first appears in the Mines Lists for 1873. Access to the LNWR was gained over a short length of the Strangeways Hall railway, from which a spur was laid in to the colliery. The layout is clearly shown on a Line Plan of the North Union[24], undated, but believed to be about 1874. It also appears on the Deposited Plans, submitted to Parliament in the 1875 Session[25] by the London and North Western Railway, for a widening from Bamfurlong to Boars Head, which in the event was not carried out.

Platt Bridge, Bamfurlong and Mains

Foggs Fold Colliery is shown as "not working" in the Mines Lists between 1883 and 1888, after which it disappears. The Strangeways Hall railway was abandoned in the early 1880s, and there is no trace of the line, or of Foggs Fold Colliery, on the Deposited Plans submitted to Parliament by the LNWR in the 1883 Session for widening the North Union line between Golborne and Springs Branch Junction[26].

The Sidings Schedules record that an agreement of 21st August 1875, between Cross, Tetley and Co Ltd and the LNWR, provided for the railway company to make a new junction between Fogg's Fold Colliery and new sidings on the west side of the main line, in substitution for the Strangeways Hall railway. As far as we are aware these alterations, which presumably would have required a bridge under the main line, were not carried out. There is no sign of any new connection on the Deposited Plans of 1883, referred to above.

The history of Cross, Tetley's Bamfurlong Colliery starts with a lease[27] which the firm obtained for forty years from 1st May 1867. It took over the pits which Adam Platt had attempted to sink in 1820s and which, as we have described earlier, had been leased by the ill fated Hull, May and Andrews partnership in the late 1840s.

Cross, Tetley and Co Ltd encountered considerable difficulty with water when the colliery was reopened and the methods which were adopted to reach the deeper seams are fully described in a contemporary paper[28]. In addition to the two original pits, a start was made with sinking two new ones in 1873.

We believe that Bamfurlong Colliery came into production around 1875. The Sidings Schedules record that a connection with the main line was provided under an agreement dated 21st August 1875. Another agreement of 6th September 1877 referred to alterations to the sidings, necessitated by the building of a new station at Bamfurlong. As well as despatching coal by rail, the colliery was able to send out part of its output by barge. Loading facilities were provided, which made use of the original canal basin constructed during Adam Platt's period of occupation.

A description of Mains and Bamfurlong Collieries as they existed at the end of the nineteenth century is provided by two articles in the Colliery Guardian for 1896[29,30]. There were two shafts at Mains and four at Bamfurlong, but unfortunately nothing is said about the railway systems at the two collieries.

At least from 1881, if not earlier, the firm seems to have worked its own trains between Mains and Bamfurlong over the main line, perhaps to take coal to the canal tip. A third line was opened between these two places in that year, and the Sidings Schedules record that this was first used by Cross, Tetley's locomotives on 14th May and by LNWR locomotives on 21st May. This additional line was retained after the two further main line tracks had been provided between Golborne and Springs Branch Junction in October 1888, but we do not know when Cross, Tetley's trains ceased to use it.

We have little information about the locomotives which Cross, Tetley and Co Ltd originally used at Bamfurlong, Mains and Foggs Fold. We know that in 1872[31] and again in 1875[32], the firm advertised for a new or second-hand locomotive to work at Platt Bridge, a description fitting either Fogg's Fold or Bamfurlong.

We have a record of a six coupled saddle tank, named BAMFURLONG, delivered new by the Hunslet Engine Company of Leeds in 1875. There is also a photograph, reproduced on here, of an unidentified four coupled saddle tank at one of Cross, Tetley's pits, which was probably taken towards the end of the nineteenth century. Apart from observing that the engine is typical of those turned out by the Scottish locomotive manufacturers, we can supply no further information.

Platt Bridge, Bamfurlong and Mains

One of Cross, Tetley's collieries, possibly Mains, showing the unidentified Scottish built locomotive.
J.A. Peden Collection

The locomotive stock was augmented around the the turn of the century and here we are on surer ground.

The Vulcan Foundry, of Newton le Willows, supplied a six coupled saddle tank in 1895, named MAINS, and a similar engine in 1904, named EDWARD. In 1900, Robert Stephenson and Company provided a six coupled saddle tank, named BOBS.

Two more locomotives were obtained from Manning, Wardle and Company in 1917. Both were six coupled saddle tanks and carried the names LIONEL and REGINALD. BAMFURLONG, the Hunslet Engine Company's locomotive of 1875, was probably taken out of service shortly afterwards, the manufacturer's records showing that spare parts ceased to be ordered after 1917.

Several of the engines were renamed during their service with Cross, Tetley and Co Ltd. According to old employees, EDWARD became ALFRED and later HERBERT. The Manning, Wardle records show that LIONEL was renamed HORACE and REGINALD became BAMFURLONG.

Cross, Tetley and Co Ltd went into liquidation in 1931. In December of that year the leasehold interest in Mains and Bamfurlong Collieries was offered for sale, together with the plant, which included three saddle tank locomotives [33]. The sale must have fallen through, as the the colliery seems to have been worked by the receiver until 31st March 1934, when the firm's assets were acquired by the Wigan Coal Corporation Ltd.

BOBS, HORACE (ex LIONEL) and BAMFURLONG (ex REGINALD) survived to be taken over by the Wigan Coal Corporation. They then had their names removed and were given numbers instead. BOBS became No 1, HORACE became No 2 and BAMFURLONG became No 3.

Platt Bridge, Bamfurlong and Mains

The two Vulcan Foundry engines, MAINS and EDWARD had already been taken out of service, perhaps soon after the two Manning, Wardles arrived in 1917.

There is a suggestion that a six coupled Hudswell, Clarke saddle tank named ALICE was hired from Thomas Wrigley of Prestwich, in the early 1930s. There is no note of this in the Wrigley records which we have of examined, nor was the engine remembered by any of the old Cross, Tetley employees whom we interviewed.

The Mines Lists show that Bamfurlong Colliery was formally abandoned in September 1936. Up to this date, it was usual for one locomotive to be stabled at Mains Colliery and the other two at Bamfurlong.

The siding connection at Bamfurlong seems to have been retained to serve the landsale yard and perhaps to give access to the canal tip. Possibly one locomotive was kept here to perform the small amount of shunting that was still necessary.

The Sidings Schedules record that, during the second world war, the Ministry of Supply took over part of the premises to store ammonium nitrate and pig lead and that additional sidings were laid in to reach the storage grounds. The Private Sidings Agreement was finally terminated on 31st December 1962 [34].

Mains Colliery continued in production and passed to the National Coal Board on 1st January 1947. It was eventually closed on 9th September 1960.

According to records at the Kirkless Workshops [35], the Manning, Wardle locomotive No 3 had already been scrapped some time before December 1940. No 1 and No 2 were taken over by the National Coal Board and the subsequent history of the locomotives used at Mains Colliery is given in the summary at the end of the chapter.

Cross, Tetley's Manning, Wardle LIONEL, later renumbered No 2, as running in National Coal Board days at Mains Colliery. Photographed on 20th April 1952. Industrial Railway Society, Ken Cooper Collection

Co-operative Wholesale Society Ltd, Platt Bridge

In 1955, the Co-operative Wholesale Society built a new factory, to produce glass bottles, alongside the Whelley Loop line, south of Platt Bridge Junction. A siding was provided which had a connection with the Up Through Line controlled by a ground frame. The Sidings Schedules state that the work was ordered on 11th November 1955, but the private sidings agreement was not signed until 19th April 1958.

The Through Lines between Bamfurlong Junction and Platt Bridge Junction were closed to traffic on 2nd October 1972 and the point work at Bamfurlong Junction taken out on 15th January 1973. A portion of the up line was retained to give access to the glass works siding. This connected with the Whelley Goods Lines near the site of the former Platt Bridge Junction, where a new ground frame was provided. Then, probably in 1976, the Goods Lines were also taken out of use, except for the portion of the up line between the new glass works ground frame and the junction with the low level lines from Springs Branch No 2 Signal Box to Bamfurlong Sidings Junction. Trains from Bamfurlong now had to make a double reversal to reach the works.

The traffic, which had latterly consisted of sand delivered to the works from Oakamoor in Staffordshire, ceased during the first week in July 1986. The private sidings agreement was terminated with effect from 1st October of the same year [36].

The works, which is still in operation, was taken over by Rockware Glass Ltd in October 1988.

LOCOMOTIVE SUMMARY

Mains and Bamfurlong Collieries

Mains Colliery

to 1866	Various firms
c1866 to 1934	Cross, Tetley and Co Ltd
1934 to 1946	Wigan Coal Corporation Ltd
After 1-1-1947	National Coal Board

Bamfurlong Colliery

c1870 to 1934	Cross, Tetley and Co Ltd
1934 to 1936	Wigan Coal Corporation Ltd
Colliery closed 1936	

BAMFURLONG	0-6-0ST	IC	HE	148	1875	14"x20"	3'4"
New							
Scrapped or sold after February 1917							
	0-4-0ST	OC	Unknown Scottish maker				
Shown in photograph							
MAINS	0-6-0ST	IC	VF	1434	1895	15"x22"	3'6"
New							
Scrapped or sold before 1934							

Platt Bridge, Bamfurlong and Mains

BOBS   0-6-0ST   IC   RS   2991   1900   15"x20"   3'6"
   New
   To Wigan Coal Corporation Ltd in 1934
   Name removed and became No 1
   To NCB on 1-1-1947 at Mains

EDWARD   0-6-0ST   IC   VF   1946   1904   15"x22"   3'6"
   New
   Reputed to have been renamed ALFRED then HERBERT
   Scrapped or sold before 1934

LIONEL   0-6-0ST   IC   MW   1925   1917   14"x20"
   New
   Renamed HORACE according to Manning, Wardle records
   To Wigan Coal Corporation Ltd in 1934
   Name removed and became No 2
   To NCB on 1-1-1947 at Mains

REGINALD   0-6-0ST   IC   MW   1926   1917   14"x20"
   New
   Renamed BAMFURLONG according to Manning, Wardle records
   To Wigan Coal Corporation Ltd in 1934
   Name removed and became No 3
   Scrapped before 1940

National Coal Board

Mains Colliery

1947 to 1950   North Western Division, Wigan Area
1960   closed

No 1   0-6-0ST   IC   RS   2991   1900   15"x20"   3'6"
   Taken over at Mains 1-1-1947
   Temporarily at Ince Moss 1952 and 1953. Returned to Mains by 11-1953
   To Chanters Colliery between 10 and 12-1960
   To Ince Moss by 5-1961
   Scrapped at Ince Moss 7-1965

No 2   0-6-0ST   IC   MW   1925   1917   14"x20"
   Taken over at Mains 1-1-1947
   Temporarily at Low Hall mid 1947
   Temporarily at Ince Moss 1951
   At Dallam Forge for repairs 12-1953
   To John Pit, Standish before 2-1955 Thence to Howe Bridge,
   Kirkless Workshops and Gibfield
   Returned to Mains by 4-1956
   To Ince Moss by 4-1961, thence to Kirkless Workshops and Standish
   Sold from Standish to Jose K Holt and Gordon 6-1965 and scrapped at their Chequerbent yard 8-1965

Platt Bridge, Bamfurlong and Mains

References to Chapter 11

1	Copy in authors' possession	2	LRO DRL 1/44
3	WRO DDX Ta 7/7	4	WRO DDX Ta 8/7
5	LG 24-12-1850	6	BC 13-3-47
7	Formerly in Ince UDC Offices	8	Copy of Sales Notice in authors' possession
9	Leeds and Liverpool Canal Company's Minutes 17-12-1833		
10	Formerly in Ince UDC Offices	11	Copy of Sales Notice in authors' possession
12	LRO DD Wa	13	LG 26-2-1858
14	BC 24-2-1866	15	PG 15-3-1845
16	BJ 13-7-1850	17	WRO DDX Ta 8/2
18	WRO DDX Ta 8/6	19	BJ 25-7-68
20	Leeds and Liverpool Canal Company's Minutes 18-5-1846		
21	WO 18-2-1870		
22	Line Plan of North Union Railway – LNWR, 1864 – 2 chains to 1 inch – at GMRO		
23	LRO PDR 764		
24	Line Plan of North Union Railway, Bamfurlong to Wigan – LNWR, n.d. – 2 chains to 1 inch – at GMRO		
25	LRO PDR 994	26	LRO PDR 1220
27	D Anderson – private communication		
28	*"The Method Adopted in Sinking through Groundwater at the Bamfurlong Colliery, Wigan"* – Walter Topping, M.E. – *Transactions of the Manchester Geological Society*, Vol XV 1879–1880		
29	CG 27-3-1896	30	CG 2-4-1896
31	CG 6-12-1872	32	CG16-4-1875
33	CG4-12-1931		
34	Line Plan of North Union Railway British Railways, 1956 – At BRPB Manchester Office		
35	Copy in authors' possession	36	British Rail Records

CHAPTER 12

LOW HALL, MAYPOLE AND WIGAN JUNCTION

In this chapter we deal with an area to the south of Platt Bridge, bounded on the west by the North Union Railway and on the east by the Wigan Junction Railway. The Moss Hall Coal Company, which we have met in previous chapters, sank pits at Low Hall around 1850. Some twenty five years later the Wigan Junction Colliery started production and this was followed by the Maypole Colliery at the turn of the century.

The maps showing the tramroads and railways in the vicinity of Low Hall will be found in Chapter 9. That relating to Maypole and Wigan Junction Collieries is on page 188.

The Moss Hall Coal Company's Low Hall and Maypole Collieries

In Chapter 6 we have already noted the early activities of the Moss Hall Coal Company in the neighbourhood of Lower Ince. The firm started to open up several small pits near Platt Bridge, on the Low Hall Estate, in the early 1850s. Low Hall Colliery is shown in Slater's Directory for 1851[1] and in the Mines Lists for 1853/4, but does not appear in the Ince Rate Books for 1850[2].

The pits were linked to the Leeds and Liverpool Canal by a series of tramroads. The first edition of the 6" map surveyed in 1845 and 1846, is too early to show them. They do, however appear on the Deposited Plans of the London and North Western Railway's Eccles, Tyldesley and Wigan Line, dated November 1860[3] and of the Lancashire Union Railway, dated November 1863[4]. Neither set of plans extends sufficiently far to show the precise route to the canal. We deduce, from what are clearly traces of a trackbed on the first edition of the 25" map, that it followed the east side of the Ashton road, and terminated at a canal basin situated alongside the main road and on the west side of Hindley Brook.

We have been unable to unravel the earlier history of this basin. It predates the Moss Hall tramroad and is shown on the 1st edition of the 1" map, surveyed in 1840 to 1842, as well as on the Ince Tithe Map of 1841[5]. The Leeds and Liverpool Canal Act of 1819[6] authorised a railway "from the east side of the aqueduct over Hindley Brook to certain estates and collieries of the Duke of Bridgewater, called Low Hall." However it is clear, from the Deposited Plans[7,8,9] that this would have terminated at the canal further east, not far from Abram Hall.

We have found no evidence that this line was ever built. If it had been constructed shortly after the canal was opened, it must have been dismantled soon afterwards. It is not shown on Stanley's map of 1833, nor on the 1st edition of the 1" map, surveyed in 1840 to 1842. Although several of the Moss Hall Company's pits were on land leased from the Bridgewater Estates, it seems that their tramroad followed a course different from that authorised in 1819.

On 22nd May 1867 the firm was turned into a limited liability company, with the title of the Moss Hall Coal Co Ltd[10,11] and the partnership was dissolved two days later[12]. The main centre of production was now the Low Hall pits, although the original Moss Hall Colliery remained in operation until 1888. Further pits were sunk at Brookside, on a site a little to the south of the Low Hall Colliery, in the early 1870s and first appear in the Mines Lists for 1873.

To provide a main line outlet from Low Hall, the Company's existing standard gauge railway was extended from Moss Hall Colliery over Amberswood Common to Low Hall. The new line was in operation by 1860, as it is shown on the Deposited Plans of the Eccles, Tyldesley and Wigan Line prepared in November of that year [13]. Until 1879 or 1880, this extension provided the only link from the Low Hall and Brookside pits to the main line railway system. It involved a haul of some two and a half miles to the London and North Western's Springs Branch and to the Lancashire and Yorkshire's Wigan to Bolton line at Ince.

Section 27 of the Wigan Junction Railway Act of 1874 [14] required that a branch be built from the main line to the Low Hall Estate. Section 33 specified that the branch was to join with the intended railway from the Moss Hall Coal Company to the Eccles, Tyldesley and Wigan Railway, that it was be to built at the expense of the Wigan Junction Railway, that it could not become the property of the Wigan Junction Railway, and that it had to be completed before the main line was opened. Section 21 of the Wigan Junction Railway Act of 1875 [15] specified that the branch was to be double track and that it was to be free of toll to the Bridgewater Trustees and to their tenants.

We believe that the branch to Low Hall was in fact opened at the same time as the Wigan Junction main line, on 16th October 1879. Certainly it was in use by August 1880, when an accident occurred near the new sidings to the main line at Low Hall. The company's workmen's train, which ran from Moss Hall to Low Hall, was involved [16].

Improved access was also provided to the London and North Western Railway. The Sidings Schedules record that, after a number of abortive proposals, including one by the LNWR Mineral manager at St Helens in 1879, an agreement was signed of 1st July 1886. The LNWR was to build a branch from Bickershaw Junction to Low Hall at its own expense, partly on railway company land and and partly on private land. The branch would be regarded as the property of the Moss Hall Company, but would be worked by the railway company's locomotives.

We have been unable to find out when the tramroad to the canal at Platt Bridge was abandoned. It was still in use in 1868 and is shown on the Line Plan of the Eccles, Tyldesley and Wigan line of that year [17]. It had certainly disappeared by the time the 2nd edition of the 6" map was surveyed in 1888 to 1892.

The 1st edition of the 25" map, surveyed in 1892, shows that considerable development had taken place at Low Hall. Nos 5 and 6 Pits, the two main coal winding shafts, are connected to a screening plant straddling the railway tracks. There is a circular railway system on an embankment which enabled empty wagons to be pushed by a locomotive to a point where they could gravitate through the screens. A branch line provides access to the nearby Low Green Nos 7 and 8 Pits, also known as Brookside Colliery.

On 9th July 1894 a financial reconstruction of the company took place [18], preparatory to further expansion of mining activities. At that time, the company owned three locomotives and 1100 wagons [18]. In January 1895, it was reported that preparations were being made for the Maypole Colliery, a mile south of Low Hall, and that work had started on the railway which was to serve it [19]. On 24th April 1895 [20], the first sod was cut at the new colliery. The railway consisted of a short connecting line to the Wigan Junction Railway north of West Leigh and Bedford station, the Sidings Schedules giving the information that the connection here was provided under an agreement dated 1st April 1896.

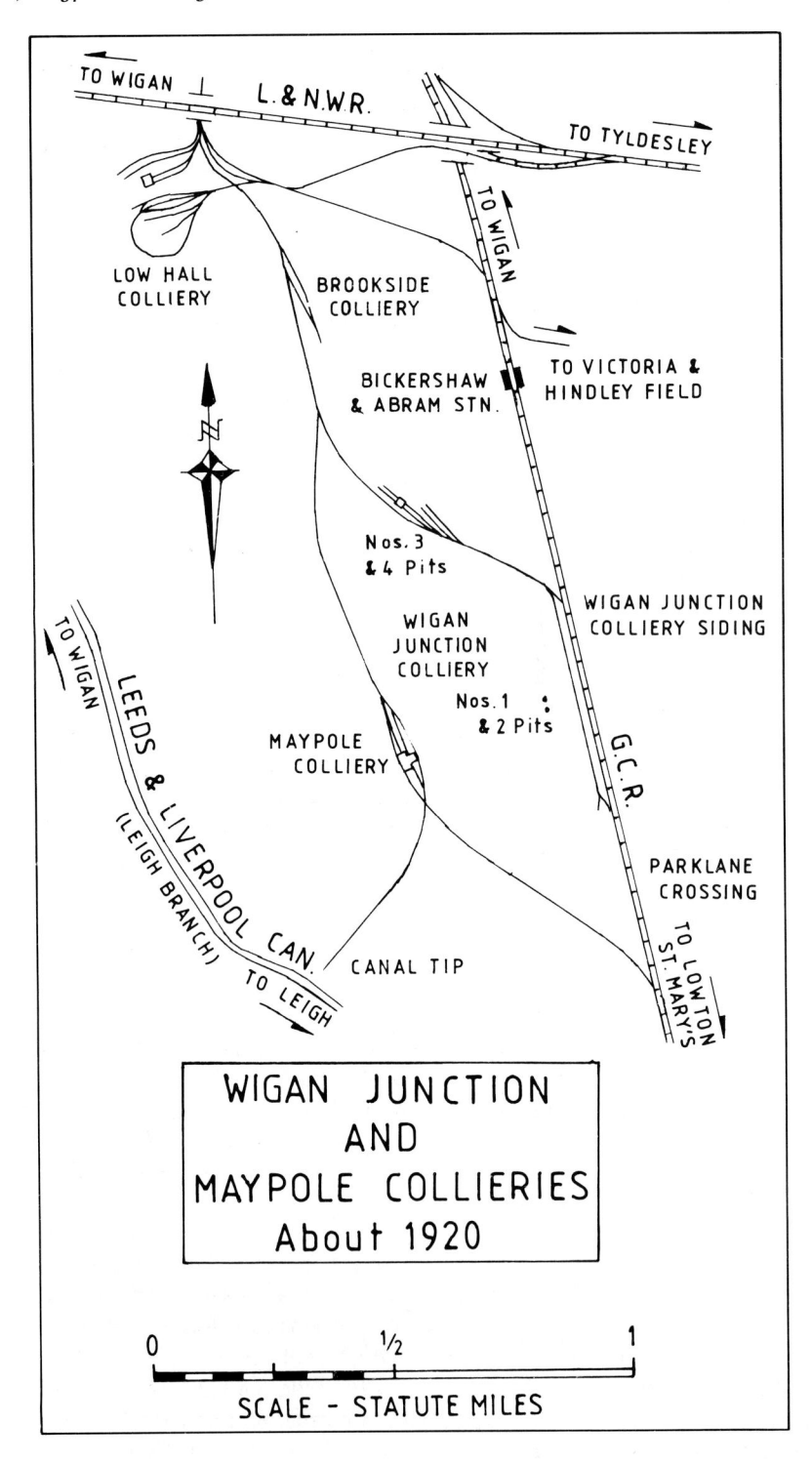

Low Hall, Maypole and Wigan Junction

WIGAN JUNCTION
AND
MAYPOLE COLLIERIES
About 1920

Low Hall, Maypole and Wigan Junction

Maypole Colliery came into production around 1905 and the Moss Hall Company's railway was extended from Brookside to join up with the siding that had been built from the colliery to the Wigan Junction line. The new bridge over Bickershaw Lane was completed before September 1905 [21].

In 1907, the Pearson and Knowles Coal and Iron Co Ltd acquired a controlling interest in the Moss Hall Coal Company Ltd and in the nearby Wigan Junction Colliery [22]. This provides a convenient break to consider the locomotives which had been used by the Moss Hall Company prior to this date.

The first locomotive that we have on record is a four coupled tender engine which was purchased second hand from the Lancashire and Yorkshire Railway in March 1854. Built by Fairbairn in 1839 for the Manchester and Bolton Railway, it had latterly been numbered 123 in the L&YR stock list [23].

Another locomotive was purchased from the Lancashire and Yorkshire Railway in March 1857. This was a small 2-2-2 tank engine, built by the London firm of George England and Co for the Liverpool Crosby and Southport Railway [23]. It had become L&YR no 124 when the Liverpool, Crosby and Southport was absorbed in 1855.

We surmise that the Fairbairn engine was acquired for working coal trains from the Moss Hall Colliery over the connection to the Springs Branch and then to Preston and elsewhere. We cannot believe that George England locomotive would have been much use for anything other than shunting at the collieries and short haul trips to the canal tips and the Lancashire and Yorkshire sidings at Ince. Perhaps it also worked to Low Hall Colliery after the line over the Amberswood Common had been opened.

We know that in 1869 the firm was still working its own trains to Preston, as its locomotive CONDOR suffered an accident there on 4th August [24]. The locomotive was being used for the first time by the Moss Hall Coal Company on that day, and it was evidently too tall to pass under a low bridge on an incline down to the coal yards north of Preston station. The chimney and the dome were knocked off. The subsequent fate of the engine is not known.

At the same period the Moss Hall Coal Company acquired some new saddle tanks locomotives. According to old colliery employees these were built at the Ince Forge and that is to some extent confirmed by old employees of the Ince Forge. We believe that a general arrangement drawing dated 1867, which is reproduced in Chapter 7, illustrates one of the six coupled engines supplied to Moss Hall. Records of neither the Ince Forge Company nor the Moss Hall Coal Company have survived, so we are uncertain of the true facts.

We have on record that Manning, Wardle and Company of Leeds supplied a six coupled saddle tank in 1873. According to the manufacturer's records this carried a plate with the inscription MOSS HALL No 4.

A further locomotive was obtained second hand around 1900, presumably to cater for the additional traffic generated from Maypole Colliery. This was a six coupled saddle tank, built by the Hunslet Engine Company in 1884 for T Nelson, the public works contractor, and delivered to him at Cardiff. The manufacturers records show that spare parts were supplied to Moss Hall in February 1902 and subsequently.

According to an old locomotive driver interviewed by the authors in the early 1950s, two six coupled saddle tanks, DOLLY and DUKE, were out of use at the Low Hall engine shed in 1908. Tradition had it that both had been built at Ince Forge. However it seems more likely that DOLLY and DUKE were the Manning, Wardle of 1873 and the second hand Hunslet of 1884, which had been given new names or nicknames. The manufacturers' records show that spare parts were last supplied in January 1900 for the Manning, Wardle and July 1906 for the Hunslet.

There was also a suggestion that two saddle tanks, named STAR and PRINCE, also allegedly of Ince Forge manufacture, had been here but had been scrapped around 1900. Our informants were not sure whether they were four coupled or six coupled engines.

Wigan Junction Colliery

The Wigan Junction Colliery Co Ltd was formed on 1st October 1875 by William and John Turner, who at that time were working the Mesnes Colliery at Wigan [25]. Sinking commenced on a site on the west side of the Wigan Junction Railway [26], then starting construction, at a point near the future Park Lane level crossing.

Considerable difficulty was encountered with water and the first two shafts had to be abandoned. In 1877, there was talk of winding up the company[27]. Other counsels prevailed and sinking of two new shafts, Nos 3 and 4 Pits, was commenced in 1878 on a site further north. The new venture proved successful and coal production started in June 1880[28].

Section 27 of the Wigan Junction Railway Act of 1875[15] required that a connection should be provided for the colliery. The 1883 Line Plan of the Wigan Junction Railway[29] indicates that sidings were laid in to serve the original sinkings, but these could have seen little use.

The Sidings Schedules refer to an agreement dated 25th February 1882. The intention appears to have been to remove the original connection near Park Lane Level Crossing and replace it with a new one more conveniently situated to Nos 3 and 4 Pits. In the event, the railway company provided a loop line, running from Park Lane Signal box to Wigan Junction Colliery Signal Box, from which leads were taken to both pairs of pits[30].

The Colliery Company had also intended to build its own line to the Leigh Branch of the Leeds and Liverpool Canal. By May 1877, land for the purpose had been leased from Mr F L Wright[31]. However, construction did not proceed, perhaps because of the financial problems facing the company.

We have found references to two locomotives owned by the company. In February 1876, the firm purchased a second hand engine for £940 from an unspecified source in Wigan, along with 60 tons of slightly defective rails[32]. This was supplemented, or replaced, by a new acquisition in 1891. In that year the Hunslet Engine Company of Leeds supplied a six coupled saddle tank, carrying the appropriate name of JUNCTION.

The Moss Hall and Wigan Junction Collieries After 1907

The controlling interest in both the Moss Hall Coal Co Ltd and the Wigan Junction Colliery Co Ltd was acquired by the Pearson and Knowles Coal and Iron Co Ltd in 1907. The two companies continued to trade under their old names, but from the point of view of the railway operations worked closely together.

The Moss Hall Company's line was extended beyond Maypole to a pier head on the Leigh Branch of the Leeds and Liverpool Canal, and a spur was put in to serve Wigan Junction Colliery. Subsequently, locomotives from the Moss Hall Company's shed at Low Hall worked the traffic to and from the Wigan Junction Colliery and performed the shunting there.

The Sidings Schedules note that the connection with the Springs Branch was removed in

1916. The level crossing over that line still remained in use to provide access to the Lancashire and Yorkshire Sidings at Ince.

After this date, all traffic for the London and North Western Railway was handled over the single line branch from Low Hall to Bickershaw Junction. The Sidings Schedules, in a note dated August 1924, stated that there was incoming traffic over this connection for Abram UDC and Hindley UDC for road repairs. A further note, dated February 1926, gives the information that Messrs Darbyshire and Jackson, who were building houses for Abram UDC, also had permission to use this connection as well as the one with the former Lancashire and Yorkshire Railway at Ince.

One of the first actions by the new management was to replace the stock of ageing locomotives. As we have mentioned above, all the former Moss Hall engines had been taken out of traffic by 1908. JUNCTION also seems to have disappeared at the same period, as no spare parts were supplied by the makers after 1906.

The replacements were two powerful six coupled saddle tanks, which came new from Peckett and Sons of Bristol in 1908. They were named DOROTHY and DELIA and were followed in 1910 by a further six coupled saddle tank which carried the name DAISY. This had been built in Pearson and Knowles own workshops, at the Dallam Forge in Warrington.

It seems to have been the usual practice to supplement these three engines with locomotives transferred from Ince Moss Colliery. According to old employees, the two Robert Stephenson engines, No 2 and No 7, were at Low Hall during or shortly after the first world war. They seem to have been exchanged with other engines allocated to Ince Moss from time to time.

One of the two large Peckett locomotives supplied to the Moss Hall Coal Company in 1908. Seen here at Low Hall engine shed in National Coal Board days. The photograph was taken in 1954. Frank Jones

191

Low Hall, Maypole and Wigan Junction

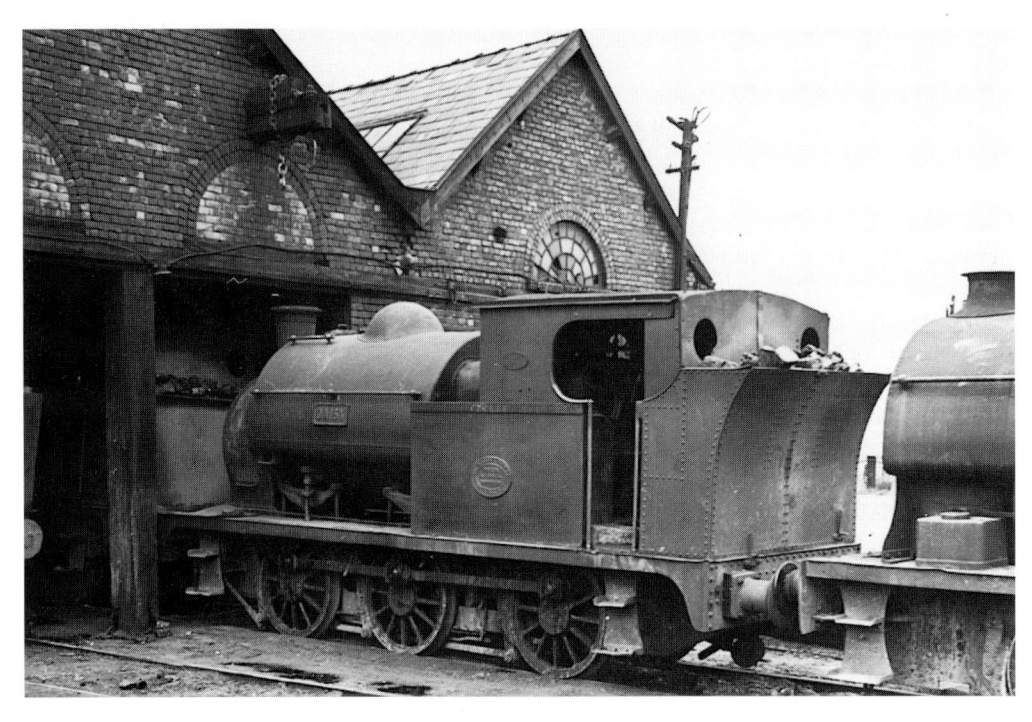

DAISY, whose large maker's plate shows that it was built by the Pearson and Knowles Coal and Iron Co Ltd at Dallam in 1910. Outside the engine shed at Low Hall on 19th August 1956. D.L. Chatfield

In 1924, as the Mines Lists show, Low Hall Nos 7 and 8 Pits at Brookside were closed, along with No 6 Pit on the Low Hall site. No 4 Pit closed the following year.

In 1930, the Moss Hall Coal Co Ltd and the Wigan Junction Colliery Co Ltd were merged into the newly formed Wigan Coal Corporation. The last of the Low Hall pits, No 5, was closed in January 1931 [33] and formally abandoned in October of the same year.

The locomotives taken over by the Wigan Coal Corporation included the Peckett six wheelers DOROTHY and DELIA and the Pearson and Knowles engine DAISY. No 2, from Ince Moss, seems to have been still here at this time, but No 7 had been returned to Ince Moss in exchange for one of the Hudswell, Clarke engines, No 5. At least, that it what we deduce from the list of locomotives compiled by the Wigan Coal Corporation in January 1932.

Subsequent lists show that No 7 had reappeared at Low Hall before 1941 and No 2 had been returned to Ince Moss. DAISY was sent to Manton Colliery, on temporary loan, at some date between 1941 and 1943, and a third engine from Ince Moss, No 1, was sent to Low Hall to replace it. Between 1943 and 1947, No 7 was sent to John Pit at Standish and No 6 was transferred from Ince Moss to Low Hall.

DOROTHY was involved in an unfortunate accident on the afternoon of Monday 30th April 1945. When it was propelling a train into a siding, built on the filled up No 7 Pit at Brookside, the ground gave way. The engine and 13 wagons fell more than 120 feet into the crater, which was described as 52 ft. long and 34 ft. wide. Sadly, the driver, Ludovic Berry, was unable to jump clear [34]. The locomotive and wagons have never been recovered.

There were some changes to the railway system during the second world war. As recorded in the Sidings Schedules, in a note dated 1943, the Wigan Coal Corporation had built a line parallel to the Wigan Junction tracks, southwards for half a mile towards Park Lane to serve a new tipping ground. By 1946 all wagons from the LNER were put in at the Maypole sidings and distributed by the colliery locomotives. The Sidings Schedules state that by this date the Park Lane connection to the Wigan Junction Colliery was out of use. The branch provided under the Act of 1874, from the former Wigan Junction Railway to Low Hall, was also taken up and does not appear on the 6" map published in 1948.

Maypole and Wigan Junction Collieries were taken over by the National Coal Board on 1st January 1947. At that time the railway system consisted of the line from Ince, past Wigan Junction and Maypole Collieries to the Leigh Branch of the Leeds and Liverpool Canal. There were connections with the London and North Eastern Railway at Maypole Colliery and with the London Midland and Scottish Railway at Ince and at Bickershaw Junction. Bickershaw Junction was reached over the single line branch from Low Hall, which was worked by exclusively by railway company's locomotives. The colliery locomotives were still stabled at the shed at Low Hall.

By vesting day, DAISY had been returned from Manton Colliery. The other locomotives at Low Hall were DELIA, No 1 and No 6. Subsequently there were numerous transfers of locomotives between collieries and these are recorded in the summary at the end of the chapter.

Maypole Colliery ceased production in June 1959 and the locomotive shed at Low Hall closed at the same time. The remaining engines, DAISY and No 6, were transferred to Wigan Junction Colliery, where the old shed was reopened. The railway from Wigan Junction Colliery to Low Hall remained in use, to serve a landsale coal yard there.

No 6, from Low Hall shed, waits to cross the Springs Branch and proceed to the ex Lancashire and Yorkshire Railway exchange sidings at Ince. There was a tramroad from Moss Hall Colliery to the canal near to this point before the Springs Branch was built.   W.S. Garth

Low Hall, Maypole and Wigan Junction

The line beyond Low Hall, over the Springs Branch, to the former Lancashire and Yorkshire Railway at Ince had closed a few years earlier, around 1955. The canal tip seems to have closed at about the same date. The track leading to it is not shown on the 6" map, revised in 1958 and 1959 and published in 1965. A stub end of the line, however, remained in situ to serve the washery.

Wigan Junction Colliery closed on 11th May 1962, but the locomotives lasted for a further three years, hauling coal, brought in by rail from other collieries, to the landsale depot at Low Hall. The depot seems to have closed early in 1965, when the railway system, or at least all that then remained of it, finally ceased operation. The private sidings agreement in respect of the connection with the former LNWR line at Bickershaw Junction was terminated on 17th May 1965[35] and the branch was formally taken out of use on 31st October 1966. There had been no traffic for some years prior to this and latterly only the connection between the Moss Hall system and the former Wigan Junction Railway had been in use.

LOCOMOTIVE SUMMARY

Moss Hall and Low Hall Collieries

Before 1867	Moss Hall Coal Company
1867 to 1930	Moss Hall Coal Co Ltd
	Subsidiary of Pearson and Knowles Coal and Iron Co Ltd from 1907
1930 to 1946	Wigan Coal Corporation Ltd
After 1-1-1947	National Coal Board

	0-4-0		Fbn	1839	13"x18"	5'0"

Ex L&YR 123, March 1854
Formerly Manchester and Bolton Railway, WOOLTON
Scrapped or sold

	2-2-2T	IC	GE		9"x12"	4'6"

Ex L&YR 124, March 1857
Formerly Liverpool, Crosby and Southport Railway, ENGLAND
Scrapped or sold

CONDOR
Damaged at coal yard at Preston on 4-8-1869. Used for the first time that day.

	0-6-0ST	IC	HE	339	1884	15"x20"	3'4"

Ex T Nelson, Cardiff 18, before February 1902
Scrapped or sold after July 1906

MOSS HALL 4	0-6-0ST	IC	MW	432	1873	13"x18"	3'0"

New
Scrapped or sold after January 1900

According to an old employee, two six coupled saddle tanks, DOLLY and DUKE were here in 1906 and were scrapped soon afterwards. Two other saddle tanks, STAR and PRINCE, were said to have been broken up about 1900. We have no other information about these four engines.

Low Hall, Maypole and Wigan Junction

DOROTHY　　　　　　　　　0-6-0ST　　IC　　P　　1148　　1908　　16"x22"
　New
　To Wigan Coal Corporation Ltd 1930
　Lost in accident 30-4-1945

DELIA　　　　　　　　　　0-6-0ST　　IC　　P　　1188　　1908　　15"x21"
　New
　To Wigan Coal Corporation Ltd 1930
　To NCB 1-1-1947 at Low Hall

DAISY　　　　　　　　　　0-6-0ST　　IC　　PK　　　　　1910　　16"x22"　4'0"
　To Wigan Coal Corporation Ltd 1930
　To NCB 1-1-1947 at Low Hall

No 2　　　　　　　　　　　0-6-0ST　　IC　　RS　　2992　　1901　　15"x20"　3'7"
　Reputedly transferred from Ince Moss during first world war
　To Wigan Coal Corporation Ltd 1930, probably at Low Hall
　From Low Hall to Ince Moss after 1932 and before 1941

No 1　　　　　　　　　　　0-6-0ST　　IC　　RS　　2880　　1900　　15"x20"　3'7"
　From Ince Moss to Low Hall after 1941 and before April 1943
　To NCB 1-1-1947 at Low Hall

No 7　　　　　　　　　　　0-6-0ST　　IC　　RS　　2848　　1897　　15"x20"　3'7"
　Reputedly transferred from Ince Moss during first world war
　From Low Hall to Ince Moss before January 1932
　To Wigan Coal Corporation Ltd in 1930, possibly at Ince Moss
　From Ince Moss to Low Hall after 1932 and before 1941
　From Low Hall to John Pit after April 1943
　To NCB 1-1-1947 at John Pit, Standish

No 5　　　　　　　　　　　0-6-0ST　　IC　　HC　　422　　1894　　16"x22"　3'10"
　Transferred from Ince Moss before January 1932
　To Wigan Coal Corporation Ltd in 1930, possibly at Low Hall
　To Ince Moss from Low Hall between April 1943 and 1-1-1947
　To Ince Moss before 1-1-1947

No 6　　　　　　　　　　　0-6-0ST　　IC　　HC　　449　　1895　　16"x22"　3'10"
　Transferred from Ince Moss after April 1943 and before 1947
　To NCB 1-1-1947 at Low Hall

Wigan Junction Colliery

1875 to 1930　　　　　　Wigan Junction Colliery Co Ltd
　　　　　　　　　　　　From 1907 subsidiary of Pearson and Knowles Coal and Iron Co Ltd. Railway system
　　　　　　　　　　　　amalgamated with that of Moss Hall Coal Company
1930 to 1946　　　　　　Wigan Coal Corporation Ltd
After 1-1-1947　　　　　National Coal Board

Second hand locomotive purchased February 1876, disposal not known

JUNCTION　　　　　　　　0-6-0ST　　IC　　HE　　546　　1891　　12"x18"　3'1"
　New
　Scrapped or sold after November 1906

Low Hall, Maypole and Wigan Junction

National Coal Board, Maypole and Wigan Junction Collieries

1947 to 1960   North Western Division, Wigan Area
1961 to 1965   North Western Division, West Lancashire Area
Maypole Colliery closed 1959
Wigan Junction Colliery closed 1962
Rail traffic ceased 1965

DAISY   0-6-0ST   IC   PK   1910   16"x22"   4'0"
   To NCB 1-1-1947
   Scrapped about 2-1965

No 1   0-6-0ST   IC   RS   2880   1900   15"x20"   3'7"
   To NCB 1-1-1947 at Low Hall
   To Dallam Forge for repairs after 12-1950, and then to Ince Moss by 2-1952

No 5   0-6-0ST   IC   HC   422   1894   16"x22"   3'10"
   To NCB 1-1-1947 at Ince Moss
   From Ince Moss by 1-1948
   Temporarily at Ince Moss 1952 and early 1952
   Scrapped at Low Hall 6-1959

No 6   0-6-0ST   IC   HC   449   1895   16"x22"   3'11"
   To NCB 1-1-1947 at Low Hall
   To Standish at end of 1962, early 1963

No 2   0-6-0ST   IC   MW   1925   1917   14"x20"
   Temporarily here from Mains mid 1947

SULTAN   0-6-0ST   IC   NW   656   1902   16"x20"   4'3½"
   Temporarily here end of 1951
   Transferred from Standish between 7-1952 and 5-1954
   Scrapped at Low Hall 6-1959

WANTAGE   0-6-0ST   IC   NW   548   1898   16"x20"   4'3½"
   Temporarily here 4-1953 to 6-1953

ACHILLES   0-6-0ST   IC   HCR   217   1880   14"x20"   3'10½"
   From Ince Moss between 2-1955 and 4-1955
   To Standish by 12-1955

BILL   0-6-0ST   IC   HE   1902   1938   15"x20"   3'7"
   From Bickershaw by 2-1956
   To Ince Moss 2-1958

No 30   0-6-0ST   IC   MW   1941   1918   17"x24"   3'9"
   Temporarily here 9 and 10-1956

GORDON   0-6-0ST   IC   RSH   7288   1945   18"x26"   4'3"
   Ex Kirkless Workshops 13-11-1958
   To Chanters 7-1959

References to Chapter 12

1	*Royal National Commercial Directory and Topography of the County of Lancaster* – Isaac Slater – Manchester, 1851		
2	Formerly in Ince UDC Offices	3	LRO PDR 717
4	LRO PDR 768	5	LRO DRL 1/44
6	59 Geo IV cap cv; 21-6-1819	7	LRO PDC 30
8	LRO PDC 35	9	LRO PDC 36
10	WRO DDX El 166/7	11	WO 1-6-1867
12	LG 7-6-1887	13	LRO PDR 717
14	37 & 38 Vic cap cxvii; 16-7-1874	15	38 & 39 Vic cap clxxxix; 2-8-1875
16	WO 13-8-1880		
17	Line Plan of Eccles, Tyldesley and Wigan Railway – LNWR Rugby, 1868 – 2 chains to 1 inch – at GMRO		
18	WO 14-7-1894	19	WO 26-1-1895
20	WO 27-4-1895	21	WRO DDX El 165/17
22	WO 14-9-1907		
23	*British Locomotive Catalogue 1825–1923, Vol 3B* – compiled by late Bertram Baxter – Moorland Publishing Co, Ashbourne, 1982		
24	CG 4-8-1869	25	WRO DDX Ap 1/11
26	CG 3-6-1898	27	WRO DDX Ap 146/35
28	CG 3-6-1898		
29	Line Plan of Wigan Junction Railway – Henry Fowler, Surveyor – 1883 – 2 chains to 1 inch – at BRPB Manchester Office		
30	WRO DDX El 165/31	31	WRO DDX Ap 146/43
32	WRO DDX Ap 146/30		
33	Directors' Report to 2nd OGM of Wigan Coal Corporation Ltd, 24-3-1932		
34	Collection of newspaper cuttings and other material in authors' possession		
35	Note on Line Plan of Eccles, Tyldesley and Wigan Railway – LNWR 1892 – 2 chains to 1 inch – At BRPB, Manchester Office		

CHAPTER 13

EDGE GREEN, BRYNN AND GARSWOOD

We now turn to a district south-west of Wigan, where mining on a significant scale did not start until the middle of the nineteenth century. The area which we shall consider was bounded on the north and west by the collieries at Winstanley, Pemberton and Platt Bridge where, as we have seen in previous chapters, the shallower seams had been exploited much earlier. To the south, in the direction of St Helens, the seams again come close to the surface and here there has also been a long history of coal mining activity.

The industrial and transport history of St Helens is far too extensive a subject to be included in the present work. We shall, however, need to stray a little over the boundary. The history of the railway systems serving the collieries which form the subject of the present chapter cannot be properly understood unless we consider the lines which were originally provided for Edge Green and its associated pits.

Evans' Edge Green and Lilly Lane Collieries

Edge Green Colliery was situated north of Golborne, to the west of what much later became the West Coast main line from Euston to Scotland. The coal here was leased as early as 12th June 1809 by William Gerard to John Evans and John Banks and the property was mortgaged to Edward Evans on 7th February 1812 [1]. The first pits to be sunk date from this period and by the early 1830s had passed into the ownership of Richard Evans [2].

The firm of Mercer and Evans was formed in 1833 [3], bringing together, under the same ownership, the collieries at Edge Green and Golborne and those at Haydock. Richard Evans and Co Ltd later took over from the partnership, the surviving collieries passing to the National Coal Board in 1947.

The interesting history of Richard Evans and Co Ltd's railways and of the locomotives which were built at the Haydock workshops is, regrettably, outside the scope of the present work. We refer those who seek further information to a booklet published by the Industrial Locomotive Society in 1980 [4]. The history of the colliery undertaking itself is described in *The Romance of Coal* [3].

Some time before the construction of the Wigan Branch Railway in the early 1830s, a tramroad had been built from Edge Green Colliery to a landsale coal yard at Golborne Smithies. The line is clearly identifiable on the 1st edition of the 1" map, surveyed in 1840 to 1842. By the period 1845 to 1847, when the 1st edition of the 6" map was surveyed, there had been further developments. A new pit had been sunk, a little to the north of the original ones, and had been provided with what is clearly a standard gauge siding from the main line railway.

A little later, probably in the early 1850s, Richard Evans opened the Dover Basin on the Leigh Branch of the Leeds and Liverpool Canal. The railway constructed by the firm to gain access to

Edge Green, Brynn and Garswood

the canal is shown on an 1864 Line Plan of the North Union Railway[5]. To reach the basin from Edge Green, the colliery trains had to draw forward on to the down main line, reverse over a cross-over on to the up main line and then proceed along the branch to the canal.

By the 1880s, these shunting operations over what was now the main line between London and Scotland, had obviously become an inconvenience and embarrassment to the London and North Western Railway. It appears that the company's records did not show how and when they had been authorised. The Sidings Schedules relate that, in March 1888, Mr Potter, the LNWR Mineral Manager at St Helens, questioned old platelayers who had worked on the construction of the Wigan Branch Railway, to find out if the Evans' railway to the canal had been in existence before the main line had been built. They recalled the tramroad to Golborne Smithies, which in 1888 was no longer in use, and confirmed that this had predated the Wigan Branch Railway. Evans' branch to the canal had, however, been built several years after the main line.

It was concluded that the canal line must have been constructed by Evans under Section 95 of the North Union Act, without any special agreement with the railway company, and that this

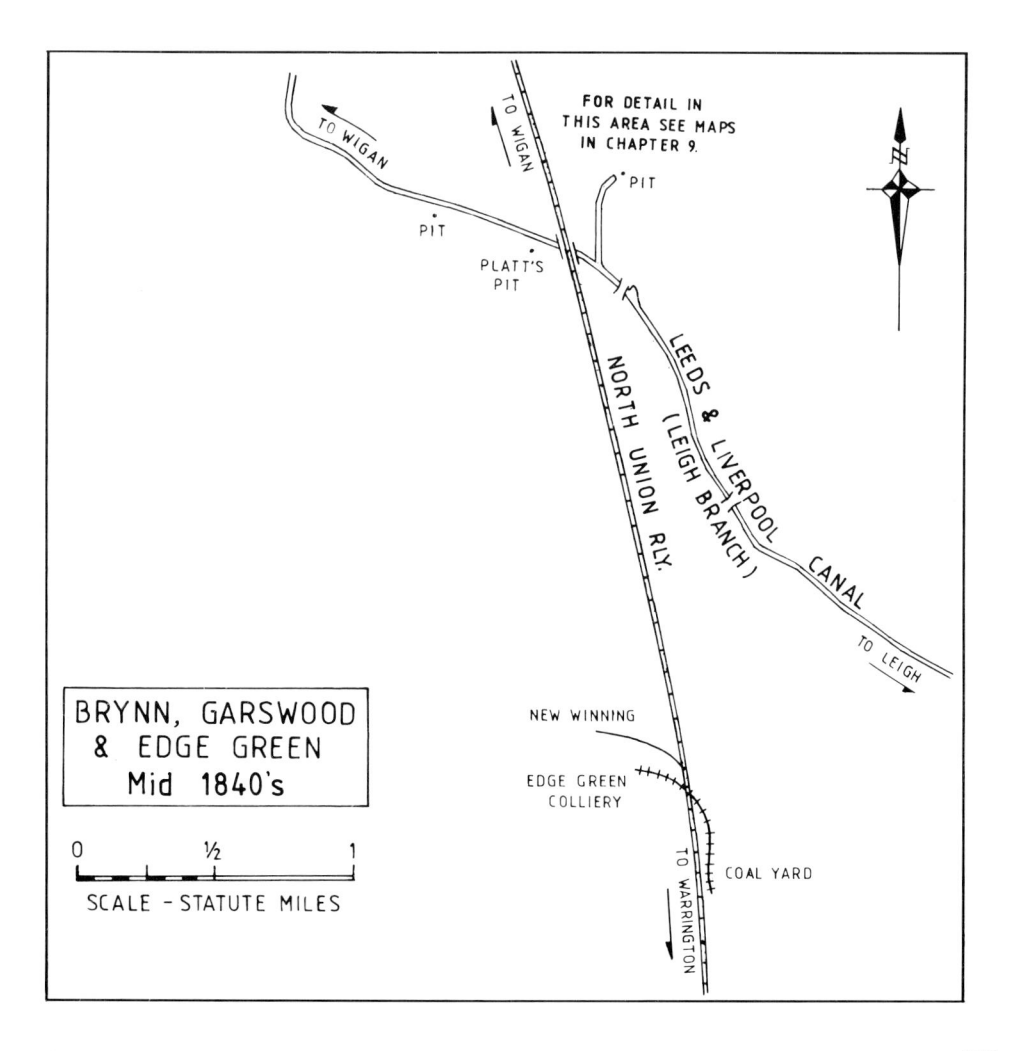

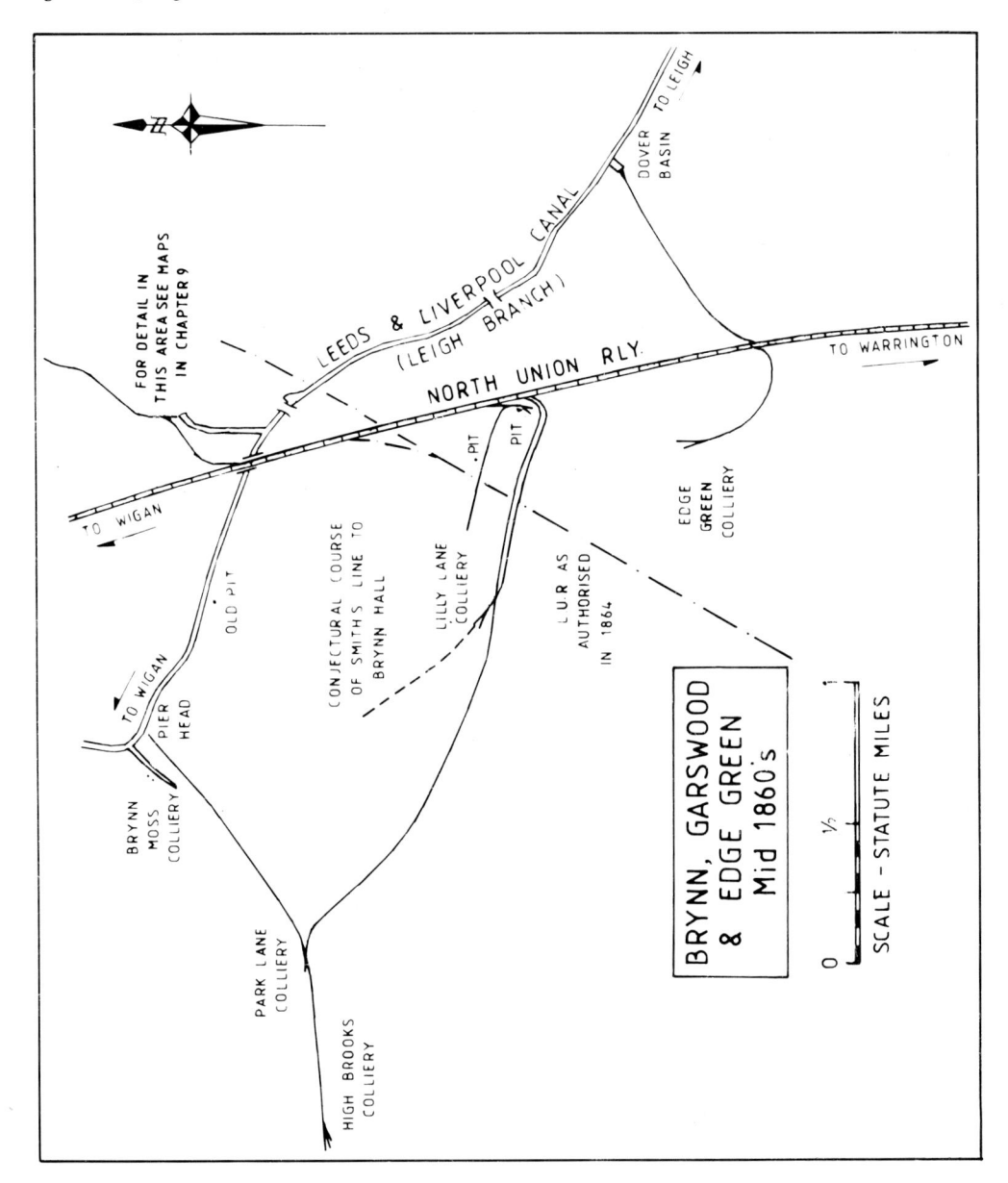

Edge Green, Brynn and Garswood

Edge Green, Brynn and Garswood

Act also conferred the right to shunt their trains across the main line. The matter was resolved by providing a bridge under the main line, to give direct access from Edge Green Colliery to the canal basin. This was done at the expense of the London and North Western Railway when the main line was being widened to four tracks under an Act of 1883[6]. The land for the diversion of the colliery line was purchased on 14th April 1888[7].

Meanwhile, Richard Evans and Company had opened their Lilly Lane Colliery, also known as Brynn, to the north of Edge Green. The mineral rights appear to have been leased from Baron Gerard as from 1st January 1864[8], but the pits do not seem to have come into operation until around 1870[3]. The railway was extended from Edge Green to serve the new workings, using, over part of its route, the trackbed of an earlier line built by Smith and Sons. The line from Edge Green to Lilly Lane appears to have been opened some time during 1871. It was stated during a court case in 1874, in which a farmer sued Richard Evans and Company for compensation for two cows killed by one of their trains, that the line had been opened three years previously[9].

There was further development of the Edge Green and Lilly Lane railway system twenty-five years later. Following the opening of the Liverpool, St Helens and South Lancashire Railway in July 1895, Richard Evans and Co Ltd extended their line southwards from Edge Green. The Sidings Schedules show that the connection with the new railway was covered by an agreement dated 30th October 1899. Coal from the Haydock and Golborne Collieries, as well as that from Edge Green and Lilly Lane, was now able to reach the canal at Dover Basin and was worked by Richard Evans own locomotives over the Liverpool St Helens and South Lancashire line.

Lilly Lane Colliery, which had latterly only been worked in a limited way, closed in 1919[3], while Edge Green Colliery ceased production, according to the Sidings Schedules, in 1928. The railway seems to have remained in operation for a few years after that and was presumably used by trains from Haydock and Golborne to Dover Basin. The Sidings Schedules record that by April 1933 the branch to the canal had been taken up and that the colliery connection with the LMS main line had been removed.

A note on the Line Plan shows that the agreement in respect of the LNER connection was transferred to T Crompton and Sons as from 11th September 1935[10]. We shall be following the subsequent history of the Edge Green site later in this chapter, but we must now return to Lilly Lane.

Smith's Lilly Lane and Brynn Hall Collieries

There had been mining at Lilly Lane before Richard Evans and Company took up their lease. The Mines Lists show that Smith and Sons had a colliery here from 1856 until 1859. From 1859 until 1864 they are shown as owning a colliery at Brynn Hall. Although the Mines Lists sometimes used different names to describe the same site, we think it probable that the firm had sunk new pits to the west of their original ones. Whatever the truth of the matter, it seems clear that the enterprise did not prosper. The plant at the Brynn Hall Collieries was up for sale on 13th February 1866[11,12] and John Smith was declared bankrupt soon afterwards[13].

In the short period that they were in occupation, Smith and Sons constructed a railway which joined the North Union line immediately to the south of what later became Mains Sidings. The line is shown in the occupation of John Smith and Company on the Deposited

Edge Green, Brynn and Garswood

Plan prepared in 1863 for the Lancashire Union Railway [14], which at that time was intended to take a more southerly course than was finally adopted. The siding connections also appear on the 1864 Line Plan of the North Union Railway, referred to earlier.

Crippin's Brynn Hall Colliery

The firm of Crippin and Smethurst first appear at Brynn Hall in the Mines Lists for 1866. We are inclined to think that the partnership probably took over from John Smith and Sons and reconstructed their earlier colliery. If so, Crippin and Smethurst may have used Smith's railway to the North Union for a year or two. Following the opening of the Lancashire Union Railway, a siding connection was put in with that line, under an agreement dated 2nd December 1869. A private line was also built to a pier head on the Leigh branch of the Leeds and Liverpool Canal.

Smethurst dropped out of the partnership around 1867, to take up an interest in the nearby Garswood Hall collieries [15], which we deal with later. The owners of Brynn Hall are variously described in the Mines Lists as Crippin and Sons in 1867 and 1868, W and J B Crippin between 1869 and 1871, William Crippin between 1872 and 1874, W and E F Crippin from 1875 to 1886 and E F and H H Crippin from 1889 to 1892.

The Mines Lists show that new pits were being sunk in 1873 by William Crippin. A Line Plan of the Lancashire Union Railway, dated 1875 [16], shows Crippin's Colliery alongside the main line, with an adjacent set of sidings leading to what is described as Brynn Hall Colliery. We are tempted to assume that the former were the new sinkings of the mid 1870s, comprising the Nos 4 and 5 Pits and that the latter were the original Nos 1, 2 and 3 Pits.

The Crippin family severed its connections with Brynn Hall Colliery at the end of 1892. The Brynn Hall Colliery Co Ltd was formed on 10th January 1893 [17,18], with Richard Fisher and Thomas Grundy as directors.

The Mines Lists show that Nos 4 and 5 Pits were abandoned in 1919, leaving Nos 1, 2 and 3 Pits, which had no doubt been modernised some time previously, still at work. The firm was clearly in poor financial shape at this time, as a shareholders' meeting on 16th April 1920 resolved to wind up the company [19]. This decision must have been rescinded, as the colliery continued in operation under the ownership of the Brynn Hall Colliery Co Ltd. According to the Sidings Schedules, there was a financial reconstruction in February 1934, when Mr Hanson, Chairman of the Central Wagon Co Ltd, took over control.

The remaining pits were abandoned, according to the Mines Lists, in November 1945. The colliery site was then taken over by S Littler Ltd, demolition contractors.

We have little information about the earliest engines which were employed at Brynn Hall Colliery. We know that a four coupled, six wheeled locomotive, with 11" x 16" cylinders, was offered for sale in July 1881 [20]. It was stated to be still at work, but too small for its present use. We assume that it had been obtained soon after the colliery opened.

The first engine for which we have authenticated information, from the manufacturer's records, was delivered in 1872. This was a six coupled saddle tank, built by the Hunslet Engine Company and carried the name BRETTARGH, after James Brettargh Crippin.

We do not know whether the colliery managed with BRETTARGH as it sole locomotive after the sale in 1881, or whether there were others which have gone unrecorded. The next definite information relates to a six coupled saddle tank, with the name SAMSON, which came second hand in 1888. Built by Manning, Wardle and Company, of Leeds, in 1867 to their M class design, it had originally been supplied to Benton and Woodiwiss, public works contractors, and delivered to Northwich. It was later used by Read Brothers, another contracting firm, and was advertised for sale by them at the new gasworks site at Padiham on 25th May 1888[21].

We think that SAMSON only lasted a few years at Brynn Hall. The manufacturer's records show that spare parts ceased to be supplied after July 1890 and its demise was probably hastened by the acquisition of another new engine in 1891. Named CHILWALL, this came from the Hunslet Engine Company and, like its predecessor of 1872, was a six coupled saddle tank. The boiler of CHILWALL exploded on 5th April 1904, killing the driver, and the engine then seems to have been scrapped. At the subsequent enquiry it was stated that the colliery had two locomotives[22], the other presumably being BRETTARGH.

A replacement for CHILWALL was obtained later in 1904 from Manning, Wardle and Company. The new engine carried the name JAMES and was an L Class six coupled saddle tank. A second identical engine was supplied by the same firm in 1921 and was named PHYLLIS.

JAMES appears to have been withdrawn from service in the late 1920s or early 1930s, followed by PHYLLIS in the mid 1930s. Thereafter, the colliery seems to have had to make do with a succession of second hand locomotives.

The records of Thomas Wrigley and Company of Prestwich[23] show that ALICE, a six coupled saddle tank built by the Hunslet Engine Company in 1901, was on hire during the period March 1927 to February 1928. This was presumably to tide the company over until their next acquisition, a six coupled saddle tank which was bought at the sale of the Swan Lane Colliery in June 1928. Built by Manning, Wardle and Company in 1892, it had been delivered new to the Arniston Coal Co Ltd, for use at a colliery near Edinburgh. Carrying the name ARNISTON, it had been purchased by the Bispham Hall Colliery Co Ltd at Orrell around 1912 and had gone to Swan Lane about 1920. At Brynn Hall it was renamed LOVICE.

The next second hand purchase was in 1932, when a four coupled saddle tank was acquired from the Winnington works of Imperial Chemical Industries Ltd, where it was named JOHN DALTON. It had been built in 1900 by Kerr, Stuart and Company, of Stoke on Trent, for Brunner, Mond and Co Ltd. It was renamed MARJORIE at Brynn Hall and had disappeared by December 1938.

A year later, in 1933, a six coupled saddle tank was purchased from the Mersey Docks and Harbour Board, where it had been numbered 41. Built in 1918 by the Avonside Engine Company of Bristol, it was named JAMES at Brynn Hall. It was disposed of some time after December 1938.

Another Avonside locomotive, built in 1909 for the Mersey Docks and Harbour Board, was purchased from Lever Brothers at Port Sunlight some time after March 1934. It took the name LOVICE from the Swan Lane engine, which was taken out of service at this time.

A third Avonside six coupled saddle tank was acquired in the 1930s from the Newport machinery dealer, A R Adams and Co Ltd. It had originally been built in 1899 for Topham, Jones and Railton for use on a contract in South Wales. It had subsequently passed through the hands of a number of South Wales companies. At Brynn Hall it was named PHYLLIS.

The list of locomotives is completed by JAMES and MARGARET, two six coupled saddle tanks built by Hudswell, Clarke and Company of Leeds in 1920 and 1921 respectively. They had been built for Cardiff Corporation, for use on reservoir construction near Merthyr Tydfil. They had later been used by Sir Lindsay Parkinson and Co Ltd on various contracts, before coming to Brynn Hall in 1939 or 1940.

Edge Green, Brynn and Garswood

MARJORIE at Brynn Hall, photographed 16th September 1933. Note that the wagon still bears the name of the former owners of the colliery.
The late B.D. Stoyel

The second PHYLLIS awaiting scrapping at Brynn Hall. In front are the remains of the second LOVICE.
G. Shuttleworth

Edge Green, Brynn and Garswood

JAMES was sold to British Sugar Corporation at Ipswich and left Brynn Hall in 1946. MARGARET went to Settle Limes Ltd at Horton in Ribblesdale during the same year. LOVICE and PHYLLIS passed to S Littler Ltd, scrap dealers, with the site. They remained for several years in a derelict condition and were broken up sometime after December 1951.

Brynn Moss Colliery

The 6" Geological Survey map of 1933 locates this colliery on the south side of the Leigh Branch of the Leeds and Liverpool canal, immediately to the west of the site of the pier head which later served Park Lane Colliery. It seems to have been sunk around 1850. It is not shown on the 1st edition of the 6" map, surveyed in 1845 and 1846, but appears in the Mines Lists for 1853/4 in the occupation of William Garstang. By 1856 it had passed to Whittle and Entwistle, who were fined for a breach of colliery rules here in January 1857 [24]. Various owners are recorded subsequently – Entwistle, Whittle and Simpson between 1858 and 1862, Entwistle and Whittle from 1863 and 1870, William Entwistle in 1871 and 1872, and William Whittle in 1872 and 1873.

The Blackrod and Brynn Moss Colliery Co Ltd was formed on 29th August 1874 [25] to take over Whittle's collieries at these two places. The firm went bankrupt shortly afterwards [26,27] and the Blackrod Collieries passed to the Blackrod Coal Co Ltd in 1876. The Mines Lists show that Brynn Moss was taken over by Dewhurst, Hoyle and Smethurst, a firm which was reformed as Smethurst, Hoyle and Grime in 1878 [28]. It passed to the Garswood Hall Collieries Co Ltd, which was founded in 1883 [29], and seems to have closed about 1887. It is not shown in the Mines Lists for 1888 and following years.

As far as can be ascertained, Brynn Moss Colliery never had a connection with the main line railway system. Its production seems to have been despatched by canal. The 2nd edition of the 6" map, surveyed in 1888 to 1892, marks the colliery, by this time dismantled, and shows that an arm about a quarter mile in length had been provided, which enabled boats to be loaded at the pit yard.

Mercer and Evans' Park Lane Collieries

Mines in the area north of Brynn were first opened out in the early 1850s. The High Brooks Colliery appears to have been started by the firm of Wright and Mercer, which worked the Cheshire Hole and Round House Collieries at Ince, described in Chapter 6. The partnership agreement in respect of High Brooks was dissolved on 3rd December 1855 [30] and the colliery first appears in the Mines Lists for 1855 in the occupation of Mercer and Evans. A separate partnership of Mercer, Thompson and Evans is stated to have begun sinking the nearby Park Lane Colliery in 1853 [31], although this does not appear in the Mines Lists until 1858. The two concerns were obviously closely linked and seem to have amalgamated in 1869. After this date the the two sites became known collectively as Park Lane Colliery, the occupiers being shown as Mercer and Evans.

A railway was constructed from High Brooks to the Leigh Branch of the Leeds and Liverpool Canal, about 1½ miles away, which also served Park Lane Colliery, part way along its route. A second railway, some 2 miles in length, ran from Park Lane to the North Union main line.

Edge Green, Brynn and Garswood

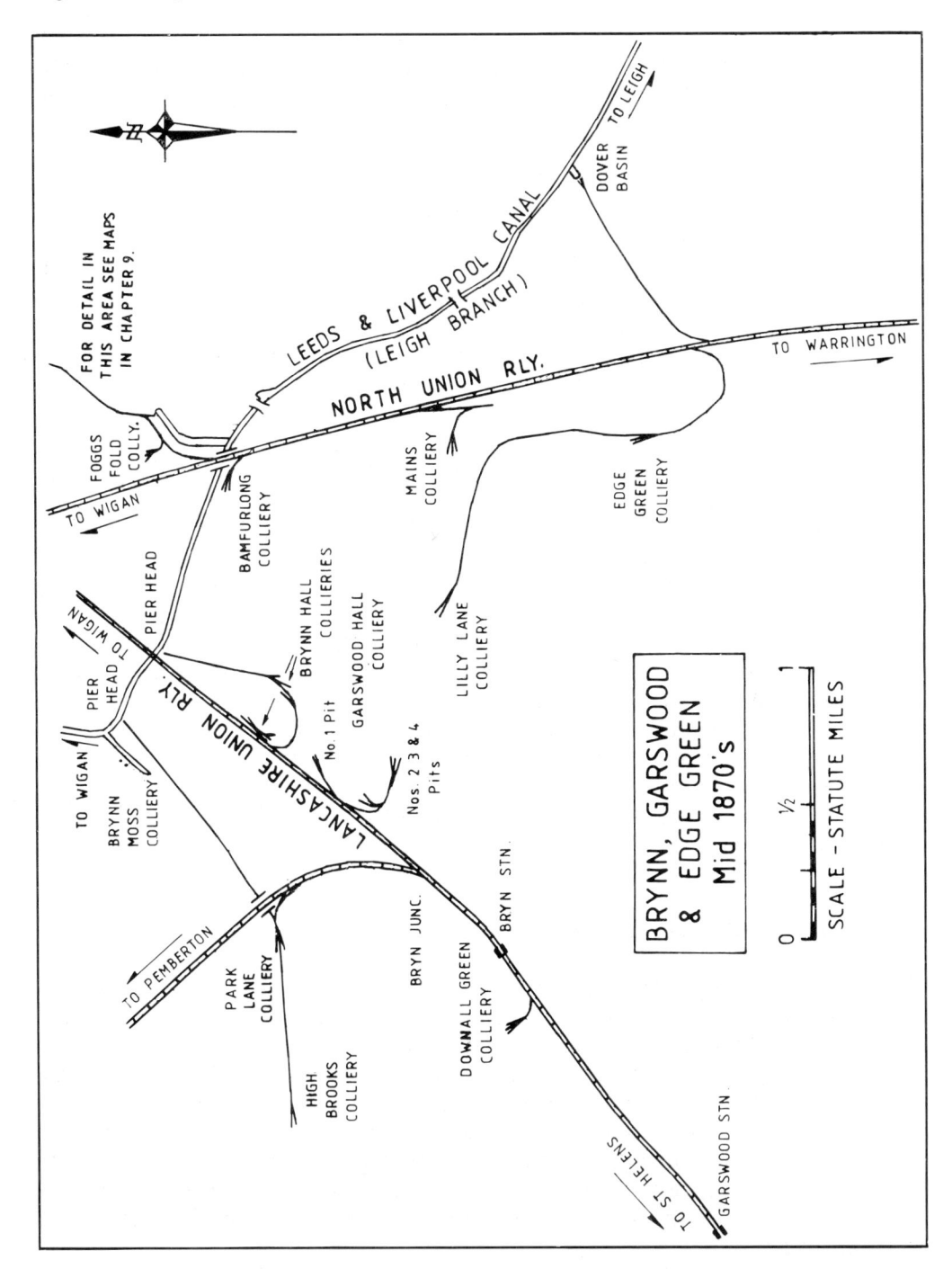

The Wigan Observer of 25th September 1959, reporting events of one hundred year previously, provides the information that the Park Lane Branch Railway, exclusively for the use of Messrs Mercer and Evans, was opened on 29th September 1859. The railway ran through the Bryn Estates and joined the North Union line 3½ miles south of Wigan. The locomotive passed up the line for the first time at about 3 pm.

Mercer and Evans' railway system is shown on the Deposited Plans of the Pemberton Branch of the Lancashire Union Railway submitted to Parliament in November 1864[32]. The line across the Bryn Estates is also shown on the Deposited Plans of the Lancashire Union Railway submitted to Parliament in November 1863[14]. The last mentioned plans make it clear that, between Lilly Lane and the North Union Railway, there were two parallel single tracks, with Smith using the southernmost line and Mercer and Evans the northernmost one. From an examination of the 1864 Line Plan for the North Union Railway dated 1864[5], to which we have referred earlier, we conclude that the two firms had adjacent, but separate, siding connections with the main line.

The construction of the Lancashire Union on its more northerly course, as authorised by the 1865 Act[33], led to changes in the rail connections to the Park Lane Colliery. In 1869 the line over the Bryn Estate to the North Union was abandoned and a new connection was laid in to join the Lancashire Union Pemberton Branch near the colliery. The private line from Park Lane to the canal was retained, and passed under the Pemberton Branch by a bridge.

To work their railway to the North Union, and also presumably that to the canal, Mercer and Evans obtained two locomotives second hand from the London and North Western Railway[34].

The first, which was purchased in October 1859, was named CALIBAN. It had been built by Sharp, Roberts and Company of Manchester in 1837 for the Grand Junction Railway and had been absorbed into LNWR stock in July 1846. Originally a 2-2-2 tender engine, we think that it may have been rebuilt with four coupled wheels, although there is no official record that this was done.

HECLA was purchased in November 1861. It had been built by the Haigh Foundry as a 2-2-2 passenger engine, again for the Grand Junction Railway. It had been rebuilt as four coupled goods engine in October 1844, before becoming LNWR property in 1846.

The Garswood Coal and Iron Company Ltd

The Garswood Coal and Iron Company Ltd was registered on 22nd November 1873[29] to take over Mercer and Evans' Park Lane Colliery. As implied by the title, the intention had been to erect blast furnaces and enter the iron manufacturing trade, but this idea was not pursued. Instead, resources were directed to developing the Park Lane Colliery and sinking new pits in the same neighbourhood, at Middle Place and Upper Park Lane.

By November 1881, when a group of students visited Park Lane, the company employed over 2000 men and owned three locomotives and over 1500 wagons [36]. An article in the *Colliery Guardian* provides a description of the collieries in the closing years of the nineteenth century[37]. Nine shafts were then in operation at Park Lane, in addition to the pits at Middle Place and Upper Park Lane.

In the late 1880s, the company began to look elsewhere for new colliery sites. The Ashton Colliery, located alongside the Lancashire Union line half a mile west of Bryn, first appears in the Mines Lists in 1888. The Sidings Lists record that the main line sidings were completed

Edge Green, Brynn and Garswood

in March 1890, under an agreement dated 13th November 1888. Ashton Colliery does not seem to have been a success, having a life of less than twenty years. According to the Mines Lists, it ceased producing coal in 1907 or 1908. It was then used as a pumping station for a few years and was abandoned in 1910. The Sidings Schedules quote Goods Traffic Committee Minute 10057 of 15th November 1911, which noted that the siding connections had been removed.

Work started in the early 1890s on a new colliery at Long Lane, to the east of Brynn. From the Mines List we deduce that Nos 1 and 2 Pits here started production in 1894. Instead of going across country to join the existing Park Lane railway system, a new line was built to the West Coast main line of the London and North Western Railway. From Long Lane, the colliery line ran for half a mile in a northerly direction on a new formation. At a point near Lilly Lane, it turned eastwards to follow the course of Mercer and Evans' 1859 line to the junction with the LNWR immediately south of Mains Colliery. The connection with the main line was provided under an agreement dated 2nd June 1892[38] and, according to the Sidings Schedules, was opened for traffic on 26th November 1893.

It is evident from the 2nd edition of the 25" map, surveyed in 1906, that between Lilly Lane and the point where the track to Edge Green diverged, both the Garswood Coal and Iron Company and Richard Evans shared the same single line of rails. The map also records the further complications which were introduced into the railway layout here after the construction of the Garswood Collieries Company's railway in the early years of the present century. However, that is a topic which we shall leave until later in this chapter.

GARSWOOD, the Hunslet of 1874, now nameless and near to the end of its days. Photographed at Garswood on 16th September 1933.
The late B.D. Stoyel

208

Edge Green, Brynn and Garswood

We have seen a copy of a draft agreement[39], which we are not sure was completed. This was drawn up in 1894 and proposed the acquisition by the Garswood Coal and Iron Company of 760 yards of Evans' line east of Lilly Lane. Evans' lease of land for the line, dating from 1864, was to be transferred by Baron Gerard to the Garswood Company. The Garswood Company was to pay £450 compensation to Richard Evans and Company, which was to have the use of the line, but was not to be liable for repairs.

The Garswood Coal and Iron Co Ltd was put into voluntary liquidation in May 1929 and its assets were taken over by the Garswood Collieries Co Ltd on the 6th of that month[29]. Before dealing with subsequent events, we need to look at the locomotive history of the Coal and Iron Company.

Shortly after its formation in 1873, the company set about ordering new locomotives. Presumably the old London and North Western engines, purchased by Mercer and Evans, were still in service at this time and were in need of replacement by more suitable designs.

In 1874, the Hunslet Engine Company supplied a six coupled saddle tank, named GARSWOOD, and, about 1877, a six coupled saddle tank, named ASHTON, was ordered from Walker Brothers of Wigan. Another engine, noted during the students' visit at the end of 1881[36], was reported to have been built by Hughes of Loughborough, but we have been unable to trace any further information about it.

A second hand six coupled saddle tank was acquired in the mid 1880s. Named SEFTON, this engine had been built by Manning, Wardle and Company of Leeds in 1882, for the public works contractor J P Edwards, for use on the construction of the Southport and Cheshire Lines Extension Railway. Subsequently, there were changes in the contractual arrangements and the later ownership of the locomotive is not clear. The plant was sold on 27th and 28th May 1885[40], following the completion of the works and we believe that this was when the locomotive was purchased by the Garswood Coal and Iron Co Ltd.

In the 1890s, additional motive power was needed to service the Ashton Colliery and the new colliery at Long Lane. Two identical six coupled saddle tanks were supplied by the Bristol firm of Peckett and Sons in 1892 and 1898. These were numbered 5 and 6 respectively at Garswood. A slightly smaller six wheeler followed from the same firm in 1900, taking the number 7.

According to old employees 5, 6 and ASHTON were associated with Long Lane colliery, and No 2, GARSWOOD and SEFTON with Park Lane, but we have no doubt that the engines were moved from one location to the other as circumstance dictated.

The Garswood Hall Collieries

The earliest pits at Garswood Hall Colliery were sunk in the late 1860s by the firm of Dewhurst, Hoyle and Smethurst and first appear in the Mines Lists for 1868. These, the Nos 1 and 2 Pits, were situated immediately to the south of Brynn Hall Colliery. They were provided with a connection to the Lancashire Union Railway, under an agreement which the Sidings Schedules say was dated 9th April 1870. In 1874 work started on Nos 3 and 4 Pits[41]. The first sod of No 5 Pit was turned on 13th April 1877[42] and No 6 Pit followed shortly afterwards.

As we shall see later, in Part 2, Chapters 25 and 26, Dewhurst, Hoyle and Smethurst were already working mines at Blackrod and Westhoughton, and later took over the Brynn Moss and Holme House Collieries. The title of the firm was changed to Hoyle, Smethurst and Grime on 17th September 1878, following the retirement of Robert Dewhurst[43]. On 24th March 1883 the

Edge Green, Brynn and Garswood

One of the two Garswood Coal and Iron Company's Peckett locomotives, No 6, photographed on 16th September 1933.
The late B.D. Stoyel

Garswood Hall Collieries Co Ltd was registered, with William Smethurst, John Smethurst, Joseph Hoyle and John Grime as directors [29, 44].

An article in the *Colliery Guardian* in 1892 provides a contemporary description of the colliery [45]. Seven pits were now in operation, No 7 having been sunk, according to the Mines Lists, in the late 1880s. The workshops must have been very well equipped, because the article states that two of the locomotives used at the colliery and the winding engines for Nos 3 and 5 shafts had been built here.

New leases near Edge Green were taken up by the Garswood Hall Company towards the end of the century. Work started on the sinking of No 9 Pit on 1st May 1901 and coal production commenced a year or two later [46]. A new railway was built from the existing sidings near Nos 5, 6 and 7 Pits past No 9 Pit to join the Liverpool, St Helens and South Lancashire line near Edge Green. The Sidings Schedules show that the connection here was provided under an agreement dated 25th October 1898.

At a point about a quarter of a mile west of the Lilly Lane level crossing, the new line joined into and immediately diverged from the Garswood Coal and Iron Company's line of 1894. The 2nd edition of the 25" map, surveyed in 1906, shows that a signal box and signals were provided here to prevent conflicting train movements.

Beyond the junction, the new line ran parallel to and on the south side of the Garswood Coal and Iron Company's line, which, as we have noted earlier, was also used by Richard Evans and Company's trains from their Lilly Lane Colliery. A quarter of a mile beyond the level crossing the Garswood Hall line turned south, and then ran parallel to Richard Evans' line as far as Edge Green, where it diverged towards No 9 Pit and the main line sidings.

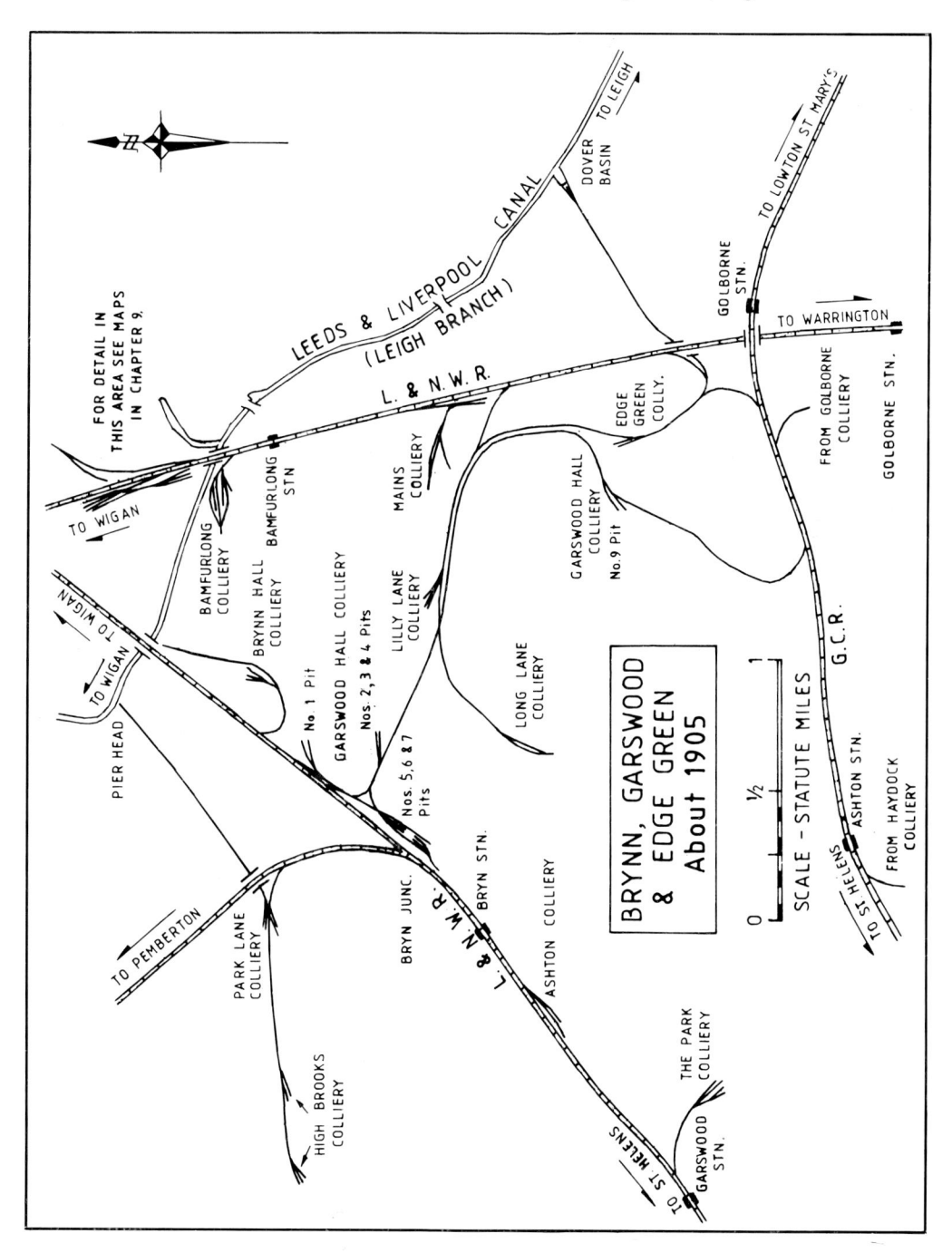

Edge Green, Brynn and Garswood

The Garswood Hall company ran a workmen's train to take colliers to and from No 9 Pit at change of shift times. A fatal accident occurred at Lilly Lane crossing in March 1917 and we learn from the newspaper reports that, on that occasion, the train consisted of the locomotive, nine empty wagons and one coach [47,48].

Before going on to describe the later history of the collieries and their railway system, we shall consider the locomotives which were here before the Garswood Coal and Iron Co Ltd assets were acquired in 1929.

We have been unable to trace any facts about the earliest locomotives used at Garswood Hall. We know that, in 1865, Dewhurst, Hoyle and Smethurst purchased two engines second hand from the Lancashire and Yorkshire Railway. It has also been suggested that a tank locomotive was obtained from the London and North Western Railway in the same year. These acquisitions predate the railway system at Garswood Hall. As we discuss in Part 2, Chapter 26, we think that the engines may have been used at the firm's collieries at Anderton Hall and Snydale Hall.

The Chronicles of Boulton's Siding [35] records that, around 1870, a locomotive named HERCULES was hired to the Garswood Park Colliery, which we assume to be that owned by Dewhurst, Hoyle and Smethurst. HERCULES is supposed to have originally been a six coupled tender engine, built by the Bradford firm of Thwaites and Garbutt. It had been purchased by Boulton as part of a job lot at Cardiff in 1866, and had been rebuilt by him as a saddle tank.

We think that this may have been the same engine which was recalled by an old employee at Garswood Hall and which was nicknamed "Black Tom". It was described as an old style of locomotive, with slide valves below the cylinders. It was reputed to have been converted to a stationary engine and later used for the sinking of No 9 Pit.

The first engine at Garswood Hall for which we have reliable information was a six coupled saddle tank, built in the colliery workshops. This was 1 ARTHUR, which carried a plate showing that it had been completed in 1884. We have no records of the second engine which the *Colliery Guardian* article implies was also constructed at the colliery. We think that the report may have been incorrect.

The next engine we have on record was 2 CYMBELINE, which had been built in 1866 for the Brecon and Merthyr Railway by Sharp, Stewart and Company of Manchester. It was one of the firm's standard types of long boiler engines supplied to a variety of railway companies at home and abroad and was sold by the Brecon and Merthyr to Garswood Hall Collieries in May 1889 [49].

This was followed by two further second hand locomotives. The first to arrive was a six coupled saddle tank, built by Manning, Wardle and Company in 1874. It had been supplied to T J Waller, who employed it on a railway contract in West Yorkshire, where it carried the name RIPPONDEN. It was later used by another public works contractor, W W Walmesley, of Manchester, who renamed it KATE. The manufacturer's records show that it was then purchased by the Garswood Hall Collieries Company, although they do not record a date for the transaction. KATE did not stay at Garswood very long, as it had been resold to the Frodingham Iron Company by 1899.

The second engine, a six coupled saddle tank built by the Hunslet Engine Company in 1887 and named IRWELL, also had a history in the public works contracting field. It had been supplied new to T A Walker for his work on the Manchester Ship Canal. It subsequently passed through the hands of several other contractors and came to Garswood Hall from T Oliver of Rugby. The manufacturer's spare parts records show that it was purchased by the colliery between September 1897 and March 1898. It lasted at Garswood Hall until the first world war, when it was sold for use at the Aintree Factory of the Ministry of Munitions, which had been established in 1917 or 1918.

To this period also belong two locomotives, LINCOLN and PERCY, which were recalled in interviews with old employees. We have been unable to trace any further information about them. LINCOLN was described as a four wheeler, and we note that an engine of this name, built by Ruston and Proctor, had been used on the Manchester Ship Canal Contract. Both had disappeared from Garswood Hall by the mid 1920s

In 1901, the company made its first purchase of a new locomotive. This was a six coupled saddle tank, named IMOGEN, which came from Robert Stephenson and Company. It was followed in 1912 by 4 ROBERT, another six coupled saddle tank, but, this time, from the Avonside Engine Company of Bristol.

Finally, in September 1916, another second hand engine was purchased from Bentley and Jubb, the Wigan dealers, perhaps as a replacement for IRWELL. Named KING, it was a six coupled saddle tank and had been built by Peckett and Sons in 1902. It had originally been supplied to the Derwent Valley Water Board and was used on the construction of a reservoir in the Peak District.

Garswood Hall Collieries Co Ltd after 1929

The assets of the Garswood Coal and Iron Co Ltd were taken over by the Garswood Hall Collieries Co Ltd on 6th May 1929[29].

The immediate result was that the Park Lane Colliery was taken out of production. By this time, only the Nos 1, 2 and 3 Deep Pits and the Ince and Middle Pits were open and the Mines Lists show that all of them were formally abandoned on 30th June 1929. The sidings Schedules record that, by October 1931, all the sidings on the colliery company's land had been removed.

Two of the pits were reopened by the Landgate Colliery Co Ltd in the early 1930s and were taken over by the National Coal Board on 1st January 1947, finally closing in 1961 or 1962. Production, however, was on too limited a scale to justify reopening the rail connections.

The closure of the Park Lane Colliery and its associated railway system left the company without an outlet to the canal. Discussions, reported in the Sidings Schedules, were held in 1930 with the London Midland and Scottish Railway with a view to opening a new tip at Bamfurlong. This was not proceeded with, as the railway company did not consider it a commercial proposition.

Instead, the colliery company built a new line, just over a mile in length, from near the now abandoned Lilly Lane Colliery to the Leigh Branch of the Leeds and Liverpool Canal. Now that Richard Evans and Company's trains had ceased to run, it was possible to rationalise the track layout in the vicinity of Lilly Lane. The former double track section was reduced to single track, with the junction between the lines to the LMS and LNER sidings now moved east of the level crossing. At the same time, a short spur was built, so that trains could run from the Long Lane pits to Garswood Hall Colliery without the need for reversal.

The run down of colliery operations led to a run down in the locomotive stock. Six locomotives appear to have been taken over from the Garswood Coal and Iron Co Ltd in 1929 – ASHTON, SEFTON, GARSWOOD, No 5, No 6 and No 7. In addition there were five locomotives previously in the ownership of the Garswood Hall Collieries Co Ltd – ARTHUR, CYMBELINE, IMOGEN, ROBERT and KING.

Edge Green, Brynn and Garswood

The Robert Stephenson locomotive IMOGEN hard at work, against a backdrop of the Wigan "Alps". Photographed on 11th May 1957.
Alex Appleton

The Avonside ROBERT poses for its photograph outside the locomotive shed at Garswood Hall on 24th May 1957.
J.A. Peden

SEFTON was presumably the six coupled locomotive, with 13½"x18" cylinders and 3'6" driving wheels, which was advertised for sale in August 1929[50]. We think that it did not find a purchaser and was broken up along with ARTHUR, ASHTON, and CYMBELINE in the early 1930s. No 7, the Peckett taken over from the Garswood Coal and Iron Co Ltd, was sold in 1929 to Sir Lindsay Parkinson and Co Ltd, for use on the East Lancashire Road contract.

Some of the remaining locomotives must have been reaching the end of their useful lives, as another six coupled saddle tank was obtained second hand at this period. Named WYNNSTAY, it had been built by Manning, Wardle and Company in 1905 for Wynnstay Collieries Ltd, near Wrexham. It had subsequently been used by the contractors for the construction of the new dock at Bromborough for Lever Brothers Ltd. The engine then appears to have been employed by Lever Brothers at their works for a few years before coming to Garswood Hall. The manufacturers' spare parts records show that it arrived at the colliery at some date between July 1929 and May 1933.

The 1930s saw further colliery closures. Nos 1 and 4 Pits at Garswood Hall had already ceased work, the former as long ago as 1905. Long Lane No 2 Pit closed in March 1931[51]. The Mines Lists show that, by 1934, Garswood Hall No 5 Pit was only used for pumping and No 2 Pit for ventilation purposes. Garswood Hall No 3 Pit was abandoned in July 1936, although it was subsequently reopened. No 9 Pit, at Edge Green, was abandoned permanently in November 1938.

With the reduction in traffic in the immediate pre-war period, the locomotives WYNNSTAY and GARSWOOD were cut up. WYNNSTAY had been out of service in the disused engine shed at Long Lane until the end of 1938.

The railway from Lilly Lane to the LNER exchange sidings closed shortly after No 9 Pit ceased work, the Sidings Schedules noting that the agreement relating to the connection was terminated on 31st October 1940. The railway from Lilly Lane to the LMS main line at Long Lane Sidings closed two or three years later. The Sidings Schedules record that the agreement here was terminated on 25th March 1943, that the sidings belonging to the colliery company had been taken up by 27th April of the same year, and that work to remove Long Lane signal box was complete by 14th October 1945. Thereafter all outgoing coal was dealt with at the Garswood Hall sidings on the Lancashire Union line at Bryn Junction or at the canal tip.

In 1943 and again in 1944, the Garswood Hall company made enquiries about the purchase of a new locomotive to supplement their ageing fleet and perhaps to cater for the increased war time output of coal. On 27th July 1944 the Hunslet Engine Company of Leeds accepted their order for a six coupled saddle tank of the War Department Austerity type. The engine, which was allocated Hunslet works number 3302, was promised for delivery in March 1945. What happened next is described in a recent article in *Locomotives Illustrated*[52].

In September 1944, one of a batch of locomotives then under construction for the War Department became available. The engine concerned was Hunslet works number 3187, which should have become War Department no 75137. However, the final tests had not been witnessed by the government inspector who therefore refused to accept it. The Hunslet Engine Company promptly despatched the engine, on 28th September 1944, to Garswood Hall, where it was put into traffic. Unfortunately for the colliery company, the War Department purchasing authorities had second thoughts and demanded that the engine should be

Edge Green, Brynn and Garswood

WYNNSTAY, the Manning, Wardle which came from Port Sunlight, not long after its arrival at Garswood Hall. Photographed on 16th September 1933. Note the smartly kept appearance. *The late B.D. Stoyel*

returned to them. It went back to the Hunslet Engine Company on 3rd November, and was subsequently given War Department no 75147. Garswood Hall Collieries cancelled their order and works no 3302 was eventually delivered to Manchester Collieries Ltd.

On the formation of the National Coal Board on 1st January 1947, Long Lane No 1 Pit and Garswood Hall Nos 3, 5, 6 and 7 Pits were still at work. They were incorporated in the St Helens Area of the North Western Division. Five locomotives, IMOGEN, ROBERT, KING, No 5 and No 6, were transferred to the new owners. All now worked from the locomotive shed at Garswood Hall Colliery, as the practice of stabling a locomotive at Long Lane had ceased some time before 1946.

The last pit at Long Lane closed in April 1955 and the colliery was dismantled in 1957. The railway from Lilly Lane to the canal was observed to be out of use in May of that year. With the reduced layout there was now only work for two locomotives and by this time the other Garswood Hall engines had been transferred elsewhere in the St Helens Area of the National Coal Board. Only one locomotive, EARLESTOWN, was moved into Garswood Hall during this period.

The remaining pits at Garswood Hall ceased work in August 1958, but the washery, which processed coal brought by rail from other collieries, did not close until four years later. The last portions of the railway system were taken out of use and the last locomotive was sent away before February 1962.

Edge Green, Brynn and Garswood

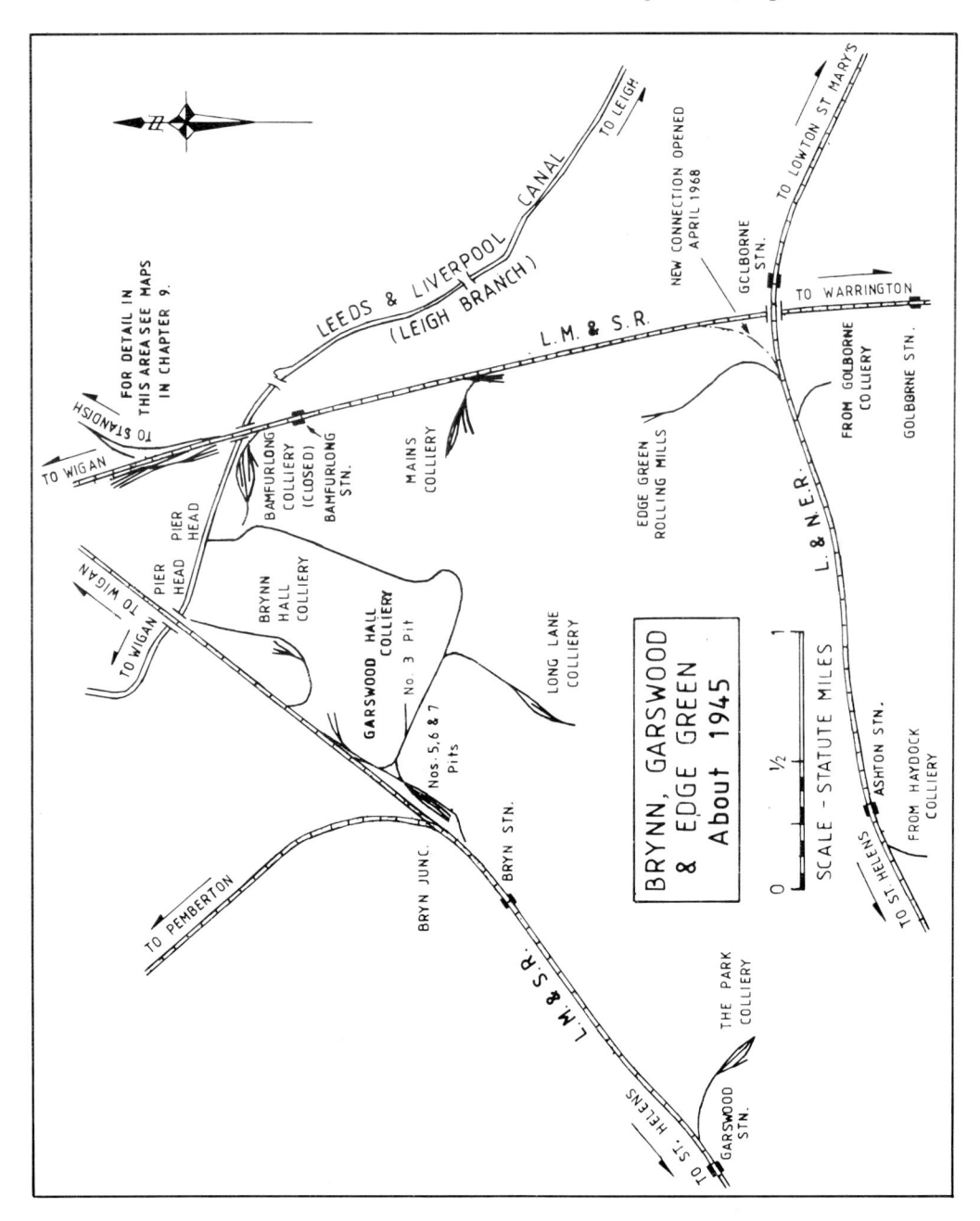

Edge Green, Brynn and Garswood

A general view of the Park Colliery, with the locomotive HORNET and loaded coal wagons. Note the pit brow lasses in the centre distance.　　　　　　　　　　　　　　　　　　　　　　　　　　　　　　　　　　　　J.A. Peden Collection

Stone's Downall Green and Park Collieries

Thomas Stone combined the businesses of railway contractor and colliery proprietor. He had associations with collieries at Bradley Hall and Hindley Green, to which we shall return in Part 2, Chapters 23 and 28. With the construction of the Lancashire Union Railway, he turned his attention to mining in the neighbourhood of Brynn.

His Downall Green Colliery first appears in the Mines Lists for 1868. It had a siding connection to the main line about a quarter of a mile west of Bryn Station, which was provided, according to the Sidings Schedules, under an agreement dated 23rd February 1870. From 1873 to 1887, the Mines List show the occupiers as Thomas Stone and Sons. Thomas Stone died on 1st July 1881 [53] and after 1887 the Mines Lists show the firm as J and R Stone. The Sidings Schedules state that in 1891 the colliery was worked out and that the siding connection was removed in October of that year.

Meanwhile J and R Stone and Company had opened out another colliery, the Park Colliery at Garswood. Sinking started in October 1887, when the first sod was cut by Mrs John Stone [54]. Coal was first wound from No 1 Pit in January 1888 and from No 2 Pit in September 1889 [55]. A siding connection was provided at a point a quarter mile on the Wigan side of Garswood station, under an agreement dated, according to the Sidings Schedules, 29th February 1888.

The colliery is described in an article in the *Colliery Guardian* in 1896 [55]. At this time there were three shafts. There was a half mile branch to Garswood Station. The colliery company's locomotive pushed the empty wagons up a 1 in 90 gradient to sidings above the screens. From here empty wagons gravitated, along one of twelve sidings through the screens, over the weighing machine, and then to the loaded wagon sidings where they were marshalled for despatch.

J and R Stone and Co Ltd was formed in 1909, and the colliery continued in the same ownership until it was nationalised on 1st January 1947.

Little information has survived about the locomotives used at Downall Green Colliery. We think it likely that Thomas Stone made use of engines which formed part of his contractors plant and that they worked at Downall Green between jobs.

Joseph Adamson, who was presumably the manager, advertised in 1877 that he needed a small tank locomotive, four wheels coupled with 8" or 9" cylinders for use at Downall Green Colliery[56].

Perhaps Manning, Wardle and Company of Leeds was one of the firms which responded to the advertisement. Later that year they sold MOLE, an F Class four coupled saddle tank, with 10" cylinders, to Thomas Stone. It is not entirely clear whether this engine went new to Downall Green or was delivered to one of Stone's contract sites; we think the former. Be that as it may, it was certainly at Downall Green by July 1883, when spare parts were supplied there.

We also know that Thomas Stone purchased two former Blackpool and Lytham Railway 2-2-2 Saddle tanks, KING and QUEEN, from the Lancashire and Yorkshire in 1877, as the sale is authorised in the Railway Company's Minutes of 31st January. Again, we are not sure whether these engines were acquired in connection with the contracting side of the business or for use at the collieries.

BUSY BEE, a typical Manning, Wardle product, in smartly polished condition, photographed at the Park Colliery.
J.A. Peden Collection

Edge Green, Brynn and Garswood

Old employees we interviewed around 1950 said that an engine named QUEEN had been the earliest engine that they could remember at the Park Colliery. It was described to us as a six wheeled locomotive and was presumably the one offered for sale in March 1892 [57]. The advertisement refers to a six wheeled, four coupled tank, with 12" x 15½" cylinders and 3'8" driving wheels. It had been replaced by a larger engine. We do not know whether the QUEEN at the Park Colliery was a rebuild of the Blackpool and Lytham engine or a later acquisition which had replaced it.

The larger engine referred to in the advertisement was undoubtedly BUSY BEE which was delivered by Manning, Wardle and Company in 1892. BUSY BEE was a six coupled saddle tank of the manufacturer's K class, with 13"x 18" cylinders. It was followed by HORNET, a somewhat bigger six coupled saddle tank, with 15" cylinders, from the same makers in 1901.

The trio of insects was made up by WASP, the former MOLE, which had been renamed after being transferred from Downall Green Colliery. A replacement WASP came new from Manning, Wardle and Company in 1915, and the four wheeler of 1877 was disposed of, finding its way to the Trustees of Robert Walker, who operated quarries at Ferriby on Humberside. The replacement engine was a six coupled saddle tank, similar to HORNET, but with 14" cylinders.

A third WASP appeared in 1945. Like its predecessor it was a six coupled saddle tank and had been built by Manning, Wardle and Company in 1902. It had been delivered new to Topham, Jones and Railton, contractors, with whom it had been named DYNEVOR. It had subsequently seen service with Nott, Brodie and Company, also contractors, before going to Cudworth and Johnson, the Wrexham based machinery merchants, from whom it was purchased by J and R Stone Ltd.

MAKERFIELD, one of a pair of well tanks built at the Haydock Foundry of Richard Evans and Co Ltd, which were transferred to the Park Colliery by the National Coal Board. Both ended their days here. J.A. Peden

Edge Green, Brynn and Garswood

The Park Colliery was taken over the National Coal Board on 1st January 1947. According to the Sidings Schedules, production ceased on 3rd June 1960. The connection with the main line does not seem to have been removed until after April 1963. The colliery was subsequently dismantled and, at the time of writing, the site and some of the old buildings are occupied as Fishwick's Trading Estate.

The locomotives BUSY BEE, HORNET and the third WASP passed to the National Coal Board. They were broken up in 1952, 1960 and 1959 respectively. KING, one of the Garswood Hall locomotives, was here for a short period between 1952 and 1954. Latterly, the shunting was performed by MAKERFIELD and PARR, two of the six coupled well tanks built at the Haydock Workshops of Richard Evans and Co Ltd. They remained out of use, locked in the engine shed, after the colliery closed and were not broken up until early 1963.

Later Developments at Edge Green

Earlier in this chapter, we noted that Richard Evans and Company's siding from the London and North Eastern Railway, which served the Edge Green Colliery, was taken over by T Crompton and Sons. This firm had been founded in 1866 and specialised in the manufacture of hinges, locks, and builders hardware, as well as carrying on a general foundry business [58]. In the mid 1930s they acquired part of the Edge Green Colliery site for a new foundry and an agreement in respect of the main line connection was signed by them on 11th September 1935.

In 1961 the works, now known as the Edge Green Rolling Mills, was absorbed into the Guest, Keen, Nettlefold Group. From 1963 it was operated by a subsidiary company with the title Crompton, Nettlefold, Stedman Ltd [58]. The factory was closed down a few years later and the private sidings agreement was terminated on 30th September 1967.

We have no record of what motive power was used by Crompton's before and during the second world war. However, in 1950 a small diesel locomotive was supplied by the Leeds firm of John Fowler and Company. This engine was taken over by the new owners of the factory in 1963. Following the closure of the Edge Green establishment it was transferred to another company in the same group, G K N Reinforcements Ltd, for use at its works on the old Douglas Bank Colliery site at Wigan.

Freight train services were withdrawn from the former Liverpool, St Helens and South Lancashire Railway beyond Ashton in Makerfield in January 1965. The portion of line from Lowton St Marys to Ashton was retained to serve the works of Lowton Metals Ltd, which had been established alongside the old goods yard there in 1963.

In April 1968, British Railways closed the line between Lowton St Marys and Edge Green. At the same time they opened a new chord between Edge Green and their west coast main line to maintain access to Ashton in Makerfield. In July 1968 the section from Ashton to Haydock was reopened to serve a oil depot belonging to Shell Mex and B P Ltd.

The traffic to the oil depot at Haydock ceased in February 1983 and the private sidings agreement was terminated as from 31st March 1984. Traffic to the Lowton Metals works ceased in March 1987 and the track between Ashton and Haydock was taken up in April 1988 [59].

Meanwhile there had been further developments at Edge Green. A tarmacadam roadstone plant had been opened by Kelbit Ltd on the old colliery site and the track had been relaid on the siding to the former LNER line. The connection was reinstated under an agreement dated 19th March 1987, the first train running to the works on 17th July 1987 [59].

Edge Green, Brynn and Garswood

The track to Ashton from a point about 1000 yards beyond Edge Green was due to be lifted towards the end of 1988[59]. The trains to Edge Green, which consist of tank wagons of bitumen from Immingham, now provide the only traffic over the chord from the West Coast main line. The main line locomotive places the wagons at the works and Kelbit Ltd do not require their own shunting engine.

LOCOMOTIVE SUMMARY

Brynn Hall Colliery

c1866 to 1892   Various Crippin family partnerships
1893 to 1945   Brynn Hall Colliery Co Ltd
Colliery closed 1945

	0-4-2 or 2-4-0					11"x16"	
For sale July 1881							
BRETTARGH	0-6-0ST	IC	HE	75	1872	12"x18"	3'1"
New, despatched from works 23-4-1872							
Scrapped or sold							
SAMSON	0-6-0ST	IC	MW	239	1867	13"x18"	3'6"
Ex Read Brothers, Padiham, 1888							
Scrapped or sold							
CHILWALL	0-6-0ST	IC	HE	497	1891	15"x20"	3'4"
New							
Boiler exploded 5-4-1904 and locomotive subsequently scrapped							
JAMES	0-6-0ST	IC	MW	1633	1904	12"x18"	3'0"
New							
Scrapped after May 1925							
PHYLLIS	0-6-0ST	IC	MW	1804	1921	12"x18"	3'0"
New							
Scrapped or sold about 1935							
ALICE	0-6-0ST	IC	HE	578	1901	13"x20"	3'0"
On hire from Thomas Wrigley Ltd, Contractors, March 1927 to February 1928							
LOVICE	0-6-0ST	IC	MW	1233	1893	12"x17"	3'0"
Ex Swan Lane Collieries Ltd 1928							
Scrapped or sold about 1935							
MARJORIE	0-4-0ST	OC	KS	729	1900	14"x20"	3'3"
Ex I C I Ltd, Winnington, 1932, JOHN DALTON							
Scrapped or sold by December 1938							
JAMES	0-6-0ST	OC	AE	1818	1918	14"x20"	3'3"
Ex Mersey Docks and Harbour Board. 41, about June 1933							
Scrapped after December 1938							

Edge Green, Brynn and Garswood

LOVICE   0-6-0ST   OC   AE   1544   1909   14"x20"   3'3"
   Ex Lever Brothers, Port Sunlight, after March 1934
   To S. Littler with site and broken up

PHYLLIS   0-6-0ST   OC   AE   1401   1899   14"x20"   3'2"
   Carried plate AE 1565 1911 in error
   Ex Adams, Newport, after 1930
   To S. Littler with site and broken up

MARGARET   0-6-0ST   IC   HC   1466   1921   13"x20"   3'2"
   Ex Sir Lindsay Parkinson and Co Ltd, after December 1938 and before May 1940
   To Settle Limes Ltd, Horton in Ribblesdale, after January 1946

JAMES   0-6-0ST   IC   HC   1429   1920   13"x20"   3'2"
   Ex Sir Lindsay Parkinson and Co Ltd, after December 1938 and before May 1940
   To British Sugar Corporation, Ipswich between April 1946 and June 1946

Garswood Coal and Iron Company's Collieries

Park Lane
1853 to 1873   Mercer and Evans
1873 to 1929   Garswood Coal and Iron Co Ltd
1929   To Garswood Hall Collieries Ltd and closed

Long Lane
c1894 to 1929   Garswood Coal and Iron Co Ltd
1929 to 1946   Garswood Hall Collieries Ltd
After 1-1-1947   National Coal Board

                      2-4-0?   SR   1837   12½"x18"   5'0"
   Ex LNWR, 17 CALIBAN, October 1859
   Originally 2-2-2 tender loco, believed tohave have been rebuilt to 2-4-0 in 1844. Possibly later rebuilt as 2-4-0T
   Scrapped or sold by 1881

                      2-4-0   OC   HF   1837   13"x20"   5'0"
   Ex LNWR, 2A HECLA, November 1861
   Originally 2-2-2 tender loco, rebuilt to 2-4-0 in 1844. Possibly later rebuilt as 2-4-0T
   Scrapped or sold by 1881

                                        HH
Stated to here in 1881, see text

GARSWOOD   0-6-0ST   IC   HE   126   1874   12"x18"   3'1"
   New
   To Garswood Hall Collieries Ltd, May 1929.

ASHTON   0-6-0ST   IC   Wkb   1367   c.1877 14"x20"   3'6"
   New
   To Garswood Hall Collieries Ltd, May 1929.

SEFTON   0-6-0ST   IC   MW   857   1882   13"x18"   3'6"
   Ex Southport and Cheshire Lines Extension Railway contract, 1885
   To Garswood Hall Collieries Ltd, May 1929.

Edge Green, Brynn and Garswood

No 5		0-6-0ST	IC	P	539	1892	16"x22"	3'10"

  New
  To Garswood Hall Collieries Ltd, May 1929

No 6		0-6-0ST	IC	P	749	1898	16"x22"	3'10"

  New
  To Garswood Hall Collieries Ltd, May 1929

No 7		0-6-0ST	OC	P	868	1900	14"x20"	

  New
  To Garswood Hall Collieries Ltd, May 1929

Garswood Hall Collieries

c1868 to 1878   Dewhurst, Hoyle and Smethurst
1878 to 1883   Smethurst, Hoyle and Grime
1883 to 1946   Garswood Hall Collieries Ltd
Took over Garswood Coal and Iron Co Ltd in 1929
After 1-1-1947 National Coal Board

HERCULES No 1   0-6-0ST   Thwaites & Garbutt
                          Rbt IWB
  Possibly came here from I W Boulton of Ashton under Lyne
  Perhaps the locomotive nicknamed "Black Tom", later converted to stationary engine

1 ARTHUR		0-6-0ST	IC	Garswood		1883/4	15"x20"	

  New
  Scrapped 1933

2 CYMBELINE		0-6-0ST	IC	SS	1666	1866	17"x24"	4'6"

  Ex Brecon and Merthyr Railway, 21 in May 1889
  Scrapped 1933

		0-6-0ST	IC	MW	511	1874	13"x18"	3'0"

  Ex M W Walmesley, Manchester, KATE
  To Frodingham Iron Co, by 1899

IRWELL		0-6-0ST	IC	HE	435	1887	13"x18"	4'1"

  Ex T Oliver, Rugby, by May 1898
  To Ministry of Munitions, Aintree about 1917

IMOGEN		0-6-0ST	IC	RS	3006	1901	17"x24"	4'0"

  New
  To NCB 1-1-1947

4 ROBERT		0-6-0ST	OC	AE	1600	1912	16"x22"	

  New
  To NCB 1-1-1947

KING		0-6-0ST	IC	P	957	1902	16"x22"	3'10"

  Ex Bentley and Jubb, Wigan, September 1916
  To NCB 1-1-1947

According to an old employee there were two other locomotives at Garswood Hall at this period named PERCY and

Edge Green, Brynn and Garswood

LINCOLN. Both had gone by 1920. We have no other information about them. LINCOLN may have been the four coupled tank engine supplied by Ruston and Proctor of Lincoln to T A Walker, for use on the Manchester Ship Canal contract.

GARSWOOD 0-6-0ST IC HE 126 1874 12"x18" 3'1"
   Ex Garswood Coal and Iron Co Ltd, May 1929
   Scrapped 1939

ASHTON 0-6-0ST IC Wkb 1367 c.1877 14"x20" 3'6"
   Ex Garswood Coal and Iron Co Ltd, May 1929
   Scrapped 1933

SEFTON 0-6-0ST IC MW 857 1882 13"x18" 3'6"
   Ex Garswood Coal and Iron Co Ltd, May 1929
   Scrapped early 1930s

No 5 0-6-0ST IC P 539 1892 16"x22" 3'10"
   Ex Garswood Coal and Iron Co Ltd, May 1929
   To NCB 1-1-1947

No 6 0-6-0ST IC P 749 1898 16"x22" 3'10"
   Ex Garswood Coal and Iron Co Ltd, May 1929
   To NCB 1-1-1947

No 7 0-6-0ST OC P 868 1900 14"x20"
   Ex Garswood Coal and Iron Co Ltd, May 1929
   To Sir Lindsay Parkinson and Co Ltd, 1929

WYNNSTAY 0-6-0ST IC MW 1646 1905 16"x22" 3'9"
   Ex Lever Bothers, Port Sunlight, by May 1933
   Scrapped after December 1938

                    0-6-0ST IC HE 3187 1944 18"x26" 4'3"
   New, despatched from Hunslet Engine Co Ltd, September 1944
   Returned to Hunslet Engine Co, November 1944 and put into traffic as WD 75147

Downall Green and Park Collieries

Downall Green Colliery

c1868 to 1891   Various Stone family partnerships
Colliery closed 1891

The Park Colliery

1887 to 1909   Various Stone family partnerships
1909 to 1946   J and R Stone and Co Ltd
After 1-1-1947   National Coal Board

QUEEN   Six wheeled loco
   Possibly a rebuild of 2-2-2ST built by Fairbairn in 1851, for St Helens Railway and later Blackpool and Lytham Railway THE QUEEN. Taken over by Lancashire and Yorkshire Railway in 1871. Sold by L&YR to Thomas Stone in 1877.

Edge Green, Brynn and Garswood

MOLE   0-4-0ST   OC   MW   652   1877   10"x16"   2'9"
  New
  Renamed WASP
  To Robert Walker Trustees, Ferriby Cliff, Lincs 1918

BUSY BEE   0-6-0ST   IC   MW   1200   1892   13"x18"   3'0"
  New
  To NCB 1-1-1947

HORNET   0-6-0ST   IC   MW   1516   1901   15"x22"   3'9"
  New
  To NCB 1-1-1947

WASP   0-6-0ST   IC   MW   1866   1915   14"x22"   3'6"
                         Rbt VF 1925
  New
  Scrapped about 1946

29 WASP   0-6-0ST   IC   MW   1726   1908   13"x18"   3'0"
  Rebuilt Cudworth and Johnson, 1945
  Ex Cudworth and Johnson, Wrexham, about 1946
  To NCB 1-1-1947

Edge Green Foundry and Rolling Mills

c1936 to 1961   T. Crompton and Sons Ltd
1961 to c1967   Various subsidiaries of GKN Ltd

                                        0-4-0DM   JF   4110009   1950   80HP
  New October 1950
  To GKN Reinforcements Ltd, Wigan, c 1967

National Coal Board

Garswood Hall Colliery

1947 to 1958   North Western Division, St Helens Area
Colliery closed in 1958, but washery remained open until 1962, being transferred to West Lancashire Area on 1-1-1961

No 5   0-6-0ST   IC   P   539   1892   16"x22"   3'10"
  Taken over 1-1-1947
  To Haydock 1956 and scrapped at Sutton Manor 12-1959

No 6   0-6-0ST   IC   P   749   1898   16"x22"   3'10"
  Taken over 1-1-1947
  To Haydock 1956 and scrapped at Lea Green 2-1963

IMOGEN   0-6-0ST   IC   RS   3006   1901   17"x24"   4'0"
  Taken over 1-1-1947
  To Haydock 8-1959 and scrapped at Haydock 9-1966

Edge Green, Brynn and Garswood

| KING | | 0-6-0ST | IC | P | 957 | 1902 | 16"x22" | 3'10" |

 Taken over 1-11-1947
 To Park after 4-1951 and before 7-1954
 To Haydock by 8-1954 and scrapped at Cronton 11-1968

| ROBERT | | 0-6-0ST | OC | AE | 1600 | 1912 | 16"x22" | |

 Taken over 1-1-1947
 To Lea Green before 2-1962. From Cronton to Jose K Holt and Gordon, Chequerbent 6-1965 and still remains there derelict

| EARLESTOWN | | 0-6-0ST | IC | MW | 1503 | 1900 | 16"x22" | 2'9" |

 From Haydock late 1958
 To Haydock 2 or 3-1960

The Park Colliery

1947 to 1960   North Western Division, St Helens Area
1960   Closed

| BUSY BEE | | 0-6-0ST | IC | MW | 1200 | 1892 | 13"x18" | 3'0" |

 Taken over 1-1-1947
 Scrapped after 4-1952

| HORNET | | 0-6-0ST | IC | MW | 1516 | 1901 | 15"x22" | 3'9" |

 Taken over 1-1-1947
 Scrapped 8-1960

| WASP | | 0-6-0ST | IC | MW | 1726 | 1908 | 13"x18" | 3'0" |

 Taken over 1-1-1947
 Scrapped at Park 4-1959

| KING | | 0-6-0ST | IC | P | 957 | 1902 | 16"x22" | 3'10" |

 From Garswood Hall by 7-52
 To Haydock 8-1954
 Scrapped at Cronton 11-1968

| MAKERFIELD | | 0-6-0WT | OC | H'dock | | 1876 | 16"x22" | 4'0½" |

 From Haydock between 6-1955 and 12-1955
 Scrapped at Park about 3-1963

| PARR | | 0-6-0WT | OC | H'dock | | 1886 | 16"x22" | 4'0½" |

 From Haydock between 3-1958 and 5-1958
 Scrapped after 4-1963

References to Chapter 13

1   WRO DDX El 95/7   2   PP November 1833
3   *The Romance of Coal* – Richard Evans & Co Ltd Albion Publishing Co n.d., about 1927
4   "Haydock Collieries – Their Locomotives and Railways" J B Latham – *Journal of Industrial Locomotive Society* 1980
5   Line Plan of North Union Railway – LNWR 1864 – 2 chains to 1 inch at GMRO
6   46 & 47 Vic cap cx; 16-7-1883
7   Line Plan of North Union Railway, Lowton to 4¼ MP- British Railways, London Midland Region, 1956 – 1/1250 – at BRPB, Manchester Office

227

Edge Green, Brynn and Garswood

8	WRO DDX El 165/4		9	WO 11-4-1874
10	Line Plan of St Helens Branch of Great Central Railway – Hanson and Davidson, St Helens, 1907 – 2 chains to 1 inch – at BRPB Manchester Office			
11	WO 5-1-1866		12	BC 13-1-1866
13	WO 27-4-1866		14	LRO PDR 768
15	WO 26-8-1870			
16	Line Plan of Lancashire Union Railway – LNWR, Rugby, 1875 – 2 chains to 1 inch – at GMRO			
17	*Iron* 20-1-1893		18	WO 21-1-1893
19	WO 24-4-1920		20	CG 1-7-1881
21	MG 26-5-1888		22	Board of Trade Boiler Explosion Report 1502
23	Copy in authors' possession		24	LC 31-1-1857
25	BJ 15-8-1874		26	WO 5-1-1877
27	BJ 5-1-1877		28	LG 1-10-1878
29	Companies House Records		30	LG 29-1-1856
31	WO 18-11-1881		32	LRO PDR 797
33	28 & 29 Viccap cxciii; 29-6-1865			
34	*British Locomotive Catalogue 1825–1923, Vol 2A* – compiled by late Bertram Baxter – Moorland Publishing Co, Ashbourne, 1978			
35	*The Chronicles of Boulton's Siding* – A R Bennett – The Locomotive Publishing Co Ltd, London, 1927			
36	WO 18-11-1881		37	CG 21-10-1892
38	LNWR Sdgs Diag No 95, dated December 1916		39	WRO DDX El 165/4
40	Engineer 22-5-1885		41	WO 24-7-1874
42	WO 16-4-1877		43	LG 1-10-1878
44	CG 6-4-1883		45	CG 9-12-1892
46	WO 25-4-1902		47	WO 17-3-1917
48	WO 24-3-1917			
49	*The Locomotives of the Great Western Railway, Part Ten* – Railway Correspondence and Travel Society, 1966			
50	CG 23-8-1929		51	WO 17-3-1931
52	*"The Hunslet Austerity 0-6-0 Saddle Tanks" – Locomotives Illustrated* – Sept and Oct 1988			
53	WEx 8-7-1881		54	WEx 22-10-1887
55	CG 17-4-1896 p 731		56	CG 20-4-1877
57	WO 12-3-1892			
58	*Industry In South Lancashire* – South Lancashire Development Corporation – Publ Ed Burrow & Co Ltd, Cheltenham and London, n.d., about 1970			
59	British Rail Records			

CHAPTER 14

SKELMERSDALE AND BICKERSTAFFE

For our penultimate chapter in Part 1, we move some five miles west of Wigan, to Skelmersdale and Bickerstaffe. We are again dealing with an area with a long mining history. It was one which was too remote from the Douglas Navigation and from the later Leeds and Liverpool Canal to take any advantage of the markets that were opened up at the end of the eighteenth century. Some development took place after the opening of the railway from Ormskirk around 1850, but most of the collieries were sunk after the line had been extended in 1858 to give access to St Helens.

Lathom and Blaguegate Collieries up to 1900

The first Lord Skelmersdale started to open up mines on the south side of his Lathom Estate in the late 1840s. The earliest pits appear to have been to the south of Slate Farm, on a site which later became known as Old Engine. We assume that these formed the Lathom Colliery, which is shown under his ownership in 1848[1]. Lord Skelmersdale died in 1853[2] and the Mines Lists indicate that the colliery continued under the trustees of his will until 1863, passing to the second Lord Skelmersdale in 1864.

Lathom Colliery appears to have been idle from 1868 to 1872. It was then acquired by Bromilow, Foster and Company, first appearing in the Mines Lists under this name in 1873. Bromilow, Foster worked the colliery until 1885, after which it reverted to the second Lord Skelmersdale, who had been created first Earl of Lathom in 1880[2].

Blaguegate Colliery, further to the north, was sunk around 1850. The Mines Lists show that in 1853/4 and 1855 it was being worked by Lord Skelmersdale's Trustees. In 1856, it is shown in the occupation of Henry Foster and then disappears from the Mines Lists. It reappears in 1873 as the Park Colliery, under the ownership of the second Lord Skelmersdale. The Park Colliery was also known as the Blaguegate Arley Colliery, the name under which it is shown on the 1st and 2nd editions of the 25" maps. We suspect that the apparent closure of Blaguegate and Lathom Collieries during the period 1857 to 1872 may be the result of inaccuracy in the Mines Lists.

Rail access was provided by a branch of the East Lancashire Railway which ran from Ormskirk, on the Liverpool to Preston line, to what was then known as Blaguegate Siding, about a quarter of a mile short of the later Skelmersdale passenger station. We have been unable to discover the exact date of the opening of this branch, but we think it was at the same time as, or shortly after, the opening of the main line from Liverpool to Preston, on 2nd April 1849. It could not have been much later, as it is shown, as far as the crossing with Coal Pit Lane, on a revision of the 1st edition of the 6" map which was published about 1850.

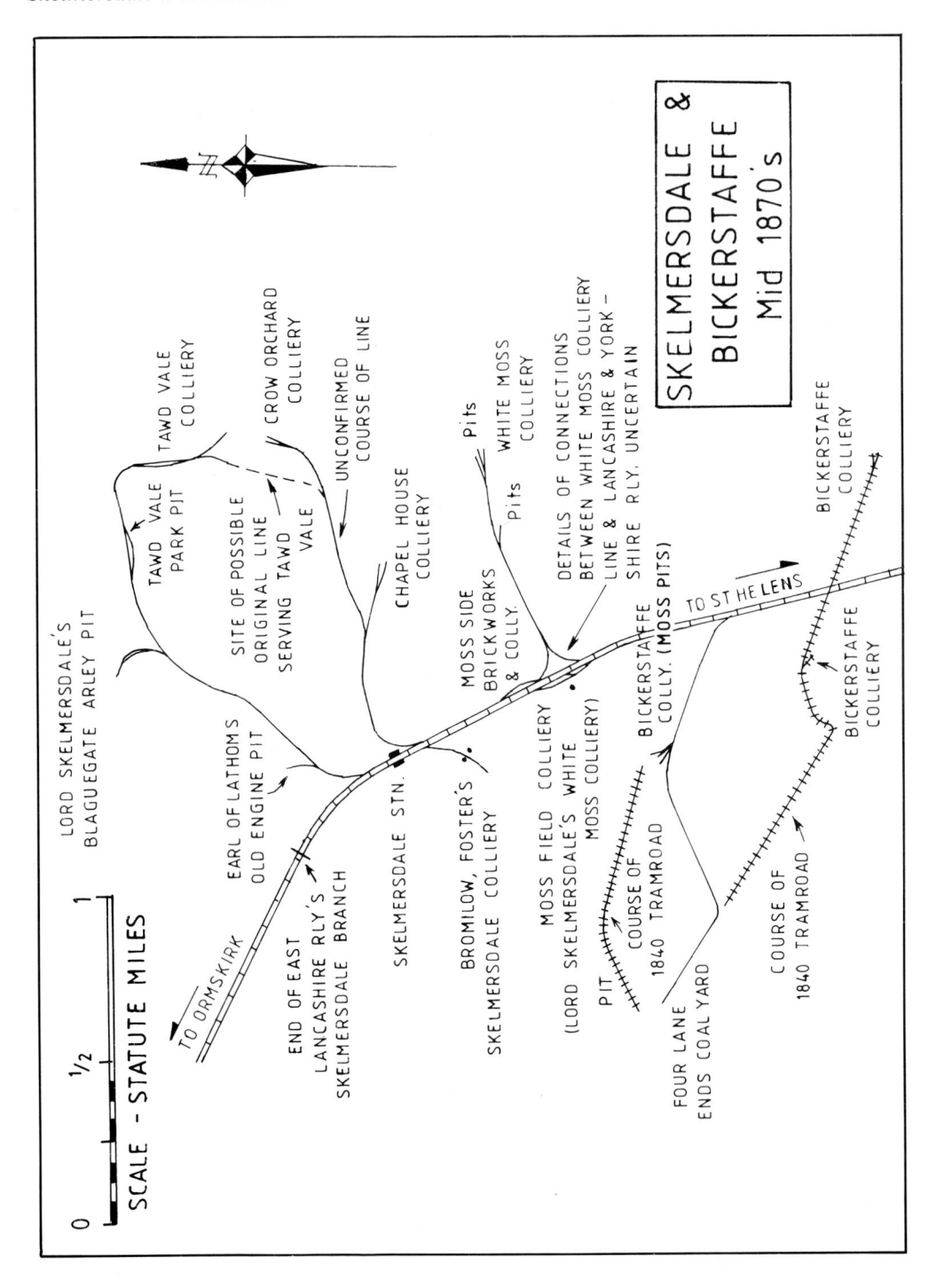

Skelmersdale and Bickerstaffe

Lord Lathom's connection to the East Lancashire branch was provided under an agreement dated 7th April 1847[3]. From here, his own railway, known as the Rutters Fold Branch, extended a little over a mile to serve the Blaguegate Colliery. Sidings near the East Lancashire line gave access to Lathom Colliery. We believe that these private lines opened simultaneously with the East Lancashire branch from Ormskirk. Although they do not appear on the revised 6" Map, this is not significant as the Ordnance Survey revisions rarely included new private railways.

We have been unable to trace any locomotive owned by Lord Skelmersdale up to the end of the century. We think it likely that the Rutters Fold Branch was worked by East Lancashire Railway Company's locomotives when it was first opened, and that Lord Skelmersdale would not need any engine of his own.

In the 1870s, or perhaps earlier, Lord Lathom's line was extended to serve pits owned by the Tawd Vale Coal Company. We shall be discussing the history of this company later in the chapter. What is of interest here is that, following the construction of this extension, the Tawd Vale Company used their own locomotives over the Rutters Fold Branch to the connection with the East Lancashire line. Old employees whom we interviewed in the 1950s were firmly of the opinion that the Tawd Vale company also worked traffic on behalf of Lord Skelmersdale from the Blaguegate Colliery. They also said that the internal shunting at Blaguegate was performed by horses.

The inundation and subsequent closure of Tawd Vale Colliery in 1898 meant that these arrangements came to an end. At the sale of the Tawd Vale Company's plant, in the middle of 1899, one of the Tawd Vale locomotives, HOLDEN, was purchased by the Earl of Lathom's agent, for use between Blaguegate and the main line.

The eastern end of the railway system, serving the Tawd Vale 11 and 12 Pits was abandoned, except for a short section from the junction near Blaguegate Colliery as far as the No 7 Pit. This pit seems to have been taken over by the Earl of Lathom, who worked it under the name of Brookfield Colliery until 1907 or 1908.

Tawd Vale Colliery was reopened by John Griffiths and Son Ltd in 1904, and renamed Glenburn Colliery. The railway was relaid between here and Brookfield Colliery. This provides a convenient point at which to consider some of the other developments which were taking place at Skelmersdale in the latter part of the nineteenth century. We return to Blaguegate and Glenburn later in the chapter.

Crow Orchard Colliery

Crow Orchard Colliery was situated to the east of Skelmersdale village. The first reference that we have found to it is in 1851. It was then owned by Thomas Stopford, who was also proprietor of a colliery at Shevington Moor[4]. The Mines Lists for 1853/4 show that Crow Orchard had been transferred to Mrs Mary Stopford, given, we assume erroneously, as Stopforth.

Mrs Stopford sold the colliery and its plant on 28th August 1860[5] and we assume that this is when the firm of Morrell and Stoner took over. The Mines Lists show that the firm had changed its name to the Crow Orchard Coal Company in 1865. From 1873 onwards the owners are given as the Crow Orchard Colliery Company Ltd.

Crow Orchard Colliery was connected to the Lancashire and Yorkshire Railway, which had by this time taken over the East Lancashire's branch from Ormskirk and the 1858 extension to

Skelmersdale and Bickerstaffe

Rainford. The junction was immediately to the south of Skelmersdale Station and the private line extended for about a mile to the pits. We think that the railway was constructed by Morrell and Stoner rather than during the period when the Stopfords owned the colliery. In December 1866 the Crow Orchard Colliery advertised that it required a new tank locomotive, with cylinders not less than 10" diameter [6]. A locomotive was certainly operating on the railway by January 1867, as there was a collision with a cart at a level crossing [7].

In July 1875 the colliery company invited tenders for the construction of a new railway 600 yards in length [8,9]. We think that this was to extend the existing line from Crow Orchard to new pits which were then being sunk to the east of the River Tawd. The new railway evidently required an additional locomotive, as the company advertised for a new six coupled tank engine in November 1875 [10].

At the same period, the Skelmersdale Wagon Company was advertising that it was the builder of coal, coke and ballast wagons [11]. We think that this firm probably had its premises adjacent to the Crow Orchard company's main line sidings.

By 1885 the Crow Orchard Colliery Company Ltd was in debt, and was being wound up in September of that year [12]. One of the creditors was the neighbouring White Moss Coal Company, which was lessor of some of the Crow Orchard mines. The White Moss Company won a judgement in the Chancery Court in Manchester on 9th January 1886 [13], and Crow Orchard Colliery was put on sale as a going concern the same month [14].

There was no bid for the colliery or its equipment [15]. In consequence, the New Crow Orchard Colliery Co Ltd was registered on 23rd January 1886 to take over the property [16,17]. The new venture did not get off the ground and the four pits together with their plant were up for sale again on 7th April 1886 [18].

The collieries were purchased by the White Moss Coal Co Ltd, and operated in conjunction with this company's existing pits, situated a short distance to the south. The Crow Orchard Company's railway, connecting with the Lancashire and Yorkshire at Skelmersdale Station, was abandoned and a new line was built to join up with the White Moss Company's system.

We have been unable to trace any information about the locomotives used at Crow Orchard in the 1860s. The earliest record which we have relates to PRESCOTT, a six coupled saddle tank which came new from the Hunslet Engine Company of Leeds in 1871. This was followed in 1876, no doubt in response to the advertisement of the previous November, by a larger six coupled saddle tank from the same makers, named THE CROW.

Both locomotives were included in the sales of January and April 1866. On the latter occasion, they were purchased by Mr T D Swift of Ince, along with the company's stock of wagons, for a total price of £3000 [18]. The manufacturer's records show that PRESCOTT was later at Hulton Colliery, near Bolton. THE CROW went to White Moss Colliery, where it was renamed SHAWE.

Tawd Vale Colliery

This colliery, located about a mile to the north-west of Skelmersdale, first appears in the Mines List in 1860 under the ownership of John Morrell. Contracts for sinking a further shaft were advertised by J C Morrell in November 1863 [19].

The Tawd Vale Coal Company Ltd was formed in 1864 to take over the colliery and was in liquidation in 1870 [20]. A new firm, the Tawd Vale Colliery Co Ltd first appears in the Mines Lists for 1875.

Old employees whom we interviewed in the 1950s told us that Tawd Vale Colliery had originally had a rail connection with the nearby Crow Orchard system, and that the Tawd Vale coal passed over the Crow Orchard railway to reach the main line. In the absence of any large scale maps for the relevant dates we have been unable to confirm this. We think, however, that there may be some substance in the story, as Morrell was associated with both collieries in the early days.

If, indeed, the original railway connection had been to the Crow Orchard system, it was certainly altered later. The 2nd edition of the 6" map shows the line taking a northerly course from Tawd Vale Colliery, up a steep incline out of the valley. From the top of the incline, it turned westwards to join Lord Skelmersdale's line near his Blaguegate Colliery.

We think that this line must have been in place at least by the early 1870s, to serve the Park Colliery, about half way between Tawd Vale and the junction with Lord Skelmersdale's line. Sinking here, on a site to the west of the original Tawd Vale pits seems to have started in the early 1870s. This Park Colliery, not to be confused with the Park Colliery of Lord Skelmersdale referred to earlier, is first shown in the Mines Lists for 1873 under Tawd Vale ownership. We presume that it was here that Mr John Morrell started up a pair of new winding engines on 15th May 1875[21].

In the late 1880s and 1890s, Park Colliery was known as Brookfield or Brookside. It was also known as Tawd Vale No 7 Pit. It seems to have closed in 1896, as it is not shown in the 1897 Mines Lists.

On 30th November 1897 the River Tawd broke through into old workings, flooded the colliery and caused considerable damage to the railway system [22,23]. The colliery was abandoned and the company went into voluntary liquidation in June 1899 [24]. The colliery plant was advertised for sale in the same month, and included three six coupled locos with 12" and 13" cylinders, built by Manning, Wardle and Company [25]. A further sale of plant was advertised in September of the same year [26].

The first locomotive which we have been able to trace at Tawd Vale came new in 1862 from Manning, Wardle and Company of Leeds. It was a six coupled saddle tank of their Old I class. According to the manufacturer's records it carried the name TAWD VALE COLLIERY. Manning, Wardle and Company supplied a second engine, of the K class design, in 1875. This was No 2 at Tawd Vale.

We have been unable to discover the fate of these two locomotives. They were probably the engines which were offered for sale by the Tawd Vale Colliery Company in August 1878 [27] and October 1882 [28]. In the second advertisement, the engine was described as six coupled, with 12" x 18" cylinders and 3'0" diameter wheels, which might fit either of them.

We know that the first two locomotives were later replaced by two second hand six coupled saddle tanks, ENTERPRISE and LIZZIE, which had also been built by Manning, Wardle and Company and had seen service with various public works contractors.

ENTERPRISE, an Old I Class engine, had been built in 1863 and had been supplied to Smith and Knight, at Alton in Hampshire, as their No 1. The manufacturer's records show that it had been acquired by Scott and Edwards before 1871 and that it was later the property of Beckett and Bentley.

LIZZIE, of the manufacturer's K Class, had gone new in 1876 to Logan and Hemingway, at Bingham in Nottinghamshire, as their No 12. It was later with Braddock and Matthews at Southport, before coming to Tawd Vale.

The colliery company also acquired HOLDEN, a rather larger six coupled Manning, Wardle saddle tank of the M class. It had been built in 1876 for John Barnes and had been delivered to one of his contracts, either at Chatburn or Southport.

Recollections of old employees were that one of the smaller Manning, Wardles, LIZZIE or ENTERPRISE, worked between the Tawd Vale pits and the incline top, taking two wagons at a time. Here, trains of between eighteen and twenty wagons were made up, which were worked to the main line sidings by HOLDEN. As we have recounted earlier, there was a strong local tradition that the Tawd Vale locomotives also hauled coal from Lord Skelmersdale's Blaguegate Colliery to the main line.

A report of the auction of colliery plant in 1899 stated that the three locomotives fetched £1188, one going to the Earl of Lathom, one to a Mr Watson of Leeds, and one to Mr Latham of Ince. The wagons went in small lots to various buyers, while Mr Flint of Ince purchased 6200 yards of railway track [29]. From subsequent records we know that it was HOLDEN that went to the Earl of Lathom, and was used at his Blaguegate Colliery. ENTERPRISE was later at the Latham Brothers' Rose Bridge Colliery at Ince. We deduce that it was LIZZIE which was purchased by Mr Watson, who we think may have been one of the proprietors of the Ellerbeck Collieries Co Ltd. One of the locomotives here, according to information from old employees, had come from Tawd Vale.

Chapel House Colliery

Chapel House Colliery, situated about half a mile east of Skelmersdale Station, first appears in the Mines Lists for 1868 and 1869, under the name of Thomas Farrimond. The colliery was advertised for sale on 20th May 1869 [30]. We believe that it was then taken over by Edward Smith, who from time to time seems to have traded as the Chapel House Colliery Company.

After Smith's death, the colliery was worked by his executors, who appear in the Mines List for 1883 and subsequent years. It was put up for auction as a going concern on 19th July 1904 [31]. There was evidently no acceptable bid, as the colliery was offered for sale by private treaty in October of the same year [32]. A further advertisement appears in March 1905, the sale this time being by order of the court [33]. Again there seems to have been no satisfactory offer and the colliery was closed down.

Chapel House Colliery was originally linked to the railway from Crow Orchard Colliery to the Lancashire and Yorkshire line. According to statements made in the early 1950s by old colliery employees at Skelmersdale, coal traffic to the main line from Chapel House was worked by Crow Orchard locomotives. However, when Crow Orchard was taken over by the White Moss Coal Co Ltd in 1886, the private railway east of Chapel House was abandoned. The Chapel House Colliery then became the sole user of the remaining portion of the line and a new sidings agreement, dated 19th August 1886, was made between Smith's executors and the railway company [34].

We do not know what arrangements were made for working the line after Crow Orchard Colliery closed. Perhaps Edward Smith's executors bought a second hand locomotive, perhaps they used horses to haul the wagons. Whatever may have been the situation initially, we know that a small four coupled saddle tank was purchased in 1893. It came new from the Hunslet Engine Company of Leeds and was named EDWARD.

We presume that it was this locomotive, described as having 13½" x 18" cylinders, which was offered for sale in 1904 and 1905. The manufacturer's records show that, by July 1905, it had become the property of Holme and King Ltd, public works contractors.

White Moss Colliery

The original pits of the White Moss Coal Company were, we believe, on a site a little to the west of Wigan Road. They first appear in the Mines Lists for 1865. The private railway, about three quarters of a mile in length, linking the colliery with the Lancashire and Yorkshire line, dates from the same period. The connection with the main line, at a point half a mile south of Skelmersdale Station, was covered by an agreement dated 5th May 1866 [35,36].

After the White Moss Company acquired the Crow Orchard pits in 1886, the railway was extended by about half a mile to enable the Crow Orchard coal to be exchanged with the Lancashire and Yorkshire Company at White Moss Sidings. The new line was stated in November 1886 to have been recently completed [37]. As mentioned earlier, the original Crow Orchard railway, past the Chapel House Colliery to the main line, was then abandoned.

The 2nd edition of the 6" map, resurveyed in 1891 and 1892, shows the White Moss railway system at what must have been its maximum extent. Starting at a triangular junction with the Lancashire and Yorkshire Railway's Ormskirk to Rainford branch at White Moss Level Crossing, the colliery railway ran due east to the original White Moss Pits and continued beyond, over the Skelmersdale to Upholland Road to serve a dirt tip. A tubway connected the Primrose Colliery, which had apparently been sunk in the early 1890s, to screening plant on the original White Moss site.

Just short of White Moss Colliery, the new line of 1886 branched off and turned north to serve the main Crow Orchard workings, which, at this period, were known as Lower White Moss Colliery. They appear in the Mines Lists under this name between 1886 and 1890, but subsequently revert to the original title.

Sidings from this line gave access to a landsale yard near the level crossing over the Wigan Road. From Crow Orchard there was another line, we believe the one constructed in 1875, running to an unnamed colliery. Beyond here, there was a further extension to stone quarries at Houghton's Delf and Elmer's Delf, just to the east of Houghton's Lane.

The Sidings Schedules state that the White Moss Company also conveyed a small amount of goods for local farmers, including Mr F Dickenson, Mr H Stringman and Mr W Hunter. There is, however, no reference to stone traffic from the quarries.

There were further colliery developments at the turn of the century. A new pit, the Park Pit, first appears in the Mines Lists for 1897. This was followed by the Prescott New Pit, which first appears in 1904. Outside the immediate environs of Skelmersdale, the White Moss Company, in 1896, reopened the old Holland Colliery formerly operated by the Wigan Coal and Iron Company. This was served by its own independent sidings connected with the Lancashire and Yorkshire Railway's Wigan to Liverpool line, and we shall be dealing more fully with its history in the next chapter.

A little later, some of the earlier White Moss workings were closed down. The old 7 ft pit was abandoned in 1910 and Primrose is last shown in the Mines Lists the same year. Crow Orchard was abandoned in 1921, although the Mines lists suggest that it had only been worked at a very much reduced level for some years previously. This left only the Prescott New Pit and the Arley and Park No 2 pits in production. In 1923 it was reported that the coal was almost exhausted, that 200 men had been given a weeks notice, and that most of the coal production would be concentrated on the Crawford Pit at Upholland [38].

Railway operations at White Moss were now on a very much restricted scale. By 1926, when the 6" map was next revised, the railway system had been reduced to the portion linking the

Skelmersdale and Bickerstaffe

original White Moss Colliery to the main line, together with the stub end of the line to Crow Orchard, which still served the landsale yard.

The Arley Pit was noted as "not working" in the Mines Lists for 1927. Prescott New Pit and Park No 2 Pit were both abandoned in May 1928. According to the Sidings Schedules, White Moss Colliery ceased production temporarily on 5th May 1928. It was also noted that the firm was sending coal from Holland Colliery to White Moss for storage.

We have no details of locomotives used by the White Moss Coal Company earlier than 1873. In that year a six coupled saddle tank, named GARDINER, was delivered by the Hunslet Engine Company of Leeds. A rather larger locomotive arrived from the same makers in 1874, and a third, larger again, in 1884. These were named OSWALD and GASKELL respectively. A further engine, THE CROW, was acquired when the Crow Orchard Colliery was purchased in 1886.

Subsequent history is confused by the fact that some of the engines were later renamed. According to the manufacturer's records, GARDINER became ROBINSON and later ROSEMARY. THE CROW was renamed SHAWE.

OSWALD was sold about 1910 to Hutchinsons Trustees at Widnes. GASKELL and ROSEMARY were later transferred to the White Moss Company's Holland Colliery. We have no record of the disposal of SHAWE.

From several former employees we learned of another locomotive which was temporarily at White Moss in the early 1930s. After the collieries had all closed, the engineer undertook to repair, presumably as a private venture, a diminutive locomotive which was thought to have come from Wigan. We are fairly certain that this was a four coupled saddle tank, with cylinders

A makers photograph of GARDINER, supplied by the Hunslet Engine Company to the White Moss Coal Company.
V.J. Bradley Collection

as small as 6", which had been built by Dick, Kerr and Company of Kilmarnock about 1915, or possibly earlier. It had been supplied to Easton, Gibb and Son Ltd, for use on a contract at Ipswich. It subsequently passed to other owners in the Ipswich area before being purchased by John Booth and Co Ltd, of the Hulton Steelworks, near Bolton. It was sold by them to H Stephenson and Sons, machinery merchants, of Hindley Green. From conversations with staff at Stephensons around 1950, we learned that this firm had sent the engine to Skelmersdale for overhaul. It seems that they were unable to resell it and we presume that it was broken up for scrap.

Moss Side Brickworks

The works was on the east side of the Lancashire and Yorkshire Railway, north of the connection with the White Moss Colliery. It was served by a short siding giving access to a loading bay. According to the Sidings Schedules, this was provided under agreement with Mr Joseph Hartley, dated 15th August 1876

The works was taken over by Moss Side Land and Brick Company, which according to the Mines Lists operated a small colliery here between 1877 and 1881. A new private sidings agreement was made on 3rd August 1878.

The Sidings Schedules state that, on June 8th 1917, the railway company received advice that the works had been purchased by Messrs Robinson and Company of Wigan. At this time the premises, or at least a portion of them, were in the hands of the military authorities. Arrangements were made for L&YR locomotives to work over the White Moss Colliery Company's siding which connected with the brickworks.

The Sidings Schedules go on to note that Messrs Robinson's business was put into the hands of a liquidator on 6th July 1922. The works was purchased, in February 1923, by Mr S T Rosbotham of the Skelmersdale Straw Rope Works. Alterations to the sidings were completed by 3rd March 1926 and there was a new agreement with Rosbotham dated 14th October 1926.

Moss Field Colliery

Moss Field Colliery was located south of Skelmersdale, on the west side of the railway, opposite to the sidings serving the White Moss Coal Company.

The colliery was originally known as the White Moss Colliery of Lord Skelmersdale. It first appears in the Mines Lists for 1865, as the property of the second Lord Skelmersdale. The siding connection with the main line was provided under an agreement dated 23rd April 1866. A further agreement in respect of the sidings was made on 3rd October 1874 [39]. The second Lord Skelmersdale was created first Earl of Lathom in 1880 [2] and Moss Field Colliery continued in his ownership until his death in 1898. After 1874, the Mines Lists rather confusingly refer to it as the Blaguegate Colliery, the name which it is given on the 1st edition of the 25" map, surveyed in 1891.

The colliery was subsequently sold to J Griffiths and Son Ltd and first appears in the Mines Lists under this owner in 1900. A new siding agreement [39] was made with Griffiths on 12th October 1900. The colliery closed down in 1905 and an endorsement on the Sidings Diagram records that the connection with the main line was taken up in 1906.

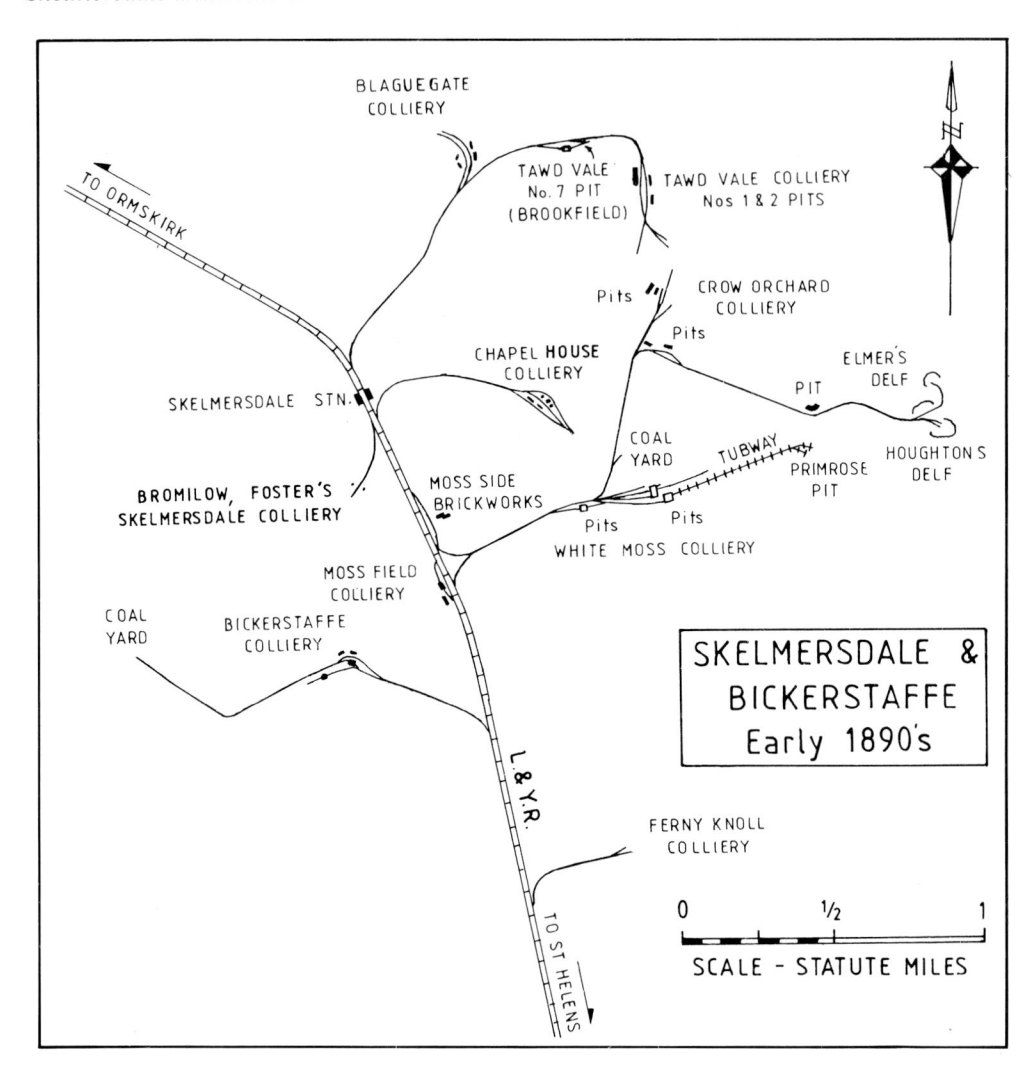

Skelmersdale and Bickerstaffe

Blaguegate and Glenburn Collieries after 1900

In 1904 John Griffiths and Son Ltd took over the derelict Tawd Vale Colliery and reopened it under the name of Glenburn Colliery. The railway track was relaid as far as Brookfield Colliery, where a junction was made with the line being worked by the Earl of Lathom. The highway at the bottom of the incline at Tawd Vale was raised to ease the gradient[40].

Shortly afterwards, the firm sank the Hilton Colliery, which first appears in the Mines Lists for 1906. This was to the east of Tawd Vale Colliery, to which it was connected by a short tubway. From 1913 the firm is also shown as owning a colliery at Dalton, remote from the railway system, and by 1915 it had acquired what is described as Lathom Colliery. We believe that this was the former Brookfield Colliery, not worked by the Earl of Lathom since about 1908 and latterly used for pumping, which had been given a new name.

Blaguegate Colliery, which had been inherited by the third Earl of Lathom after he succeeded to the title in 1910[2], was purchased by John Griffiths and Son Ltd. The firm first appears as occupier in the Mines Lists for 1923.

Meanwhile, Griffiths' other pits had ceased production. The Mines List show that Hilton closed in 1919, Lathom and the isolated Dalton Colliery in 1921 and Glenburn in 1923.

After 1923, the whole of the railway system east of Blaguegate Colliery was closed, only the western section being retained to provide an outlet from Blaguegate to what was now the London Midland and Scottish Railway. The Sidings Schedules state that a new agreement in respect of the main line siding was made by John Griffiths and Son Ltd on 1st June 1927.

Blaguegate Arley Colliery looking north. Date of photograph unknown. John Ryan Collection

Skelmersdale and Bickerstaffe

According to the Sidings Schedules, Blaguegate Colliery itself closed in February 1933 and the Mines List show that it was formally abandoned in November 1934. The Old Engine Pit, also used by Griffiths, had already been abandoned in December 1932.

By December 1933, the colliery railway had been dismantled and the Private Sidings Agreement was terminated in January 1934. Removal of the main line connections was ordered on 1st November 1934 and reported to be complete on 21st March 1935.

To work the reopened railway from Glenburn to the main line sidings, John Griffiths and Son Ltd bought three second hand locomotives. According to old employees we interviewed they were named KEYHAM, NORTHFIELD and WINIFRED.

KEYHAM was a six coupled side tank which had been built by Hudswell Clarke and Company of Leeds in 1889. It had been delivered to T A Walker at Ellesmere Port for use on the construction of the Manchester Ship Canal, where it had been named HEATON. It had subsequently been purchased by Sir John Jackson, another public works contractor.

NORTHFIELD, a six coupled saddle tank, had been built by Peckett and Sons of Bristol in 1898 for Abraham Kellett, who used it on the construction of a reservoir for Birmingham Corporation at Rubery. It seems to have come direct to Glenburn from Kellett.

We have records of two other engines which were employed at Glenburn at this period. One was a small four coupled saddle tank, which had been built 1888 by the Hunslet Engine Company for the Whitecross Company and used at their Peasley Cross Colliery at St Helens. The manufacturer's records show that it was still at Peasley Cross in February 1905 but that spare parts were supplied to John Griffiths and Son at Glenburn in March 1911 and August 1912. The locomotive was named CHAMPION at Peasley Cross, but could have been renamed WINIFRED after coming to Skelmersdale.

The other engine which is known to have been at Glenburn was a four coupled saddle tank which had been built by Peckett and Sons in 1900. It had been originally supplied to James Carter and Sons Ltd, who owned quarries and limeworks near Clitheroe, where it was named DELAMERE. It seems to have been sold by them about 1907. It was at Peckett's works in Bristol for repairs in December 1912.

It would seem that traffic from Griffiths' collieries declined during the first world war and this led to the disposal of some of the locomotives. NORTHFIELD was sold to James Pain Ltd for use at their ironstone quarries at Byfield in Oxfordshire. KEYHAM was evidently the six coupled saddle tank, with 15" x 20" cylinders, built by Hudswell Clarke, which was offered for sale in October 1919 [41]. The manufacturer's records show that it was with Firth, Blakely, Son and Company, at Church Fenton, by 1921.

On taking over the Blaguegate Colliery, John Griffiths and Son Ltd acquired the locomotive HOLDEN. This, it will be remembered, had been purchased by the Earl of Lathom from the old Tawd Vale Colliery in 1899 and had been used for working the section of line between Blaguegate and the main line sidings since then.

HOLDEN continued to perform this duty for the new owners and was the engine mentioned by old employees as being used up to the closure of the colliery. It seems that DELAMERE was also kept on for a time by John Griffiths and Son Ltd, perhaps as a spare engine. The firm's other locomotives appear to have been scrapped or sold in the early 1920s.

Our old employees recalled that HOLDEN was cut up at the LMS exchange sidings in 1933 or 1934, after the closure of Blaguegate Colliery and after the remaining part of the railway system had been dismantled.

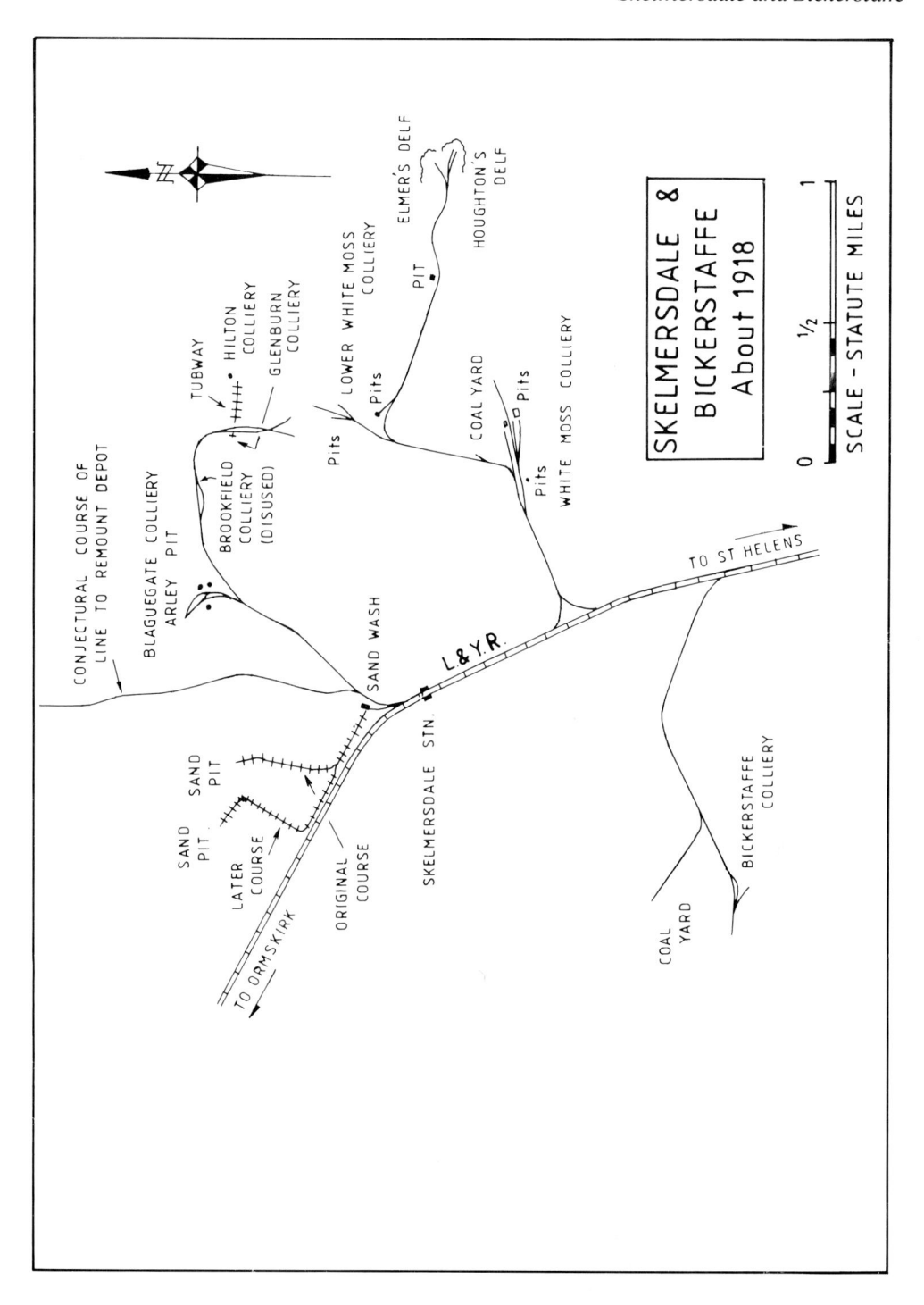

Skelmersdale and Bickerstaffe

Skelmersdale and Bickerstaffe

The colliery site was later occupied by the Lathom Brick Company Ltd, which opened its works here in 1935 [42,43]. The old locomotive shed was converted into a garage for lorries and was still being used for this purpose in 1954. In 1951 the Lathom Brick Company erected new works at Dalton [43]. At the time of writing, both works had been closed. That at Dalton has been dismantled, while the premises at Blaguegate are now used for storage.

Skelmersdale Sand Pits

Towards the end of the nineteenth century, Cannington, Shaw and Co Ltd opened out sand pits to the north of Skelmersdale, to provide raw materials for their glassworks at Sherdley, near St Helens. A sand washing plant was erected near the the Lancashire and Yorkshire Railway's line, and a siding was provided under an agreement dated 21st February 1894 [44]. A 2'0" gauge tramway connected the sand pits with the washing plant.

We think it likely that horses provided the motive power for the tramway system at least at the beginning. Some modernisation seems to have taken place after Cannington, Shaw and Co Ltd was absorbed by United Glass Bottle Manufacturers Ltd 1n 1913 [43].

Latterly internal combustion locomotives were used and two, supplied by Honeywill Brothers, and probably of Hibberd make, were observed here in March 1954.

The Sidings Schedules mention that, during the second world war, the firm was unable to obtain Belgian sand and reopened their Crown Dale Quarry at Llanfynydd in North Wales. Sandstone was brought by rail to Skelmersdale, where a new crushing plant was set up. After treatment, the sand was despatched to the Sherdley Works at St Helens. Additional sidings were installed and were passed for traffic on 7th December 1940.

We think it unlikely that either United Glass Bottle Manufactures Ltd or their predecessors used locomotives on the standard gauge siding. The sand pits had been abandoned by June 1959 and the Sidings Schedules record that the private sidings agreement was terminated on 31st December 1959.

Lathom Park Remount Depot

Some of the older inhabitants of Skelmersdale, to whom we talked in the 1950s, told us about an Army Remount Depot which was established during the 1914–18 war, in the grounds of Lathom Hall. We have been able to obtain additional information from a short history of Skelmersdale written by Revd Nigel Sands [45].

The depot was under construction in September 1914 and the first batch of horses arrived on 18th and 19th October [46,47]. A railway was built and was in use by February 1915 [48]. This left the Earl of Lathom's line in the vicinity of Blaguegate Colliery, passed Slate Farm and then through the Spa Farm lands near the Big Wood. War Office locomotives were said to have been used, but we have been unable to trace any further information about them.

The depot remained operational until December 1920. By this time the railway was used to store surplus wagons and was later taken up.

Skelmersdale and Bickerstaffe

The sand washing plant at Skelmersdale, in September 1954, showing the network of narrow gauge track. J.B. Horne

Bromilow, Foster's Skelmersdale Colliery

We now return to the area south of the town, to deal with a colliery associated with the firm of Bromilow, Foster and Company. This was connected to the Lancashire and Yorkshire line, immediately to the south of Skelmersdale Station, by a short branch, about 400 yds in length. We assume the branch dates from the late 1860s, since there was a private siding agreement with Bromilow Foster and Co dated 7th July 1869 [49].

We have been unable to trace much of the history of the colliery, because of the difficulty of identifying individual pits in the Mines Lists for the Skelmersdale area. A further confusion is that the 1st Edition of the 25" map, surveyed in 1892, gives the name Bickerstaffe both to this colliery and to the Moss Pits, about half a mile further south.

Skelmersdale Colliery was probably sunk in the late 1860s, around the time the private sidings agreement was concluded. We think that it may have occupied the site of the Swifts Fold Colliery, which is shown in the 1853/4 Mines Lists under James Shaw and was operated by Shaw and Foster between 1855 and 1868.

On 30th June 1898, the colliery was up for sale, along with Bromilow and Foster's other Bickerstaffe Colliery [50]. Included in the sale were 28 8-ton wagons and 1450 yards of rails.

We believe that the Skelmersdale Colliery closed at the time of the sale and never reopened. It is recorded that the sidings were taken up in 1898 [49]. Bickerstaffe Colliery continued under new ownership, as we shall see below.

Skelmersdale and Bickerstaffe

The Bickerstaffe Collieries

The 1st edition of the 6" map, surveyed in 1844 and 1845, shows two tramroads which predate the main line railway system.

One, over three quarters of a mile in length, ran from what is described as Bickerstaffe Colliery to a coal yard at Four Lane Ends, on the north side of the road to Skelmersdale. This Bickerstaffe Colliery was near to the later Moss Pits.

The other tramroad was considerably longer, some two miles in all. It started at a group of pits, again described as Bickerstaffe Colliery, near Two Barns Farm on Nipe Lane. It ran in an east-north-easterly direction to a third Bickerstaffe Colliery, where a number of pits and engine houses are marked in the vicinity of Yew Tree House. After a further mile, it terminated at another coal yard at Four Lane Ends, on the south side of the road to Skelmersdale.

The tramroad from Two Barns was still in use in the 1850s, and is shown on the Deposited Plans for the East Lancashire Railway Company's Skelmersdale Branch Extension to Rainford, dated November 1852[51]. We are unclear what happened to it after the Rainford Extension was completed in 1858, but we assume that it was subsequently abandoned.

The tramroad serving the Moss Pits was replaced by a standard gauge branch from the main line. This was built, as far as the Moss Pits, by the Lancashire and Yorkshire Railway, which had taken over the East Lancashire Railway in 1859. The Sidings Schedules note that it was in substitution for a branch from the Liverpool and Wigan main line which the railway company was required to lay down for the convenience of collieries on Lord Derby's land at Bickerstaffe. The land required was obtained under a lease from the the Earl of Derby, granted on 10th September 1860.

The Lancashire and Yorkshire Railway Minutes for 29th May 1860 reported that the contract for earthworks had been let to Rich and Fawkes of Leigh, with completion in 12 weeks. The line was later known as the Moss Pits Branch and the company charged a toll of 1d per ton for traffic passing over the 57 chains which it had built[52].

The branch was extended as a private line, built by the colliery company, to the coal yard on the south side of Four Lane Ends. For the last six hundred yards this used the track bed of the earlier tramroad from Two Barns.

We have had difficulty in tracing who worked these pits at this time. Both Lord Skelmersdale and Bromilow, Foster and Company are shown with collieries at Bickerstaffe in 1848[1] and 1851[4]. We assume, without concrete evidence, that Lord Skelmersdale operated the pits near Two Barns and Yew Tree House. The Mines Lists show the Trustees of Lord Skelmersdale were in occupation until 1865, followed by Foster, Shaw and Company in 1866. After that date, the colliery disappears from the Lists.

We equate Bromilow, Foster and Company's Bickerstaffe Colliery with the Moss Pits. The Mines Lists show that the colliery was worked by Bromilow, Foster and Company from 1854 onwards, except for a period from 1856 to 1858, when Henry Foster is shown in occupation. Latterly the partnership had consisted of David Bromilow, James Whitehead, Richard Manley Fisher, Henry George Bromilow and James Shaw. It was dissolved on 2nd December 1866[53] and its assets were taken over by Bromilow, Foster and Co Ltd, which had been formed in late 1866 or early 1867[54].

Bromilow, Foster's Bickerstaffe Colliery, along with their Skelmersdale Colliery, was advertised[50] for sale on 30th June 1898. We think that the firm may have been in financial difficulties following what seems to have been an unsuccessful venture to the east of the Lancashire and Yorkshire line.

Ferny Knoll Colliery, near the site of the earlier pits at Two Barns, first appears in the Mines Lists for 1894, although it may possibly have been the same as the Far Moss Colliery which is shown in the occupation of Bromilow, Foster between 1877 and 1893. The 2nd edition of the 6" map, surveyed in 1892, shows a short branch line serving Ferny Knoll, but very little obvious activity at the colliery itself. Ferny Knoll has disappeared from the Mines List by 1896.

Following the sale, Bickerstaffe Colliery was taken over by the firm of Foster, Williams and Co Ltd, preparatory to a programme of expansion. The first sod of a new colliery, on the west side of the St Helens to Ormskirk road was turned in March 1899 [55].

The railway was extended to connect with the new colliery, which was producing coal in August 1900 [56]. The old workings at the Moss Pits were abandoned, but the branch serving the coal yard at Four Lane Ends was retained. There were further agreements in respect of the main line connection, with the Earl of Derby on 6th July 1899 and with Foster, Williams and Co Ltd on 31st October 1900 [52].

The earliest locomotive which we have on record was delivered in 1871. This was a D class four coupled saddle tank which came from the Leeds firm of Manning, Wardle and Company and was named BICKERSTAFFE. This engine seems to have lasted until the new colliery developments at the turn of the century, the last spares being supplied in June 1901. In that year it was replaced by a four coupled saddle tank bearing the same name, built by Peckett and Sons of Bristol.

From conversations with old employees we were told that, during the present century at least, the colliery only had this one locomotive. When it needed repairs it was usual to hire a small engine from the Lancashire and Yorkshire Railway and later the London Midland and Scottish Railway. Our informants also recalled that a locomotive named GLADYS was here for a period during the early 1930s. We presume that GLADYS was the six coupled saddle tank, built by Fox Walker and Company of Bristol in 1871. In the 1930s it was the property of Thompson and Co Ltd of Ince and was hired to a number of collieries in and around Wigan.

In February 1928, Alderman S T Rosbotham took over the controlling interest in Bickerstaffe Collieries Ltd [57], but it seems that the firm was in poor shape financially. According to the Mines Lists, No 1 Pit was discontinued on 22nd June 1929 and formally abandoned on 29th June. Closure of No 2 Pit and the Wash Drift does not seem to have been notified to the Mines Inspectorate. The Sidings Schedules state that a receiver was appointed on 23rd July 1929.

In April 1930, the property was disposed of to Mr P H Swift, trading as Bickerstaffe Collieries (P H Swift Proprietor), who agreed to abide by the private sidings agreement of 3rd October 1900. He subsequently reopened No 1, No 2 Pit and the Wash Drift, although the last mentioned was abandoned again in November 1931.

The Earl of Derby's lease of land to the railway company for the Moss Pits Branch was due to expire in 1932, but was renewed for a further 17 years and 6 months from July 1932. The private sidings agreement was endorsed on 27th February 1933 by Prescot Proprietary Ltd as successors in title to the 2nd Earl of Derby.

The Mines Lists show that Nos 1 and 2 Pits at Bickerstaffe Colliery were abandoned by Mr Swift in September 1936. By this time the branch was also being used for incoming traffic, presumably for the landsale yard at Four Lane Ends. The Sidings Schedules, in a note dated August 1936, record that F Marsh and Company had permission to deal with occasional wagons of coal. The line must have closed shortly afterwards, as the private sidings agreement was terminated by letter of 20th May 1938 [58]. The Sidings Schedules state that the main line connection was taken out in December 1938 and that the signalling was being removed under an economy scheme in 1940.

Skelmersdale and Bickerstaffe

A little later, Messrs William Evans and Co (Manchester) Ltd, acting on behalf of a group of timber importers, secured an area of land in the vicinity of the old Moss Pits. The purpose was to store imported timber, which it was necessary to disperse from the ports immediately on arrival to avoid the possibility of destruction by enemy action.

The Sidings Schedules state that arrangements were made for the reinstatement of the private sidings facilities to deal with timber coming to the site from Garston Docks. The work was ordered on 11th April 1941 and completed on 28th April 1941. The cost of restoration was £753-12-8d and an account for this was submitted to Widnes Timber Storage Co Ltd. This was the company formed to operate the site and in which Messrs Evans was a constituent.

The Widnes Timber Storage Co Ltd, in a letter to the railway company dated 20th December 1945, stated that they had decided to vacate the site and that traffic would cease as from 1st January 1946. Work to remove the main line connection and the track on the railway owned part of the branch was ordered on 17th June 1947. It had been completed by 9th August 1947.

In 1951 the timber storage area was reopened by Messrs Craig and Evans, who applied for the siding facilities to be reinstated. This was not done, as the firm decided to use road transport.

During the period that the Widnes Timber Storage Company used the site, a locomotive was transferred from the Widnes yard of the parent company, William Evans and Co (Manchester) Ltd. The engine, KENYON, a four coupled saddle tank, built by Black, Hawthorn and Company of Gateshead in 1875, seems to have arrived shortly after the Bickerstaffe operations commenced. Before returning to Widnes, it was sent to Hough and Sons Ltd for repairs. These were carried out by Houghs in premises at the Rose Bridge Colliery at Ince.

KENYON, after it had returned from Bickerstaffe to William Evans' timber yard at Ditton, near Widnes. Photographed in 1953. F. Jones

The land occupied by the colliery railway and the timber yard has now reverted to agricultural use. A petrol station and cafe have been built at Four Lane Ends on the site of the landsale coal yard. The spoil heaps of the Moss Pits and the later Bickerstaffe Colliery remain in place at the time of writing.

Bickerstaffe Sand Pits

Pilkington Brothers Ltd, of St Helens, operated sand pits in the area immediately north of Four Lane Ends in the 1970s. The workings at Bickerstaffe lasted for only a short period, probably less than two years. Narrow gauge lines were laid from the pits to a loading point and the sand was taken away by road vehicles. Several internal combustion locomotives, built by the Motor Rail company of Bedford, were used.

At this time the firm was exploiting a number of scattered sites to the north and west of St Helens, many of which only had short life. The railway equipment was transferred from one location to another, as necessary. The history of these operations is more properly dealt with in a work dealing with the industries of St Helens and can only have a brief mention here.

LOCOMOTIVE SUMMARY

Crow Orchard Colliery
To Hilton Colliery Company, 1886, via T D Swift, Ince

c1850 to 1860	Various Stopford family firms
1860 to 1873	Morrell and Stoner, later trading as Crow Orchard Coal Company
1873 to 1886	Crow Orchard Colliery Co Ltd
1886	Sold to White Moss Coal Co Ltd

PRESCOTT   0-6-0ST   IC   HE   66   1871   12"x18"   3'1"
  New
  To Hulton Colliery Company, 1886, via T.D. Seift, Ince

THE CROW   0-6-0ST   IC   HE   160   1876   15"x20"   3'4"
  New
  To White Moss Coal Co Ltd, 1886, via T D Swift, Ince.

There was another unidentified locomotive here in 1867, see text

Tawd Vale Colliery

c1860 to 1864	John Morrell
1864 to 1870(?)	Tawd Vale Coal Co Ltd
1870(?) to 1897	Tawd Vale Colliery Co Ltd
1897 to 1904	Colliery closed
1904	Taken over by John Griffiths and Son Ltd and renamed Glenburn (see below)

TAWD VALE COLLIERY   0-6-0ST   IC   MW   64   1862   12"x17"   3'2"
  New, despatched from works 19-12-1862
  Scrapped or sold after October 1885

Skelmersdale and Bickerstaffe

| 2 | | 0-6-0ST | IC | MW | 175 | 1865 | 12"x17" | 3'2" |

   New, despatched from works 8-9-1865
   Scrapped or sold

| ENTERPRISE | | 0-6-0ST | IC | MW | 91 | 1863 | 12"x17" | 3'2" |

   Ex Beckett and Bentley, contractors.
   To W and T Latham, Rose Bridge Colliery, Wigan, 1899

| LIZZIE | | 0-6-0ST | IC | MW | 610 | 1876 | 12"x17" | 3'0" |

   Ex Braddock and Matthews, contractors, Southport, about 1884
   To Mr Watson, Leeds, 1899
   Possibly later to Ellerbeck Colliery

| HOLDEN | | 0-6-0ST | IC | MW | 603 | 1876 | 13"x18" | 3'0" |

   Ex John Barnes, contractor, Chatburn.
   To Earl of Lathom, Blaguegate Colliery, 1899

Chapel House Colliery

1868 to 1869   Thomas Farrimond
1869 to 1882   Edward Smith, sometimes trading as Chapel House Colliery Company
1883 to 1904   Executors of Edward Smith

| EDWARD | | 0-4-0ST | OC | HE | 411 | 1886 | 13"x18" | 3'1" |

   New
   To Holme and King, contractors, by July 1905

White Moss Collieries

1865 to 1928   White Moss Coal Co Ltd
   Purchased Crow Orchard Colliery 1886
   Last pit closed 1928

| GARDINER | | 0-6-0ST | IC | HE | 76 | 1873 | 12"x18" | 3'1" |

   New, despatched from works 20-9-1873
   Later renamed ROBINSON
   Later renamed ROSEMARY
   To Holland Colliery

| OSWALD | | 0-6-0ST | IC | HE | 120 | 1874 | 13"x18" | 3'1" |

   New, despatched from works 16-4-1874
   To Hutchinsons Trustees, Widnes about 1910

| GASKELL | | 0-6-0ST | IC | HE | 338 | 1884 | 15"x20" | 3'4" |

   New
   To Holland Colliery

| SHAWE | | 0-6-0ST | IC | HE | 160 | 1876 | 15"x20" | 3'4" |

   Ex Crow Orchard Colly Co Ltd, 1886, THE CROW

Blaguegate Colliery

c1850 to 1922   Successive Lords Skelmersdale and Earls of Lathom
1923 to 1933   John Griffiths and Son Ltd

Railway worked by owners of Tawd Vale Colliery c1860 to c1899
Railway worked by John Griffiths and Son Ltd after 1922 (see below)

| HOLDEN | 0-6-0ST | IC | MW | 603 | 1876 | 13"x18" | 3'0" |

Ex Tawd Vale Coal Co Ltd, 1899
To John Griffiths and Son Ltd about 1923

Glenburn Colliery (also Blaguegate after 1922)

Glenburn Colliery (Tawd Vale renamed)
    1904 to 1923 John Griffiths and Son Ltd
    1923 Last Pits closed

Blaguegate Colliery
    1923 to 1933 John Griffiths and Son Ltd

| NORTHFIELD | 0-6-0ST | OC | P | 717 | 1898 | 14"x20" | |

Ex A. Kellett, Rubery
To James Pain Ltd, Byfield.

| KEYHAM | 0-6-0T | IC | HC | 318 | 1889 | 15"x20" | 3'6½" |

Ex Sir John Jackson, contractor
Offered for sale by Griffiths, October 1919
At Firth, Blakely, Son and Company, Church Fenton, by 1921

| CHAMPION | 0-4-0ST | OC | HE | 428 | 1888 | 13"x18" | 3'1" |

Ex Whitecross Co, Peasley Cross Colly after February 1905
Possibly named WINIFRED at Glenburn
Believed to have been scrapped or sold in early 1920s

| DELAMERE | 0-4-0ST | OC | P | 796 | 1900 | 12"x18" | |

Ex James Carter and Sons Ltd, Clitheroe, about May 1907
Scrapped, possibly in 1933

| HOLDEN | 0-6-0ST | OC | MW | 603 | 1876 | 13"x18" | 3'0" |

Ex Earl of Lathom, about 1922
Scrapped 1934

Skelmersdale Sand Pits

?1897 to 1913   Cannington, Shaw and Co Ltd
1913 to c1959   United Glass Bottle Manufacturers Ltd

2'0" gauge

| | 4w PM | | FH | (?) | | | |

Sold or scrapped about 1959

Skelmersdale and Bickerstaffe

| | | 4w PM | | FH | 2017 | 1936 | | 40HP | |

New, presumed to this site
Sold or scrapped about 1959

Bickerstaffe Colliery

c 1845 to 1866   Bromilow, Foster and Company
1866 to 1898   Bromilow, Foster and Co ltd
1899 to 1904   Foster, Williams and Co Ltd
1905 to 1929   Bickerstaffe Collieries Ltd
1930 to 1936   Bickerstaffe Collieries (P H Swift Proprietor)

BICKERSTAFFE   0-4-0ST   OC   MW   372   1871   8"x14"   2'9"
 New, despatched from works on 31-5-1871
 Scrapped or sold after June 1901

BICKERSTAFFE   0-4-0ST   OC   P   881   1901   14"x20"
 New
 Scrapped or sold

GLADYS   0-6-0ST   OC   FW   342   1871   13"x20"   3'6"
 Hired from Thompson and Co (Wigan) Ltd, Ince, 1934.

Bickerstaffe Timber Yard

1941 to 1946   Widnes Timber Storage Co Ltd (Subsidiary of William Evans (Manchester) Ltd

KENYON   0-4-0ST   OC   BH   296   1875   12"x19"   3'2"
                           Rbt VF 1936

References to Chapter 14

1 *Royal National Commercial Directory and Topography of the County of Lancaster* – Isaac Slater – Manchester, 1848
2 *Who Was Who* – Adam and Charles Black, London 1962
3 L&YR Sdgs Diag No 147, dated 27-7-1897
4 *Royal National Commercial Directory and Topography of the County of Lancaster* – Isaac Slater – Manchester, 1851
5 WO 17-8-1860
6 CG 15-12-1866
7 BC 19-1-1867
8 WO 15-7-1875
9 WO 22-7-1875
10 CG 12-11-1875
11 CG 19-1-1875
12 WO 11-9-1885
13 MJ 23-1-1886
14 CG8-1-1886
15 WO 30-1-1886
16 *Iron* 5-2-1886
17 WO 6-2-1886
18 WO 10-4-1886
19 WO 20-11-1863
20 WO 23-12-1870
21 WO 22-5-1875
22 WO 11-12-1897
23 WO 24-12-1897
24 WO 8-7-1899
25 WEx 17-6-1899
26 WEx 9-9-1899
27 CG 16-8-1878
28 CG 17-10-1882
29 WO 5-8-1899
30 WO 14-5-1869
31 WEx 2-7-1904
32 *Engineer* 28-10-1904

33	*Engineer* 24-3-1905	34	L&YR Sdgs Diag No 74A, dated 30-10-1899
35	L&YR Sdgs Diag No 64, dated 7-4-1896	36	L&YR Sdgs Diag No 64A, dated 6-7-1916
37	WRO DDXEl 35/4	38	WO 10-2-1923
39	L&YR Sdgs Diag No 65A, dated 25-4-1904	40	WO 20-8-1904
41	CG 24-10-1919	42	OA 17-1-1935
43	*Industry In South Lancashire* South Lancashire Development Corporation – Publ Ed Burrow & Co Ltd, Cheltenham and London, n.d.,about 1970		
44	L&YR Sdgs Diag No148, dated 27-7-1897		
45	*The Skelmersdale Story* Revd Nigel Sands – locally published – March 1970		
46	OA 17-9-1914	47	OA 22-10-1914
48	OA 11-2-1915	49	L&YR Sdgs Diag No 66, dated 7-4-1896
50	WO 11-6-1898	51	LRO PDR 591
52	L&YR Sdgs Diag No 315, dated 21-11-1903	53	LG 17-5-1867
54	WO 25-5-1867	55	WO 25-3-1899
56	WO 1-9-1900	57	WO 3-3-1928
58	Line Plan of Skelmersdale Branch L&YR n.d. – marked up on 25" ordnance survey map – at BRPB Manchester Office		

CHAPTER 15

RAINFORD, UPHOLLAND AND ORRELL

In this chapter we first move south of Skelmersdale, to consider the the collieries in and around Rainford. Developments here followed the opening of the Lancashire and Yorkshire Railway Company's Liverpool and Bury line in 1848.

We shall then look at the later developments which took place in the neighbourhood of Upholland and Orrell, and conclude our tour of the southern and western part of the Wigan Coalfield where we began. Although we have covered the earlier history of this area in Chapter 3, it is more appropriate to deal with what happened in the latter part of the nineteenth century and in the twentieth century here.

Rainford Colliery

The original Rainford Colliery was situated on the north side of the railway from Wigan to Liverpool, to the east of the St Helens to Ormskirk road. It appears to have been sunk in the late 1840s, and is marked on the revised version of the 1st edition of the 6" map which was produced shortly after the opening of the railway in 1848. The Mines Lists show that it was owned by William Harding between 1854 and 1856, and from 1857 by the Moss Hall Coal Company. As we have seen in Chapters 6 and 12, this firm had extensive colliery interests at Ince and Platt Bridge, but in the mid 1850s was expanding its activities further afield. The Mines Lists for 1873 show that the Rainford operations had been taken over by the Rainford Coal Company Ltd.

New pits were sunk to the west of the St Helens to Ormskirk road, but still on the north side of the Wigan to Liverpool railway. The original colliery was subsequently abandoned and is not shown on the 2nd edition of the 6" map, resurveyed in 1892. We have been unable to find out when these developments took place. They may date from the mid 1860s, as the Sidings Diagram relating to the new colliery refers to agreements of 4th October 1866 and 26th September 1867[1]. Lord Derby's Manure Siding, provided under agreements of 26th May 1846 and 19th June 1846, was adjacent to the connections to the new colliery[2]. The Rainford Coal Company opened a brickworks adjacent to the colliery in 1895[3].

The Rainford Coal Co Ltd was in liquidation in September 1903[4]. The colliery was taken over by Bromilow, Foster and Co Ltd, which had already made successful trial borings for coal in 1896 and 1897, on the west side of Rainford Village[5]. Rainford Colliery restarted under its new owners in December 1903[6]. A new agreement in respect of the sidings was made with the Lancashire and Yorkshire Railway on 24th October 1905[7,8].

We have no record of the earliest locomotives used at Rainford Colliery. We know that in 1877 the Rainford Coal Company purchased a small four coupled saddle tank from Manning, Wardle and Company of Leeds. The manufacturer's records show that this engine was later the

Rainford, Upholland and Orrell

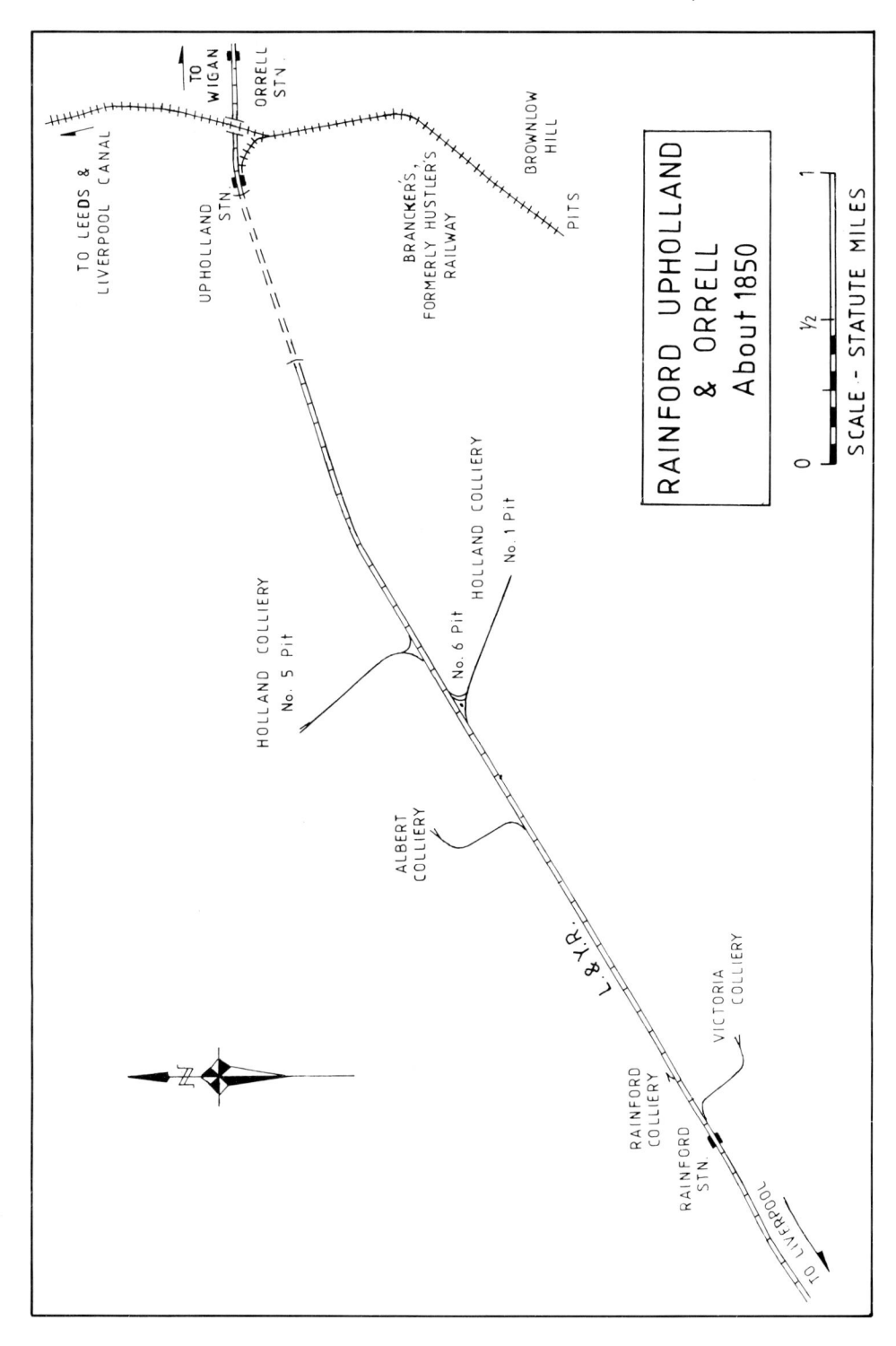

property of the machinery merchants C D Phillips and Company of Newport, Monmouthshire. It may have been the four coupled engine with 10" cylinders which was advertised for sale by the Rainford Coal Company in February 1900 [9].

After acquiring the colliery, Bromilow, Foster and Co Ltd went to Manning, Wardle for a rather larger four coupled saddle tank. This was delivered in 1907 and carried the name PREMIER. According to old employees we talked with, this was the only engine based at Rainford. When it needed repair, a temporary replacement was supplied from Bromilow, Foster's Ashtons Green Colliery, at St Helens. KING and QUEEN, four coupled saddle tanks built by Andrew Barclay, Sons and Company of Kilmarnock, appeared at Rainford from time to time.

Rainford Colliery closed in the late 1920s, last appearing in the Mines Lists in 1929. PREMIER was used to dismantle the colliery and the sidings. According to our old informants, it was then cut up for scrap.

Victoria and Albert Pits

Victoria Colliery was situated on the south side of the Lancashire and Yorkshire Railway's Wigan to Liverpool line, and was served by a short branch which joined the main line near the first Rainford Colliery. Albert Colliery was about a mile further east, on the north side of the Wigan to Liverpool railway.

Both collieries seem to have opened in the late 1840s and are shown on the revision of the 1st edition of the 6" map, published about 1850. They were both started up by A F and D Mackay and Company. Part of the land required for the railway serving the Albert Colliery was leased by the Earl of Derby to Edward Ellison of Upholland from 20th November 1849 and released by him to the Hugh, Archibald, James and Daniel Mackay from 3rd March 1850. Mineral rights here were leased by Ellison to the Mackays for 30 years from 20th November 1849 [10].

The firm of A F and D Mackay and Company was dissolved on 22nd April 1852 [11]. Included in the sale which took place the following month were 40 hopper wagons for traffic to Stanley Dock at Liverpool and one good locomotive. There were also 700 yards of railway line at the Victoria Colliery and 1250 yards at the Albert Colliery [12].

From the Mines Lists for 1853/4 we learn that the two collieries became the property of the Victoria and Albert Coal Company. Albert Colliery is not shown in the Mines lists for 1855 and later. We think it may have been taken over by the Earl of Crawford and Balcarres and worked in conjunction with his Holland Colliery, which we deal with later in this chapter. In 1858, the Earl's agent was negotiating with the Lancashire and Yorkshire Railway Company about charges for coal traffic to Liverpool from both the Albert and Holland Collieries. A special rate of 1/- per ton was agreed in place of the 13d charged previously [13].

Victoria Colliery was advertised to be sold on 18th September 1856, the plant including 900 yards of railway track and an unspecified number of railway wagons [14]. It was purchased by the Moss Hall Coal Company, which the Mines Lists record in occupation in 1857 and subsequently. Between 1864 and 1870 the owners are shown in the Mines Lists as Walmesley and Company, and from 1871 as the Victoria Colliery Company.

By 1892, when the survey was carried out for the 2nd edition of the 6" map, the original Victoria Colliery had been abandoned. Nos 3 and 5 Pits had been sunk further south, near

Rainford village. The railway had been extended to connect with the St Helens to Rainford line, by this time absorbed in to the London and North Western Railway. At the north end of the colliery line, a triangular junction with the Lancashire and Yorkshire Railway had replaced the original connection facing towards Liverpool.

The Victoria Colliery Company Ltd had already gone into voluntary liquidation at the end of 1891. There was a sale of plant on 18th November and this included 100 wagons[15,16]. A further auction took place on 22nd June 1892[17]. The sales catalogue[18] refers to a locomotive built by the St Helens firm of Borrows and Co.

The colliery did not reopen and was dismantled along with its railway system. By 1906–1907, when the survey was made for the 3rd edition of the 6" map, all the track had gone. The connection with the London and North Western railway now served an engineering works, and a note on the Line Plan[19] shows that a new sidings agreement was made with Mr W A Taylor on 1st December 1905. According to old inhabitants of the district with whom we talked in the early 1950s, Taylor was killed during the first world war. The site was later occupied by an oil works belonging to Leslie Allen and Co Ltd, but some engineering activities were still carried on.

Mr H W Johnson, brother of the oil works manager Jack Johnson, occupied premises within the works boundary and built three small well tank locomotives to a design developed by E Borrows and Sons of St Helens. The site was occupied in the period immediately after the second world war by the firm of Robertson, Buckley and Co Ltd and used as a store. At the time of writing, the buildings had been demolished and a new housing estate was in the course of construction.

We think it possible, in view of the sales advertisement of 1852, that the Mackay partnership worked its own coal trains to the docks at Liverpool. If this interpretation is correct, it seems likely that the Moss Hall Coal Company continued the practice. However, we have no documentary evidence to support this statement, nor do we have any information about the locomotives which were used.

We believe that we can identify the locomotive offered for sale in 1892. We know that a four coupled well tank, named VICTORIA, came new in 1876 from E Borrows and Sons. This firm built a number of small industrial locomotives at its works near St Helens Junction and further information about them can be found in an article by Bernard Roberts[20]. As mentioned above, three engines of this type were later turned out by Johnson at Rainford.

Moss House Colliery

We identify this colliery with the one described by old inhabitants in the neighbourhood of Rainford as being situated near Kings Moss and connected to the Lancashire and Yorkshire line at Holland Moss by its own branch. The recollections were that a locomotive had been employed here in the 1880s.

The colliery and its railway system are not marked on the revision of the 1st edition of the 6" map, published around 1850. By 1892, when the surveys were prepared for the 2nd edition of the 6" map, the colliery had disappeared. The are however traces on the map which we believe represent the course of the old railway.

Moss House Colliery first appears in the Mines Lists in 1865, under the ownership of Horn and Kelly, who also appear to have traded as the Moss House Colliery Company. Thomas Bird and Company took over in 1873 and by 1888 the colliery was out of use. It is not shown in the Mines Lists for 1891 and subsequent years.

In the 1920s, a moss litter works was established near where the colliery railway had crossed Cat Lane. A short narrow gauge tramway was laid on the trackbed of the old line to bring peat to the works. The tramway first appears on the revised 6" map, published in 1928 and is still shown on the revision of 1955. It had disappeared by the time that a further revision was published in 1967.

Holland Colliery

Soon after the opening of the Liverpool and Bury Line in 1848, the Earl of Crawford and Balcarres sank a number of pits on Holland Moss. The revised 1st edition 6" map, published about 1850, shows No 6 pit adjacent to and on the south side of the main line, with which there is a triangular junction. A railway connects No 6 Pit with No 1 Pit, situated to the south of Pimbo Lane. To the north of the main line, another branch, again with a triangular junction, serves No 5 Pit. In January 1852, it was reported that a private electric telegraph was being installed to link the Holland Colliery with the Earl of Crawford's headquarters at Haigh Colliery[21]. The work had been completed by 20th February of that year[22].

The coal trains between Holland Colliery and Liverpool over the Lancashire and Yorkshire Company's line were worked by engines owned by the Earl of Crawford and Balcarres. These operations must have commenced soon after the colliery came into production, as from 1852 onwards there are reports of a series of accidents and incidents concerning the trains and the locomotives which hauled them.

These workings continued after Holland Colliery became the property of the Wigan Coal and Iron Company in 1865, but we have not been able to trace when they finished. They were often mentioned by old employees of the company with whom we talked in the 1940s, although not from first hand experience. They were relating what previous generations of their families had told them, some of whom had driven the engines working the Liverpool trains. The impression we formed was that, in later years, one of the tender engines from the shed at Kirkless did a return trip to Liverpool each day, calling at Holland Colliery en route. It seems that locomotives for this traffic, and perhaps for internal shunting duties as well, were also stabled at Holland Colliery. Pay abstracts for 1869 have survived and contain entries for locomotive cleaning and locomotive driving[23]. We shall return to the subject of the locomotives owned by the Earl of Crawford and Balcarres and by the Wigan Coal and Iron Co Ltd in Part 2, Chapters 16 and 19.

The Wigan Coal and Iron Company's operations at Holland Colliery were suspended in June 1880. Part of the site had been leased from Henry Gaskell and, following his death, his executors gave notice to determine the lease. The ventilating fan, the upcast shaft and the engine house for the locomotives were on this property. The remainder of the colliery was leased from the Earl of Lathom, but rail access could only be obtained over Gaskell's land[24]. The colliery was therefore abandoned, and we presume that the locomotives and rolling stock were transferred elsewhere within the company.

In 1896, after a lapse of sixteen years, Nos 6 and 9 Pits at Holland Colliery were reopened by the White Moss Coal Co Ltd[25,26]. The new winding engine at No 9 pit was brought into operation in August[27].

Rainford, Upholland and Orrell

We have already dealt with the history of the White Moss Company's railway system at Skelmersdale in Chapter 14. We were fortunate to meet several old employees who had been with the White Moss Company at Holland Colliery who were able to tell us something about the locomotives used there in later days.

One engine which our informants remembered was BAINBRIDGE, a six coupled saddle tank built by Manning, Wardle of Leeds. It was stated to have come second hand to Holland Colliery and had carried the name FRECKLETON when it arrived. It was reputedly sold to Hough of Ince. We can identify FRECKLETON as a locomotive which was built in 1890 for the Executors of T A Walker for use on the construction of Preston Docks. It subsequently saw service with another public works contractor, Holme and King, who used it on various jobs.

There seems to have been some interchange of locomotives between Holland and White Moss Collieries. GASKELL, the 1884 Manning, Wardle six coupled saddle tank, which we have mentioned previously in Chapter 14, was remembered as being at Holland for a time. The manufacturer's records show that it was still in existence in February 1930, when spare parts were supplied.

ROSEMARY, the Hunslet six wheeler which had been delivered to White Moss Colliery as GARDINER, also was said to have spent some time at Holland. The manufacturer's records show that a new boiler was provided in May 1924.

Two second hand locomotives were purchased in the 1930s. The first to arrive, in 1933[28], was a four coupled saddle tank, fitted with a vacuum brake. This engine had been built by Manning, Wardle of Leeds, in 1901, for the Cambrian Railways for use on the Van Branch. It was numbered 22 in the Cambrian Railways stock and was sold in 1916 to Messrs Armytage and Jones of Sheffield, who were acting on behalf of the Government. It was used at the camp at Prees Heath and subsequently became Air Ministry Works Department No 128. The former colliery engineer told us that it was at Cardington, near Bedford, when he purchased it.

In January 1935, the colliery acquired another four coupled saddle tank with main line railway associations. This came from the London Midland and Scottish Railway, in whose stock it had been numbered 16019. The engine had originally been built in 1889 by the Caledonian Railway at its St Rollox Works in Glasgow.

Coal production had already started to decline in the 1930s. The Crawford Pit was abandoned, according to the Mines Lists, in February 1932 and No 6 Pit in July 1936. The Crawford Day Eye and No 9 Pit continued until 1939, when they too were closed. At a sale of plant on 23rd August 1939 two locomotives were included, the ex Cambrian Railways and the ex Caledonian Railway engines. They appear to have been broken up for scrap.

The colliery must have been dismantled shortly after the sale. No rail connections are shown on a Line Plan of 1940[29].

Crawford Sand Pits

There was a short lived narrow gauge tramway in the vicinity of Holland Colliery, serving what are described as silver sand pits. The line is shown on the 1928 and 1938 revisions of the 6" map. It had been dismantled by the time there was another revision in 1948.

The tramway ran from sand quarries in the fields opposite Crawford School to a washing plant on the south side of Pimbo Lane. From here it crossed Pimbo Lane on the level and then took a northerly course across country. It terminated at Ditton Brook Sidings on the Wigan to

Upholland Brick and Tile Works

The Ditton Brook Coal and Iron Company, a firm with iron works near Widnes, opened out a colliery on Holland Moor, south of the Upholland to Skelmersdale road. The colliery was sunk in the early 1870s and first appears in the Mines List for 1873. It was served by a private branch which joined the Lancashire and Yorkshire Railway's Wigan to Liverpool line at Ditton Brook Sidings and which was in operation by September 1871 [30].

The iron works at Widnes was severely damaged by an explosion on 6th October 1876 [31,32] and the company went into liquidation eighteen months later [33]. It is clear that by 1878 clay as well as coal was being exploited at Upholland, for there is reference to the sale of the Holland Moor Colliery and Firebrick Works of the company on 23rd July of that year [34]. A tank locomotive was included in the sale.

The colliery and clay works were taken over by Upholland Brick and Coal Company, under which name they are shown in the Mines Lists between 1886 and 1893. They subsequently passed in to the ownership of the Upholland Brick and Tile Co Ltd, which had been registered on 30th September 1889 [35,36]. In 1908, the premises were taken over by the Ravenhead Sanitary Pipe and Brick Co Ltd, a firm incorporated in 1875 [37] which already operated similar works at St Helens.

The successive owners retained the rail connection with Ditton Brook Sidings but the dates of the various private sidings agreements are not shown on the relevant Sidings Diagram [38]. However, from an endorsement on the Line Plan of the Liverpool Bolton and Bury Railway [29], we know that the agreement with the Ravenhead Sanitary Pipe and Brick Co Ltd was signed on 12th March 1908.

We have very little authenticated information about the locomotives which were used at the works in the early days. From about 1930, the railway system was operated by a rather unusual machine, which went by the name of UPHO. It had been constructed according to the designs of the Sentinel Wagon Company of Shrewsbury. It incorporated a boiler and engine unit similar to those fitted the firm's road vehicles, mounted on the chassis of a conventional steam locomotive which had been stripped of its boiler and cylinders.

The Sentinel records show that the parts needed for the conversion were sent to the United Alkali Co Ltd, at Muspratt Works, Widnes, between January and July 1925, where they there were fitted to the frames of an unidentified locomotive belonging to the works. After about five years service at Widnes, the rebuilt locomotive was sold to the Upholland brickworks.

The records of Thomas Wrigley, the Prestwich contractor, show that his locomotive SEDGLEY was on hire at Upholland between July 1920 and February 1921 at a charge of £10 per week. It was presumably deputising for one of the earlier engines that was under repairs.

We also have on record that the Ravenhead company owned a 2'0" gauge diesel locomotive. This, we understand, was used in the firm's clay pits. It had been built by Ruston and Hornsby Ltd of Lincoln.

The standard gauge railway system was abandoned in the mid 1950s and UPHO was scrapped around 1957. The narrow gauge locomotive was sold to Chris Holden Ltd, machinery dealers, of Blackburn.

Rainford, Upholland and Orrell

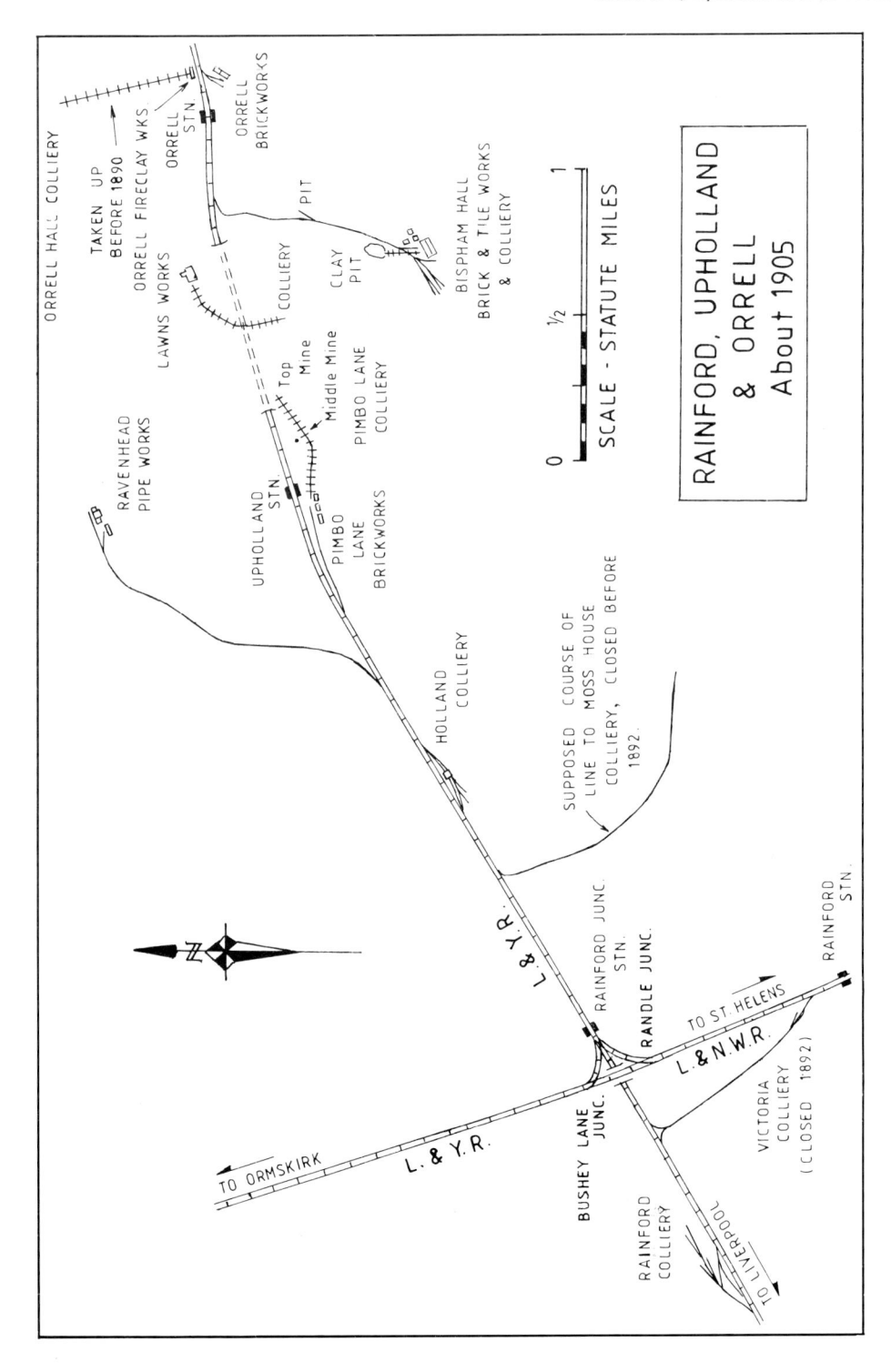

Rainford, Upholland and Orrell

The works is still operational at the time of writing. It was taken over by Henry Foster Building Products Ltd in April 1970 and became the property of Gibbons (Dudley) Ltd in November 1974. Since 1979 it has been owned by Steetley Brick Ltd, a member of the Steetley Group of companies[39].

Pimbo Lane Brickworks and Mountain Mine Colliery

The first Pimbo Lane Brickworks was located on the south side of the Lancashire and Yorkshire Railway's Wigan to Liverpool line, adjacent to Upholland Station. It appears to date from around 1900, as neither the works nor the collieries later associated with it are shown on the 2nd edition of the 6" map, surveyed in 1892. The siding which served the works had been put in under an agreement with the Pimbo Lane Brick and Tile Co Ltd dated 20th October 1899[40] and we assume that the works came into operation around this time.

The 3rd edition of the 6" map, revised 1906 to 1907, shows a narrow gauge tramway about half a mile long linking the brickworks with two small collieries on the high ground adjacent to Upholland Tunnel. Pimbo Lane Top Mine is at the eastern end of the tramway and Pimbo Lane Middle Mine is nearer the brickworks.

We think that these were originally the property of the Pimbo Lane Colliery Company and had been sunk in the middle of the 1890s. They appear in the Mines Lists for the period 1896

A view of Ditton Brook Sidings, looking towards Wigan. The line to the Upholland brickworks can be seen on the left of the main line. The connection serving the Pimbo Lane brickworks, the Mountain Mine Colliery and the later coking plant had been taken out before the photograph was taken. It was to the right of the main line, beyond the signal box.

C.H.A. Townley

to 1900 under this ownership. Between 1901 and 1908, Pimbo Lane Nos 1 and 2 Pits are shown under the Pimbo Lane Brick and Tile Company.

The colliery and brickworks were taken over, in 1911, by the Mountain Mine Colliery Co Ltd and a new agreement in respect of the private siding was signed by this company on 13th May 1912.[40]. The colliery was redeveloped and the standard gauge line was extended from the brickworks to serve it, replacing the earlier tramway. The level crossing over Pimbo Lane was the subject of an agreement with Upholland Urban District Council, dated 19th August 1912[41].

The brickworks itself was demolished and the site was conveyed on 12th August 1912 to the Simplex Coke Oven and Engineering Co Ltd[42]. This firm then built a battery of 35 ovens and a by-products plant there[43].

A new brickworks was erected, without rail connection, north of the Lancashire and Yorkshire line. This continued in operation until about 1975, latterly under the ownership of the Southern family[39] and was subsequently demolished. In November 1989, the old clay pits were being used by Lancashire County Council as a landfill site.

The Mountain Mine Colliery was acquired in 1916 or 1917 by the Bispham Hall Colliery Company Ltd. We will digress to deal with the earlier history of this company before continuing with that of the Pimbo Lane site.

Bispham Hall Colliery and Brickworks

At the turn of the century there was a revival of mining activities immediately to the north of the area worked by William Hill Brancker thirty years earlier and which we have described in Chapter 3. The Mines Lists record that William Hilton occupied a colliery at Bispham Hall from 1894 to 1898. From 1899 the owners are shown as the Bispham Hall Colliery Company, the title adopted by the partners William Hilton and James Marsden. The partnership was dissolved on 9th February 1900[44], on the formation of the Bispham Hall Colliery Co Ltd

As well as coal, there were supplies of good quality clay in the vicinity and there are records of brick and tile making here in the late 1860s. The Bispham Hall works of William Moorfield was advertised for sale by auction on 23rd January 1867[45]. The Bispham Hall Colliery Company also went into the brick and tile business, but we do not know whether they took over existing premises or whether they built a new works themselves.

To serve the colliery and brickworks, the Bispham Hall Company constructed a railway about half a mile in length to join the Lancashire and Yorkshire line at Orrell West. The connection here was provided under an agreement of 21st September 1901 with James Marsden, trading as the Bispham Hall Colliery Company[46]. At its northern end the line crossed the corner of the Lancashire and Yorkshire Company's reservoir by means of a timber bridge. The Sidings Schedules note that, by 1931, the bridge was in need of repair. To save expense, it was decide to fill in the corner of the reservoir, the work being ordered on 21st December of that year.

The railway system and its locomotives have been described in an article by Mr C A Appleton, published in the Journal of the Industrial Locomotive Society[47].

To work the new line from the brickworks and colliery to the Lancashire and Yorkshire Railway, the Bispham Hall Colliery Company purchased a six coupled saddle tank from Peckett and Sons of Bristol. Delivered in 1901 and originally named WALTER, it was, according to former employees, rechristened HILDA around 1926.

Rainford, Upholland and Orrell

HILDA, the locomotive supplied by Peckett and Sons of Bristol to Bispham Hall Brickworks in 1901.
Alex Appleton Collection

As we have seen earlier in this chapter, the Bispham Hall Company took over the Mountain Mine Colliery during the first world war. The coke ovens and by-products plant seem to have remained the property of the Simplex Company until this firm sold up in 1920 [41]. A new railway, about a mile in length was built from Bispham Hall to link up with the existing sidings at the coke works.

To cater for the extra traffic, additional locomotives were required. Old employees who were interviewed in the 1950s recalled that GLADYS, a six coupled saddle tank built by Fox, Walker and Company, was on hire for a time from Hough and Sons Ltd. There was also mention of a four coupled saddle tank, named ADAM, which was stated to have worked at the coke works.

We know that the Bispham Hall Company purchased a six coupled saddle tank second hand around 1916. This engine had originally been built by Manning, Wardle and Company of Leeds in 1893 for the Arniston Coal Company for use at collieries near Edinburgh and, appropriately enough, bore the name ARNISTON.

In the 1925, the coke works and the Mountain Mine Colliery were sold to the Upholland Coking and By Products Co Ltd. A six coupled saddle tank, built by Hudswell, Clarke and Company of Leeds in 1907, was brought from the Crigglestone plant of the parent company, Benzol and By Products Co Ltd, to perform the shunting here.

There was only a brief period of activity under the new owners. The colliery closed in February 1930 [48] and the Mines Lists show that it was formally abandoned in March the same year. The coke works ceased production at about the same time. There was a sale of plant on 28th to 30th May 1930, which included the locomotive [49]. The manufacturer's records show it was bought by Sir Lindsay Parkinson and Co Ltd, the civil engineering contractors.

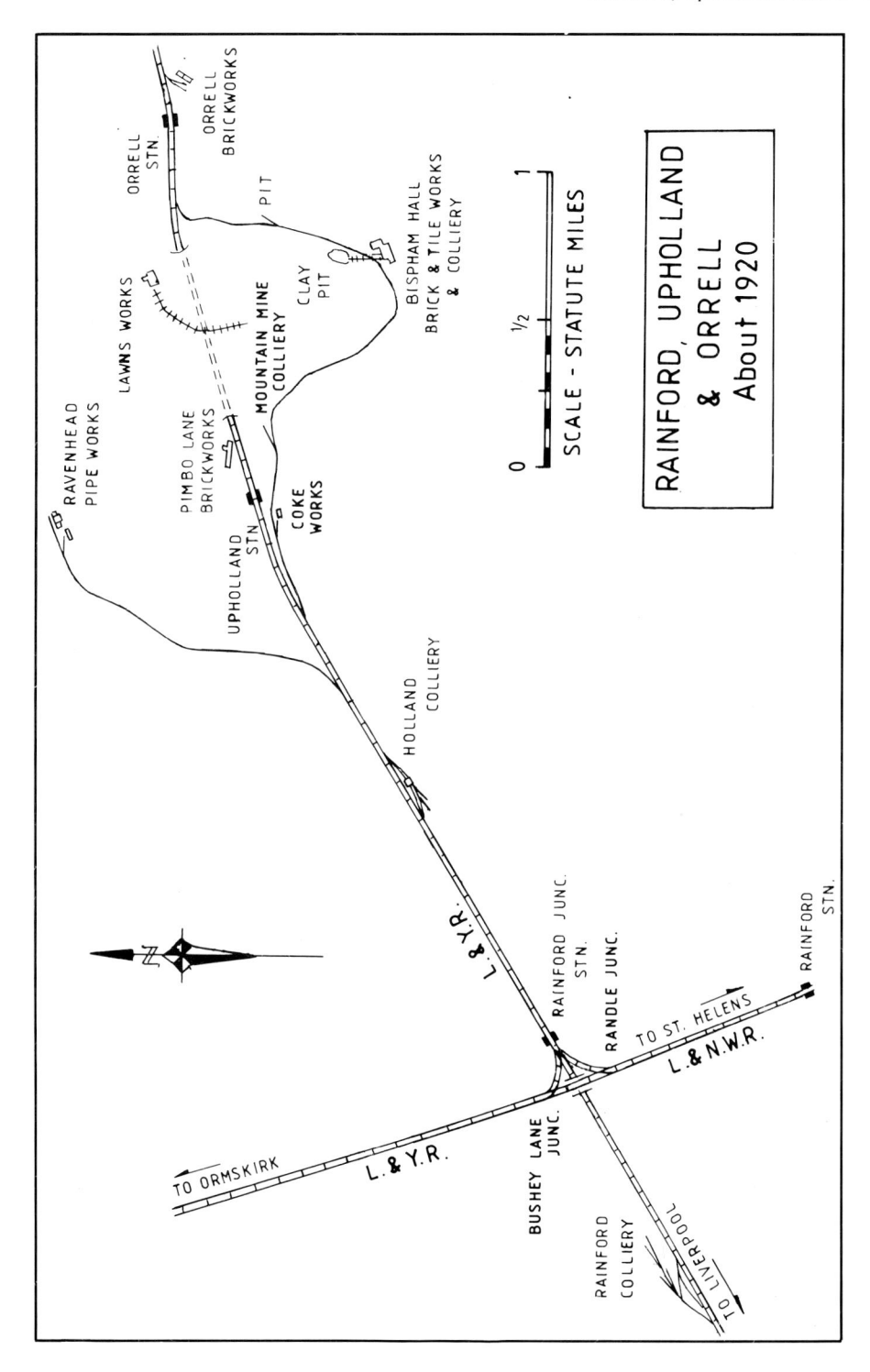

Rainford, Upholland and Orrell

The private sidings agreement relating to the connection with what was now the London Midland and Scottish Railway was also terminated in 1930[29]. The site was later levelled and is now, in part, occupied by Pimbo Nurseries.

The Bispham Hall Brick and Terra Cotta Co Ltd was formed in 1925 to take over the brickworks and its associated clay and coal mines. The railway between the brickworks and the Mountain Mine was abandoned, but that from the works to Orrell Station was retained. The Sidings Schedules show that a new agreement in respect of the connection at Orrell West was signed on 26th November 1925.

With the now reduced track mileage, the Bispham Hall Company sold the Manning, Wardle locomotive, which later worked at the Swan Lane Collieries, described in Part 2, Chapter 27. The Peckett engine of 1901, now named HILDA, was left to carry on on its own. When HILDA needed repairs, it was usual practice to hire a spare locomotive from one of the Wigan dealers. KING, a four coupled saddle tank, built by Andrew Barclay of Kilmarnock was here for a short period in the early 1930s.

As was usual on many of the private railway systems around Wigan, the Bispham Hall Company conveyed traffic for other individuals with premises near to its line. The Sidings Schedules record that in September 1925 traffic was being handled for a Mr J J Mayers, W Gaskell and Company, builders and contractors, Mr J Gibbons, a farmer, and Littler Brothers, farmers. In December 1928, manure and farm produce was being conveyed for Mr H Middlehurst and, in 1931, manure and lime for D Lucas and William Ashton.

The Bispham Hall Brickworks abandoned rail transport in 1952 and HILDA was cut up towards the end of that year[47]. The Gauntley Pit, adjacent to the works, continued to provide

Bispham Hall Brickworks before the closure of the railway system.   John Ryan Collection

supplies of coal and clay, and remained in operation until 1967. The wooden headgear, a survival from the turn of the century, was dismantled and later re-erected in the Haigh Country Park[50]. Terra cotta production had already ceased at the start of the second world war. Manufacture of bricks finished in 1973 and earthenware a year later[39].

The works itself survives, still largely intact, no longer in production but serving as a distribution depot for bricks and clayware brought from elsewhere. It merits detailed attention by industrial archaeologists to record and possibly conserve what remains.

Lawns Brickworks

The 2nd edition of the 6" map, surveyed in 1892, marks a brick and tile works, which it names as Lawns Works, near to the Tontine at Upholland. A tramway is shown running for about half a mile in a southerly direction to bring coal from a colliery on the opposite side of Upholland Tunnel. The layout changed little, if at all, over the next forty years, and the same features appear on the 3rd edition of the 6" map, surveyed in in 1906 and 1907, and on the revision of 1926.

The pits were known as Lawns Delf and, according to tradition, worked both coal and stone. They first appear in the Mines Lists for 1874, in the occupation of John Laithwaite. We think that the brickworks may date from the same period. John Laithwaite, presumably a son of the original owner, was still in occupation in July 1935, when the Mines Lists show that the colliery was abandoned. The brickworks appears to have closed shortly afterwards. The pits and the tramway connecting them to the works are shown disused on the 1938 to 1940 Line Plan of the Liverpool to Wigan Line[29].

The brickworks was reopened and enlarged after the second world war by the Lawns Brick Company. This firm was controlled by the Simpkins and Gaskell families, who also owned the Wigan Brick Co Ltd[39]. The works closed again in 1953 or 1954, this time permanently, following a partial collapse of the kiln. The buildings were subsequently demolished and the site cleared.

Orrell Hall Colliery and Brickworks

The Orrell Hall Colliery of John Holt and Company is first shown in the Mines Lists for 1872. It was taken over two years later by the Orrell Hall Coal and Fireclay Co Ltd, which had been formed by William Jones of Liverpool early in 1874[51]. This firm was in liquidation in 1879[52] and between 1883 and 1891 the Mines Lists describe the establishment as the Orrell Fireclay Works or, alternatively, as the Orrell Coal and Fireclay Works.

The colliery itself was situated adjacent to Moor Road. It was connected by tubway to a siding alongside the the Lancashire and Yorkshire Railway at a point opposite Orrell Goods Yard. A valuation exists of what was described as the Orrell Bank Company's assets, made on 12th August 1873, when John Holt was trying to sell the colliery[53].

The shafts were quite shallow, Nos 1 and 2 Pits being 41 yards and 26 yards deep respectively. There were 750 yards of tramway laid with 15 lbs per yard rail. What were apparently the main line sidings were described as 386ft in length, 304 feet being laid with 50 lbs per yard rail. The brickworks was not included in the valuation and perhaps had not been built at this time. Its location was at the end of the tubway, adjacent to the main line.

Rainford, Upholland and Orrell

Both colliery and tubway had disappeared by the time the 2nd edition of the 6" map was surveyed in 1892. We assume that the brickworks, although still marked on the map, had also closed.

Orrell Brick and Tile Works

The 2nd edition of the 6" map also marks extensive brick and tile works on the opposite side of Lancashire and Yorkshire Railway's Wigan to Liverpool line, adjacent to Orrell Goods yard. The works was connected with the main line through a siding in the goods yard, which served a series of loading docks.

The Mines Lists show that a William Ormrod was working a small colliery at Orrell in the period 1891 to 1893. The earliest reference we have in the Sidings Schedules is to an agreement with J Ormrod and Sons Ltd, dated 1st June 1895. There was a subsequent agreement with the Orrell Brick and Tile Co Ltd on 8th February 1904, after this firm had taken over the works [54,55].

Rail traffic ceased around 1940. The Sidings Schedules show that the Private Sidings Agreement was terminated as from 31st December 1940 and instructions were given to remove the sidings on 30th December 1941. We believe that shunting had always been performed by main line engines and that the brick and tile works had never possessed a locomotive of its own.

Around 1930, the works appears to have passed into the hands of the Southern family, who also owned the works at Pimbo Lane. The Orrell works closed around 1969 [39]. It was demolished in 1973, the site then being owned by L T Farrell (Liverpool) Ltd of Prescot [56].

Triangle Valve Co Ltd, Lamberhead Green

We conclude with a modern 2'0" gauge railway system which was built at the premises of the Triangle Valve Co Ltd. This firm opened a new factory on the Lamberhead Green Trading Estate in the mid 1950s and the railway was provided to transport materials around the site. There was a level crossing where the line passed over a public road separating the east and west works.

Motive power was in the form of a small diesel locomotive, supplied by Listers of Dursley in 1957. Internal transport at the factory was reorganised in 1979 and the railway was noted to be out of use in May of that year. The locomotive was transferred to the works of another company in the group, Triangle Alloys Ltd, at Clay Cross in Derbyshire, in 1980.

At the time of writing the works is still run by the Triangle Valve Co Ltd. The only reminder of the railway system is a short length of track embedded in the road surface where the level crossing used to be.

LOCOMOTIVE SUMMARY

Rainford Colliery

c1850 to c1856	William Harding
c1857 to c1867	Moss Hall Coal Company
1867 to c1873	Moss Hall Coal Co Ltd
c1873 to 1903	Rainford Coal Co Ltd
1903 to c1929	Bromilow, Foster and Co Ltd

Colliery closed c1929

RAINFORD	0-4-0ST	OC	MW	660	1877	8"x14"	2'8"

New
This locomotive may have passed to Bromilow, Foster and Co Ltd
To C D Phillips, Newport, by 1915

PREMIER	0-4-0ST	OC	MW	1670	1907	14"x18"	3'0"

New
Scrapped about 1930

KING	0-4-0ST	OC	AB	1448	1919	14"x22"	3'5"

On loan from Ashtons Green Colliery from time to time.

QUEEN	0-4-0ST	OC	AB	1784	1923	14"x22"	3'5"

On loan from Ashtons Green Colliery from time to time.

Victoria and Albert Pits

c1849 to 1852	A F and D Mackay
1852 to c1856	Victoria and Albert Coal Company

Albert Pit closed c 1854

c1857 to c1863	Moss Hall Coal Company
c1864 to c1870	Walmesley and Company
c1871 to 1891	Victoria Coal Co Ltd

Victoria Colliery closed 1891

Locomotive for sale May 1852

VICTORIA	0-4-0WT	OC	EB	6	1876	

New
Scrapped or sold about 1892

Moss House Colliery

1865 to 1872	Horn and Kelly, trading sometimes as Moss House Colliery Co
1873 to 1890	Thomas Bird and Company

Locomotive reputed to be here in 1880s

Rainford, Upholland and Orrell

Holland Colliery

c1849 to 1865	Earl of Crawford and Balcarres
1865 to 1880	Wigan Coal and Iron Co Ltd
1880 to 1896	Colliery closed
1896 to 1939	White Moss Coal Co Ltd

Colliery finally closed 1939
For locomotives used by Earl of Crawford and Balcarres and Wigan Coal and Iron Co Ltd, see Part 2, Chapters 17 and 19

Locomotives used by White Moss Coal Co Ltd :-

ROSEMARY   0-6-0ST   IC   HE   76   1873   12"x18"   3'1"
   Ex White Moss Colliery
   Scrapped or sold after March 1924

FRECKLETON   0-6-0ST   IC   MW   1155   1890   14"x20"   3'6"
   Ex Holme and King, contractors
   Reputedly renamed BAINBRIDGE
   Reputedly to Hough and Sons Ltd, Wigan, about 1921

GASKELL   0-6-0ST   IC   HE   338   1884   15"x20   3'4"
   Ex White Moss Colliery
   Scrapped or sold after February 1930

                        0-4-0ST   OC   MW   1523   1901   12"x18"   3'0"
   Ex Air Ministry,128, 1933; originally Cambrian Railways, 22
   For Sale 23rd August 1939, still here 10th September 1939, subsequently presumed scrapped

16019   0-4-0ST   OC   St Rollox   1889   14"x20"   3'8"
   Ex L.M.S. 16019, January 1935
   For Sale 23rd August 1939, still here 10th September 1939, subsequently presumed scrapped

Upholland Brick and Tile Works

c1871 to 1878	Ditton Brook Coal and Iron Company
1878 to c1890	Upholland Brick and Coal Company
c1890 to 1908	Upholland Brick and Tile Co Ltd
1908 to 1970	Ravenhead Sanitary Pipe and Brick Co Ltd
1970 to date	Various owners – see text

Rail traffic ceased about 1955

Locomotive for sale 29-6-1878

UPHO   4wTGV   S   6006CH
   Rebuilt from conventional locomotive at United Alkali Co Ltd, Muspratts Works, Widnes, in 1925
   To Upholland brickworks about 1930
   Scrapped about 1957

SEDGLEY   0-6-0ST   IC   MW   1376   1898   12"x17"   3'1⅜"
   On hire from Thomas Wrigley, contractor, Prestwich, July 1920 to February 1921

2'0" Gauge

                        4wDM   RH   172332   1935   10HP
   New
   To Chris Holden Ltd, Blackburn.

Upholland Coking Plant

1912 to 1920   Simplex Coke Oven and Engineering Co Ltd
1925 to 1930   Upholland Coking and By-products Co Ltd
Closed 1930
May have been worked by Bispham Hall Colliery Co Ltd from about 1916 to 1925

ADAM	0-4-0ST	OC				12"	

According to former employee a locomotive of this name was here and was disposed of about 1920

BILLY No 1	0-6-0ST	IC	HC	795	1907	14"x20"	3'7"

   Loaned from Crigglestone Colliery and returned

No 2	0-6-0ST	IC	HC	820	1907	14"x20"	3'8"

   Ex Crigglestone Colliery, by 1927
   To Sir Lindsay Parkinson, by 1931

Bispham Hall Colliery and Brickworks

c1894 to c1898   William Hilton
c1898 to 1900   Bispham Hall Colliery Company
1900 to 1925   Bispham Hall Colliery Co Ltd
Mountain Mine Colliery acquired c1916 and sold to Upholland Coking and By-products Co Ltd in 1925
1925 to date   Bispham Hall Brick and Terra Cotta Co Ltd
Rail Traffic ceased 1952

WALTER	0-6-0ST	OC	P	924	1901	14"x20"	

   New
   Renamed HILDA 1926
   Scrapped March 1953

ARNISTON	0-6-0ST	IC	MW	1233	1893	12"x17"	3'0"

   Ex Arniston Coal Co Ltd, 1916
   To Swan Lane Collieries Ltd, about 1922

GLADYS	0-6-0ST	OC	FW	342	1877	13"x20"	3'6"

   On hire from Hough and Sons Ltd, Wigan, possibly about 1916

KING	0-4-0ST	OC	AB	1448	1916	14"x22"	3'5"

   On hire from Hough and Sons Ltd, Wigan, about 1930

Triangle Valve Co Ltd

Rail system closed 1979/1980

2'0" gauge

	4w DM		L	50191	1957

   New
   To Triangle Alloys Ltd, Clay Cross, Derbyshire, 1980

Rainford, Upholland and Orrell

References to Chapter 15

1	L&YR Sdgs Diag No 155, dated 5-1-1898	2	L&YR Sdgs Diag No 156, dated 5-1-1898
3	BC 8-8-1896	4	WO 26-9-1903
5	WO 23-1-1897	6	WO 12-12-1903
7	L&YR Sdgs Diag No 155A, dated 5-9-1906	8	L&YR Sdgs Diag No 155B, dated 16-6-1908
9	CG 9-2-1900	10	WRO DDX El 269/1
11	LG 27-4-1852	12	BC 22-5-1852
13	WRO DD Hai 10/8	14	BC13-9-1856
15	MG 14-11-1891	16	BC 14-11-1891
17	CG 10-6-1892	18	Copy in authors' possession
19	Line Plan of St Helens Railway – LNWR, Rugby, 1871 – 2 chains to 1 inch – at BRPB, Manchester Office		
20	*"The St Helens Well Tanks"* B Roberts – *Journal of Stephenson Locomotive Society* December 1950		
21	WO 9-1-1852	22	WO 20-2-1852
23	WRO DD Sc B1		
24	Wigan Coal and Iron Co Ltd, Directors' Report for half year, ending 30-6-1880		
25	WO 15-2-1896		
26	Wigan Coal and Iron Co Ltd, Directors' Report for half year, ending 31-12-1895		
27	WO 8-8-1896		
28	*Locomotives of the Great Western Railway, Part Ten* – Railway Correspondence and Travel Society, 1966		
29	Line Plan of Liverpool, Bolton and Bury Railway – LMSR Euston 1938 to 1940 – 2chains to 1 inch – at BRPB, Manchester Office		
30	WO 8-9-1871	31	WO 13-10-1876
32	BC 14-10-1876	33	WO 24-5-1878
34	WO 29-6-1878	35	*Iron* 11-10-1889
36	WO 12-10-1889		
37	*Industry In South Lancashire* South Lancashire Development Corporation – Publ Ed Burrow & Co Ltd, Cheltenham and London, n.d., about 1970		
38	L&YR Sdgs Diag No 247, dated 17-9-1901	39	Information supplied by Mr Ted Cheetham
40	L&YR Sdgs Diag No 248, dated 17-9-1901	41	WRO DDX El 36/23
42	WRO DDX El 36/27	43	WO 18-3-1913
44	WO 21-2-1900	45	WO 11-1-1867
46	L&YR Sdgs Diag No 327, dated 3-9-1906		
47	*"Bispham Hall Colliery and Brickworks, Upholland By-products Plant"* – C A Appleton – *Journal of Industrial Locomotive Society* Vol 6, No 5, June 1953		
48	WO 15-2-1930	49	CG 16-5-1930
50	*Mining and Geology Trail to Haigh Plantations, Wigan* Robin Grayson, Donald Anderson and Robert E Fry – Metropolitan Borough of Wigan, Department of Leisure, Booklet No 4 – 1979		
51	WO 11-4-1874	52	WO 23-5-1879
53	WRO DDX El 140/31	54	L&YR Sdgs Diag No 52, dated 5-2-1896
55	L&YR Sdgs Diag No 52A, dated 11-7-1900	56	WO 25-5-1973

To be published as a separate volume:

Part II

North and East of Wigan

Contents:

Haigh and Aspull

Kirkless

The Wigan Coal and Iron Co Ltd and the Wigan Coal Corporation Ltd

The Locomotives of the Wigan Coal and Iron Co Ltd and the Wigan Coal Corporation Ltd

Shevington, Appley Bridge and Gathurst

From Douglas Bank to Westwood

North of Wigan

Standish

Coppull

Chorley and Adlington

Blackrod and Westhoughton

Westleigh

Bickershaw and Hindley Green

Locomotives built by Walker Brothers and Atkinson Walker

Locomotives built at the Haigh Foundry

Locomotive Dealers in Wigan

The Steam Ships of the Wigan Coal and Iron Company

Index to Part I and Part II